Relational "(e)pistemologies"

Studies in the Postmodern Theory of Education

Joe L. Kincheloe and Shirley R. Steinberg
General Editors

Vol. 226

PETER LANG
New York • Washington, D.C./Baltimore • Bern
Frankfurt am Main • Berlin • Brussels • Vienna • Oxford

Barbara J. Thayer-Bacon

Relational "(e)pistemologies"

PETER LANG
New York • Washington, D.C./Baltimore • Bern
Frankfurt am Main • Berlin • Brussels • Vienna • Oxford

LIBRARY OF CONGRESS CATALOGING-IN-PUBLICATION DATA
Thayer-Bacon, Barbara J.
Relational "(e)pistemologies" / Barbara J. Thayer-Bacon.
p. cm. — (Counterpoints; v. 226)
Includes bibliographical references (p.) and index.
1. Critical pedagogy. 2. Knowledge, Theory of. 3. Feminism and education.
4. Postmodernism and education. I. Title: Relational "epistemologies".
II. Title. III. Counterpoints (New York, N.Y.); v. 226.
LC196 .T53   370.11′5—dc21   2002066143
ISBN 978-0-8204-6172-4
ISSN 1058-1634

Bibliographic information published by DIE DEUTSCHE NATIONALBIBLIOTHEK.
DIE DEUTSCHE NATIONALBIBLIOTHEK lists this publication in the "Deutsche
Nationalbibliografie"; detailed bibliographic data are available
on the Internet at http://dnb.d-nb.de/.

Cover design by Joni Holst

© 2003, 2017 Peter Lang Publishing, Inc., New York
29 Broadway, 18th floor, New York, NY 10006
www.peterlang.com

All rights reserved.
Reprint or reproduction, even partially, in all forms such as microfilm,
xerography, microfiche, microcard, and offset strictly prohibited.

*For the women in my life,
who taught me to see the world
as connected and whole,
as a living, breathing world in relation.*

Contents

Foreword		ix
Preface		xi
Acknowledgments		xv
Introduction		1
Chapter 1.	Why "(e)pistemology?"	14
	Traditional Epistemology 17	
	Some Feminist Concerns 26	
	Some Pragmatist Concerns 35	
	Some Postmodern Concerns 41	
Chapter 2.	Embracing *Qualified Relativism*	49
	James's Truths 50	
	James's Radical Empiricism 54	
	James's Radical Pluralism 58	
	Dewey's Warranted Assertability and Democratic Inclusion 62	
	Conclusion 71	
Chapter 3.	Why *Relationality?*	73
	Personal Relations 77	
	Social Relations 81	
	W/holistic Relations 85	
	Ecological Relations 90	
	Scientific Relations 94	
	Conclusion 99	

viii   Relational "(e)pistemologies"

Chapter 4.   Personal Relations   100
             Subject as Infant Cared-for   101
             I/Thou Relationships   115
             Conclusion   125

Chapter 5.   Social Relations   127
             Subject as Acculturated Social Being   129
             Power and Culture Issues   140
             Conclusion   151

Chapter 6.   W/holistic Relations   153
             Nonduality   156
             Great Spirit, Dreams, and Holy Wind   168
             Conclusion   182

Chapter 7.   Ecological Relations   183
             Human/nonhuman Nature   186
             Women and Nature   199

Chapter 8.   Scientific Relations   212
             The Universe as Unified, Complementary, and Dynamic   216
             Compassionate, Connected Science   236

Chapter 9.   Educational Implications   243
             Personal Relations   245
             Social Relations   251
             W/holistic Relations   255
             Ecological Relations   261
             Scientific Relations   264
             Conclusion   271

Notes   275

Bibliography   283

Index   295

Foreword

Relational "(e)pistemologies" offers us a thoroughly relational account of human interactions with the world—its objects, fellow humans, ideas, and events. A relational approach avoids the most troubling errors of both individualism and communitarianism. Before individuals, communities, or sub-cultures come into existence, there is a relation—encounter and response. Relation is ontologically basic.

Why is this important? What errors are avoided? First, we avoid the error of supposing that rational individuals provide the foundation of community through free choice and consent. On the contrary, we see that individuals themselves are products of countless interactions with others and with themselves (through reflection). The much celebrated autonomy of individuals may be an illusion; interdependence—even intelligent heteronomy—better describes the reality of selves. Second, we avoid the exclusiveness of community. Without denying the bonds of community and its great attactions, we can see that relation is more fundamental and, because it *is* more basic, we can go beyond the bounds of present community to form new connections and to refine and strengthen present patterns of interaction. The author makes all this clear in discussions of both ordinary and scientific communities.

Thayer-Bacon challenges us to seek connection across both similarity and difference. Some relational approaches obliterate difference by assimilating both parties to a "oneness" of some sort, but a deeply relational account recognizes that those beings we call "individuals" emerge from relations and enter (never fully formed) new relations in which differences will always be present. Indeed, we can never entirely remove the differences even between our present and past selves. This suggests a continuing need to connect and re-connect, and this is so in our pursuit of knowledge and truth as well as satisfying social relations.

Thayer-Bacon shows courage and ingenuity in presenting the case for intuition and relation in the world of non-human entities. Biographical accounts strengthen her arguments. We know that great scientists, mathematicians, composers, writers, and artists have "listened" to the objects of their study. They have been involved in co-creation with non-human partners, not in the autonomous investigation of "objects." Topics that seem mystical in other settings become real and practical in this relational account.

The relational approach should be particularly attractive to educators. When, as so often happens today, caring relations fail to develop in schools, it may not be the fault of individuals called "teachers" or "students." It may be that the social organization of schools fails to supply the structure in which caring relations can develop. What sort of space must be created for the growth of caring relations? It is not enough for carers (teachers) to want to care and for cared-fors (students) to want caring. The conditions of schooling must make caring possible.

In closing this brief foreword, I want to mention the potential power of a relational approach for world peace. Instead of continually arguing over who is right and who wrong, we should ask how we can establish the conditions under which people might relate peaceably. A relational approach recognizes difference, is slow to fix blame, and probes beneath the surface of individual actions to find both causes and solutions. The approach is familiar to good parents and teachers everywhere.

Nel Noddings

Preface

Relational *"(e)pistemologies"* is designed for graduate students in philosophy of education, philosophy, education, religion, sociology, ecology, cultural studies, and women's studies who are enrolled in courses which consider epistemology as a topic. It is also intended to make a significant contribution to scholarship in the field of epistemology, from a feminist perspective, so it should be of special interest to scholars in epistemology, and feminist theory, philosophy, philosophy of education, education, and women's studies. It may be of interest to scholars in religion, and sociologists as well.

As a scholar, my theoretical background is in philosophy of education, and my interests include: critical thinking, epistemology, feminist theory, ethics, social/political theory, and school reform. My perspective is a pragmatic, social feminist one.

This project is one of redefining Epistemology in a nontranscendent manner, and reclaiming the traditional Epistemological concerns of standards and criteria for warranting arguments and determining truth from falsity. These concerns must be reclaimed in order to make them visible and hold them accountable as well as make them pragmatically useful, but on socially constructed grounds, not on transcendental grounds. I use Rorty's (1979) lead and capitalize Epistemology to mark traditional transcendental Epistemology from the nontranscendent epistemology I want to discuss, which I represent in a lower case *e*. I also use Berger and Luckmann's (1966) technique of reminding the reader that when s/he reads *epistemology* within the text, I mean to place quotes around the word "epistemology" metaphorically to make sure it is not confused with its Transcendental look-alike, even though I don't actually use quotes throughout the text, for ease of reading. Just to make absolutely sure I am not misunderstood on my topic of discussion, I also employ a postmodern technique of placing () around the *e* in epistemology, like so: *(e)pistemology*. It is my goal to write a feminist (e)pistemology that can still address important epistemological concerns without getting tangled up in the shimmering ontological nets of universal essences. I present in *Relational "(e)pistemologies"* an alternative theory of knowing as well as many other examples of relational (e)pistemologies.

xii   Relational "(e)pistemologies"

Organization of the Text

I use *Relational "(e)pistemologies"* as a way to examine the issues and concerns pragmatists, feminists, and postmodernists are voicing about Epistemology, as well as to offer my own feminist (e)pistemological theory, which I show is capable of addressing these concerns. I begin by describing my position and the basic assumptions I assume in the Introduction, as well as my plan for the book. Here I qualify what I intend to accomplish so that it is clear this book is not meant to be a comprehensive history of the field of Epistemology, nor is it meant to be a thorough discussion of traditional Epistemological theories, past or present. It is mean to be a presentation of one feminist's relational (e)pistemological theory in comparison to others.

I start in the Introduction by describing my approach and what my goals are for this text. Chapter 1 describes the current debate about whether we even need Epistemological theory or not, from pragmatist, feminist and postmodernist perspectives. I use this chapter as a way to position myself within the traditional Epistemology vs no epistemology debate, as a feminist philosopher. Chapter 2 is a discussion and response to the fears of relativism traditional Epistemologists express concerning a relational approach. Chapter 3 is the place where I define what I mean by *relational*. There are many uses for this term, and I wish to show how my theory encompasses them all in a wholistic manner. The following chapters will more closely discuss particular forms of relational knowing.

Chapter 4 specifically addresses personal relations, in an intrapersonal manner. Chapter 5 turns to the interrelational qualities of social relations. Chapter 6 moves to dissolve the Epistemological subject/object distinction by emphasizing a w/holistic relational approach. Chapter 7 considers ecological relations, and works to view the knower in naturalistic terms. Chapter 8 considers the relational qualities of our world in terms of more recent scientific ideas in the fields of physics, chemistry, and biology. Chapter 9 is a concluding chapter that considers the implications this theory has for education.

I am able to write this book because of longstanding conversations shared with other philosophers, in texts and in person, in particular pragmatic, feminist, and postmodern philosophers such as: Belenky et al., Benhabib, Bordo, Code, Flax, Gilligan, Greene, Grimshaw, Haraway, Harding, Jaggar, Martin, Noddings, Ruddick, Seigfried, Buber, Dewey, Foucault, James, Levinas, and Rorty. I bring out their voices throughout the text.

Features of the Text

Relational "(e)pistemologies" is a book graduate students will find accessible, and yet it also offers high quality scholarship, and numerous sources for topics and issues students will want to pursue on their own. Professors will find *Relational "(e)pistemologies"* is a valuable text to add to their class list of books. It is timely, and forward thinking, as well as addressing major theories from the past that have contributed to the author's feminist epistemological theory. The timely quality of this book will make it possible for students to not only be aware of the history of feminist epistemological theory, but also help them understand the current issues and concerns being debated. From a professorial standpoint, this is also an attractive feature as the current feminist perspectives are usually in article or paper form, or within an edited volume. Rarely are they found discussed throughout one text, as they are presented here.

Relational "(e)pistemologies" is a valuable book for professors to use in graduate courses which consider feminist epistemology as a topic. This includes at least people who teach graduate courses in philosophy of education, philosophy, ethnic studies, and women's studies. *Relational "(e)pistemologies"* has a wide reach and is applicable to most fields of study, for it includes discussions of work from the fields of psychology, sociology, religious studies, ethnic studies, and science. It is multidisciplinary in its approach.

As a final feature of *Relational "(e)pistemologies,"* since my goal is to offer my own relational epistemological theory, I hope that what I write will be a significant contribution to the scholarly discussion on feminist epistemology. If I am successful at this task, *Relational "(e)pistemologies"* will be a text graduate students and scholars in the field of feminist epistemology will want to read for its scholarly value and the contributions it makes toward furthering our understanding of feminist epistemology.

Ways to Use this Text

Due to its detailed treatment of current feminist epistemological issues, it is possible to use *Relational "(e)pistemologies"* as a central text in a course on feminist epistemologies, epistemological theories, or sociology of knowledge, and then give students assignments to research other individual scholars cited within the text on their own. A *Relational "(e)pistemology"* is recommended for use as one of several equally weighed assigned texts in a quarter or semester long course or as a main text with students doing research on scholars discussed in the text, or others not discussed, on their own. It could also be used as the main text in a shorter course, such as a six-week summer session.

Acknowledgments

I have benefited from help in many forms during the process of writing this book. My first thank you's must go to my family, for their support is always there with me, and they suffer through endless conversations about the topics and issues I ponder, especially my loving partner and best friend, Charles Bacon. Thank you, Thayer, for your efforts to read Chapter 8. Next, I must thank my three professors in philosophy of education at Indiana University, Denis Phillips, Elizabeth Steiner, and especially George Maccia, as well as Milton Fisk from philosophy, for first introducing me to this topic, which has become a major strand of my research and the manuscript before you now.

I have had the great advantage of working at a supportive institution of higher education for 9 years, and I must thank Bowling Green State University for their support, which has come in many forms. I especially want to thank Marie Clemons, my research graduate assistant in 1999–2000, for her careful reading and editing of all but the last chapter of the text. She also spent many hours in the library tracking down the sources I needed, or thought I did. I also wish to thank Cathy Long, the EDFI department secretary, for her secretarial assistance throughout this process. And, I am very grateful for the sabbatical BGSU awarded me in fall 1998, that helped me get started on this book.

I was a Visiting Scholar at Teachers College, Columbia University for my sabbatical, fall 1998, and thank you's must go to the students, faculty, and staff at TC, for their suggestions and assistance during this beginning stage, in particular Nel Noddings. I also visited Jane Roland Martin several times during that fall and must thank her for her insightful questions that helped me clarify just what I mean by 'relational.' The answer to that question shaped the entire structure of this book.

Just as my sabbatical was ending I received word that I had been awarded a Spencer Foundation small grant that would give me the gift of a half year more time and a graduate assistant for the year. The Spencer Foundation's support for June, 1999 to May, 2000 was what made this project possible to see through to completion. It was a tremendous gift of time and assistance just when I needed it the most.

There are many others who have given me feedback and suggestions along the way at conferences and in my classrooms whom I wish to thank, although I regret I can not name them individually. I shared particular chapters of this text with several colleagues with particular expertise in topics I discuss, and I have benefited from their careful reads and responses: Kathleen Knight Abowitz, Haithe Anderson, Malcolm Campbell, Clint Collins, Jim Garrison, Susan Laird, Huey-li Li, Conrad Pritcher, and Rosalie Romano. I also used part of this text in my fall 1999 "Feminist Epistemologies and Education" class at Bowling Green State University, and I want to thank those students in particular for their feedback.

As I was nearing the end of this project I found myself in the great fortune of being offered and accepting a new job at the University of Tennessee. Thank you's must go to my new colleagues at UT, especially Bill Morgan, Joy DeSensi, and Clint Allison, for their excitement and enthusiasm for my work and for their warm welcomes to Knoxville, Tennessee. I am sorry to have had them as colleagues for such a short time, as I have already lost them due to retirement, relocation, and restructuring. Such is life in higher education! It is due to Clint Allison's presence that I realized I should send the manuscript to Joe Kinchelow (a former UT grad and student of Clint's) and Shirley Steinberg, as editors of the Counterpoint Series at Peter Lang. Thank you's must go to Joe and Shirley for their enthusiastic reception and recommendation and to Chris Myers for his acceptance of the manuscript for Peter Lang. It has been a great pleasure to work with them, as well as the publishing staff at Peter Lang, especially Lisa Dillon.

Introduction

In 1966 two sociologists, Peter L. Berger and Thomas Luckmann, published a small yet influential book, titled *The Social Construction of Reality*, in which they argue that reality is socially constructed and that it is the task of the sociology of knowledge to analyze the process in which this occurs (p. 1). They acknowledge in their Introduction that "reality" and "knowledge" are two terms with a long philosophical history, and they are careful to claim they are not using the terms in a philosophical way, but rather within the context of sociology. Berger and Luckmann describe the task of the philosopher as one of trying to differentiate between valid and invalid assertions about the world, in a general sense, whereas sociology of knowledge is concerned with reality and knowledge within the context of various social settings. The sociologist must keep quotation marks around the terms *reality* and *knowledge*.

Berger and Luckmann (1966) wish to make it clear in their Introduction that they are bracketing out any epistemological or methodological questions. While they do not say this, they are also bracketing out metaphysical questions. They describe their task, as sociologists of knowledge, as an empirical task focusing on commonsense "knowledge," on trying to understand the "reality" of everyday life rather than "ideas" (theory). Later, in their description of the philosopher's role within a society, philosophers are described as "legitimators" of social institutions, who supply "universe-maintenance." Legitimators explain and justify social orders "by ascribing cognitive validity" to the social institution's meanings, and "by giving a normative dignity to its practical imperatives" (p. 93). The legitimation process is very similar to what Foucault (1972, 1978, 1979, 1980) describes in his efforts to clearly connect knowledge to power. For Berger and Luckmann, philosophers are not the only legitimators, scientists and theologians are too. They are the definers of the universe. They supply the conceptual framework, the theory, that explains why things are the way they are.

Berger and Luckmann's (1966) definition of philosophy as knowledge that is general and removed from everyday living and ordinary life, is just what I want to question in this text. Their sharp distinction between sociology's empirical task of looking at commonsense knowledge, and philosophy's validity task is just what I want to collapse. Like Dewey, I argue that "the most pervasive fallacy of philosophic thinking goes back to neglect of context," to philosophy's effort to describe itself in a transcendental manner, removed from the context of the everyday, common world (1960, "Context and Thought," p. 92). Dewey goes on to point out: "All statements about the universe as a whole, reality as an unconditioned unity, involve the same fallacy" (p. 95). Berger and Luckmann describe philosophy as decontextualized, in contrast to sociology, which is embedded in context, in particular social context. Berger and Luckmann's effort to bracket out epistemological, and metaphysical, questions from sociological concerns is one I wish to argue is an impossibility doomed to failure. We cannot divorce ourselves from epistemological and metaphysical questions, for they form the very weaving of the net we use to catch up our everyday commonsense concerns. That Berger and Luckmann believed they could separate and bracket out philosophical questions was itself based on certain philosophical views that they embraced. I do not mean to single Berger and Luckmann out in particular, or other sociologists of knowledge, I just am using their distinctions as an example of what points to the heart of my own project here.

I do not question that Berger and Luckmann (1966) are accurate in their distinction between philosophy and sociology, in terms of how the two disciplines have historically been separated. The social sciences developed out of philosophy, and sought to distinguish themselves from philosophy by striving to be more empirical and thus more scientific. What I question is philosophy's assumed ability to tell us what is *a priori* Truth and Goodness and Beauty, as well as science's assumed ability to avoid philosophical questions. I agree with the accuracy of Berger and Luckmann's description of the historical assumed role of philosophers as social legitimators and universe-maintenance workers. It is because of my agreement with their description of the philosopher's role, that I join feminists and postmodernists in reasserting the need to uncover the philosopher's assumption of power. Along with other pragmatists, I agree that the philosopher's role should be one of cultural critic, and helping to develop ideas to deal with the actual crises of our lives. Philosophers can help "to imagine a future which is the projection of the desirable in the present, and to invent the instrumentalities of its realization" (Dewey, 1960, "The need for a recovery of philosophy," p. 69). Philosophers can help to guide historical change intelligently because not only do they legitimate conformities, they also question conformities that have become so habitual that they are taken to be Reality or Truth.

Because I question philosophy's ability to be transcendental, I must question the epistemological definition Berger and Luckmann embrace, in their effort to distinguish sociology of knowledge from epistemology. Berger and Luckmann assume epistemology is a study of knowledge without quotation marks, Knowledge that is really true, whereas the sociology of knowledge studies common people's claims to "knowledge" that are assumed beliefs, maybe even justified beliefs, but not necessarily true. Epistemologists establish the criteria and standards necessary to prove validity and truth. As epistemology has traditionally defined knowledge, only what we believe is true, have good reason to believe is true, and in fact is true, can we call knowledge. Knowledge = Truth. Because knowledge is defined as what is justified true belief, then it is necessary for sociologists to qualify their studies because they are not claiming that what common people believe is "true" is really true. They are not claiming that what people believe is "real" really is. Their task is to study how beliefs come to be viewed as real and true. Philosophers, according to the tradition which Berger and Luckmann reflect rather than question, have the task of proving the validity of truth claims, of making the case for warranted assertions that are justified as necessarily so.

I question that it is possible to accomplish what transcendental epistemologists claim to be able to do. I want to suggest that we can never remove the quotation marks from around *knowledge* and *reality*. I join others in arguing that none of us have access to transcendence, none of us can know what is True or Real, in a universal sense, and so we must all be content to continue to talk about "knowledge" and "reality" as Berger and Luckmann do, with quotation marks around the terms. I do not intend to offer an extensive argument for the demise of epistemology in this text, Richard Rorty has already done that very well (*Philosophy and the Mirror of Nature*, 1979), as did John Dewey before him, with his *Logic* (1938). There are many others who have contributed to the death of transcendental philosophy, and epistemology in particular, as well.

One of my main tasks here is to describe a non-transcendent epistemology. Like Burger and Luckmann, I want the reader to know up front that I symbolically place quotation marks around the concept "epistemology" to distinguish it from the philosophical definition of epistemology as transcendental, even though I will not literally place " " around the term each time I use it, for ease of reading. I will follow Richard Rorty's lead and capitalize Epistemology when I use the term in the traditional sense, with an assumption of absolutism. However, I am not just striving to use the term 'epistemology' in a traditional sociological way here either. I want to redefine *epistemology*. I want to reconstruct the meaning of the term. I will adopt a methodological tool often used in postmodern discourse and place parentheses around the *e* of *epistemology*, like so, (e)pistemology, to further remind the reader when I am using the term *epistemology* in a non-transcendent way, meaning within the context of this world, not removed from our ordinary, everyday experiences.

The reader might ask, why bother with this technique? Won't this be too confusing? Why not just use a different term and avoid Epistemology altogether? Believe me, I have wrestled a great deal with this very question. I have the advantage of hindsight and can see the pitfalls my brother and sister pragmatists and feminists have fallen into because of the use of common philosophical terms in new ways, and the resistance and confusion this creates. I can also see the confusion created by using new terms, such as Dewey's use of *inquiry*, to replace Epistemology, because he was seeking to avoid ontological status, and thus transcendence (See: "In defense of the theory of inquiry," 1960).

I am well aware that traditional Epistemologists will criticize me for misusing the term *epistemology*, saying that what is included in this text is not Epistemological theory (they will also distain my capitalizing of the term as a ploy). However, they are absolutely right in their criticism, I am not claiming to offer an Epistemological theory, as traditionally defined, and I want to make that very clear. Philosophy has a long history of eminent scholars who have written Epistemological theories, as well as present-day philosophers contributing to the Epistemological discussion. I do not claim to be one of them. My voice is one that is attempting to contribute to the demise of traditional Epistemology. If the reader wishes a comprehensive historical presentation of Epistemological theories, or a discussion of current Epistemological issues, the reader will have to look elsewhere for these, and there are many fine sources. While I will offer some discussion of Epistemology, past and present, it will not be an indepth discussion for my main task is a different one. I seek to describe my own feminist (e)pistemological theory, a relational way of knowing, as well as others.

Feminists and postmodernists will criticize me, as well, not for misusing the term *epistemology* but instead for clinging to the term. In recent years questions concerning the philosophical field of Epistemology, as well as philosophy in general, have been raised by postmodern philosophers. Lyotard (1984) uses the term 'modern' "to designate any science that legitimates itself with reference to a metadiscourse of this kind [i.e., a discourse of legitimation with respect to its own status, a discourse called philosophy] making an explicit appeal to some grand narrative, such as the dialetics of the Spirit, the hermeneutics of meaning, the emancipation of the rational or working subject, or the creation of wealth." With this as his starting point, 'postmodern' is defined as "incredulous towards metanarratives." Lyotard goes on to ask "Where, after the metanarratives, can legitimacy reside?" (p. xxiii, pp. xxiv-xxv). Richard Rorty (1979) uses capital letters to distinguish Philosophy that claims to be transcendental and able to tell us what is *a priori* Truth and Goodness and Beauty, from philosophy that serves as cultural critic, and as a guide for historical change. Lower case (p)hilosophy is warranted by truths that are assertions justified to our social communities' satisfaction.

Given the strong arguments made by postmodernists against Philosophy being able to offer a God's eye view of the world, Rorty (1979) ends his *Philosophy and the Mirror of Nature* with the suggestion that Philosophy as we have know it is dead, as are the fields of Metaphysics and Epistemology. For Rorty, philosophers are generators of new descriptions, rather than describers of accurate descriptions, and "edifying philosophy aims at continuing a conversation rather than at discovering truth . . . " (p. 373). "If we see knowing not as having an essence, to be described by scientists and philosophers, but rather as a right, by current standards, to believe, then we are well on the way to seeing *conversation* as the ultimate context within which knowledge is to be understood" (p. 389). Rorty (1977) suggests "we can eliminate epistemological problems by eliminating the assumption that justification must repose on something other than social practices and human needs" (p. 62).

At the same time that postmodernists are questioning the role of Epistemology in Philosophy as well as the role of Philosophy itself, several feminists have been striving to write feminist epistemologies. Thus we find feminist standpoint epistemology, by Harding, Hartsock, Hill, and Smith for example. Feminist standpoint epistemology has been criticized by traditional Epistemologists for focusing on social/political and ethical questions, at the expense of traditional Epistemological questions concerning criteria and standards for justification. Postmodernists criticize feminist standpoint epistemology for relying on the traditional Epistemological assumption of epistemic agency, a transcendental God's eye view, and just shifting the assumption of transcendence from the center of the tradition to the margins, describing those who have been cast in the past as outsiders as those now most able to offer a clear perspective. As Bar-On (1993) points out, such a move still relies on using the tools of the master's game. "Although the claim to epistemic privilege as a tool may seem to be a claim of the oppressed, due to some of its history, it nonetheless reveals itself also as a master's tool" (p. 97). The need to authorize speech is felt when silence is the rule. Traditional, transcendental Epistemology is based on the silence of particular, everyday experiences.

Some feminists, such as Lorraine Code and Charlene Haddock Seigfried, conclude there can be no feminist epistemology given traditional conceptions of Epistemology which rely on a transcendental "something" such as God, Reason, Intuition, or the Universal Forms and the individual cognitive ability of autonomous reasoners.

> The more we explore and reflect on a rationality which has evolved over time as a means of intelligently transforming ourselves and our environment, a rationality which is inevitably informed by our multiple relationships of gender, sexuality, color, nationality, and class, to name a few, the more it seems that feminists would be better off abandoning the misguided epistemological project we've inherited, rather than to continue tinkering with it. A more radical and productive feminist approach would be to continue developing a transformative model of interested, not disinterested, inquiry into experience; in short, to engage in an unapologetic feminist philosophy of inquiry rather than epistemology. (C. H. Seigfried, 1997, pp. 8–9)

Many feminists have made extensive cases for transcendental Philosophy's exclusionary qualities, showing how women, and other minorities, have routinely been classified as lacking in the abilities and qualities necessary to know Truth, Goodness, and Beauty. Given Philosophy's problematic assumption of transcendence, and its exclusionary results, why would any feminist wish to write a feminist epistemology, as I do here? Seigfried's advice is very tempting. Given that I am aware of many pitfalls which I seek to avoid (I am sure there are even more I will discover along the way), why choose to continue to walk down an *epistemological* path, even one marked "(e)pistemology" instead of Epistemology?

My answer is that I do not think it is possible for us to avoid epistemological questions about what counts as evidence in research problems, what criteria we should use to judge the quality of someone's reported results, and how we avoid harmful biases in our judgments, for example. These are extremely important and serious questions and how we answer these questions have beneficial as well as debilitating results. If we do not address epistemological concerns, how can we make them visible and hold them accountable for the tremendous power they hold over people's lives? Thus, I do not want to walk away from epistemology, as a field of study, I want to redescribe epistemology in a way that does not assume transcendence. While Epstemology has been declared dead in its transcendental forms, it still continues to show its ugly transcendental shapes and falsely judge many as lacking in knowledge, and as inferior. Epistemology still continues to hold powerful sway in determining who is heard and who is silenced, who gets hired and promoted and who is fired or impeached.

My project is not only one of redefining Epistemology in a nontranscendent manner, I also want to reclaim the traditional Epistemological concerns of standards and criteria for warranting arguments and determining truths from falsities. These concerns must be reclaimed in order to make them visible and hold them accountable as well as make them pragmatically useful, but on socially constructed grounds, not on transcendental grounds. Dismissing Epistemology as a topic allows it to become/remain invisible and continue to gain in power, or at least not lessen or be removed from power. Epistemology is allowed to remain the given, the norm, against which everything else is measured. It is like not discussing race or gender, for the fear is if we continue to discuss race and gender, we continue to recreate a racist, sexist world. Ideally, many of us hope to live in a world where race and gender become meaningless categories. Yet, that is not the world in which any of us have grown up, it is not the world in which we have all been acculturated, the world that has been socially constructed for us by our elders. Given the contextuality of a racist, sexist world, if we ignore that contextuality we do not remove it, we allow it (Whiteness, Maleness) to remain the hidden ruler, the assumed standard by which everything else is measured. Ignoring essentializing categories does not make them go away: it is the vigilant effort to confront them and deconstruct them that dissolves them.

If we just embrace a new concept, such as Dewey's *inquiry*, for (e)pistemology, my fear is that we will easily make the mistake of another attempt at transcendence. We replace one form of transcendence for another, just as Truth has been represented as The Forms, God, Reason, Spirit, the hermeneutics of meaning, the emancipation of the rational or working subject, or the creation of wealth. Given the philosophical contextuality of having inherited a world of Epistemological transcendence, I worry that if we ignore Epistemology it will be allowed to remain the invisible standard by which all other theories concerning ways of knowing are measured. We must confront Epistemology, and deconstruct it, so that we can dissolve the dualisms it creates and move on. These dualisms include for example: absolute/relative, subjective/objective, mind/body, knower/known. So, as much as I would like to ignore it and not use the term *epistemology* at all, I think doing so will not solve our problems. Hopefully, it will not recreate them as well, which is why I choose to symbolize a redescribed epistemology as "(e)pistemology." We cannot let go of the term *epistemology*; we must coopt it.

My project is one of analysis and critique, as well as redescription. What I offer is one pragmatist social feminist view, a relational perspective of knowing, embedded within a discussion of many other relational views. In *Relational "(e)pistemologies,"* I seek to offer a feminist (e)pistemological theory that insists that knowers/subjects are fallible, that our criteria is corrigible (capable of being corrected), and that our standards are socially constructed, and thus continually in need of critique and reconstruction. I offer a self-conscious and reflective (e)pistemological theory, one that attempts to be adjustable and adaptable as people gain further in understanding. This (e)pistemology must be inclusive and open to others, because of its assumption of fallible knowers. And this (e)pistemology must be capable of being corrected because of its assumption that our criteria and standards are of this world, ones we, as fallible knowers, socially construct. Let me explain further what I mean by these concepts.[1]

I begin with the assumption that all *people are social beings*. Our lives begin in and are lived in relationships with others. The quality of these relationships directly affects our abilities to become knowers. This is because *we develop a sense of "self" through our relationships with others*, and *we need a sense of self in order to become potential knowers*. Our ability to develop a sense of "self" is greatly enhanced if the relationships we experience are caring ones. Thus, the reader will find my perspective is greatly influenced by feminist scholarship on caring, although one of my original contributions is to help us understand caring's connection to (e)pistemology.

Not only are all people social beings, *we are contextual social beings*. All of us have unique contexts that affect who we are and how we interpret the world. We are situated people who are embedded in a particular setting as well as embodied within a particular body. With our unique bodies we experience the world around us certain ways and not others. And, due to our embeddedness we inherit a past at birth, and are affected by our environment, including our social environment. The social practices that surround us promote us to believe certain beliefs and not others. How people begin to make sense of the world is due to their contextuality, including their own subjective experiences as well as their social setting, and its past. This means that all knowledge is value-laden or interest-laden, and that cognitive pursuits and their social organization are not independent entities.

All of us begin our relational lives in someone else's trusting arms. What they teach us we believe; we do not begin our lives as independent, self-reliant, autonomous knowers. We must trust others, for lack of trust impedes the growth of knowledge. We are not autonomous knowers sitting in a social setting struggling with whether we have good reasons to believe that someone is an expert and we should believe what s/he tells us. We do not just trust others because to do so quickens our growth of knowledge. We really have no choice but to trust those others with whom we are in social relation. We are social beings who learn from others (we believe); because we are able to develop caring relationships based on such qualities as trust, we begin to develop a sense of self and eventually learn to think more autonomously (we can question our beliefs).

Like other feminist, critical, and postmodern theories, my theory relies on the insights "that the personal is political, that there is direct relation, however complex it may be, between sociality and subjectivity, between language and consciousness, or between institutions and individuals . . . " (de Lauretis, 1986, p. 5). However, I argue that it is possible for us to gain insights into the contexts of our lives. I describe us as contextual beings, and I acknowledge the dominance of culture, yet I also describe us as people who are able to begin to understand the settings we are born into and how they have affected and shaped us. We gain insights into our contextuality through our interactions with other people. As we begin to understand this contextuality, we begin to develop the ability to offer fresh, unique perspectives. Not only do we develop a sense of self due to the relationships we have, but we all become aware, to varying levels and degrees, of that sense of self and how our social contexts have affected the way we view the world through our relationships with others. *Other people help us become aware of our own embeddedness.* Our ability to improve our awareness as knowers is enhanced if we are able to experience sustaining caring relationships.

Since none of us have a God's-eye view of the world, and none of us can claim to be all-knowing, we must reach out for each other to add to our limited perspectives. This feminist (e)pistemological theory insists on the need for pluralism, to help compensate for our fallibility. I do not claim to offer the best, or truest Epistemological theory, for to do so would be a claim of transcendence, which I deny any of us have. I also do not claim to offer a theory that is original and uniquely my own, for such a claim is contrary to my own thesis that we are contextual social beings influenced by our surroundings. So much of what I think has been affected by others. Still, I am uniquely embodied and I experience the world in certain ways and not others. I also have been exposed to experiences that are uniquely my own, including opportunities to participate in many, many conversations with others. These conversations with others have helped me gain my own insights and that is what I bring to this text. I bring my slant, my perspective. I offer my voice to the conversation. And my errors and faults are my own, as much as anything that I think belongs to me. It is important to remind the reader that this conversation has been going on long before me, and will continue long after me. I am a qualitatively unique self-in-relation with others. I am a contextual social being who has learned how to be critical and creative, to be constructive, with the help of many others. I will try to bring out many of their voices throughout this text.

Given my assumption that we are contextual social beings who are not omniscient, I agree with Berger and Luckmann (1966) that what we take to be Reality is one that we have socially constructed by the signification we have given to it. Since our "reality" is human-created it is continually subject to error and in need of change. The good news is that because we have defined and described the world in particular ways, we always have the possibility of defining and describing the world other ways as well. We *can* correct our errors and adapt and change. In order to help us figure out what is an error, we need standards and criteria to help us determine what is right/wrong. However, the standards and criteria we have available to help us make judgments are themselves socially constructed too. Thus, our standards and criteria are also vulnerable to error. Again, the good news is that given that we do not receive our standards and criteria from an omniscient force, we create them, *we* can improve upon them. Given the fallibility of human beings, due to our contextual social embeddedness, we must assume that our criteria and standards potentially are subject to error. But they are also correctable, and so a relational (e)pistemology assumes criteria and standards are corrigible.

With an (e)pistemological theory that does not assume transcendence but instead embraces a view that knowledge is socially constructed by fallible human beings, there is no role for Truth to play. I do not offer Truth here; what I have to offer is a pragmatist perspective concerning truths. I offer what Dewey called *warranted assertability* (*Logic*, 1938) and what James called satisfactory truths. This position is one I have labeled *qualified relativism*, in response to the charge of relativist that is often made against pragmatists, feminists, and postmodernists. I will defend a qualified relativist position in Chapter 2 of the text.

My relational (e)pistemology is a pragmatic social feminist perspective calling for active engagement, aiming at democratic inclusion, joining theory with praxis, striving for awareness of context and values, tolerating vagueness and ambiguities. I argue that knowing is something people develop as they have experiences with each other and the world around them. People improve upon the ideas that have been socially constructed and passed down to them by others. They do this improving by further developing their understandings and enlarging their perspectives. With enlarged perspectives people are able to create new meanings for their experiences. In summation: *My relational (e)pistemology views knowing as something that is socially constructed by embedded, embodied people who are in relation with each other.*

I have already explained what I mean by the term "(e)pistemology." I would like to turn now to the term *relational*, which is also central to the title of this book. The term *relational* is ambiguous in that we use it in many ways. Relation signifies the existential connections of things, a dynamic and functional interaction, and it also signifies the logical relationships of terms. We speak of the overlapping and interconnecting of concepts and meanings that have reference to each other, and we describe how things affect each other existentially. Relationships can be personal, one-on-one exchanges as between a teacher and a student, a parent and their child, or two lovers. We also use the term *relational* in a general manner, as with social relationships between a citizen and their country, or the relationship of men to women. We speak of relations in terms of kinship, that so-and-so is related to someone else, and we say we can relate to someone else meaning we feel sympathy toward that person. We can compare our experiences to the other. The plural use of the term, *relations*, is even used to mean sexual intercourse. Given all the different ways we use this term, *relations* has a common theme of 'connection' to others which is what I want it to signify. I offer a theory of knowing based on an assumption of connection in many forms. I find it an advantage, not a disadvantage, that *relational* means connections in so many ways. My hope is that its many uses will remind us of the transactional nature of knowing (in the Deweyian sense of the term).

For one, I will be exploring the many connections knowers have to the known, and I will be working to collapse the strong distinction and split that has built up between the knower and the known. It is a split that works to sever us from each other, and our world. I argue that we cannot separate Reality from ourselves. It is not possible for us to function as spectators who view and describe the world around us. I present a case that we are connected to our world in a wholistic manner. There is no objective Reality for us to try to understand and know. What we are trying to understand includes us: we are part of this world. Thus we cannot function as surveyors who stand outside of Reality, and describe it, we are embedded in "it." The problem of how the self, mind, etc. can reach knowledge of an external world becomes a meaningless problem when we stop assuming the knower (mind, self, etc.) is separate from the world. We will find that collapsing the distinction between Reality and ourselves dissolves traditional Epistemology, which is based on this assumed distinction. Because of this strong connection between knowers and the known, like the Eastern concept of yin/yang they only exist together as a unity, I will describe knowledge as knowing. Using the term *knowing* reminds us that it is a verb always in process, emphasizing knowing's transactional qualities and not describing "it" as a finalized object or product.

I will also be exploring the connection between individual knowers to other knowers, at a personal level as well as at a social level. Historically, Epistemology is based on an assumption of individual autonomy, that individuals by themselves can discover Truth. These individuals are usually represented as if they sprouted out of the ground as adults, with the ability to think for themselves. I describe individual knowers as beginning their lives in relation with others, in particular their biological mother and whoever becomes their care providers. We begin our lives already in relation with an other, and we expand that relationality to include more others, as we grow and begin to obtain a language, and extend our means of communicating. Our others that we are in relation with are also in relation with more others, so the connection between individual knowers at a personal level very quickly becomes a larger social relation. The distinction of individual and social blurs as well when we try to chase down differences between public and private lives, for example. What we find is a blending together of one into another. Thus, I will consider personal and social ways of knowing.

I also want to develop connections between ourselves, as knowers, and our world around us, in terms of an ecological view of nature in relation to human beings. Not only do we exist in relation to other human beings, we also live our lives in relation to our environment. Enlightenment Epistemology represents knowers as autonomous individuals who are separate from their environment and are therefore able to manipulate that environment to meet their individual needs. The world in which we live becomes one we can measure and quantify and shape to conform to our desires. Yet, many argue that this severed view of individuals in contrast to nature is leading us to ecological disaster. I will turn to Eastern philosophy and Indigenous tribal views, as well as deep ecological and ecofeminist views, to help us understand the (e)pistemological connections between ourselves and the natural world with which we live in relation.

We have already found that historically Epistemology embraces a metaphysical assumption that knowledge in general is sharply distinct from knowledge in particular. Thus philosophy is given the task of concentrating of generals and essences, as opposed to science, which tries to understand the specifics of this world. We saw this distinction with Berger and Luckmann's (1960) theory, in their effort to distinguish philosophy from sociology, and Epistemology from the sociology of knowledge. I will describe the particular (such as personal relations) and the general (such as social relations) in a connected manner. The fields of philosophy and science (and religion) are not nearly as sharp and distinct as we have historically tried to represent them. Like the individual/others split or the human being/nature split, the general/particular split dispels when we explore connections. Thus, the reader will find in this project not only philosophical influences, but scientific and religious ones as well. There are discussions within this text that are relevent to ethics, politics, sociology, psychology, aesthetics, ecology, and spirituality, not just (e)pistemology.

It is now easy to understand the structure of this text. I will start in Chapter 1 by describing the current debate about whether we even need Epistemological theory or not, which I sketched in this Introduction. This will allow me to define traditional Epistemology in a favorable light, with Harvey Siegel's help, as well as describe in more depth feminists' and postmodernists' problems and concerns about Philosophy in general and the field of Epistemology in particular. I will further develop my case for why I choose to continue to use the term *epistemology*, in its altered form (e)pistemology, and why I think it is important to do so. I will use this chapter as a way to more clearly position myself within the traditional Epistemology vs no epistemology debate, as a feminist philosopher. Chapter 2 is a discussion and response to the fears of relativism traditional Epistemologists express concerning a relational approach. I will turn to James's truths and Dewey's warranted assertability for help. It is here that I will define and defend my qualified relativist position.

Chapter 3 will be the place to further define what I mean by *relational*. There are many uses for this term, as we have already found, and I wish to show how my theory encompass them all in a wholistic manner. The heart of this book will involve exploring many ways of knowing and their relational qualities and Chapter 3 will supply the road map for our exploratory trip. Thus we find that there are personal relations, social relations, w/holistic relations, ecological relations, and scientific relations. As I describe each of these forms of relationality, I will point to key scholars whose work highlights a certain relational form. Then the following Chapters will more closely discuss each particular form.

Central to my relational "(e)pistemological" theory is the role of subjects of knowing to objects of knowing. I do not want subjects to get lost and disappear from discussions of knowing, as tends to happen when Epistemologists focus on the objects of knowledge, and not the subjects as knowers. I also do not want subjects to be denied their infancy, and social embeddedness. And, I do not want subjects to be denied their multiplicity and fractured qualities, as well as their embodiments. Chapter 4 will specifically address personal relations, in an intrapersonal manner. Here I will discuss work by feminists such as Nel Noddings, Sara Ruddick, and Jane Flax, concerning subjects as infants-in-relation-with-caregivers. They help to describe a relational ontology, and begin to explore the effects such an ontology has on (e)pistemology. Martin Buber and Simone Weil will offer us ways to consider a personal relationship between knowers and the known with their views on I-Thou relationships. I will critique the personal from a social level throughout the discussions.

Chapter 5 turns to the interrelational qualities of social relations. Here I will discuss Mead's work on the development of a self out of one's social community, and Dewey's extension of Mead's work with his transactional description of I <-> others. This chapter will help us explore subjects as acculturated, situated social beings. It helps us consider ways to address Epistemological fears of relativism, through the concept of selves-in-relation-with-others. Peter Berger, Thomas Luckmann, and Dorothy Smith help me describe how we come to better understand our own social embeddedness and find ways to address concerns about power, for example.

Chapter 6 moves to dissolve the Epistemological subject/object distinction by emphasizing a w/holistic relational approach. Buddhism's concept of nonduality and Native American's Great Spirit, Dreams, Holy Wind, and Sacred Hoop will be important contributions to this discussion. Chapter 7 works on dissolving the distinction between human beings (man) and nature, by considering ecological relations, and viewing knowing in naturalistic terms. The deep ecological perspective of Arne Naess will be explored, as well as the ecological perspectives of several feminists such as Carolyn Merchant, Mary Daly, Ynestra King, and Karen Warren. Buddhist and Native American views will have much to contribute here too.

Chapter 8 considers more recent scientific relational ideas, such as relativity theory, quantum mechanics, general systems theory, and symbiosis, for example. I explore work in the science areas of physics, chemistry, and biology by scientists such as Einstein, Bohr, Bohm, Lovelock, Margulis, and McClintock. Here we find an emphasis on the collaborative relationships and connections at the subatomic, and genetic level, as well as at the macro level of the whole universe. Chapter 9 is a concluding chapter which considers the implications relational (e)pistemological theories have for education.

In questioning philosophy's transcendence, I walk down the path that pragmatists, feminists, and postmodernists walk. I declare philosophy's naturalism and philosophers' fallibilism in a pluralistic universe. I reveal philosophy's gendered, subjective biases and its tendency to neglect its own contextuality. I decry the need for metanarrative in philosophy, and insist on the importance of considering philosophers' powerful role as legitimators. I walk down this path as a fallible social critic who understands that we can redescribe what has already been described, we can recreate and envision anew, we can reform, but we need each other to help us in this process. Not one of us, alone, knows the Answers. I invite your contributions to the conversation, for as Dewey points out, inquiry only ends when we have solved all of our problems, and answered all of our questions, and we are a long way from there. Not only do I think we will never get to that point, I doubt it is even a desirable point to reach. Disharmony, discontent, and diversity help us continue to grow and further our knowing.

CHAPTER 1

Why "(e)pistemology"?

I begin this chapter with a difficult task, one of trying to describe the given, the norm, Epistemology as it has historically been shaped within the Philosophical world. This task is so enormous that it is impossible to accomplish without being vulnerable to charges of over-generalizing and reductionism. There is a long history to Epistemology, and there are a variety of interpretations and forms it has taken. Still, there are some general characteristics that do apply across time, and help to define what we mean by Epistemology, as we use the term today. In order to help us understand the norm that we know today as modern, Enlightenment Epistemology, I think it is helpful to begin by placing this field of study within the larger context of Philosophy. Many may think that to do so just places me in an even bigger mess, yet I argue that the field of Epistemology has been shaped by its described role within Philosophy, and therefore it is impossible to ignore that larger context without participating in what Dewey called "*the* philosopher's fallacy" of neglecting context (Dewey, 1960, "Context and Thought"). Bear with me on what may seem very basic for some of you, for a feminist epistemology must begin by questioning the basic structure of Philosophy, as well as key assumptions made historically in the field of Epistemology.

Philosophy means the love of wisdom. It involves inquiry into "the nature of things" based on logical reasoning rather than empirical methods, which are science's realm. Philosophers analyze and critique "fundamental beliefs," and they investigate causes and laws "underlieing reality." Here, we find that we must capitalize Philosophy right from its beginning because the assumption of universality is built right into its definition. Inquiry into the nature of things, into fundamental beliefs, and underlying reality, is inquiry in a universal, general way, divorced from its particularity. Some questions to explore in this text are: Is it possible for philosophy to be general as well as particular? Can philosophy avoid essentializing, and thus avoid dogmatism, or is it the case that a particularized philosophy is no longer philosophy at all but some other subject such as science or literature instead?

Why "(e)pistemology? 15

Historically, philosophers try to answer questions such as: what is the essence of life? what is virtue? what is truth? what is beauty? and these general questions have come to symbolize the different fields of study within Philosophy. Thus we find that questions about virtue and goodness represent the field of ethics, questions about beauty signify the field of aesthetics, questions about essential categories (first principles) are metaphysical, and questions about truth are epistemological concerns. Logic is also considered a field of study in Philosophy; it is the study of the principles of reasoning, and reasoning is the method used by philosophers in all the fields of study to answer their questions.[1]

Over time a hierarchy of value and importance has developed for these philosophical fields of study, and this hierarchy is reflective of biases in Euro-western Philosophy.[2] One bias is a valuing of abstraction over practice. Plato started us on this bias by arguing that philosophers should trust their ideas in trying to understand objects in their abstract, universal, Ideal, Forms, rather than trusting their individual experiences which are limited to particular objects (see, for example, *The Meno*). He also argued that the guardians of an Ideal state should be those people who are best able to understand theorical ideas, philosophers (the gold, in his metal analogy), rather than more practical-minded people such as craftspeople (the bronze), or more action-oriented people such as warriors (the silver) (*The Republic*, 1979).

Thus, we find that Metaphysics and Epistemology have come to enjoy a higher status in Philosophy due to their questions being perceived as more abstract and less practical. Both Metaphysics and Epistemology operate only in a realm of abstraction and universality, as historically defined. Whereas ethics, which looks at goodness in terms of good behavior, is always connected to the practical world of human beings and therefore suffers a lower ranking as a philosophical field of study. Of course, my field of study, philosophy of education, is even lower in status because it deals with philosophical questions in regards to the very practical world of teachers and students. In the Euro-western world, the more abstract the field of philosophical study is, the more value it enjoys.

We can find this valuation expressed in the historical tracing of feminists' contributions to Philosophy. In *Feminist Epistemologies*, Linda Alcoff and Elizabeth Potter (1993) note in their introductory essay that feminists began contributing to Philosophy from the margins, and they have moved to the center. The margins are the applied fields, in particular applied ethics, which is where feminist work was first published. "Feminist philosophers began work in the applied areas because feminism is, first and last, a political movement concerned with practical issues, and feminist philosophers understood their intellectual work to be a contribution to the public debate on crucial practical issues" (such as the right to equal job opportunities, and to own property) (p. 2). The center, or what Alcoff and Potter call "the 'core' areas" are Epistemology and Metaphysics.

Alcoff and Potter (1993) inform us that when feminists began working in the field of Epistemology, their contribution was as critique of the tradition, as was their contribution in the other philosophical fields of study. If Epistemology is defined as a theory of knowledge in general, then a feminist epistemology which refers to women's experiences, is an oxymoron, due to its efforts to focus on the particularity of women instead of the generality of human beings. And, indeed, when feminists began contributing to Epistemology they were criticized for not doing Epistemology, as it has been historically defined. Feminists found that they can only begin to contribute to Epistemology by first challenging the Philosophical premise "that a general account of knowledge, one that uncovers justificatory standards a priori, is *possible*" (p. 1, emphasis in original). Feminists argue that while 'human beings' is a concept that claims to include "all people," it really has historically been an androcentric concept that represents a male perspective. Since traditional Epistemology has *not* been able to present a generality but rather has represented a male perspective as if it is general, neutral, and inclusive of women, then there is the possibility of offering a feminist epistemology. This is why critique of the tradition has to come first, in order to create a space where feminists can begin to actually do constructive and reconstructive work in (e)pistemology. That work is just beginning to emerge now, and this text is meant as a contribution to that effort.

My plan is to consider Epistemology more specifically, in terms of its traditional meaning, and how it is represented currently in philosophical discussions. I will describe Harvey Siegel's Epistemological theory, which still takes a universalizing approach, yet in a limited way. I offer Siegel's theory as an example of Enlightenment Epistemological theory in its best and in its most recent form. I will then present the feminist, pragmatist, and postmodern side of this debate, turning to Richard Rorty's and Charlene Haddock Seigfried's work, with contributions from John Dewey, for he is an important source for Rorty, Seigfried, and myself. Lorraine Code's concern for a "responsibilist" epistemology and Sandra Harding's feminist standpoint epistemology will also come into the discussion. Siegel attempts to address postmodern, multicultural, and feminist concerns, seeking to avoid dogmatism while at the same time clinging to absolutism. We will see if he succeeds in having it both ways, as he strives for particularity and universality. I will end by coopting (e)pistemology and removing its absolute status, even in its non-vulgar form, in exchange for a qualified relativist status. I will reclaim the value and importance of being able to make judgments and present our arguments based on criteria which are socially constructed and therefore open to criticism and improvement. I will keep in check (e)pistemology's will to transcendental power and its desire to embrace dualisms such as knower/known, mind/body, theory/practice, subject/object. Thus, the reader should end this chapter with a good sense of my positon within the epistemological debate, as well as a better understanding of why I continue to use the word *epistemology*, though in its altered form of (e)pistemology.

Traditional Epistemology

Historically, Philosophy has been perceived as the "foundational" discipline which "grounds" knowledge claims. Earlier on, Philosophy struggled against religion for status as the foundational source of knowledge, and succeeded in defeating religion by relegating religion to *faith* and claiming *justified true belief* for Philosophy. More recently Philosophy has been at risk of losing its foundational status, as science has gained in status. Thus we find more recent philosophers such as Russell, Husserl, Peirce, and Dewey concerned with keeping Philosophy "rigorous" and making it "more scientific." Even more recently, Philosophy's foundational status has been under attack by postmodernists who have declared Philosophy irrelevant and dead (Lyotard). Philosophers are being replaced by scientists (Quine), leaving poets, novelists, and storytellers (Rorty, Foucault, Derrida) as our moral teachers.

Philosophers historically defined Epistemology as the branch of Philosophy that develops theories concerning what counts as knowledge. Epistemologists look at questions about the *justification* of people's beliefs and concern themselves with the normative status of knowledge claims. They attempt to *verify* claims that are made, and to prove the *validity* of arguments. Traditionally, epistemologists do not concern themselves with how people come to believe certain things or how they learn, saving those questions for sociology, psychology, and education. Epistemologists are concerned with what *warrants* the knowledge claims we make, therefore they ask normative questions such as what counts as good evidence, not causal questions concerning how beliefs are developed.

Epistemologists concern themselves with finding Knowledge, and they have historically defined absolute Truth as a necessary condition for Knowledge. Only that which is absolutely True is Knowledge; if we are not sure that something is True, we must call that something a *belief* instead of *knowledge*. Beliefs are not necessarily true, but Knowledge is necessarily True. There are different categories of beliefs, which depend on how close the beliefs are to being declared Knowledge, which is *True belief*. *Mere beliefs*, or right opinions, are stated as "S believes that p," with "S" symbolizing the subject of the belief, and "p" signifying the object of the belief. *Rational beliefs* are beliefs that are supported by compelling reasons ("S has good reason to believe that p"). We only call "p" Knowledge if what S believes about p, and S has compelling reasons to believe about p, is really True ("S knows that p").

There are many kinds of Epistemological theories which have developed throughout time. Plato's theory is that we know 'that p' because our souls are immortal and therefore know all knowledge. Knowing is an act of remembering what our souls already know. Aristotle argues, in disagreement with his teacher, that it is not enough to recollect Truth, thus relying on thought as reality and the origin of knowledge. Aristotle suggests that we must test out our ideas with our experiences to be sure they are true, thus asserting that material things are the reality, and the origin of knowledge. If our ideas correspond to our experiences then we can conclude they are True. Aristotle's correspondence theory follows a path that leads us to present-day science and the scientific method. Following a similar vein as Plato, Descartes argues that what we know is what is beyond doubt. By using Descartes's doubting method to dismiss everything we can doubt, until we come to what we take to be self-evident, we can find Truth. Peirce follows Aristotle's path into the future, arguing that we will not know Truth until the end of time. Truth is something that we are getting closer to as we continue to test out our ideas with our experiences, but none of us can be guaranteed of certain knowledge in our own lifetimes. Thus, we find today that while epistemologists still strive for clarity and coherence, most have rejected certainty as a condition of knowledge, following Peirce's lead.

Foundational epistemologists seek to establish that we can ultimately justify our claims by relying on "foundational" beliefs which are justified, but not in terms of other beliefs. Coherentists seek to establish that claims fit coherently into the existing body of knowledge. Some describe foundationalists as embracing a pyramid model, and coherentists as embracing a raft model. The pyramid model attempts to establish basic "foundational" beliefs (undisputed Truths) and builds upon these. The raft model allows that specific truths may change over time, as we change in our understanding, so that individual logs on the raft may need repair or replacement, yet the raft continues to hold us and support us down the river of Truth.

There are some key metaphysical assumptions embedded in traditional Philosophy's definition of Epistemology, no matter which particular theory one embraces. These assumptions are based on several dualisms, which we have already come across in my above description. We find that Philosophy distinguishes itself from science, for example, based on the separation of theory from practice, and universality from particularity. Epistemology talks about knowers and the known (subjects/objects, S and p), and separates itself from science and religion by drawing a sharp distinction between relative (individual) belief and absolute (universal) Truth. The metaphysical assumption I wish to address in this section is the assumption of absolutism, in contrast to relativism. I will turn to knowers and the known in the feminist section, particularity/universality in the postmodern section, and theory/practice in the pragmatism section.

Harvey Siegel (1997) describes his epistemological theory as a modernist, Enlightenment view that aims to secure Truth by offering rational justification for claims made. He realizes his theory is an absolutist Epistemology based on a traditional view of Philosophy.

> On my (admittedly traditional) view, philosophy is fundamentally concerned with reasons, arguments, and, with Socrates, is committed to following the argument wherever it leads—i.e. to basing belief, action and judgment on epistemically forceful reasons. The aim of the exercise is the discovery of philosophical truths (p. 187).

Seigel insists on the need for a concept of absolutism in Epistemology in order to be able to make objective, non-question begging judgments. He argues that without an assumption of absolutism, we slide into relativism, the position that all views are possibly right or wrong for all truths are relative to the individual, and to the time and place in which s/he acts. Siegel describes relativism as incoherent, self-defeating, arbitrary, or impotent. As Seigel (1987) states in *Relativism Refuted*, "absolutism is a necessary precondition of epistemological inquiry" no matter what one embraces for a theory of truth (correspondence or coherence), theory or justification, the analysis of knowledge ("standard analysis, a causal theory, a defeasibility theory, a reliabilist theory, an explanatory theory, or virtually any other theory"), and theory of evidence (p. 165).

Siegel (1987) is very careful, however, to define what he means by "absolute." Indeed, this is one of his main tasks in *Relatism Refuted*. Siegel does *not* wish to be aligned with what he terms "vulgar absolutism." He agrees with feminists and postmodernists that vulgar absolutism leads to dogmatism (see arguments below). But he disagrees with them in regards to their rejection of the Enlightenment project, for Siegel argues that rejecting the Enlightenment project means denying the need to ground a position with reasons which justify holding the position. To hold a position seriously, as feminists and postmodernists want to do, and at the same time deny the need to rationally justify the holding of that position with the epistemic force of transcendental arguments is a logical contradiction, according to Siegel. As soon as feminists or postmodernists use reasons to attempt to make any claims, they must assume reasons are legitimate and can be used to justify and warrant arguments. However, we will find that feminists and postmodernists (and pragmatists) do not deny that reasons are needed to warrant arguments; they just deny the transcendental force modernist Enlightenment philosophers want to assign to reasons. They do take (e)pistemology seriously, but they deny (e)pistemology its transcendental legitimacy, insisting (e)pistemology's legitimacy lies in the natural world instead, which is a contingent, ever-changing world in which we are active participants. (E)pistemology's legitimacy lies within the generalizability of our limited, particular, biased, socially constructed experiences.

Siegel (1987) argues in *Relativism Refuted* that "absolutism" does not entail certainty if that means there is no room for us to be fallible, make mistakes, and correct our errors. While *vulgar* absolutism is based on a fundamental belief that knowers can have direct access to Reality and be certain that they are right, *non-vulgar* absolutism admits of possible error. Non-vulgar absolutism recognizes that "(t)here is no such completely neutral perspective from which to judge. Our judgments are in *this* sense unavoidably contextual, and, consequently, are forever fallible, forever open to challenge from perspectives and viewpoints both already in view and not yet anticipated" (Siegel, 1997, p. 127, emphasis in original). Seigel's non-vulgar absolutism accepts Peirce's argument that knowledge is revisable, thus he does not wish to claim that Knowledge = Certain Truth. He accepts Peirce's *fallibilism*, which he takes to mean in a very general way "*all* claims are fallible and open to challenge, and *no* claims are certain" (Siegel, 1997, p. 121, emphasis in original). However, Siegel (1997) argues that fallibilism entails some standard of evaluation that allows us to judge alternative beliefs or frameworks. "The predicament of fallibilism" is that no one can get beyond *all* contexts, yet Siegel argues this does not mean "there is no principle barrier to getting beyond any particular context, or to judging it from a perspective which enjoys critical leverage over both it and its alternatives" (Siegel, 1997, p. 127). Thus we find that while Siegel does not claim that he has a God's-eye view of what is Right/True, he does want to claim the possibility of epistemic agency. I will come back to this later in our discussion of feminist standpoint epistemology, for they also want to claim critical leverage.

In agreement with traditional Philosophy, Siegel's non-vulgar absolutist Epistemology describes the philosopher's task as one of trying to determine the extent to which reasons for a claim offer it warrant. Philosophers rely on criteria to help them with this task. Criteria act as norms, standards, and principles. Siegel argues that to avoid relativism, philosophers must treat criteria as if they are binding upon all reasoners. Criteria must presuppose an objective or absolute status in order to function as criteria and allow us the possibility of comparison and evaluation across alternatives. However, Siegel admits he does not want to claim that criteria are incorrigible; in fact he wants to claim just the opposite. The criteria we use to judge reasons and arguments can be self-correcting and corrigible (capable of being improved). Siegel (1988) describes his position on criteria (principles) this way:

> Principles embody rationality and define and assess reasons in a tradition at a time. As the tradition evolves, so do the principles which define and assess reasons. So what counts as a good reason in a tradition may change over time; today's compelling reason may be seen as less compelling tomorrow. . . . Still, the principles which determine the compellingness of reasons at a time apply to all putative reasons impartially and universally. . . . (T)he principles which define reasons and determine their force may change, but rationality remains the same. (Siegel, 1988, p. 135)

Siegel (1987) wants to avoid absolutism and relativism, by embracing a non-vulgar absolutism. He defines his "absolutism" as: "a non-dogmatic, non-certain, corrigible, fallible, non-unique absolutism" (p. 164). What is absolute about such a concept? Siegel (1987) argues that his non-vulgar absolutism offers "the possibility of objective, non-question-begging evaluation of putative knowledge-claims, in terms of criteria which are taken as absolute but which nonetheless admit of criticism and improvement" (p. 162).

Siegel (1997) sums up his view this way:

Specifically, I argue ... for a fallibilist but absolutist conception of truth: absolutist in that truth of a proposition, sentence, belief or claim is independent of the warrant or justification it enjoys on the basis of relevant evidence, and fallibilist in that our judgments concerning truth are always open to challenge and revision; for a view of justification as a fallible indicator of truth; and for the rejection of epistemological relativism. (p. 6)

There is a tension in Siegel's theory between wanting to admit contextuality and the possibility of subjective, human error, on the one hand, and needing to insist on impartial generalizability and the possibility of objectivity, on the other hand. Siegel's insistence on hanging on to absolutism, even in its non-vulgar form, and the need to remain within the structure of traditional, modern, Enlightenment Epistemology undermines Siegel's desired softened categories. We can find two examples of how Siegel's non-vulgar absolutism undermines his own softened categories in his more recent collection of essays titled *Rationality Redeemed?* (1997). With each of these examples Siegel embraces dualisms in order to support the dichotomy he wishes to retain between (non-vulgar) absolutism/relativism. The dualisms do help him remain in an absolutist Epistemological world, but at the expense of hardening the very categories he wishes to soften. Thus, we will find that Siegel is subject to the very criticisms of privileged framework, incorrigibility, and certainty he seeks to avoid. He is also subject to being accused of performance contradiction; the same criticism he uses regularly with feminists and postmodernists.

In 1991 Siegel participated in a healthy debate with Nicholas Burbules concerning Siegel's concept of non-vulgar absolutism.[3] Burbules published his views in a book review essay of Siegel's two books (*Relativism Refuted*, 1987; *Educating Reason*, 1988) for *Educational Theory*, 1991. Their debate was published in *Philosophy of Education 1991*, and Siegel republished his views in *Rationality Redeemed?* (1997). The debate refers to Siegel's critical thinking theory, which I have addressed elsewhere and therefore will not address again here (Thayer-Bacon, 2000). It is not necessary to engage in a discussion of Siegel's critical thinking theory to make the point I wish to make here about epistemology. Burbules begins the debate by complimenting Siegel for his efforts to reconceive rationality in a more contextualized manner. Burbules describes Siegel as holding a view that is in agreement with his, which Burbules calls a *substantive* conception of rationality. A substantive conception of rationality includes the importance of considering the individual character of the person doing the reasoning, the subject of rationality, not just the object of rationality. (We will find below that Lorraine Code discusses this issue in her *Epistemic Responsibility* and "Taking Subjectivity into Account.") Siegel (1992) describes the substantive side of his critical thinking theory, "the critical spirit." Burbules calls his own substantive conception of rationality, "reasonableness" (p. 218). Burbules

(1992) says: "I want to incorporate into the very idea of reason the elements of personal characteristics, context, and social relations that support and motivate reasonable thought and conduct. That is, *to be reasonable* means to be a certain kind of person, in a certain kind of situation, related to certain kinds of other persons" (p. 218, emphasis in original).

While Siegel (1992) agrees with the need to reject a formal conception of rationality, and to "regard rationality as a substantive epistemic notion, involving the contents of sentences rationally related" (p. 228), he has problems with Burbules's notion of "reasonableness," believing that "he overstates the contextual dimensions of rationality" (p. 228). If rationality is determined by "the actual activities, decisions, and judgments which people make, then I see a big problem: namely, there is no room on this view for actual activities, decisions, and judgments to be irrational, for there is no role for criteria to function in assessing specific activities, decisions, and judgments as rational (or not)" (Siegel, 1992, p. 229). We find that Burbules and Siegel do not really agree in their substantive concept of rationality/reasonableness, for Burbules acknowledges that theories, such as rationality, are ones that people construct, thus arguing for a strong version of contextuality. Siegel (1997) is willing to accept that rationality "manifests itself" in the activities, decisions, and judgments of persons but he is not willing to say rationality "is constituted by" this context, suggesting that rationality is determined by the activities, decisions, and judgments of persons (p. 105). Siegel tells us:

> This "constitutive" view of rationality is strongly contextual, for it implies not only that the rationality of particular judgments, etc. is relative to context—which it surely is, since the evidence one has at one's disposal is context-bound—but also that rationality itself is determined by context, in the sense that what "rationality" means, and whether and why it is to be valued, themselves are determined by context. (p. 105)

For Siegel, rationality is a regulative ideal, in the Kantian sense. He does not want rationality to lose its transcendental status where truth is independent of epistemic justification, even as he embraces fallibilism. He protects rationality from strong contextuality by reinstating the traditional sharp distinction between generalizable philosophy and particular science. Siegel (1997) claims that Burbules confuses *causal* questions with *philosophical* ones, mistaking causal efficacy for epistemic support (p. 108-109). Thus we find Siegel must reinstate a sharp dichotomy between existential causal factors in the natural world and rational ideals in a transcendent world in order to maintain his absolutism/relativism distinction, for the admission of contextuality threatens to dispel the dualism. Siegel is willing to admit some contextuality into his Epistemological theory, but not too much. He wants Philosophy to maintain its privileged position of supplier of the standards of (fallible) criteria for Rationality and Truth.

In 1992 Siegel responded to another book review essay discussing his two books, *Relativism Refuted* (1987) and *Educating Reason* (1988). The review, written by Mark Weinstein (1992), was published in *Studies in Philosophy and Education*, as was Siegel's response. Siegel republished his response in *Rationality Redeemed?* (1997). Again, we find Weinstein compliments Siegel for the scope and quality of his work. Siegel's analyses are detailed and clarificatory. Weinstein also wants to defeat relativism, highlight the importance of giving reasons to ground claims and judgments, reject any privileged perspective, embrace fallibilism, and admit the possibilities of objective reasons and rational criticism (Siegel, 1997, p. 128). Weinstein (1992) tells us his view on "epistemology across the disciplines ... relies essentially on what seems to be the most important contribution that Siegel makes.... His arguments free us from immodest relativist fears by guaranteeing the reflexivity of the rational enterprise in a way that yields modest foundational support" (p. 248).

Weinstein (1992) focuses his discussion on the type of argument Siegel employs to make his points. Weinstein calls this type of argument "a priori" or "foundational" argumentation which is "based on logical truth alone" (p. 249). Weinstein argues this type of argument is very limited in its reach for while it can yield certainty, it cannot solve outstanding practical problems concerning educational reform. Weinstein also questions Siegel's "non-vulgar absolutism," suggesting this version of absolutism is either dogmatic or arbitrary. Weinstein offers instead an argument "for the primacy of communities as the foundation of reasoning" (p. 249). Weinstein's community-based rationality is another example of strong contextualism.

Siegel (1997) responds to Weinstein's essay by first pointing to confusion in Weinstein's use of the term "foundational" in terms of consistency of use as well as in terms of coherence with the customary use in Epistemology, where "foundational" "refers to a sort of belief, not a set of argument-types or a class of discourse frames" (p. 113). Siegel then moves to question Weinstein's assumption that logical argumentation can yield certainty, for, as we have already found, Siegel embraces fallibilism and does not claim that philosophical arguments can yield certainty. He agrees with Weinstein that philosophical arguments are limited in their reach, they "cannot resolve outstanding, largely extra-philosophical problems which are in need of resolution" (p. 115). These are empirical, practical problems, not philosophical ones. Siegel describes his project as a "traditionally conceived, philosophical project" of challenging epistemological relativism (1987) and defending critical thinking as an educational ideal (1988). Thus we find again Siegel's distinction between existential causality and essential Philosophy.

In response to Weinstein's (1992) criticism that Siegel's non-vulgar absolutism is either dogmatic or arbitrary, the same criticisms Siegel uses against relativism, Siegel employs another dualism to answer these charges. He admits that all our justified beliefs are open to challenge. However, even though our justified beliefs do not yield certainty, they can still afford warrant to a claim and end with credibility. "In order to afford warrant, it need not be certain, but only itself justified" (1997, p. 121). Siegel (1997) tries to demonstrate that Weinstein mistakenly assumes "that something *is* a good reason" means the same thing as "that something is taken to be a good reason." The difference between is-taken-to-be/is-a-good-reason is the difference between *doxastic* justification and *propositional* justification, according to Siegel. Propositional justification refers strictly to the relationship between belief and potentially justified belief; it is independent of context. Propositional justification is independent of subjects (communities), whereas doxastic justification requires the believers (the subjects) and their beliefs. Doxastic justification "is contextualist, in the sense that it requires that beliefs be 'based on' their justifiers in particular (and philosophically contentious) ways" (Siegel, 1997, p. 123). Doxastic justification resides within space, time, and causal conditions whereas propositional justification resides in Philosophy's transcendental, ideal, decontextualized world. Again we find Seigel seeking to distinguish between a weak and strong sense of contextuality, in order to maintain his absolutism/relativism distinction, and remain within the structure of traditional, modern Enlightenment Epistemology. Again we find the admission of contextuality threatens to undermine the distinction between the causal, natural world and the transcendent, philosophical world. And, once again, we find Siegel embraces a dualism in order to support the dichotomy he wishes to retain between (non-vulgar) absolutism/relativism. As a consequence of Siegel's efforts to retain traditional Philosophy's (non-vulgar) absolutist Epistemological aim, he ends up shoring up the very categories he claims to want to soften, thus making himself vulnerable to the very criticisms of privileged framework, incorrigibility, and certainty he seeks to avoid.

Jim Garrison (1999a, 1999b) has also written a review of Siegel's work; in fact he has written two reviews, both of which focus on Siegel's 1997 *Rationality Redeemed?* In Garrison's *Educational Theory* essay in particular, he brings out many of the tensions and criticisms I discuss here.[4] Siegel's (2000) response to these was just printed at the time of my writing. In Siegel's response he accuses Garrison of distorting and misconstruing his positions, saying he hardly recognizes himself in Garrison's description. Garrison argues that Siegel's commitment to rationality as criteriology (fixed first principles as ultimate premises) and epistemological absolutism require him to reject strong contextualism. We have found that this is a fair description, for in the examples above Siegel insists on the need to reject strong contextualism and warns that to not do so leads us to epistemological relativism. Garrison (1999a) describes Siegel's strategy as one of first decontextualizing "by severing language from its roots in existential operations and the coordination of social action. He then commits the philosophic fallacy and hypostatizes decontextualized abstractions" (p. 332). Thus language and reason, as abstract concepts, are treated as if they have a real identity of their own, divorced from any context (Siegel's propositional justification and rationality). In Siegel's (2000) response he does reiterate that for him "truth is independent of justification. . . . (S)uitably formulated, sentences and/or propositions do not typically change truth-value with change of time, culture, or other aspects of context—though our evidence for them, and so our estimates of their truth, do" (p. 129). Further along he says, "'(T)ruth' [is] a semantic notion, truth is a property of some beliefs, sentences, and so forth" (p. 130). Siegel describes his "non-epistemic conception of truth" as requiring a minimal realism consistent with minimalist conceptions of truth in order to insure truth's independence, what is the case, from what we take to be the case.

Garrison (1999a) ends his essay by showing how the sharp distinction between decontextualized propositional justification and contextualized doxastic justification is easily dissolved, and how doxastic context can always be restored.

> The intuition that allows one to always recognize and reject Siegel's question-begging arguments for self-justifying rationality is this: *No one just gives reasons; they give reasons to someone in some context because they desire some consequence.* . . . All reasons are given to someone in some context of action (p. 333, emphasis in original). . . . Context may always be restored, even to formal propositional arguments, by asking, acceptable to whom? (p. 334). . . . Siegel only conceals context, he does not destroy it. (p. 336)

Siegel (2000) responds that he does not "conceal context," he simply ignores it in the cases where it is irrelevant.

By reintroducing contextuality, Garrison (1999a) also demonstrates how Siegel is guilty of "performative contradiction," the very same charge Siegel makes against feminists and postmodernists. A performative contradiction "occurs in a situation where the very act of arguing contradicts the propositional content that is argued for" (Garrison, 1999a, p. 336). When feminists and postmodernists question the value of an absolute Epistemology, Siegel accuses them of performative contradiction for they assume the value of Epistemology in offering reasons for why it should be questioned. Garrison (1999a) points out that performative contradiction is a double-edged sword:

> By reversing his strategy, we see that *Siegel* himself is caught in a performative contradiction. In the very act of arguing for the self-justification of decontextualized foundationalist epistemology he employs a strategy that contradicts his claim because it requires a context to determine that it is not question-begging. (pp. 336–337, emphasis in original)

I do not think Siegel escapes the criticisms I have sketched here and will further develop below. Once we embrace fallibilism and a pluralistic universe, we must let go of the hope of absolute Truth, and learn to live with truths that are satisfactory (James), with what Dewey called "waranted assertability." Once we acknowledge we cannot escape contextuality, we cannot argue for the self-justification of decontextualized absolutist Epistemology without performatively contradicting ourselves. In this chapter and the next I will make the case that pragmatists, feminists, and postmodernists show us the way out of Epistemology's absolute/relative dichotomy and the charge of performative contradiction from either side of the sword. Since what I offer here is a feminist (e)pistemology, I turn first to some feminist concerns.

Some Feminist Concerns

As we have found, feminists must begin their discussion of Epistemology by questioning its assumption of generalizability. They must make the case that their voices have not been historically included in the general concept of knowers, but rather an androcentric (male) perspective has been presented.[5] Many feminists have contributed to the argument that *girl/woman* is excluded from the concept "human beings" ("mankind") and treated as "other" in Euro-western philosophy.[6] Once establishing that the female voice has been excluded from Philosophy in general, which I think most philosophers would agree has been successfully accomplished, the next step is to establish the exclusion of the female voice within the field of Epistemology, as described above.

A significant example of androcentrism in Philosophy is demonstrated by the association of Philosophy with the mind, which is linked to males, in contrast to the body, which is connected to females. Although Descartes usually gets blamed for splitting the mind from the body in Euro-western philosophy (Bordo, 1987; Rorty, 1979), I argue that we can go back to ancient Greece and find many examples of Plato severing the mind from the body, and assigning the body to a lesser status (Thayer-Bacon, 2000). A most vivid example of Plato's separation and assigned value can be found in his theory of knowledge. Plato describes each of us as having an immortal soul that knows all, and we forget what we know when our souls inhabit our bodies at birth. Thus, our bodies cause us to forget all knowledge, and we are doomed to spending our lifetimes trying to remember what we already knew.

Once the body is split from the mind, and given a lesser status as that which serves as a barrier, deceives us, and lures us away from seeking Truth due to its earthly passions, then it is an easy next step to associate women with the body. Simone de Beauvoir (1952/1989) carefully makes the argument that there are only two things that distinguish women from men when we look at cultures around the world and throughout time, and yet the two things have been used to assign women an inferior, Other, status in many cultures. Given the inferior status of the body, it is not surprising to find that these two things that distinguish women from men have to do with women's physical bodies: that they have weaker muscles and they menstruate. De Beauvoir points toward the future when technology will help women compensate for their weaker muscles, and birth control will bring their reproductive systems within their control. When that day comes, de Beauvoir predicted that women may finally be given an equal status. That day that de Beauvoir predicted is here for many women, still women have not yet reached an equal status. Neutralizing bodily differences is not enough to change women's status; the status of the body must be raised and it must be reconnected to the mind. Feminists realize now that in order to help put an end to the androcentrism in Philosophy, we must call into question the body/mind split, and make the case for a wholistic *bodymind*. That argument comes from many diverse camps, and will be represented in this text in the chapters on personal relations, w/holistic relations, ecological relations, and scientific relations, for example.

Traditional Epistemology shows its androcentricism with its embrace of Rationality as an Ideal, for rationality (or reason) is again associated with the mind, which is linked to males. Irrationality, in contrast, is associated with the emotions and intuitions, which are normally attributed to women. So, historically within the field of Epistemology, males function as the model for rationality and females serve as the model for irrationality. Feminists have argued for the value of intuition and emotions (and imagination) in reason, by turning to womens' experiences and describing womens' ways of knowing (Belenky et al., 1986; Gilligan, 1982; Martin, 1994; Ruddick, 1989). Along with traditional androcentric Epistemological models, we now have examples of gynocentric (female) Epistemological models (Duran, 1991). However, claiming a distinctive status for women as knowers not only serves to raise their status, it also continues to maintain a gender split. As long as a gender split is maintained, women still serve in the role of Other defined in contrast to rational males. Once again, feminists have learned that the best way to gain women's status as rational beings who are potential knowers is to call into question the rational/irrational (mind/body) split, and to show that all of us use many tools to help us construct knowledge, our reason, emotions, intuition, *and* imagination, for example (Thayer-Bacon, 2000).

Another good place to look for androcentrism in Epistemology is with the "subject," 'S' in "S knows that p" statements. The subject, the knower, the epistemic agent, are all quite objective, neutral terms that could represent anyone, so it seems. In fact, not only is the knower represented with neutral terminology, the importance and weight of considering 'S's' contribution to 'that p' is minimalized, thus devaluing the importance of 'S' even more. Historically, Epistemology has been based on an assumption that subjects (S) do not need to be taken into consideration in determining 'that p.' As Epistemology has historically developed, the subject, S, has been severed from 'that p' and the attention of epistemologists has been focused on 'that p,' at the expense of 'S.' Euro-western Philosophy concerns itself with the product of knowers' efforts. Knowers are separated from what is known, and devalued in importance.

Lorraine Code (1987) argues that not taking subjects into account leads us to the following traditional Epistemological conclusions:

> (1) that knowledge properly so-called is autonomous in that it is of no epistemological significance whose it is; (2) that knowledge acquisition may be of psychological interest but it is irrelevant to an epistemologist's quest for criteria of justification, validity, and verification; and (3) that knowledge is objective in the sense that discussion of the character and epistemic circumstances of subjects has nothing to contribute to the proper epistemological task of assessing the product. (p. 25–26)

If we can ignore knowers in our quest for knowledge, then we can ignore questions such as how do we come to be knowledgable, and for what purpose is such knowledge? We can ignore questions that draw our attention to the context of knowing, show the connection of knowledge with values, and point to issues of power. We can ignore gender, class, ethnicity, and race as categories of concern, for example. If we diminish the importance of subjects, then we can pretend to offer a neutral, general theory of knowledge, when what we really offer is an androcentric Epistemology. The androcentrism is visible in the objectification and neutralization of the subject.

Lorraine Code's work has contributed to a feminist effort to bring the subject, 'S,' more directly into discussions of epistemology. In *Epistemic Responsibility* (1987) her focus is on making the case that there are moral implications to knowledge claims, and that we need to understand how directly connected morality is to epistemology. Code's (1987) central claim is "that knowing well is as much a moral as it is an epistemological matter" (p. 252). The way we understand that knowing well is a matter of considerable moral significance is to pay attention to the character of would-be knowers. Code tells us she is trying to shift the emphasis of investigation and evaluation so that knowers come to bear as much of the onus of credibility as "the known" (pp. 8–9). She wants to put "epistemic responsibility" in a central place in theories of knowledge. She wants to insist that knowers must be held accountable to their community as well as to the evidence.

In "Taking Subjectivity into Account," published in *Feminist Epistemologies*, Code (1993) again takes up the topic of looking at 'S' of 'S knows that p' statements. Here she makes the case these statements are representative of a "received" knowledge model that is very narrow and limited in scoop. By "received" knowledge, she means "conditions that hold for any knower, regardless of her or his identity, interests, and circumstances (i.e., her or his subjectivity)" (p. 15). This dominant Enlightenment Epistemological theory, as we saw above with Siegel, relies on Ideals of objectivity and value neutrality (Siegel's non-vulgar absolute), to argue that Reason allows 'S' to transcend particularity and contingency. Thus 'S' is suppose to represent anyone and everyone (no one in particular).[7] Code wants to seriously entertain a model of "constructed" knowledge, that "requires epistemologists to pay as much attention to the nature and situation—the location—of S as they commonly pay to the content of p; . . . [she maintains] that a constructivist reorientation requires epistemologists to take subjective factors—factors that pertain to the circumstances of the subject, S—centrally into account in evaluative and justificatory procedures" (p. 20).[8] Thus, gender, race, class, ethinicity become recognized as primary analytic categories as we move to take subjectivity into account.

Code (1993) makes the case, similar to Garrison (1999a) above, that subjectivity is always there, hidden, despite disclaimers, and that we can always find the context that is being suppressed. Subjectivity is found in the examples selected for discussion, and the experiences used to represent "human thought," for example. Contra to Siegel, Code (1993) argues that "taking subjectivity into account does not *entail* abandoning objectivity" (p. 36, emphasis in original). What it does is help us guard against reductivism and rigidity. It allows us to accommodate change, by letting knowledge claims be provisional and approximate. Code describes herself as a "mitigated relativist," who argues that epistemology has no ultimate foundation, "but neither does it float free, because it is grounded in experiences and practices, in the efficacy of dialogic negotiation and of action" (p. 39). This is similar to my *qualified relativist* position which I will further develop in Chapter 2.

What we have found out so far in this section is that feminists have successfully made the case for Philosophy's androcentrism, as well as Epistemology's androcentrism. Feminists have argued soundly for the dissolving of the body/mind dualism and for taking subjectivity into account as they make the case for viewing knowledge in relation to knowers. As we found above with Siegel's epistemological theory, current male philosophers are careful not to claim a spectator's view of knowledge, and are willing to acknowledge their own embeddedness. Yet they do not want to relinquish the claim to epistemic privilege that they have held for so long, for fear they will be left with nothing (relativism). In their efforts to hold back subjectivity and contextuality so that they admit some, but not so much that all is lost, some traditional Epistemologists such as Siegel have found allies amongst feminists, in particular spontaneous empiricist feminists and standpoint feminists, as labeled by Sandra Harding (1991, 1993). Like her, these feminists tend to work in various fields of science.

According to Harding (1993), spontaneous empiricist feminists, such as Lynn Hankinson Nelson, Elizabeth Potter, and Helen Longino,[9] argue that insufficient care and rigor in following the existing methods and norms is what has caused sexist and androcentric results in research. They do not think the problem lies in the basic canons, but rather with how we *do* science and philosophy. They recommend that what we need is more precision and clarity, what we need is to do *good* science and philosophy that is more careful and rigorous. Like Siegel in regards to Philosophy, empiricist feminists accept the inescapablity of social influence on the content of science. Longino's (1990, 1993) work helps us understand the deep hostility science and philosophy have historically expressed toward women. Elizabeth Potter (1993) and Lynn Nelson (1990, 1993) shed light on the negotiating process that goes on in science, within epistemological communities.

Nelson, Potter, and Longino each argue for a community's approach for establishing warrantability, as a way to undermine Epistemology's traditional transcendental perspective, as well as to avoid not being able to offer critique at all. Rather than thinking individuals are epistemic agents, that 'S' is a single knower, they recommend we think of communities as the primary epistemic agencies. Code (1987, 1993) recommends this as well. This strategy to combat science and philosophy's hostility, Longino (1993) describes as "multiplying the subjects," or as "*views* from *many wheres*" (p. 113, emphasis in original). If we treat science (and philosophy) as a practice, that commits us to viewing inquiry as ongoing and theories as partial, then "we can recognize pluralism in the community as one of the conditions for the continued development of scientific knowledge in this sense" (p. 116). Longino concludes no segment of the community can claim epistemic privilege. She recommends the creation of what she calls a "cognitive democracy," of "democratic science," using public and common standards (p. 118).

Harding (1993), however, thinks "the methods and norms in the disciplines are too weak to permit researchers *systematically* to identify and eliminate from the results of research those social values, interests, and agendas that are shared by the entire scientific community or virtually all of it" (p. 52, emphasis in original). The scientific method cannot rid itself of bias. Thus she recommends her strong objectivity method, which places the subjects of knowledge on the same critical, causal plane as objects of knowledge. Harding's "strong objectivity" requires that scientists (and philosophers) and their communities (Subjects) be critiqued as well as 'that p' (p. 69).

> All of the kinds of objectivity-maximizing procedures focused on the nature and/or social relations that are the object result of observation and reflection must also be focused on the observers and reflectors—scientists and the larger society whose assumptions they share. But a maximally critical study of scientists [philosophers] and their communities can be done only from the perspective of those whose lives have been marginalized by such communities. (p. 69)

Harding's strong objectivity method is based on a feminist standpoint epistemological theory. Harding and others,[10] have made important points about who gets left out of communities of inquirers. They argue for the need to expand epistemological communities to include those on the margins, those outsiders who are not traditionally viewed as experts, such as women, people of color, and people lacking in property. Using Marx, Engels, and Lukacs (and Hegel) as their sources initially, feminist standpoint theorists seek to understand the relations between power and knowledge, by looking at collective subjects, groups with shared histories and shared locations in relation to power. They try to generate different accounts from the dominant ones and explore the intersections of different outsider perspectives (e.g. feminists of color, gay and lesbian accounts, etc.). They do not claim to have a traditional Epistemological goal of seeking Truth; rather their project is to understand power relations, in order to be able to change them, by privileging the speech of marginalized subjects. Their Subject focus is also not of individuals, but collective subjects, groups who share histories, experiences, based on their shared positionality in relations of power.

Feminist standpoint epistemologists adopt the traditional Epistemologist's claim to epistemic privilege by claiming epistemic privilege for those traditionally excluded from mainstream philosophy. According to Harding (1993), their claim is "that all knowledge attempts are socially situated and that some of these objective social locations are better than others as starting points for knowlege projects [to] challenge some of the most fundamental assumptions of the scientific [and Philosophical] world view . . ." (p. 56). Looking from the margins helps us see the dominant culture and its assumptions of superiority. Marginalized lives provide us with the problems and agendas for standpoint theories, but not the solutions. Feminist standpoint theory starts from womens' lives, but these women are embodied and visible, and they are multiple and heterogenous, contradictary or incoherent. These marginal views are not just from our own marginalized lives, as women, but from other, different, and often oppositional womens' lives as well (p. 58).

Harding (1993) describes standpoint epistemologists as "sociological relativists"—but not epistemological relativists (p. 61). Like Siegel above, standpoint epistemologists want to have it both ways, they accept "the idea of real knowledge that is socially situated" (p. 50). Notice that like Siegel, while Harding does not want to claim she has a God's eye view of what is Right/True, she does want to claim the possibility of epistemic privilege, just with different subjects. She shifts the claim of critical leverage from the center to the margin, from philosophers and scientists, to those excluded from philosophy and science's androcentric theories. By doing so, she continues to use an absolutist tool (epistemic privilege) to try to dismantle absolutist Epistemology, in effect using a master's tool to try to dismantle the master's house (Bar On, 1993).[11] Another absolutist tool Harding insists on maintaining is "objectivity," even though she is well aware of how objectivity has been used in scientific projects that are now judged to be sexist, racist, classist, homophobic, etc. Harding (1993) argues "(t)he notion of objectivity is useful in providing a way to think about the gap that should exist between how any individual or group wants the world to be and how in fact it is" (p. 72). Thus we find she reveals her realist leanings. Longino (1993) describes Harding's standpoint theory as using the strategy of "changing the subject" to combat science and philosophy's hostility to girls/women, and she suggests Harding's standpoint theory begs the question.

Harding (1993) tries to deny that her project is an epistemological one, arguing instead that she is looking at political and social concerns. However, this sharp separation between epistemology and social and political theory undermines her own claim that "the grounds for knowledge are fully saturated with history and social life rather than abstracted from it" (p. 57). What Harding needs to deny is that her project is a transcendental Epistemological one. She, and other feminists, make a significant contribution to the collapse of absolutist Epistemology by highlighting the relationship between knowledge and power. By showing transcendental Epistemology's biases and limitations, Harding contributes to the description of a transformed (e)pistemology on socially constructed grounds. If Harding's theory is an accurate description of knowing, then she cannot avoid using (e)pistemological theory in her own project. What she can do is avoid transcendental Epistemology, and the use of its tools (such as epistemic privilege and objectivity).

I agree with empiricist feminists and standpoint feminists that there is a need to embrace pluralism, and in fact I will argue in Chapter 2 that (e)pistemological fallibilism entails (e)pistemological pluralism, contra to Peirce and Siegel. However, I do not think any of us, as knowers, can escape our own social embeddedness completely, and therefore I do not think any one standpoint has the chance of offering us a privileged, clearer, sounder view. There are as strong limitations on women's ways of knowing, as on men's, on Blacks' as on Whites', on lower-classes' as on middle or upper-classes', on homosexuals' as on heterosexuals' ways of knowing, just to name a few categories. The argument for standpoint epistemology risks sliding into determinism on one end of the spectrum and reaffirming a spectator's view on the other end. I argue that where we fall is somewhere in-between. We are greatly determined by our social setting, as social beings, but we are also able to become aware of our embeddedness, because we are social beings. Others shape our views but others also help us become aware of how views differ. I do not want to argue that any of us has a privileged perspective; I do not think any of us has a spectator's view on Reality; we are always embedded within it. We do not have views from nowhere, and we are also never able to see the world from everywhere. We are always situated and limited, our views are from *somewhere*. We are able to gain more critical leverage the more we experience and expose ourselves to others' standpoints, but we are never able to gain complete understanding. Contra to Peirce, I do not think the process of gaining understanding is linear, and the last person on earth will know Truth, at the end of time. The last people on earth will still be struggling with trying to understand from within their limited standpoints and they will still need each other to help them inquire and develop greater insight.

Some feminists argue that feminists should give up the task of trying to write a feminist epistemology, given the way Epistemology has historically been framed, in terms of its assumptions of generic transcendence (Code, Seigfried). Others argue there is value in developing a gynocentric epistemology in contrast to the androcentric ones we have inherited (Duran). I agree with Code and Seigfried, that it is impossible to write a feminist epistemology given the constrictions of Epistemology as historically defined. A feminist epistemology must include a gendered subject. Any attempt to include gender will be judged by traditional Enlightenment epistemologists as over-reaching the boundaries of Epistemology and asking Epistemology to stretch beyond its healthy limits, as we found above with the Weinstein/Siegel debate. Weinstein accused Siegel's epistemological theory of being too limiting, and Siegel responded by reaffirming the value of the limits of Philosophy in general, and Epistemology in particular.

Seigfried (1997) argues that there is a current hegemony of epistemology in philosophical and theoretical discourse, and this hegemony is due to the model of rationality many feminists are trying to challenge. Seigfried turns to pragmatism to help make the case that rationality includes "at least four dimensions, intellectual, aesthetic, moral, and practical," whereas our current model of rationality focuses only on the intellectual dimension (James, 1909/1977, p. 55). Like Dewey and James, Seigfried rejects "the myriad dualisms informing centuries of philosophic speculation and the spectator theory of knowledge that emerged from them" (p. 2). She describes the need to replace "traditional models of knowing as rationally speculative or empirically passive, as abstracting essences, satisfying *a priori* criteria, and producing certainty" with a model of knowing as a way of doing (p. 3). She warns that when feminists attempt to "add back the other dimensions" to the intellectually focused rationality model they are vulnerable to the charge of undermining the model itself. What feminists need to do is transform the model of rationality, and thus the traditional models of Epistemology.

Following Dewey's ("The Need for a Recovery of Philosophy," 1960) lead, Seigfried (1997) rejects what she calls "the very problem which forms the core of epistemology," that experience attaches to a private subject, and develops independently of the world of facts, thus creating "the problem of how the mind or subjective consciousness can understand the external world" (p. 3). For her, this separation of the knower from the world of facts (the known) is based on a false metaphysics that separates experience from existence. This false assumption is the basis for the spectator view of knowers. Seigfried also rejects Epistemology's conceived problem of knowledge *in general*. The Epistemological problem of knowledge *in general* is derived from assuming that there is a knower in general, who is outside of the world to be known. Seigfried warns that unless this assumption is undermined, feminist contributions to epistemology "will never be taken as anything other than at best a distraction from and, at worst a distortion of, the epistemological enterprise" (p. 4). She charges Epistemologists with continuing "to tinker at perfecting a perfectly rational account of knowledge in itself, while ignoring the question of what such knowledge is for, as well as how it arises in experience" (p. 5).

Seigfried (1997) encourages feminists to reject the Epistemological turn that has dominated twentieth-century philosophy departments, as pragmatists did earlier. She encourages feminists to embrace a pragmatic theory of knowledge as inquiry that satisfactorily resolves problematic situations.[12] Seigfried recommends that:

> (f)eminists do not have to defend themselves against hostile charges that they are not doing rigorous philosophy, that is, epistemology. They are not doing sloppy epistemology, but have understood that theories of knowledge must continue to develop into theories and practices of inquiry in order to get out of the cul-de-sac in which epistemology has been stuck ever since it went into business for its own sake. (p. 14)

I agree with feminist efforts to reject Epistemology, given the standard philosophical definition of Epistemology. However, I do not think feminists should be willing to accept this traditional definition, we need to redefine "epistemology." I recommend redefining "epistemology" because I think Siegel is right, that it is not possible to hold a position seriously and yet deny the need to ground a position with reasons which justify holding it. It is impossible to avoid epistemological concerns, such as what counts as criteria and standards for judging and critiquing reasons used to justify arguments, without risking sliding into dogmatism. And, it is vital that feminists actively engage in epistemological concerns in order to insist that criteria and standards remain open to critique. Feminists need to actively participate in efforts to continually improve upon the criteria and standards that our communities use. We need to confront epistemological concerns, not avoid them because of the transcendental baggage attached to them. However, we can only confront absolutist Epistemology with some tools of our own, such as an (e)pistemological theory offers.

The canons of Epistemology cannot stand up to the criticisms they are receiving from feminists (pragmatists and postmodernists, below). The current absolutist definition of Epistemology (even in Siegel's non-vulgar form) has problems with it which affect all philosophers, not just women, for all philosophers live in a gendered society. Not allowing Epistemology to address gender issues affects men and women alike. Epistemology must be redefined so that Subjects are able to be recognized as gendered subjects who are also social beings living in-relation-with others. Epistemology must be redefined so that it can be sensitive to actual outcomes, and require awareness of diverse contexts. A redefined (e)pistemology must include: "the emotional dimensions of understanding, the mutuality of facts and values, the exploration and rejection of pervasive prejudices, recognition of multiple standpoints, cooperative problem-solving, and valuing the other in their distinctiveness" (Seigfried, 1997, p. 9).

We already know that traditional Epistemologists will respond to my suggestion with a fear of the strong contextuality it introduces to theories of knowledge, as Siegel responded to Burbules's *substantive* proposal. But we also have learned from Garrison and Code that any efforts to limit or remove context are doomed to eventual failure. As long as Epistemologists continue to be willing to recognize we need knowers in order to have knowledge, then knowers will bring with them their contextuality, including their gender. I move on to some pragmatist concerns, as John Dewey recommended philosophy let go of Epistemology many years ago. Dewey's theory of inquiry inspires Garrison, Seigfried, Rorty, and myself, and serves as an example of an (e)pistemological theory.

Some Pragmatist Concerns

Along with Epistemology's embracing of an absolutism/relativism dualism that values transcendental Truth instead of contingent truths, a mind/body dualism that values the mind at the expense of the body, and a subject/object dualism that separates knowers from what is known and assigns higher value to the objects of knowledge, we also find that Epistemology has historically embraced a theory/practice dualism. Epistemologists are suppose to be concerned with the judging of reasons and reasons (theories, ideas) are usually descibed as being in contrast to experiences (practice). Thus we find some philosophers argue that we cannot trust our experiences and must tune into our ideas (Idealists), while others describe our experiences as our source of knowledge (Empiricists). Overall, ideas have held a higher status in the Euro-western world, as being more abstract, objective, and general than experience, which is judged to be more immediate, subjective, and concrete. Both types of argument still embrace a theory/practice dualism, favoring one side or the other. When treated as separate, contrasting entities then philosophers can ignore their transactional qualities, and again attempt to avoid issues concerning context, values, and power.

Classical pragmatists, usually represented as Peirce, James, and Dewey (as well as Mead and Royce), contribute significantly to the collapse of the theory/practice categorical bifurcation. Their contribution is what I want to explore in this section, in particular Dewey's contribution. The place to look for classical pragmatism's contribution is in the two key concepts of *fallibilism* and *experience*. These two concepts form the epistemological and metaphysical netting that catches up classic pragmatists' philosophical ideas. Here I want to focus on Dewey's contributions to the dispersion of the theory/practice dualism through his development of the concept *experience*, which was significantly influenced by James's writings on 'experience.' I will return to James's and Dewey's work on dissolving the absolutism/relativism split in Chapter 2, in my discussion on *fallibilism*.

I will argue in this text, as I have elsewhere (Thayer-Bacon, 2000), that James and Dewey were both successful in their dissolution efforts, though each have their own flaws which get in their way. James clings to the Subject as an individual, which makes him more vulnerable to relativism charges. Dewey embraces a democratic community of inquirers model, which is the direction feminists and postmodernists recommend, yet he reaches out to science as a method for solving doubts, and we found above that feminists have much to say about the inability of science to be objective and impartial. Classic pragmatists do not address adequately issues of power, and we already know that feminists have much to say to ensure we understand the connections between power and knowledge. We will find in the next section that postmodernists contribute significantly to our understanding of the connections between power and knowledge as well. However, even though Dewey did not focus his discussions on power issues, the way current feminists and postmodernists do, his discussion of *the* philosophical fallacy of neglecting context moved us to a better understanding of philosophy's own limitations due to its own embeddedness. His discussion on context is also a way into understanding his concept of 'experience.'

In "Context and Thought," Dewey (1960) looks at language to demonstrate how words and sentences are saturated with context. He shows how the meaning of words and sentences are dependent on "the contextual situation in which they appear and are used" (p. 90). Dewey defines *context* as including background (which is both temporal and spatial) and selective interest. Contextual background is what we take for granted, which is tacitly understood, as we draw our attention to that which we are immediately thinking of, through our selective interest.

> Surrounding, bathing, saturating, the things of which we are explicitly aware is some inclusive situation which does not enter into the direct material of reflection. It does not come into question; it is taken for granted with respect to the particular question that is occupying the field of thinking. Since it does not come into question, it is stable, settled. (p. 99)

Of course, background context can come into question, in fact that is one of the main contributions philosophers can make, helping to disturb what we take to be given, and causing us to bring an aspect of our background context to our selective interest. "Philosophy is criticism; criticism of the influential beliefs that underlie culture..." (Dewey, 1960, p. 107). This task of making the familiar strange is what standpoint theorists suggest is the role of the marginalized, the outsider who has been oppressed by the background context. Dewey argues that while we can learn to question our background context, we can never completely escape our background context, any more than we can step outside of our own skins in order to see them from an outsider perspective. We can only get partial glimpses.

Selective interest is the bias or attitude that exists for each of us in every particular thought we have. This attitude is what determines the questions we choose to ask and the way we choose to go about answering our questions. This bias is what causes us to notice certain qualities and not others, and to attend to certain experiences and not others. "There is care, concern, implicated in every act of thought" (Dewey, 1960, p. 101). Selective interest is what we have discussed above in the feminist section as the 'subjective.' Dewey explains how interest is equivalent to individuality or uniqueness, when framed in modest terms, and it is genuis and originality when framed in magnified terms. ". . . (S)elective interest is a unique manner of entering into interaction with other things. It is not a part or constituent of subject matter; but as a manner of action it selects subject matter and leaves a qualitative impress upon it" (Dewey, 1960, p. 102). The opposite of subjective is not objective, but rather the merely repetitive.

Dewey (1960) points out in his essay, "Context and Thought," several different fallacies "that tend to haunt philosophizing" (p. 96). These fallacies are examples of ways that philosophers commit the fallacy of ignoring context, what Dewey sometimes calls "apart thought." In philosophical analysis, philosophers commit the analytic fallacy when they ignore "the context in which and for the sake of which the analysis occurs" (p. 93). The fallacy of unlimited extension or universalization occurs when philosophers try to move beyond the limiting conditions that set up a contextual situation to a single and coherent whole. "All statements about the universe as a whole, reality as an unconditioned unity, involve the same fallacy" (p. 95). He then points out examples of the harmful effects caused from ignoring context in the accounts given of the history of thought. Historians often write about philosophers' work without paying attention to the conditions of the times in which they originally wrote, thus commiting the fallacy of ahistoricity. This is again an example of ignoring context. Dewey (1960) warns us:

> There exists at any period a body of beliefs and of institutions and practices allied to them. In these beliefs there are implicit broad interpretations of life and the world. These interpretations have consequences, often profoundly important. (p. 106)

Dewey (1960) tells us the significant business of philosophy is the disclosure of the context of beliefs, and he names *experience* "the last inclusive context. . . . The significance of 'experience' for philosophic method is, after all, but the acknowledgment of the indispensability of context in thinking when that recognition is carried to its full term" (p. 108). Dewey reveals his pragmatic leanings, which he called instrumental leanings, with his concept of 'experience,' for Dewey's logic of experience is one that argues meaning is "primarily a property of behavior" (Dewey, 1925/1981a, p. 141). Dewey adopted from Peirce his notion of meaning, that our conceptions are analyzed in terms of the consequences of our action. According to Peirce (1958), we cannot separate our ideas from our experiences. "A belief is that upon which a man is prepared to act" ("The Fixation of Belief," p. 91). Peirce argues that we determine how clear our concepts are by running them through a functional test, grounding them to experience. Thus, meaning is defined in terms of its effects.

In *Democracy and Education* (1916/1966) Dewey describes experience as having an active and passive element, trying and undergoing. "We do something to the thing and then it does something to us in return; such is the peculiar combination" (p. 139). In *Experience and Nature* (1925/1981a) Dewey describes experience this way: "Experience is not a veil that shuts man off from nature . . . but rather a growing progressive self-disclosure of nature itself" (p. 5). He goes on to say experience is:

> a double-barrelled word . . . it includes *what* men do and suffer, *what* they strive for, love, believe and endure, and also *how* men act and are acted upon, the ways in which they do and suffer, desire and enjoy, see, believe, imagine—in short, processes of *experiencing*. . . . It is "double-barrelled" in that it recognizes in its primary integrity no division between act and material, subject and object, but contains both in an unanalyzed totality. (p. 18, emphasis in original)

Jim Garrison (1994) further explains Dewey's concept of experience. "Experience for Dewey was simply what happened when human beings *actively participated in transactions* with other natural experiences. . . . Experience, for Dewey, is simply *how* the human organism interacts with its environment" ("Realism, Deweyan Pragmatism, and Educational Research," p. 9, emphasis in original).

Dewey's understanding of philosophy's own limitations due to its own embeddedness caused him to recommend the need to turn away from Epistemology, because of its assumption of absolutism and neglect of context. He recommended we turn toward a theory of inquiry, which is best presented in his book *Logic: The Theory of Inquiry* (1938, 1955). This book is one that Dewey said later in his life he misnamed, wishing he had just used the subtitle as the title of the book, for his book is much more about inquiry than it is about logic, as traditionally conceived (1960, "In Defense of the Theory of Inquiry"). Calling it a book on logic only led his readers in the wrong direction and hindered the book's reception, he later realized. Today philosophers are rediscovering Dewey's *Logic* and engaging in exciting discussions about it (Cahn, 1977; Sleeper, 1986; Garrison, 1995). Given Dewey's desire to rename his book, I will call it by its subtitle to help focus our discussion as he intended.

In *The Theory of Inquiry* (1955), Dewey points out that logic, as a branch of philosophy, is embedded in a context of philosophical assumptions. He argues that logic is a naturalistic theory and a social discipline (biological and cultural influences), that logic is a progressive discipline that involves a circular process. It is inquiry into inquiry. He argues that ". . . all logical forms (with their characteristic properties) arise within the operation of inquiry and are concerned with control of inquiry so that it may yield warranted assertions" (pp. 3-4). Inquiry is due to doubts—when doubts are removed, inquiry ends. For Dewey, knowledge is "that which satisfactorily terminates inquiry" (p. 8). He tells us that he has no problem with the term 'knowledge' if we mean by knowledge, the end of inquiry. That is a tautology, a truism. But if we take knowledge to have a meaning of its own *apart from inquiry*, then inquiry becomes subordinated to this meaning. This renders logic "subservient to metaphysical and epistemological preconditions" (p. 8). Dewey rejects *a priori* principles for logic which determine the character of inquiry. The conditions for logic are to be determined in inquiry. In other words, Dewey presents a contextual theory of logic as inquiry. His *The Theory of Inquiry* is an account of what takes place in inquiry; he says he was "undertaking an inquiry into the facts of inquiry" (Dewey, 1960, p. 135). For Dewey, logic is the method of intelligent behavior.

Dewey's (1960) formal definition of inquiry is: "*Inquiry is the controlled or directed transformation of an indeterminate situation into one that is so determinate in its constituent distinctions and relations as to convert the elements of the original situation into a unified whole*" (p. 116, emphasis in original). Inquiry has a common structure or pattern which Dewey discusses in many of his books (see for example *Democracy and Education, Experience and Education*). This structure is similar to the scientific method. Dewey does not distinguish between common sense and scientific inquiry, for he says the difference is in the subject matter (difference in the problems), not in their basic logical forms and relations. First we have doubts or questions, the institution of a problem. Knowing begins with a "felt need." Something causes us to inquire, something disturbs us, unsettles us, interrupts "the smooth, straightforward course of behavior" (Dewey, 1960, p. 136). The indeterminate situation evokes questions and attracts our attention. However, as no situation is completely indeterminate, some of the constituents of a situation must be assumed to be settled. This is Dewey's idea about background context: we cannot possibly question all of our background assumptions in order for us to proceed, some of which we take to be settled and are likely not even aware. Then we search out the constituents to help us define the problem. Next we search for a possible solution, an idea, a suggestion, which we test out to determine if it settles our doubts. When our doubts are settled, our inquiry of this particular situation ends.

For Dewey (1960), "the unsettled, indecisive character of the situation with which inquiry is compelled to deal affects all of the subject matters that enter into all inquiry" (p. 136). The subject matters of the problem and the solution are both in question "since both are equally implicated in doubt and inquiry" (p. 137). Dewey perceives this as his original contribution in his theory of inquiry, his bringing the *problem* into question and declaring the problem belongs "in the context of the conduct of inquiry and not in either the traditional ontological or the traditional epistemological context" (p. 138). Dewey (1960) describes, late in his life, how he used an historical approach to help elucidate his original contribution. In other words, he tried to give a larger, historical context to the philosophical ideas he was trying to bring into question. By taking a larger view, he hoped to make what we take for granted seem strange, and questionable. He looked at problems "in the context of the use they perform and the service they render in the context of *inquiry*" (p. 138, emphasis in original). He tried "to convert all the *ontological*, as prior to inquiry, into the *logical* as occupied wholly and solely with what takes place in the conduct of inquiry as an evergoing concern" (p. 142, emphasis in original).

As is typical of Dewey's historical style of argumentation, he spent a great deal of his time in The Theory of Inquiry (1955) exploring the history of logic, to demonstrate how logic historically neglects context. On hindsight, he says: "As I look back I am led to the conclusion that the attempt conscientiously to do my full duty by these treatises is acountable for a certain cloudiness which obscures clear vision of what the book was trying to do" (Dewey, 1960, p. 149). A little less time on placing his theory within the context of others before him, and more time on explaining his in particular (less time on the problem and more on the solution) might have gone a long way.

Dewey (1960) dissolves the bifurcation between theory and practice by showing that the subject matter of theory (the abstract) grows out of and returns to the subject matter of everyday concrete experiences. He shows that a problem that appears to be unsolvable if its terms are placed in an ontological context, collapses when treated in the context of inquiry. "When the issue pertaining to and derived from this contrast is placed and treated in the context of different types of *problems* demanding different methods of treatment and different types of subject matter, the problem involved assumes a very different shape from that which it has when it is taken to concern ontological 'reality'" (p. 146). Dewey points out that what has helped science make such great headway in its methods and conclusions is its experimental conduct, and the fact that even its best theories remain hypothetical in their status (p. 148). A hypothesis used to mean that which was beyond doubt or question, and now its meaning has radically changed to an assertion that is subject to verification or proof.

Dewey saw science as a good model of his theory of inquiry, but more recently science has been shown to be just as vulnerable to subjectivity and bias as philosophy (Kuhn, 1962; Gilligan, 1982; Keller, 1985; Harding, 1986). Dewey's theory of inquiry, which was written within the context of Darwin's evolutionary theory and was affected by that context, still holds, not because it points us to absolute Truths, but because it is useful and purposeful for answering our questions and solving our problems. It helps us question our specific interests as well as our background assumptions. It stands up to the test of time as a way of establishing knowing and meaning, for it starts with experience and it is never beyond questioning itself. It represents a form of naturalistic (e)pistemology for it still strives to yield warranted assertions that are not arbitrary, yet it does not rely on *a priori* principles to do so. Dewey's theory of inquiry eliminates the need for an absolutist Epistemology by assuming justification relies on social practices and human needs, and nothing more.

We begin to understand how Dewey's concept of experience in relation to knowing opened up a space for feminists to argue for the need to examine the contextual qualities hidden in absolutist Epistemological theory, from different standpoints of experience. Feminists' insistence on the inclusion of women's experiences, and even more specifically Black women's, or Latina women's, or lesbian women's experiences in philosophical discussions, is an effort to underscore the importance of context. Clearly, Dewey does not embrace a transcendental view of Epistemology. In fact, he is very critical of Epistemology due to its *a priori* principles and its metaphysical assumptions. But this does not mean that Dewey does not use (e)pistemology, for certainly he gives reasons to justify his arguments and evidence to warrant his claims. Dewey's theory of inquiry relies on a rehabilitated (e)pistemology. We shall find in the next section that Rorty is no more able to avoid (e)pistemology than Dewey is, although he certainly tries. We shall also consider Siegel's (1997) suggestion that Rorty is wrong in his claim that epistemological claims cannot be both particular and general. And we will need to consider Rorty's advice to feminists to forego 'experience' for language.

Some Postmodern Concerns

The American pragmatists, Dewey and James in particular, helped push philosophers to let go of transcendental, universal arguments. Richard Rorty, as a contemporary pragmatist, continues to push against universalizing tendencies. Continental philosophers such as Lyotard, Foucault, Derrida, and Deleuze, influenced by Nietzsche and Heidegger, have also contributed significantly to efforts to undermine philosophy's tendency to legitimate itself with reference to a metadiscourse. These people, who hold significantly different views, share in common their focus on critiquing transcendental philosophical assumptions, and so they are usually categorized together as "postmodernists" or "deconstructionists." It is not easy to even call these people 'philosophers,' because they have each in their own way severely criticized Philosophy's claims to transcendence, as well as Philosophers' assumptions that they can accurately describe the world through their God's-eye view. They each have declared Philosophy dead, with the use of different methodologies and with different targeted focuses. However, they all serve as philosophers in the Deweyian sense of cultural critics who help to disturb influential beliefs that we take to be given.

It seems that Rorty (1989) follows Dewey's lead, and describes philosophers as "prophets, poets, and soothsayers." Rorty, like Hegel and Dewey before him, uses historical analysis to draw our attention to previous background assumptions, in an effort to contextualize philosophy. Foucault also uses historical analysis to do archeological digs on key social concepts, such as discipline and punishment, sexuality, and insanity, in order to demonstrate how these concepts become institutionalized and powerfully impact particular people's lives. Derrida turns to language, and Deleuze to literary analysis, to explore *différance* and the lack of any master word, any ultimate foundation of meaning. These "philosophers" work to point out how our world is shifting, unstable and uncertain, lacking a center or a circumference. They break down the solid Metaphysical Categories and Epistemological Truths Philosophers have worked so hard to build, creating ruptures, deconstructing and problematizing fixities, in an effort to affirm openness towards the other. We have already met the Other in the feminist section, she is the excluded, the marginalized, the one objectified and distanced from Us. Postmodernists share in common with feminists a desire to acknowledge what is different, to recognize what is left out, and to respect what is queer.

In *Philosophy and the Mirror of Nature* (1979), Rorty turns his focus specifically on the history of the development of Epistemology, in an effort to draw us to the conclusion that we no longer need Epistemology for we can access reality directly. Rorty dismantles the idea of the mind as a great mirror. In agreement with Wittgenstein, Heidegger, and Dewey, he recommends we abandon "the notion of knowledge as accurate representation, made possible by special mental processes and intelligible through a general theory of representation" (p. 6). Because of his focus on the tradition of Epistemology, I turn to him for our discussion of postmodern concerns.

In *Philosophy and the Mirror of Nature* (1979), Rorty places particular emphasis on the development of the concept of "mind" and the idea of a mental domain. As a pragmatist, Rorty looks at the functions that the different stages and developments of epistemology have fulfilled. For example, he argues that Descartes's idea of a mental domain served the purpose of getting science out from under religion. Descartes sought certainty (that which he could not doubt), and he invented the mind/mental to give us a solid foundation (correspondence theory of truth). However, the concern for foundational knowledge is a hold-over from Cartesian doubt, which has outlived its usefulness. Rorty proposes that philosophy's role now is not foundational, rather one of edifying discourse.

Rorty (1979) does not deny there is justification for knowledge, but he works to soften the distinction between justified belief and knowledge. Like Siegel, Rorty argues that "true" is corrigible and fallible. Rorty does not even deny incorrigible knowledge (not open to doubt), for example the report that I am in pain, or that this paper is white. His point is just that these claims do not require us to have mental entities/minds. Rorty looks to sociology and history for justification and criteria for knowledge. "Epistemology" becomes descriptive science, not transcendental norms. He's looking for causal links, not eminent norms. Also like Siegel, Rorty recommends we should continue to improve our criteria. This is because our only criteria are socially acceptable rules. Justification is in social practice, which is corrigible, self-correcting. Rorty wants us to have conversations with each other rather than confrontations. He describes philosophy's task as one of building bridges between disciplines, and opening communication.

Rorty (1979) tells us he agrees with Wittgenstein that language is a tool rather than a mirror, and he finds Heidegger's historical awareness helps us distance ourselves from "the tradition." But it is Dewey who offers Rorty a vision of a new kind of society, a culture no longer dominated by the ideal of objective cognition, but by aesthetic enhancement. Rorty agrees with Quine that there are no distinctions between facts and beliefs. And he agrees with Davidson that we are just a "network of beliefs." Similar to James, he argues there is no way of knowing what's true apart from our own terms. In *Philosophy and the Mirror of Nature* (1979), Rorty describes himself as a realist, in a common sense way, not a philosophical realist. In *Consequences of Pragmatism* (1982), he describes himself as a pragmatist, and later in *Contingency, Irony, and Solidarity* (1989), he calls himself a liberal ironist.

Rorty's position is that language is contingent (therefore, there are no universal claims), and self is contingent (therefore there is no human nature, and other postmodernists add, the self is multiple and fractious). Truth is not "out there" or "in here" but "what is better for us to believe" (James's words). "True" or "right" or "just" is whatever the outcome of undistorted communication happens to be. It is whatever view wins in a free and open encounter, not "the accurate representation of reality." Rorty doubts the distinction between morality and prudence. These positions commit him to a lot of apparent paradoxes, and make him suspected of relativism, irrationalism, and immorality. But Rorty says these disadvantages of his position are outweighed by the advantages of being free of dogmatic universal claims of unchanging essences, of ahistorical natural kinds with permanent sets of intrinsic features. Rorty emphasizes differences, over sameness, and accommodation over synthesis. Rorty describes the philosopher's role as one of telling new stories, using new metaphors, not relying on argumentation. Like Dewey, he recommends that we keep philosophy connected to culture and we learn to live with plurality.

While Harvey Siegel is complemented by other modernist philosophers for trying to take postmodern positions seriously, I do not think postmodernists are so quick to complement him. Indeed, in *Rationality Redeemed?* Siegel (1997) does address Rorty's work, however not at any depth as he tends to find postmodernism in general contradictory and incomprehensible and easily dismissed. As Siegel explains: the postmodern stand—that epistemology is irrelevant—holds a position seriously and yet denies the need to ground it with reasons which justify holding it; this is a logical contradiction. We have found, though, that Rorty does not deny the need to justify a position with reasons, it's that he denies the reasons have transcendental force. Like Dewey, Rorty shows that Epistemology assumes absolutism and denies its own situatedness, its own contextuality. His historical analysis aims to expose the embeddedness of Epistemology. Rorty's position is that justification is socially constructed, similar to the position I argue for a non-transcendent (e)pistemology. People do argue and debate with each other, and offer reasons for their positions. They engage in conversations. Whatever view wins in their free and open conversation is what is considered "right."

Siegel (1997) worries especially about Rorty's effort to separate the universal from the particular. In *Philosophy and the Mirror of Nature*, Rorty (1979) does say "the universal-particular distinction is the *only* metaphysical distinction we have got" (p. 31, emphasis in original). Rorty approaches particularity from the angle of language, which is based on his own embeddedness within the philosophical tradition of language analysis. For Rorty (1991), Sellar's attack on "givenness" and Quine's attack on "necessity" are the crucial steps in undermining the possibility of a "theory of knowledge." He takes seriously the idea "that interpretation goes all the way down: that what a human being is, for moral purposes, is largely a matter of how he or she describes himself or herself" (p. 244). People are located within certain communities, and they are fundamentally ethnocentric. They cannot ever completely step outside of their own skins, or outside of their own community "long enough to examine it in the light of something that transcends it, namely that which it has in common with every other actual and possible human community" (Rorty, 1989, p. 36). Rorty (1989) says that striving after objectivity is "an attempt to avoid facing up to contingency" (p. 46).

Siegel (1997) focuses on Rorty's particular/universal distinction by first demonstrating that the argument: "language, self and community are contingent; therefore, universality is impossible or unachievable—is simply a non sequitur" (p. 215, ftnt. 21). He shows that one cannot coherently reject universality in general, or all metanarratives. The denial of all universality is itself a universal statement. "In denying the universal, it appears, one embraces it; one can't escape the universal by denying it" (p. 174). Siegel moves on to attempt to show that the idea that the universal and the particular are mutually exclusive is wrong. We already know that Siegel agrees that we are embedded in our own contextuality, and that we do not have a spectator's view, "(w)e always judge from the perspective of our own conceptual scheme" (p. 175). But Siegel does not agree that this fact of particularity entails that "a perspective unencumbered by our particular situation is impossible" (p. 175). He agrees that we cannot transcend all perspectives, but this does not mean that we cannot transcend any particular perspective. Siegel (1997) gives counterexamples from mathematics, science, morality, and social/political domains to demonstrate that "though we judge from the perspectives of our own schemes, our judgments and their legitimacy regularly extend beyond the bounds of those schemes" (p. 176). According to Siegel, "there is no contradiction, or even tension, between acknowledging particularity and at the same time constructing universalistic theories" (p. 178). Any argument must presuppose transcultural normative reach. Siegel charges that Rorty's "strong perspectivism" becomes merely description; it cannot hold any normative claim.

Rorty would say, exactly. It is his goal to have philosophy fulfill the role of edifying discourse. All Siegel has done is re/describe Philosophy as presuming transcendence. This is why Rorty says he is not trying to make a Philosophical argument, for to do so is to try to make normative claims. To offer a Philosophical argument is to immediately be caught in the Metaphysical and Epistemological web of absolute assumptions that Rorty claims we no longer need. Rorty offers a descriptive science, he's looking for causal links, not ontological conclusions.

It is interesting to look at what Rorty thinks pragmatism has to offer feminists, and why it doesn't address their needs. While it seems that Rorty (1989) follows Dewey's lead, in describing philosophers as "prophets, poets, and soothsayers," we find that Rorty (1991) wants to limit the philosopher's role to one of clearing the road for prophets and poets, "to make intellectual life a bit simpler and safer for those who have visions of new communities" (p. 240). He describes pragmatism as being in a supportive role for prophetic feminists, for example, in terms of being able to offer new metaphors and help for "imagining a community whose linguistic and other practices are different from our own" (Rorty, 1991, p. 239). Philosophy can free up our imaginations so our future practices will be different from our past. But Rorty maintains a separation between pragmatism and political radicalism, in that pragmatism cannot supply a general theory of oppression, or a universalist, ahistorical claim concerning the intrinsic nature of "woman" or the essence of "human being," as political radicalism is want to do. And he maintains a separation between pragmatism and postmodernism, claiming that pragmatism "offers all the dialectical advantages of postmodernism while avoiding the self-contradictory postmodern rhetoric of unmasking" (Rorty, 1991, p. 237). "(P)hilosophy is not . . . a source of tools for path-breaking political work" (Rorty, 1993, p. 100). Rorty says pragmatism is neutral between feminism and masculinism. Pragmatism cannot provide help for feminist doctrines. "Neither pragmatists nor deconstructionists can do more for feminism than help rebut attempts to ground these practices on something deeper than a contingent historical fact—the fact that the people with the slightly larger muscles have been bullying the people with the slightly smaller muscles for a very long time" (Rorty, 1993, p. 101).

Dewey also denies pragmatism can offer a generalist theory or make universal claims; he does not think pragmatism can unlock the secrets of history or society as Marx claimed historical materialism could do. However, Dewey insists on describing the problems of philosophy as inseparable from the problems of collective life, thus connecting pragmatism, as philosophy, to political issues, such as feminism must address. Dewey says that philosophers help make us aware of background assumptions we take for granted (such as sexist views), and in helping us become more aware of cultural context, philosophers serve as social critics. Rorty seems to want to separate pragmatism from political issues of power. But this is a dangerous separation that other postmodernists and feminists work hard to dismantle.

46   Relational "(e)pistemologies"

Rorty (1991) advises feminists to forego experience, in particular "women's experiences," for language. For Rorty, 'experience' connotes a natural kind with a fixed set of intrinsic features, whereas language covers our experiences without any metaphysical assumptions. As we found above, in the feminist section, Rorty is right to criticize feminists for describing women's experiences as a natural kind which gives access to a deeper reality, a superior claim of epistemic agency, as feminist standpoint theorists want to claim. Rorty contends that we should not find talk of women's "experience" any more credible than talk about woman's "nature." Rorty recommends that feminists, as separatist groups, need to gradually put together a new language that "succeeds in achieving semantic authority over its members" (1991, p. 247). This is because "what you experience yourself to be is largely a function of what it makes sense to describe yourself as in the languages you are able to use" (1991, p. 244). As Kaufman-Osborn (1993) describes Rorty's position:

> Language's grammar, i.e., the impersonal system of rules defining what can be said at any given moment in time, effectively dictates the parameters of meaning within which persons are constituted as identifiable subjects. There is, therefore, no meaningful way to distinguish between someone's experience and the language used to talk about it. For experience is a linguistic event, and so the object of feminist inquiry must be the discursive constitution of the subjects that are women. (p. 128)

Rorty pries language loose from the social practices in which it is embedded, in order to speak about it abstractly. The move to abstract language, while necessary for thinking about it, is problematic "when Rorty effectively 'forgets' that language is always relationally implicated in palpable webs of immediate experience that must be 'had' before anything caught up within them can be 'known' as a determinant subject of discursive inquiry.... Rorty's fear of essentialism, when joined to his claim that 'all awareness is a linguistic affair,' requires that he reject the reality of anything that might plausibly be called nondiscursive experience" (Kaufman-Osborn, 1993, p. 128).

There is a direct relationship between experience and meaning. True, the language we inherit from our social contexts has a tremendous impact on our lives. Language affects how we view the world and how we make sense of the experiences we have. But "the approriation of meaning, no matter how oppressive, is always a matter of active transformation rather than mere assimilation" (Kaufman-Osborn, 1993, p. 133). It is also true that much of what we experience remains unnamed and cannot be reduced to its articulated meanings. For feminists, the indeterminacy of experience is what makes 'experience' so important to their work. Feminism encourages us to be receptive and attentive to the inarticulate, too, not just what is named, which is why they cannot forego 'experience.' Language gives determinate form to what is nondiscursively had. Appealing to 'experience' reminds us that no telling is ever the whole or final story. As Dewey (1925/1981b) explained, "(E)xperience warns us that all intellectual terms are the products of discrimination and classification, and that we must, as philosophers, go back to the primitive situations of life that antecede and generate those reflective interpretations, so that we re-live former processes of interpretation in a wary manner" (p. 386).

Dewey (1981b) concludes:

> When the varied constituents of the wide universe, the unfavorable, the precarious, uncertain, irrational, hateful, receive the same attention that is accorded the noble, honorable and true, then philosophy may conceivably dispense with the conception of experience. But till that day arrives, we need a cautionary and directive word, like experience, to remind us that the world which is lived, suffered and enjoyed as well as logically thought of, has the last word in all human inquiries and surmises. (p. 372)

Rorty (1977, 1979) has many good things to say about Dewey as a critic of philosophical tradition, and it is clear that Dewey and James have inspired Rorty, a self-described pragmatist. Yet Rorty is also critical of Dewey, and where he is particularly critical is in regards to Dewey's concept of *experience*. Rorty supports Dewey's strong renouncement of transcendental metaphysics, but he thinks Dewey makes a mistake when he tries to rehabilitate "metaphysics" into an empirical metaphysics with the help of his concept of 'experience.' Rorty recommends that Dewey should not have tried to offer a reform, a new program. Rorty accuses Dewey of becoming transcendental in his philosophy with his metaphysical discussion of experience in *Experience and Nature* (1925/1981).

Dewey avoided metaphysics as a topic for over 20 years. However, while at Teachers College, he came to realize his logic has ontological implications. But Rorty misunderstands Dewey when he accuses Dewey of becoming transcendental in *Experience and Nature* (1925/1981), similarly to the misunderstanding Dewey experienced about his *Theory of Inquiry*, due to his use of the term *Logic*. Dewey's "metaphysics" insists on the relativity of ontological commitments. Dewey attempts to establish a "metaphysics" of existence. He is a naturalist, not a supernaturalist. He argues for a conception of nature as changing through the interaction of existences (Sleeper, 1986).

Dewey's "metaphysics" is not transcendental, but he later realized that he should have never used the terms 'metaphysics,' or 'experience,' due to the confusion the words caused because philosophers attached traditional meanings to the two common terms, instead of being careful to use the terms as Dewey redefined them. This is a difficulty I may run into as well, if readers do not carefully read my explanation of the use of the term 'epistemology,' and instead make the false assumption that I mean the word in its traditional transcendental way. Dewey suggested later he should have used the word 'culture' instead of 'experience' to help avoid misunderstandings that he later had to clear up and defend his theory against.

Rorty thinks he can avoid "ontology" just as he tries to avoid "epistemology" but he cannot. What he can do is avoid transcendental Metaphysics and Epistemology. However, I do not think philosophers can avoid "ontology" any more than they can avoid "epistemology," for the two together form the netting that we use to catch our ideas for our theories. They form our background context that we use to help us selectively attend to problems. 'Language' becomes Rorty's ontological category, instead of 'experience.' 'Relations' is my ontological category. I think Dewey was on the right track with his efforts to rehabilitate "metaphysics" in *Experience and Nature* and his efforts to rehabilitate "epistemology" in *Theory of Inquiry*. Dewey shows us how these concepts can retain their pragmatic uses while at the same time being held accountable for their potential misuses. This is exactly what I am trying to do with (e)pistemology.

The (e)pistemological theory I offer is steeped in a feminist and postmodern understanding of the need to address power and its affects on theories of knowledge. It is also steeped in the classic pragmatist focus on addressing context (background and selected interest). Like my pragmatic, feminist, and postmodern colleagues, I am working to dissolve dualisms traditional Philosophy and Epistemology embrace, such as theory/practice, subject/object, mind/body, and relative/absolute. I describe knowers as fallible human beings who are connected to knowledge, in a knowing relation. I question that a general account of knowledge, based on *a priori* standards for justification, is possible.

What I present is not a Transcendental Epistemology, for I do not have any Truth to offer. I do not have the Right Answer. I offer truths, that are assertions warranted by as much evidence as I can muster, with the understanding that our criteria and standards are socially constructed and therefore fallible, and corrigible. It is the need to warrant our assertions and justify our claims that causes me to continue to use the term 'epistemology' in its altered form (e)pistemology. I do not deny the need to justify claims, I just deny that any justification I can offer has transcendental force. (E)pistemology's legitimacy lies in the natural world, which is a contingent, ever-changing world in which we are active participants. It is important to address questions about what counts as good evidence, and criteria used to help us make decisions and solve our problems. As we continue to strive for solutions, to inquire, problem solve, and constructively think (e)pistemological questions will continue to arise. Can we avoid these? I think not. I am not letting go of (e)pistemological concerns, just the concept of Epistemology that assumes absolutism, even in Siegel's non-vulgar form. I present knowing as a relational process between the knower and the known, steeped in strong contextuality. Let me move on to address fears of relativism that my (e)pistemological theory will trigger.

CHAPTER 2

Embracing Qualified Relativism

We found in Chapter 1 that Harvey Siegel (1997) tells us he embraces Peirce's theory of *fallibilism*, and he claims most philosophers today do so as well. Yet, within classic pragmatism there is disagreement on what fallibilism entails, just as there is disagreement concerning the key pragmatist concept of *experience*. These disagreements still exist today between current pragmatist philosophers. In their own lifetimes Peirce, and Dewey each published essays publicly declaring their views differed from each other, and from James, while James tended to consider his views as being in alignment with both Peirce and Dewey. It appears today that James and Dewey were more in agreement, and they both differed from Peirce, for Peirce fought to hang on to a concept of absolutism, and James and Dewey worked to dissolve the absolutism/relativism dichotomy, each in their own unique ways.

I want to use this Chapter to show how James and Dewey were both successful in their dissolution efforts, and hopefully clear up some common misconceptions philosophers make about their positions. James and Dewey both have some flaws that get in their way, but feminists can help them with those flaws by further presenting the need to embrace a pluralistic universe. I will argue that (e)pistemological fallibilism (belief in the impossibility of attaining knowledge that is certain) entails (e)pistemological pluralism (belief in the impossibility of attaining knowledge that is universal), contra to Peirce and Siegel. I will also argue that democratic communities always-in-the-making are what protect us from fears of vulgar relativism, as we openly argue and discuss and debate our concerns within our own communities as well as among other communities, even communities we can only imagine. My plan is to begin with James's position, in contrast to Peirce's, and then consider Dewey's perspective. I will then extend Dewey's position and add feminist contributions to this debate. By the end, it should be clear what my qualified relativist position is, and how it differs from Siegel's (1987) non-vulgar absolutism. Our differences follow the same lines as that which distinguishes Peirce from James and Dewey.

James's truths[1]

While James is classified as a classical American Pragmatist by pragmatist scholars such as Seigfried (1990, 1996) and West (1989), he certainly held views that differed from his fellow pragmatists, in particular C. S. Peirce. James often compares his views to Peirce, and considers his own arguments as contributing to Peirce's views, yet Peirce went to great lengths to disassociate his own views from his friend's, James. There are reasons for this disassociation, and these reasons not only help us distinguish James from Peirce, they also point to James's unique contribution to pragmatism. The key to understanding the differences between James and Peirce is through an examination of the epistemological and ontological netting they each use to catch up their theories. Because they use different netting, they catch up different ideas, even though they start out using the same terms. For example, it is well known that Peirce is credited by James as originating the concept of 'pragmatism' in the early 1870's at their Metapysical Club meetings, and both of them used the same term to describe their theories. However, Peirce later renamed his own view 'pragmaticism' in order to distinguish his ideas from what he judged were James's, and others such as Schiller's, more relativistic approaches ("What Pragmatism Is," 1958).

In Peirce's early writings, he made a significant contribution to pragmatism by insisting that we cannot separate our ideas from our experiences, that the continuity of experience and nature is revealed through the outcome of directed action. This contribution is a hallmark of what distinguishes a pragmatist from other philosophical perspectives, and it is an idea Peirce, James, and Dewey all share in common. Peirce (1958) states his famous Pragmatic Maxim this way: "(C)onsider what effects, which might conceivably have practical bearings, we conceive the object of our conception to have. Then, our conception of these effects is the whole of our conception of the object" ("How to Make Our Ideas Clear," p. 124). And, again, in "What Pragmatism Is," we find Peirce (1958) defining meaning in terms of what effects it has on life. Peirce's theory is "that a *conception*, that is the rational purport of a word or other expression, lies exclusively in its conceivable bearing upon the conduct of life" (p. 183).

For pragmatists, we determine how clear our concepts are by running them through a functional test, grounding them to experience. Peirce's connecting and relating of experience and ideas, theory and practice, belief and action, heals the subject/object (mind/body) split that Descartes widened in Euro-western philosophy. Peirce shows the way for pragmatists to reject the central problems of modern philosophy as presupposing false dichotomies. We discovered in Chapter 1 that Dewey approaches this healing through his concept of 'experience.' In James's hands this healing takes the form of radical empiricism, which emphasizes a primal, integral, relational unity. I will return to James's radical empiricism in the next section.

Another major contribution Peirce made to pragmatism was his fallibilism argument, contra to Descartes, that we can never attain knowledge that is certain, and that what fixation we can attain is not done by ourselves. However, both of these claims are controversial and take on different forms in other pragmatists' hands. Peirce (1958) argued that each person is not absolutely an individual ("What Pragmatism Is," p. 191). Each person is embedded within a social setting that necessarily influences our individual beliefs. We have a critical self within us, that we have to persuade, and we also have a person's circle of society that is a sort of loosely compacted person. Therefore, our problem is not how to settle our belief, individually, but how to settle the community's belief (Peirce, 1958, "The Fixation of Belief," p. 103). While Peirce insists others must be included in our efforts to fix our beliefs, he describes 'others' as an educated community of scholars, other scientists, not a pluralistic community as defined by feminists and multiculturalists. Peirce (1958) argues that the only method out of Descartes's *a priori* speculation is the self-corrective scientific method. The scientific method's experimental results are always subject to revision by future evidence ("The Fixation of Belief," p. 92). The scientific method is a social, communal process, for even if one person can individually find the answer to a problem, that person can only settle doubts by testing out the idea with others who are members of the community of scholars.

Seigfried (1996) defines pragmatism as embracing fallibilism and pluralism. While this is true for James and Dewey, I am not so sure it accurately describes Peirce's position. While Peirce (1958) suggests our beliefs must always be subject to change, he also tells us he seeks a method for fixing our beliefs that will lead us to absolute Truth, in the end. "[T]rue opinion must be the one which they would ultimately come to" ("How to Make Our Ideas Clear," pp. 133–134). While Peirce denies certainty, for us, he does not deny the possibility of certainty ever. Peirce seems to suggest that in the end, the knowledge we attain will be something we all agree on; it will be universal. Peirce's (1958) standard for the method he seeks to fix beliefs is: "It must be something which affects, or might affect, every man. . . . the method must be such that the ultimate conclusion of every man shall be the same, or would be the same if inquiry were sufficiently persisted in. Such is the method of science" ("The Fixation of Belief," p. 107). And again, in "How to Make Our Ideas Clear," Peirce (1958) suggests, "all the followers of science are fully persuaded that the processes of investigation, if only pushed far enough, will give one certain solution to each question to which they can be applied" (p. 132). Peirce (1958) postulates Truth to be something we are emerging toward, thus while he does not declare our current ideas to be vulgarly absolute (certain), it appears our final, permanent set of beliefs will be universally True. "The opinion which is fated to be ultimately agreed to by all who investigate is what we mean by the truth, and the object represented in this opinion is the real. That is the way I would explain reality" ("How to Make Our Ideas Clear," p. 133).

Others criticize Peirce for embracing what seems to be a deterministic stance in regards to Truth, yet Peirce writes later in his career:

> We cannot be quite sure that the community ever will settle down to an unalterable conclusion upon any given question. Even if they do so for the most part, we have no reason to think that unanimity will be quite complete, nor can we rationally presume any overwhelming *consensus* of opinion will be reached upon every question. All that we are entitled to assume is in the form of a *hope* that such conclusions may be substantially reached concerning the particular questions with which our inquiries are busied. (*Collected Papers*, 1933-58, 6: 610, p. 420, emphasis in original)

Thus, as West (1989) points out, for Peirce "ultimate agreement" is simply meant to function as a regulative ideal, for "of course, such ultimate agreement never comes" (p. 51). And so we find that it is possible to interpret Peirce as embracing a doctrine of non-vulgar absolute Truth (as Siegel defines his own absolutism, 1987), or absolute chance, for there are infinite possibilities for making connections, interactions, and significations of reality. James takes the absolute chance route. We will also find in the next section that James does not embrace Peirce's assumption that Truths are objectively real.

Peirce's idea of Truth as an emerging absolute which demands of us endless investigating becomes truths which are relative to an individual's situation, in James's hands (*The Meaning of Truth*, 1909, 1975a). James follows Peirce's radical lead of incorporating contingency and revision into a theory of truth, yet he unties his theory of truth from Peirce's view of the evolutionary process of inquiry toward Truth. James postulates with Pierce an end of Truth but knows that this is just a belief.

> The 'absolutely' true, meaning what no farther experience will ever alter, is that ideal vanishing-point towards which we can imagine that all our temporary truths will some day converge.... Meanwhile, we have to live to-day by what truth we can get to-day, and be ready tomorrow to call it falsehood. (1907/1975b, p. 106)

For James a belief is true if it yields sensibly satisfactory results in experience when acted upon. "(T)o say something is true is to say that it is satisfactory" (Seigfried, 1990, p. 314). In *Pragmatism*, James (1907/1975b) italicizes the following definition of truth: "*True ideas are those that we can assimilate, validate, corroborate and verify. False ideas are those that we cannot*" (p. 97).

Truth grows and expands in James's hands, and takes on a changing, relational quality, rather than a futuristic essential quality. Truth means that ideas (which are themselves just parts of our experience) become true in so far as they help us get into satisfactory relation with other parts of our experience. "(T)ruth is only our subjective relation to realities" (James, 1909/1975a, p. 89). James says:

> Truths emerge from facts; but they dip forward into facts again and add to them; which facts again create or reveal new truth (the word is indifferent) and so on indefinitely. The 'facts' themselves meanwhile are not *true*. They simply *are*. Truth is the function of the beliefs that start and terminate among them. (1907, 1975b, p. 108, emphasis in original)

In James's own time he was criticized for emphasizing the subjective side of truth and ignoring the objective side. Philosophers equated 'satisfaction' with personal feelings. However, James's 'satisfaction' is meant to encourage us to look away from first principles or categories (metaphysics) and to look forward to fruits and consequences. James went to great length to refute the subjective/objective dualism. As Seigfried (1990) points out: "The charge of subjectivism can be sustained only by clinging to the dogmatic view of reality characteristic of rationalism, which was already refuted by him [James]" (p. 311). "There is no loss in substituting tentative for absolute standards if absolute standards are impossible" (p. 298). James took the notion of absolute Truth to be dogmatic, a foreshadowing of feminist and postmodern concerns we found in Chapter 1. James (1907/1975b) responded to what he called slanderous criticisms of relativism by asking: "Pent in, as the pragmatist more than any one else sees himself to be, between the whole body of funded truths squeezed from the past and the coercions of the world of sense around him, who so well as he feels the immense pressure of objective control under which our minds perform their operations?"(pp. 111–112).

According to James we call "knowledge" or "truth" ideas that we can assimilate, validate, corroborate, and verify. True ideas are ones we have resolved and no longer doubt. "Truth *happens* to an idea. It *becomes* true, is *made* true by events. Its verity *is* in fact an event, a process; the process namely of its verifying itself, its veri-*fication*" (James, 1907/1975a, p. 97). James's view is Peirce's without the assumption of Truth at the end of time and without an assumption of universality.

> For James, pragmatism is a proposal which is vindicated in a range of areas of application by its varied fruits. For Peirce, on the other hand, it is a technique which is to be defended by showing that it helps us to achieve a definite purpose: making scientific progress. (Hookway, 1997, p. 159)

James's pragmatic view is not a form of vulgar relativism (also called strong relativism, radical relativism, or the view from everywhere), as he is often accused of, nor is his view as absolute as Peirce's qualified universal view. What James presents is a qualified relativistic view which aims to dissolve the absolute/relative distinction. However, James's view is vulnerable to criticism because he embraces an individualistic model for knowers rather than a social model, like Dewey describes. While James argues for the sacredness of individuality, Dewey (1916/1966) argues for a transactional relationship between individuals and others, and for the importance of inquiring within democratic communities. I will come back to this point in the Dewey section.

Suffice it to say at this point, I use the term *qualified relativism* in an effort to distinguish this perspective from vulgar relativism. Unfortunately, most scholars do not make such a distinction, but rather describe relativism in glossed, extreme terms. Even Siegel (1987), who is so careful in his definition of absolutism, is guilty of this charge in regards to relativism. Pragmatism is often accused of being relativistic because it is described as relying on a view of reality as a function of human belief and truth as a function of human practice. However, pragmatism does not represent a view from everywhere, what it opens up is the possibility of views from somewheres. James and Dewey show us how. A qualified relativist view is different from Siegel's non-vulgar absolutist view, in the same way that James's view differs from Peirce's. I suggest that the difference lies in our logic and ontology, for Siegel remains clearly within the traditional Enlightenment paradigm, even as he describes inquirers in non-vulgar absolutist terms. And Peirce remains clearly within the same paradigm, even though he describes inquiry in terms of the scientific method. Both Peirce and Siegel embrace (e)pistemological fallibilism but neither of them embrace (e)pistemological pluralism. Peirce's desire to defend pragmatism against charges of relativism is based on an acceptance of a binary absolutism/relativism distinction which James and Dewey work hard to dissolve. What a qualified relativist proposes is nothing less than a transformation of the Enlightenment paradigm by dissolving the binary logic supporting that paradigm.

It is ironic that Peirce's pragmatic method and his concept of fallibilism is what first inspired James to question distinctions between subject/object, knower/known, and relativism/absolutism. For Peirce's ontological realism caused him to strive to separate himself from his fellow pragmatist. Perhaps we can better understand the difference between non-vulgar absolutism and qualified relativism if we further explore the ontological differences between Peirce and James. Their ontological views affect their epistemological theories, and vice versa. We will find that James offers us clear guidelines for distinguishing non-vulgar absolutism from qualified relativism. James shows us how the absolutist/relativist distinction dissolves with his theory of radical empiricism and pluralism. I return to James to further examine his ontological differences from Peirce and demonstrate how these differences affect their concepts of truth(s). I explore James's radical empiricism and then I consider James' radical pluralism, in contrast to Peirce's views.

James's Radical Empiricism

Peirce developed an ontology that has been labeled scholastic realism, or what he preferred to call "Scotistic realism." He was greatly influenced by the medieval scholar, Duns Scotus, and his theory of hacceity (thisness), and common nature. Scotus tried to find a way between the one and the many, between a transcendental ontology and a relativistic one. "Scotus asserts that being *qua* being is the proper object of the human intellect, as 'being has the same limits as the intelligible'" (Borden-King, 1989, p. 11, inside quote Bettoni, 1961, p. 33). Being *qua* being is what Peirce describes as his category of Firsts, "existent singulars." Peirce (1958) describes Firstness as "the mode of being of that which is such as it is, positively and without reference to anything else" (p. 383). The objects in the universe of Firsts are "ideas or possibilities" (Peirce, 1958, p. 404).

Scotus argued that "(t)hings are singular, but they are not exclusively such" (Bettoni, 1961, p. 55). Things have a "common nature" which is neither universal nor singular. "The common nature has 'singularity in concrete things, universality in the intellect'" (Borden-King, 1989, p. 12, inside quote Bettoni, 1961, p. 55) and thus is not itself properly universal. Peirce described this relationship between and among existent singulars as "Seconds." Secondness is constituted by existents and facts. Existents are "Objects whose Being consists in their Brute reactions" while facts are "reactions, events, qualities, etc. concerning those Objects" (Peirce, 1958, p. 405).

For Peirce, the univerality in the intellect that Scotus described, the logical universe that is the extension to generality of the physical and metaphysical universal, becomes "Thirds," general laws of relation. Thirdness is "the mode of being of that which is such as it is, in bringing a second and third into relation to each other" (Peirce, 1958, p. 383). Or, put another way, Peirce says that the Third universe "consists of the co-being of whatever is in its nature *necessitant*, that is, is a Habit, a law, or something expressible in a universal proposition" (Peirce, 1958, p. 405, emphasis in original).

Borden-King (1989) argues that Scotus's idea of 'common nature' is clearly reflected in Peirce's three modes of being.

> Secondness is the common nature as physical universe, Firstness is the common nature as metaphysical universe, that is, the common nature 'as it is apprehended by the intellect,' while Thirdness is, like the logical universal, the mediation which gives determinate generality to Secondness and thus is tied to both Firstness and Secondness. (p. 18, quote within is Bettoni, 1961, p. 56)

Peirce's ontology is not dualistic, the one and the many, but rather triadic. Reality is in the encounter between Firstness and Secondness with Thirdness transcending the encounter, as Peirce's bridge between particularity and universality. As Borden-King (1989) describes this: *"Thirdness is not chained to reality but it is anchored there"* (p. 19, her emphasis).

Peirce strove to distinguish his pragmaticism from pragmatism because pragmatism had come to denote a concern with actions/events (Peirce's Seconds) and

Peirce was concerned with understanding (Thirds). With Duns Scotus's help, through his realism, Peirce postulates a real world that is mind-independent: "That is *real* which has such and such characters, whether anybody thinks it to have those characters or not. At any rate, that is the sense in which the pragmaticist uses the word" (Peirce, 1934, CP 5.430, p. 287, emphasis in original). Peirce also holds to the existence of universals and general principles operative in nature. "Despite his stress on the contingency and revisability of scientific claims and theories, Peirce preserves the permanency and independence of what those claims and theories are about" (West, 1989, p. 51). Thus, we can describe Peirce as offering a non-vulgar absolutism, for he clearly recognizes historical contingency and context, the fallibility of inquirers, and the need to provide a method for achieving revisable knowledge-claims. Peirce insists on the need for continual critical assessment of epistemological criteria that are corrigible, and he turns to the scientific method and logic to fulfill that need. Yet, Peirce preserves a final grounding of knowledge claims in his postulation of real existents and the "external permanency," which exists independent of human thought. Peirce offered a theory of synechism, which was "intended to connect the real—. . . with what is 'destined' to be believed as a consequence of the continuity of experimental inquiry" (Sleeper, 1986, p. 45). Chris McCarthy (1997) labels Peirce's view "pragmatic realism." Unfortunately, Peirce's hold on to a destined reality that is mind-independent points us back to the binary logic of absolutism/relativism.

James does not maintain the same position as his friend Peirce, in terms of a triadic ontology. He also does not embrace a dualistic ontology, rather he strives to describe a unifying one. Thus, we find that while Peirce can be labeled a non-vulgar absolutist, James is what I call a qualitifed relativist in that he insists on dissolving the absolute/relative distinction. Even "qualified relativist" may be a misnomer if it reinscribes the absolutist/relativist distinction. Because James was accused in his own lifetime of being too subjective, and too relativistic, he addresses head-on the topic of binary logic in his debates with rationalists about his theory of truths. James defends his epistemological theory with the help of a complimentary ontological theory, which he calls *radical empiricism*.

In *The Meaning of Truth* James (1909/1975a) defines *radical empiricism* thus:

> Radical empiricism consists first of a postulate, next of a statement of fact, and finally of a generalized conclusion. The postulate is that the only things that shall be debatable among philosophers shall be things definable in terms of experience. The statement of fact is that the relations between things, conjunctive as well as disjunctive, are just as much matters of direct particular experience, neither more so nor less so, than the things themselves. The generalized conclusion is that therefore the parts of experience hold together from next to next by relations that are themselves parts of experience. (pp. 6–7)

In James's (1912/1976) final work, *Essays in Radical Empiricism*, which was published posthumously, he describes his radical empiricism this way:

> There is, I mean, no aboriginal stuff or quality of being, contrasted with that of which material objects are made, out of which our thoughts of them are made; but there is a function in experience which thoughts perform, and for the performance of which this quality of being is invoked. That function is *knowing*. (p. 4, emphasis in original)

Thus, we find James (1912/1976) describes a relational ontology that begins as a unity, not as separate entities. James calls his unity "primal stuff" or "pure experience," the *thatness* of being. With his radical empiricism, knowing is therefore easily explained as "a particular sort of relation towards one another into which portions of pure experience may enter" (p. 4). There is only one primal stuff or material in the world, a stuff of which everything is composed. James's radical empiricism moves to get rid of dualisms in reality. For him, experience has no inner duplicity. Experience just is, in its pure *thatness*. Experience is subjective *and* objective, it is private *and* public, it is internal *and* external, it is thought *and* thing. What we do with pure experience, when we categorize and separate it and create lines of order for it, is by way of addition, not subtraction to pure experience (James, 1912/1976, pp. 6–7). Experience can serve different functions, and may be different kinds. When it is taken in different contexts, in different associations, it plays different parts. Thus, in a binary logic experience is forced to be either absolute or relativistic, either universal or particular. However, with James's radical empiricism we understand that it is not contradictory to say that experience is both absolute and relative, it is both particular and universal. This tremendous insight James brings to pragmatism is an offer which scholars are still exploring, as I am here, in this chapter and text. James does not present a pragmatic realism, as Peirce does.

James explains in *Essays in Radical Empiricism* (1912/1976) why he calls his ontology 'radical empiricism.' Rationalism, as the opposite of empiricism, starts with the one, a unified whole, but cannot address particulars, the many. Empiricism starts with particulars, the many, but cannot unify them into a whole. James's description starts with the parts, what he calls pure facts, which is why he calls it 'empiricism.' It's 'radical' because the "*relations that connect experiences must themselves be experienced relations, and any kind of relation experienced must be accounted as 'real' as anything else in the system*" (p. 22, emphasis in original). Empiricism over-emphasizes the bare *withitness* between parts and rationality tends to ignore it, whereas "(r)adical empiricism, on the contrary, is fair to both the unity and the disconnexion" (p. 24). The radical empiricist argues that the relation of continuity is a *whatness* just as empirically real as the whatness of separation and discontinuity.

James (1912/1976) tells us he emphasizes the relation of continuity in his discussions because conjunctive experiences have been discredited by empiricists and rationalists and disjunctivity has been over-emphasized. Knowers are separated from the known, subjects from objects, and treated as absolutely discontinuous. James reminds us, we add to pure experience, by differentiating and distinguishing, but we always start with "sensible realities" that come to life "in the tissue of experience" (p. 29). Knowledge "is *made*; and made by relations that unroll themselves in time" (p. 29, emphasis in original). Or, put another way: "The instant field of the present is always experience in its 'pure' state, plain unqualified actuality, a simple *that*, as yet undifferentiated into thing and thought, and only virtually classifiable as objective fact or as someone's opinion about fact" (pp. 36–37, emphasis in original).

The charge of relativism is something James and I can only be guilty of if one assumes there is a distinction between relativism and absolutism. Then absolutism represents what is universally true, and relativism represents what is individually true. However, this false distinction between relativism/absolutism is based on the assumption that knowers are divorced from what is known, that the world exists independently of us and what sense we make of it. This distinction is shown to be false by James's radical empiricism. We find that when the dualism between knowers and the known (subjects/objects) collapses, so does the dualism between relativism and absolutism. What I describe as a qualified relativist position, one based on a pluralistic, fallibilistic perspective and a relational ontology, is the only position I argue any of us are justified to take. Even non-vulgar absolutist positions such as Peirce's and Siegel's require a leap of faith that cannot be warranted by our reasoning abilities, as fallible, embedded and embodied social beings.

James tells us his philosophy "harmonizes best with a radical pluralism," so I would like to turn now to an exploration of just what he means by 'radical pluralism,' and see how his pluralism compares to the pluralism to which feminists refer. Feminists argue the need to include outsiders (others) in any testing of "truths," as women have historically been categorized as the Other (feminist standpoint epistemology). They find support for this position with Dewey, but what about James? Given that James argues for radical empiricism from within an individualistic perspective, maybe his radical pluralism further protects him from charges of relativism, since he does not turn to a social democratic model for support? I turn to James's radical pluralism to help us further understand his qualified relativistic view.

James's Radical Pluralism

In *A Pluralistic Universe*, James (1909/1977) argues that the world we experience is more than we can describe. "(C)oncrete reality and experience are richer, more dynamic, and thicker than can possibly be expressed by our concepts" (Bernstein's

Introduction, 1909/1977, p. xiv). James describes reality as genuinely continuous and active. "Reality is not a closed system; it is ontologically open" (Bernstein's Introduction, 1909/1977, p. xxv). He describes our theories as incomplete, open, and imperfect. He shows how conceptual knowledge is very valuable, but it stays on the surface of things. Conceptual knowledge is knowledge about things, it does not penetrate to the inner reality of things and it is not capable of capturing reality's continuously changing nature. For James, "What really *exists* is not things made but things in the making" (p. 117, emphasis in original). "Reality, life, experience, concreteness, immediacy, use what word you will, exceeds our logic, overflows and surrounds it" (p. 96). Reality is nonrational, it is where things *happen*.

James (1909/1977) shows over and over again how philosophy is guilty of "vicious intellectualism" due to its reliance on the use of concepts which are unable to penetrate and capture the flux and depth of concrete reality and experience. It's not that certain concepts are limiting, but that all concepts are. *Vicious intellectualism* is: *"The treating of a name as excluding from the fact named what the name's definition fails positively to include"* (p. 32, emphasis in original). James criticizes various forms of vicious intellectualism: absolute idealism, and atomistic empiricism, for example. Empiricism explains wholes by parts (each-form), and rationalism explains parts by wholes (all-form). James suggests there are degrees in rationality and that the universe is loosely connected. Rather than taking either side of the each/all debate (relativism/absolutism), James suggests we embrace the notion of *some*.

> Radical empiricism and pluralism stand out for the legitimacy of the notion of *some*: Each part of the world is in some ways connected, in some other ways not connected with its other parts, and the ways can be discriminated, for many of them are obvious, and their differences are obvious to view. (pp. 40–41)

With James, the classical absolutism/relativism dualism collapses, as does monism and even atomistic pluralism. James does not solve the absolutism/relativism problem he dissolves it.

James (1909/1977) discusses the work of Henri Bergson, a French philosopher who was first a mathematician before becoming a philosopher. He tells us Bergson is who made him bold, for Bergson criticizes intellectualism. Bergson helped James understand that Plato began vicious intellectualism by teaching us "that what a thing really is, is told to us by its *definition*" (p. 99, emphasis in original). James argues that first we have immediate experience, his radical empiricism, the mere *thatness* of experiences. Then we frame our experiences, we name them, with concepts. However, our immediate experiences always overflow concepts and logic, conjunctions and disjunctions. "Concepts are only man-made extracts from the temporal flux" (p. 99). So, we find that first concepts become a method, then a habit, and finally a tyranny. "Concepts, first employed to make things intelligible, are clung to even when they make them unintelligible" (p. 99).

Since Plato and Aristotle, we have valued fixities over change, concepts over immediate experiences. Bergson inverts Plato, and moves away from concepts toward perceptions. As James (1909/1977) describes this inversion, he contrasts theoretical or scientific knowledge to speculative knowledge (Bergson's perceptions). Theoretical or scientific knowledge is knowledge *about* things. It touches on the outer surface of reality. "Thought deals thus solely with surfaces. It can name the thickness of reality, but it cannot fathom it, and its insufficiency here is essential and permanent, not temporary" (p. 112). Speculative knowledge is a passive and receptive listening, intuitive sympathy, a dive back into the flux itself to *know* reality, in terms of direct acquaintance. Concepts negate the inwardness of reality. Because concepts are fixities, they help us avoid context. "When we conceptualize we cut out and fix, and exclude everything but what we have fixed. A concept means *that-and-no-other*" (p. 113, emphasis in original). Logic makes static cuts, and "real life laughs at logic's veto" (p. 115).

To sum up James's (1909/1977) argument:

> Our intellectual handling of (it) [life] is a retrospective patchwork, a postmortem dissection, and can follow any order we find most expedient. We can make the thing seem self-contradictory whenever we wish to. But place yourself at the point of view of the thing's interior *doing,* and all these back-looking and conflicting conceptions lie harmoniously in your hand.... What really *exists* is not things made but things in the making. (p. 117, emphasis in original)

Thus, we find that James's doctrine of pluralism means

> that nothing real is absolutely simple, that every smallest bit of experience is a *multum in pravo* plurally related, that each relation is one aspect, character, or function, way of its being taken, or way of its taking something else; and that a bit of reality when actively engaged in one of these relations is not *by that very fact* engaged in all the other relations simultaneously. (p. 145, emphasis in original)

"Whenever we try to describe our experiences "something always escapes" (p. 145). Logic will always fail to reach completely adequate conclusions, for it always omits something. Absolutism insists everything is present to *everything* else, but James proves that with our concepts, "(t)hings are 'with' one another in many ways, but nothing includes everything or dominates over everything" (p. 145).

In his Appendix C to *A Pluralistic Universe,* James (1909/1977) compares Bergson's work to Peirce's. While they reach their views so differently, one as a mathematician the other as a logician, James points out what he thinks they have in common. James says that Peirce, Bergson and he all believe in a synechistic pluralism (p. 154). James is wrong though, in thinking his radical pluralism is in sympathy with Peirce's views. Peirce invokes 'synechism,' or continuity, to explain how his developing system fits together. Synechism is formulated in order to reconcile and unite "his doctrine of absolute chance [fallibilism] with the 'real Necessity' that is the backbone of his logical realism" (Sleeper, 1986, p. 218, ftnt 4). Synechism united Peirce's logical realism with his objective idealism, and the tychism of objective chance "with its consequent thorough-going evolutionism" (Peirce, 1933–58, 6.163, p. 113). Tychism is the genuine feature of existents of all kinds—that chance everywhere mitigates necessity in the natural order of things. However, there's a flaw in Peirce's philosophy with his implicit commitment to an ontology of fixed essences. There is a "contradiction between Peirce's tychism and the fallibilism of his doubt-belief theory of inquiry and his contrasting commitment to what he liked to call his 'Scotistic Realism' and his conviction that the object of eventual knowledge consists in the 'permanent possibility of sensation'" (Sleeper, 1986, p. 50).

Again we find that the difference between Peirce and James highlights James's unique contribution to pragmatism. Peirce clung to absolutism, even though a nonvulgar absolutism, thus undermining his own fallibilism with his ontological realism. Siegel still clings to ontological realism today, thus undermining his embrace of Peirce's fallibilism by insisting on maintaining an absolutism/relativism bifurcation. James dissolved the absolute/relativist dichotomy with his theory of radical empiricism and pluralism. For James, and myself, the universe is unfinished.

How does James compare to feminists who consider themselves qualified relativists? Certainly his argument for the limitations and tyranny of man-made concepts is one that is very helpful to feminists, as they make the case that concepts have fixed the world in ways that exclude them, and that concepts are in need of constant critique and revision. James's idea of sympathetic acquaintance, of passive and receptive listening, is also in harmony with work feminists are doing to describe women's ways of knowing and caring reasoning (Belenky et al., 1986; Gilligan, 1982; Keller, 1983, 1985; Noddings, 1984; Ruddick, 1989; Thayer-Bacon, 1993, 1997, Summer 2000).

However, one weakness James has, is his clinging to an individual model. James embraces the United States' democratic philosophy, live and let live, and maintains a democratic respect for the sacredness of individuality. He argues for pluralism in terms of experiences that are fluid and in flux, that are many, and in terms of respect for individual experiences. Yet, he does not address pluralism in terms of the diversity of human beings within his epistemological theory. While James powerfully makes the case for the limitations of concepts and logic, he does not take up Peirce's fallibilism and expand upon it, as Dewey does, to include the limitations of human beings, in general, due to their own situatedness. James makes a strong argument and is successful at avoiding the charges of relativism, but Dewey and feminists have much to offer that help make James's case even stronger. Let's step outside of James's worldview and look at the issue of qualified relativism from a Deweyian perspective with 'warranted assertability,' before turning to feminist perspectives. I will contrast Dewey's argument for pluralism, in terms of democratic communities, to Peirce's and Siegel's arguments for communities of scholars.

Dewey's Warranted Assertability and Democratic Inclusion

In *Logic: TheTheory of Inquiry*, Dewey (1938/1955) credits Peirce with being "the first writer on logic to make inquiry and its methods the primary and ultimate source of logical subject-matter" (footnote 1, p. 9). He tells us that he accepts Peirce's (1958) idea of Truth as "the opinion which is fated to be ultimately agreed to by all who investigate" ("How to Make our Ideas Clear," p. 133). Peirce's *fallibilism* is the source of Dewey's ideas concerning logic as inquiry into inquiry, for fallibilism made Dewey aware of the historical context of logic, as a subject matter of philosophy. Dewey realized that logic is viewed in a variety of ways by different people, depending on their philosophical assumptions. Dewey adopts Peirce's doubt-belief theory, his pattern of inquiry, but he interprets it more liberally than Peirce intended. For Dewey, it becomes a logic of scientific method. Because he takes seriously Peirce's claim that we will never know Reality, it is a futuristic Ideal, this causes Dewey to distinguish between ontological Truth (the nature of truth) and epistemic validity (the test of truth). Dewey works out a logic of experience that argues that the principles of logic are not "*a priori* principles fixed antecedently to inquiry" (p. 12), but rather the principles of logic are "generated in the very process of control of continued inquiry" (p. 12). Dewey's theory of logic as inquiry undermines Peirce's doctrine of synechism (connecting the real to what is destined). For Peirce, logic is a normative science. As we have already found, Peirce is implicitly committed to an ontology of fixed essences. Dewey questions Peirce's commitment, arguing that we ought to get our logic from our ontology, not our ontology from our logic.

In *The Theory of Inquiry* Dewey (1938/1955) makes it clear that we inquire because we have doubts. When doubts are removed, inquiry ends. Doubts make us feel uneasy and unsettled. When our doubts are settled, we have genuine belief or knowledge. Dewey tells us he chooses *not* to use the term 'settled belief' to describe the end of inquiry, because of the ambiguity associated with the term 'belief.' He means 'genuine belief' to signify "the settled condition of objective subject-matter, together with readiness to act in a given way when, if, and as, that subject-matter is present in existence," (p. 7), but people commonly use 'belief' to also mean "a personal matter; something that some human being entertains or holds, . . . merely a mental or psychical state" (p. 7). Due to this ambiguity, Dewey recommends we not use the term 'genuine belief,' thus avoiding the charge of relativism.

Dewey (1938/1955) also seeks to avoid the charge of dogmatism. He tells us that the end of inquiry, when doubts are settled, can also be called 'knowledge,' but due to the ambiguity from which that term also suffers, he seeks to avoid its use. 'Knowledge' has come to signify a fixed and eternal end, absolute Truth, as we found in Chapter 1, which is contrary to the meaning Dewey wants to stress. For Dewey, inquiry is a *continuing* process (his emphasis), and settled beliefs are not necessarily settled for all time, so that they are not exposed to more inquiry. All settled beliefs are open to possibly becoming unsettled by further inquiry. "It is the convergent and cumulative effect of continued inquiry that defines knowledge in its general meaning" (p. 8). Dewey suggests the use of a different term that is free from the ambiguity of *belief* and *knowledge*. This term is *warranted assertion* (p. 9).

> When knowledge is taken as a general abstract term related to inquiry in the abstract, it means "warranted assertibility." The use of a term that designates a potentiality rather than an actuality involves recognition that all special conclusions of special inquiries are parts of an enterprise that is continually renewed, or is a going concern. (p. 9)

Dewey rejects any correspondence or coherence theory of Truth. He argues that what we need to focus on is the agreement process that we use to try to establish epistemic claims. Focusing on the agreement process, inquiry, helps us understand that the testing of truth is a social practice. To determine whether our ideas are reliable and worthy of action, we must look at how we warrant our assertions. As fallible, contextual human beings, the only truths we have access to are derived through our own error-prone yet self-correcting procedures. Even our logical forms are developed from within our own contextuality. Therefore, our truth claims are forced to be tentative and revisable, and any argument for Truth as corresponding to reality, or as coherence, must fall back on warranted assertability in practice. Thus, we call 'knowledge' or 'truth' by 'warranted assertibility' what we can assert to the best of our abilities, based on our best efforts to consider all options and solve all doubts so that we can say that what we assert is warranted by our best evidence, based on our best criteria. Or, as James put it, until we are satisfied.

Dewey's pragmatic view, like James's, is a qualified relativistic view that aims to dissolve the absolute/relative distinction. Dewey found James's concept of 'experience' to be significant, not only for an adequate behavioristic theory of meaning, as James uses it in *Principles of Psychology* (1890/1950), but also as an adequate basis for a theory of truth. "Dewey took James to mean we can account for the origins of our most stable and reliable norms of inquiry without postulating any source other than experience" (Sleeper, 1986, p. 51). Even metaphysics can be seen as a consequence of experience. Inquiry itself shapes our concept of 'being'—not the other way around. Judgment is intimately and indissolubly connected with affection, appreciation, and practice (Sleeper, 1986, p. 63). Dewey restores reason and thought to the same ontological plane as objects and things (Sleeper, 1986, p. 65). For Dewey, reality is always in process, it is not fixed. He holds a radical naturalist and radical empiricist view, for he argues for the naturalizing of epistemology and metaphysics. Like James's pluralism, he treats essences as provisional rather than as permanent. Both Dewey and James show us a way clear of the binary logic of absolutism/relativism.

However, Dewey's view is less vulnerable to criticism of subjectivism than James's because he describes knowing in relation to knowers who are members of social communities, whereas James embraces an individualistic model. James holds a democratic respect for the sacredness of individuality, and believes there is no point of view absolutely public and universal. For James (1975a), pragmatism is a reconciler and mediator, it is a way of testing probable truth. Pragmatism's only test is "what works best in the way of leading us, what fits every part of life best and combines with the collectivity of experience's demands, nothing being omitted" ("What Pragmatism Means," p. 522). Feminists agree that there is no view from everywhere, but they do not wish to embrace a view from nowhere either. Qualified relativists insist on acknowledging our own particularities and situatedness, which we learn about through our social interactions with others not like us. Because James embraced individual values, and a "live and let live" attitude, he never had to place his own sexist views under scrutiny. Thus, his individualism made it possible for him to avoid confronting his own limitations, which were harmful, and had exclusionary results for women (Seigfried, 1996). James's insistence on individualism makes it difficult to call him a friend of feminism, although we can call him an associate.

Feminists do find a friend in Dewey, who embraces a social emphasis for inquirers, as does Peirce, yet Dewey offers his own significant contributions to pragmatism. One of Dewey's contributions is his accenting of the context in which philosophical theory develops, not just at the micro-level of fallible human beings (Peirce), but also at the macro-level, in terms of ideas being developed within the context of social institutions such as schools. As West (1989) describes Dewey's contribution, he adds "a mode of historical consciousness that highlights the conditioned and circumstantial character of human existence in terms of changing societies, cultures, and communities" to the pragmatic argument of contingency and revisability (pp. 69–70). For Dewey, inquirers must appeal to the experiences of their fellow community members for confirmation and correction of their individual results. Due to his appeal to others in democratic, pluralistic terms, Dewey is less vulnerable to the criticism of subjectivism than James is, or to the charge of elitism that Peirce is vulnerable to because he describes communities in terms of scholars (see below). Dewey is indebted to Peirce for his doubt-belief theory, and to James for his metaphysical pluralism. But Dewey's transactional view of selves-in-relation-to-others is his own.

I will explore Dewey's transactional view further in Chapter 5, but suffice it to say, for now, that Dewey argues in *Democracry and Education* (1916/1966) that individuals and social communities function interactively, and interrelationally. Dynamic changes take place with the self and the community, because of their interaction with each other, and all are affected. Individuals do not develop on their own and then decide to join up with communities because it benefits them to do so. Individuals develop out of their social communities, as Mead argues with his social behaviorist model (1934). Dewey, with Mead, recognizes that individuals start out as members of communities. However, for Dewey individuals are not socially determined by their communities, they interact with their communities and affect each other. Dewey's description of democratic communities recognizes the interactive, interrelational, interdependent qualities of individuals and others. He measures the worth of social life by "the extent in which the interests of a group are shared by all its members, and the fullness and freedom with which it interacts with other groups" (1916/1966, p. 99).

In *Democracy and Education* Dewey (1916/1966) begins his discussion with human beings as social beings. His focus is on language, in its broadest sense, as the means of communication between social beings, the way to establish meaning, as he turns to the problem of how communities maintain themselves through renewal and social continuity (education). For Dewey, social discourse, or language, is the cultural matrix of inquiry. The development of language out of biological activities is the key to transformation of purely organic behavior into intelligent behavior. In *The Theory of Inquiry* (1938/1955), Dewey places logic as inquiry within the context of people's problems, and these people are encultured, relational beings. *The Theory of Inquiry* is a book about language and meaning; it insists on viewing knowledge in relation to knowers. Inquiry is an effort to settle the disturbed relation of organism-environment.

Dewey (1938/1955) begins his discussion on his theory of inquiry by choosing to focus on inquirers, as biologically habituated beings, and as cultural beings. He ends his discussion by reminding us that "(a)ll inquiry proceeds within a cultural matrix which is ultimately determined by the nature of social relations" (p. 487). "The notion of the complete separation of science from the social environment is a fallacy which encourages irresponsibility, on the part of scientists, regarding the social consequences of their work" (p. 489). Dewey credits Peirce as being "notable among writers on logical theory for his explicit recognition of the necessity of the social factor in the determination of evidence and its probative force" (ftnt 3, p. 490). Peirce did not think Truth was found by one person seeking it on his own, it is found by us testing out our ideas with others, as a community of scholars. Since individuals are limited, contextual beings who are fallible, it is only possible to get closer, and clearer on our understanding of "truths" if we are able to explain and test out our ideas with others. Ideally, we learn and share what we learn with each other, as a community of scholars seeking Truth, and working together toward that goal.

However, Peirce carefully restricts his community of scholars to scientists who are involved in rational inquiry and are considered experts in their fields of study. Given Peirce's pragmatic realism and his doctrine of synechism, it makes sense that it is only important to him to include those who are considered most knowledgeable in discussions attempting to further advance knowledge. Peirce does not describe "others" (nonexperts) as needing to be necessarily included in the discussion for not everyone has the background knowledge necessary to do the investigating. Peirce's community of scholars is not friendly to feminists, for science has a long history of excluding women and not considering them as equal members of the scholastic community. This exclusionary move by Peirce is one that has the dangerous potential of limiting our inquiring as well as reassuring inquirers they need not worry about trying to negotiate with others who are not considered members of the scientific community.

Peirce uses the standard of relevant qualifications or expertise to exclude "nonexperts." Given Harvey Siegel's agreement with Peirce's pragmatic realism and his doctrine of synechism, it should come as no surprise that Siegel (1997) offers a present-day argument that exclusion on the basis of lack of relevant qualifications or expertise, or failure to meet relevant standards, is both permissible and consistent with the ideal of inclusion. Let's trace the lines of Siegel's (1997) argument. In his Presidential address to the Philosophy of Education Society in 1995, "What Price Inclusion?" Siegel defines inclusionary discourses and theories as "discourses which seek out, make room for, and take seriously, and theories which adequately reflect, the voices, views, and interests of those who are and have traditionally been excluded from discussion and/or consideration" (p. 168). He argues, à la Kant, that we should endorse the ideal of inclusion on moral grounds. To exclude is to fail to treat people with respect. However, he goes on to argue that we should not endorse inclusion on epistemic grounds, that

> inclusive theories are not *in general* more likely than exclusive theories to be true, or justified, and inclusive discourses are not *in general* more likely than exclusive discourses to yield such epistemically worthy theories; there is no *necessary* connection between inclusion and epistemic worthiness, or between exclusion and epistemic defectiveness. (p. 171, emphasis in original)

Siegel (1997) turns to science for examples to show that common shared beliefs people held have not yielded Truth but rather have turned out to be false (e.g. the earth is flat, handling frogs causes warts). Siegel also turns to science for examples that exclusion does not necessarily lead to false claims (e.g. many of the claims of contemporary science which were forged in exclusionary discourses, yet enjoy impressive epistemic credentials, such as jet airplanes and radio transmissions). He concludes: "Since inclusion is routinely conjoined with epistemic weakness, and exclusion with epistemic strength, it sems to me a mistake to regard inclusion as an *epistemic* virtue. Rather, inclusion is a *moral* virtue, and should be valued as such" (p. 172, emphasis in original).

While Siegel (1997) is not willing to grant that people and groups deserve inclusion because of any special epistemic privilege they enjoy, or because including them necessarily increases the probability of obtaining true or justified theories, he is willing to acknowledge that "inclusion, by adding previously ignored perspectives to scientific research and debate, can and often does serve to correct and enhance ongoing theorizing" (points made by Bordo, Keller, Harding, Longino, Nelson, and many others) (p. 172). However Siegel considers this qualification a matter of principles of *conduct* for inquiry, not criteria of evaluation of the *products* of inquiry.[2] Any theory can be defective, and not necessarily because it has been exclusive, but for many reasons, including lack of information, inadequate sources of evidence, etc. And inclusive theories can also be defective, due to lack of imagination or failure to criticize theoretical presuppositions, for example (p. 172).

Siegel (1997) is willing to admit that mainstream philosophy excludes others by relying on disciplinary standards which are portrayed as unbiased and neutral, which in fact are not. He credits recent feminist scholarship for exposing the ways in which extant standards are defective. The admittance of faulty standards should lead us to conclude the need to reject our current standards for ones that are superior, not to reject standards altogether. For, as Siegel rightly points out, standards are needed to make the case for inclusion. I have already pointed out that this is a "false worry" on Siegel's part as no one suggests we should reject standards altogether. Rather, others insists on the need to recognize that our standards are faulty (see Chapter 1).

Siegel (1997) also admits, "there *is* a genuine tension between inclusion and one common standard, namely that of *qualifications* or *expertise*" (p. 181, emphasis in original). He argues that not everyone is qualified or competent to participate in some discourses, and on the grounds of (lack of) appropriate expertise, exclusion is perfectly legitimate. "(F)or conversations to be maximally functional, or maximally interesting, informative, or communicative for their participants, some potential participants may well be best left out" (p. 182). Thus, he concludes: "Exclusion on the basis of lack of relevant qualifications or expertise, or failure to meet relevant standards, is both permissible and consistent with the ideal of inclusion" (p. 182[3]). At the same time, Siegel hastens to add that if someone feels wrongfully excluded, they can protest and "try to show how their exclusion is in some way or other unjust or otherwise mistaken" (p. 182). He suggests that the way to protest one's exclusion is "by arguing that she is in fact qualified and sufficiently expert to be entitled to participate" (p. 182). He also adds that for many discourses everyone is qualified, and conversations can be expanded in ways that require the inclusion of more people, as well as people can acquire expertise and thus come to merit inclusion. "The point remains nevertheless that for some conversations, exclusion is perfectly legitimate or the basis of (lack of) appropriate expertise" (p. 182).

Of course, as a feminist I have to point out the dangers of Siegel's argument. Siegel admits that philosophy and science have both used standards to exclude women from the conversations. These sexist practices continue today. Just recently the Massachusetts Institute of Technology (MIT) admitted to current sexist practices in its treatment of its few women scientists on its campus. (Religion can easily be added as another example of exclusionary discourse that still continues today.) Siegel admits that the more recent inclusion of women in philosophical and scientific conversations has helped philosophers and scientists become more aware of their own biases. Doesn't this improved awareness of biases constitute an example in favor of inclusion on epistemic grounds?

Siegel admits that standards are fallible and that someone can be wrongfully excluded due to misjudgment of lacking expertise based on faulty qualifications. Women have only recently been allowed to ride in space shuttles or pilot jet planes. In the past they have been judged inferior and inadequate for these tasks because of a variety of reasons, using physical, psychological, and logical criteria, all of which have been proven to be false. In fact, women have proved themselves superior at these tasks, with equal access to education and training. How does one ever get to question the criteria used to determine the relevant qualifications of expertise if outsider views are not included? How do we become aware of our own faulty biases and the hidden assumptions our standards impose on all to the advantage of some and the disfavor of others? Again we find a value for inclusion on epistemic grounds for inclusion is what allows us the means to question the accepted standards for judging.

Siegel is correct to point out that including others does not guarantee Truth, just about any example would do to support his claim since we are continually adjusting and adapting our theories as we seek the ever-elusive Truth. However, he is wrong to think that exclusion leads to Truth. The examples "that enjoy impressive credentials" which Siegel points to (e.g. jet airplanes and radio transmissions) do not look so impressive when they are viewed from outsider perspectives. Jet airplanes look like major polluters of our air and significant users of our limited fossil fuels. Radios look like capitalist exploitation of cheap labor in colonized Third World nations where the radios are manufactured. The splitting of the atom may look like an impressive scientific contribution toward a new source of energy from a United States perspective, but it looks like radioactive fallout, environmental destruction, and the decimation of thousands of people's lives from a Japanese perspective. These examples show us that exclusion is dangerous and that while it may not lead to false claims (a small group of scientists did learn how to split the atom), it certainly leads to claims with a much wider range of significance than any one group of scientists can fathom, wisely consider, and critique.

What about Siegel's conduct/product distinction, in which he acknowledges that inclusion does serve to correct and enhance ongoing theorizing but this has to do with principles of *conduct* for inquiry, not criteria of evaluation of the *products* of inquiry? What we find here is that Siegel attempts to draw a sharp distinction between ethical behavior and epistemological results, as if how we treat each other in our inquirying is not related to the results we find from our inquirying. However, the very work Siegel points to, work by Bordo, Keller, Harding, Longino, and Nelson, belies this distinction. These feminist scientists have contributed significantly to the reshaping of their fields of study, as well as to adaption and changes in methods of inquiry within their fields. Recent changes in how we conduct research in psychology, biology, anthropology, and education, for example, have caused significant changes in the research results.

Indeed, tremendous changes have occurred in educational research due to the uses of newer qualitative research methodologies, which dominate educational research today. In the past, researchers in education have tried to follow the principles of conduct for inquiry established by scientific quantitative researchers, only to find the products of their research very limited due to the innumerable variables a teacher in a classroom of 30 children present. Because there have been changes involving the criteria for evaluating the products of inquiry, we now find qualitative research techniques such as case studies, interviews, and focus groups count as sound methods of inquiry. Due to changes in the criteria for what counts as evidence or data, personal letters and diaries count as evidence in research studies today, for example. Education now finds itself in a position where teachers' experiences in the classroom are no longer just viewed as antidotal, personal witnessing, but teachers are considered researchers. Due to changes in our standards for research, researchers can now go into the classroom and study what teachers and students do in their natural setting, and have their work considered an important contribution to educational research. Siegel's false distinction between conduct and product is a slip into the distinction between knowers and knowledge, between subjects and objects, that Peirce, and other pragmatists, worked so hard to reconnect and heal.

One last point regarding Siegel's (1997) argument against inclusion on epistemic grounds. Siegel softens his exclusionary approach by encouraging those who are excluded on expertise grounds to protest on the grounds that "she is in fact qualified and sufficiently expert to be entitled to participate" (p. 182), or seek out and acquire the necessary expertise, or seek to expand the conversation topic so that she can be included. Siegel's respondent, Kathryn Morgan (1996) warns us about the perils of inclusion. One peril she titles "Theories R Us," points to how Siegel continues to presuppose that his theories are the norm, the ones doing the including, as he graciously includes others in his discourse and as objects of his theories (my theories are the best like my toys are the best, and my theories apply to everyone, like Theories R Us) (p. 32–33). She warns that Siegel's proposal places women and minorities in an "experimental data" category of pseudo-inclusion while he continues to occupy an epistemological and institutional place of pride. Women and minorities must either conform to the given criteria and attempt to meet it, or show that they have already met it, thus giving up on their "differences," or change the conversation so that they can be included. In all of their options, they must comply, rather than take an oppositional stance. Their particularized epistemic subjectivity is eliminated (p. 33).

The roots of American Pragmatism developed at the same time that science was gaining in status in the Euro-western world, and the value and status of scientific thinking is assumed by Peirce, James, and Dewey in their work. It continues to be assumed today by scholars such as Siegel. Still, we find in James's radical pluralism a criticism of philosophy and science (theoretical or scientific knowledge) as being just knowledge *about* things, which only touches the outer surface of reality. Thus, James offers support for feminist arguments that science itself is embedded in values that cause scientists to describe the world in certain ways and not others. Given Dewey's agreement with James's radical pluralism and his central claim that all inquiry (and logic itself) is affected by philosophical assumptions which are culturally bound, Dewey also offers support for feminists. Later in his career, Dewey turned toward art as a model for inquiry and this turn helped further open the door for feminist redescriptions of inquiry as constructive thinking (Thayer-Bacon, 2000).

Dewey's greatest support for the argument I want to make here, that fallibilism entails pluralism, comes from his unique contribution to pragmatism, his transactional view of selves-in-relation-to-others. If we are relational social beings who are fallible and limited by our own embeddedness and embodiment, at a micro level as well as a macro level, then none of us can claim Epistemological, privileged agency. None of us has a God's-eye view of Truth. Our only hope for overcoming our own individual limitations, as well as our social/political limitations (cultural and institutional) is by working together. Through our use of language, as "the tool of tools," and our efforts to attempt to communicate and relate with each other, including others from our past and others we can only imagine in our future, we can enlarge our thinking and improve our inquirying. We can reach beyond our micro- and macro-limitations and continually revise and improve our theories, with the help of each other. Our embeddedness constitutes a strong reason for inclusion on epistemic grounds.

If we limit the others we are willing to attempt to relate to and communicate with to "scholars" or "experts," then we limit the reach of our understandings. For the standards we use to determine expertise are also fallible and embedded within social contexts. Our standards of epistemic worth are not independent of the particular inquirers seeking to establish the standards, yet our standards can become more independent and more general the more we include other inquirers in the establishing of standards. Our standards need to be continually questioned and this can only happen at a deep level, reexamining foundational background assumptions, if we allow in outsiders' perspectives. Given our fallibilism (a doctrine of absolute chance and radical contingency), then we must embrace the value of inclusion on epistemic grounds in order to have any hopes of continually improving our understandings. Inclusion of others perspectives in our debates and discussions allows us the means for correcting our standards, and improving the warrants for our assertions.

Given that the universe is unfinished and pluralistic, rather than evolving to one necessary conclusion, then we can only hope for temporary alliances and agreements, and truths that satisfy our corrigible standards. This is quite all right, for in the disagreements and disharmony come the stimulation of more awareness and growth, and the chances of improving our understanding of our own unquestioned background assumptions as well as expanding our selected interests. Inclusion of others' perspectives in our conversations allows us the means for adjusting for our own limitations, correcting our standards and improving the warrants for our assertions, and recognizing the role of power and privilege in epistemological theories.

Conclusion

We found that Dewey follows James's lead and embraces a unity, a totality, a relational ontology. However, James applied his relational ontology to criticisms concerning concepts, not social relationships. Dewey expanded James's relational ontology to include social relationships. As we will find in subsequent chapters, feminists also argue for a relational ontology on the grounds of social relationality. Their work has much to offer James in helping to extend his arguments against individual relativism, just as James has much to offer feminists by extending their arguments against conceptual relativism.

Depending on one's own ontological leanings, it is possible to find support for absolutism as well as relativism in classic pragmatism, for Peirce represents a nonvulgar absolutist perspective with his pragmatist realist view, and James and Dewey represent qualified relativist perspectives with their radical empiricist and pluralist views. However, to make absolutism/relativism one's focus for argumentation is really to miss the tremendous insight pragmatism has to offer, which is a way to dissolve this dualism. Although James and Dewey spent significant energy in their own lifetimes trying to clarify this point, it seems to be one that continually resurfaces, for the desire for a separate Reality and transcendental Truth runs long and deep in Euro-western philosophical traditions.

I hope that my exploration of Peirce's, James's, and Dewey's epistemology and ontology has helped shed light on what distinguishes Peirce's pragmatic realism from James's, Dewey's, and my, qualified relativism. Even calling our position "qualified relativism" is a misnomer if it encourages us to maintain an absolutist/realist distinction. Peirce strove to maintain that distinction, whereas, like James and Dewey, I strive to dissolve it. James and Dewey offer us a way out of dualistic thinking, by embracing a concept of experience as an unanalyzable totality. Our analysis is what we add to pure experience. Experience can take on many shapes and forms, depending on its functions. We understand experience in terms of its relations. I also hope that by comparing and contrasting James's views to Peirce's and Dewey's, the reader has gained a greater appreciation of each philosopher's unique contribution to pragmatism.

With the help of Peirce's fallibilism, James's radical empiricism and radical pluralism, and Dewey's transactional, democratic view of selves-in-relation-to-others, one can make the case that (e)pistemological fallibilism entails (e)pistemological pluralism. I argued that epistemic agency can only be assured through interaction with others, and that assurance is tenuous, open to further revision. As world travelers of a radical democratic community-always-in-the-making, we must negotiate with each other in order to come to an agreement of what is, and then pass our efforts on to the next generation for them to debate and discuss further. Individuals can/do make individual contributions to knowledge, but they do not do so as isolated individuals: they are community members. I embrace a fallibilistic view of truths, as I believe most scientists and philosophers currently embrace, although we certainly argue about what Peirce's fallibilism logically entails. With qualified relativism, I am not necessarily suggesting a linear, progressive model that postulates universal Truth at the end of time. I place the range of fallibilism in Jamesian terms, in an open universe. Like James, I do not postulate a world of Forms, or material Reality, that is separate from us and our efforts. And, like Dewey, to further avoid a charge of vulgar relativism I place emphasis on the social negotiating process that inquiry must go through, to help us settle our doubts and satisfactorily end our inquiry. I move on to begin to redescribe (e)pistemology in a relational way.

CHAPTER 3

Why Relationality?

Now that I have explained what I mean by (e)pistemology, and have defended myself against charges of relativism, I would like to turn to the other central concept in the title of this book, *relationality*. 'Relations' form the heart of this (e)pistemological theory and is a unique contribution I have to offer, in terms of drawing our attention to relational forms of knowing as opposed to individual descriptions, which have dominated Euro-western Epistemological theories for so long. I certainly do not want to claim to have discovered relational approaches to knowing. In fact, to make such a claim contradicts my own theory. I will argue that we become knowers and are able to contribute to the constructing of knowledge due to the relationships we have with others. None of us are able to make contributions without the help of others, and none of us discover new ideas all on our own. I will describe a theory of knowledge that aims to show how interconnected we all are, not just to each other personally, but also to our social environments, our cultures, past, present, and future, as well as our surrounding natural environment, and the forces of the universe as a whole. I will also describe how much our individual, unique ideas are caught up within webs of related ideas.

The reader will find in the following chapters that many will be able to contribute to the discussions on relationality and have much to say. In fact, I will have to limit my explorations of what others have to say to a select few, in order to conserve space as well as give some focus to the discussions. We should be able to consider enough views, though, that we will gain an appreciation of the wealth of diverse voices there are on this topic, as well as a variety of ways relationality can be applied to (e)pistemology. I want to underscore and highlight many ways we already describe knowing in a relational manner, across genders, cultures, and fields of studies, including philosophy, religion, and science.

As I pointed out in the Introduction, the term *relational* is ambiguous in that we use it in many ways. It is fascinating that we use 'relations' in so many different ways, and still not only know what we mean by the term in the context that we use it, but also find it an important term to use. To be related to someone else means to be a kin. Our family members are our relations. We can also be related to people who are not kin, as in when we have personal relations with our neighbors, friends, and partners. Additionally, we can be related to others in a general, social group sense, as with other citizens of our country, state, or town, or other members of a religious community such as fellow Muslims, Buddhists, or Christians, or an ethnic community such as Hispanics, Native Americans, or African Americans. To have relations with someone else can mean, at a very personal level, to have sexual intercourse.

We use 'relations' in a variety of ways when we talk about concepts and try to establish meanings for terms. For example, we use relations to draw comparisons. When we want to determine how wide, or tall, or heavy something is in comparison to another similar object, we relate the one object to the other. Parents know how confusing it can be to try to teach children the concepts tall, taller, tallest, when the category changes depending on whom the child stands next to. And of course it changes over time as well. The oldest child in a family can be the tallest child for a long time, and end up the shortest, as has happened in my family where the oldest is a girl and her younger brothers now tower over her. Another interesting comparison is the category 'spicy.' We determine spicy in comparison to bland, mild tastes, but some people consider food that is salted and peppered to be spicy, while others need cumin, cayenne, chili or jalapeño peppers in order to call their food 'spicy.'

We use 'relations' to make logical or natural associations. An old, favorite love song on the radio will remind us of someone who was dear to us when the song was first released. We say, "I can relate to that song." We smell something cooking and we associate that smell with a special holiday, or someone we know. The smell of waffles cooking reminds me of my grandmother, because she use to make them for us when my family came to visit. We learn to relate a comb to a brush, a toothbrush to toothpaste, and mittens to hats as logical associations. We learn to associate certain body language with fear, for example a loud, angry voice, a scowl, or a clinched fist. We relate a windy day to a change in weather pattern, thunder is associated with lightening, and large, dark cumulonimbus clouds cause us to predict rain.

We use 'relations' in terms of dynamic and functional interactions. We learn that an object that drops on a hard surface will likely break. In relation to the hard surface, what was a solid object can become shattered glass. We also learn that most objects that fall do not come back up to us, due to the relation gravity has to falling objects, unless it is something like a ball that bounces. We watch with amazement the first time we discover ice melts when it comes in contact with heat, and the first time we knead dough and it rises and bakes into delicious bread. These are all examples of dynamic interactions that we describe in relational terms. In terms of functional interactions, think about how we relate the waving of a white flag to the function of surrender in a battle situation. Around the world, a smoke signal symbolizes alarm, and can be used to warn us of danger or signal a person's location for rescue efforts.

We use the term 'relate' when we talk about how one idea is relevant to another. We say, "I see how these concepts relate." Scientists make important discoveries when they are able to see relevance and make connections that before others could not make. Water splashing out of a tub when a person gets into a too-full bath becomes relevant when Archimedes relates the dispersing of liquid by a solid mass (his body in the too-full bathtub) to the problem of how to weigh the king's crown for gold content. Philosophers help us understand how to make sense of our world in new ways when they redescribe family, church, school, and state as institutions of oppression that shape our lives. When they help us understand the relevance between women starving themselves and a cultural norm for feminine beauty, we can relate to a new concept such as the cultural inscription of physical bodies. Artists make original creations that move us when they are able to show us relevance that before had missed our attention and we are able to relate to their demonstration. They help us see "anew"; they make strange what we take for granted, or cause us to notice something lacking that before went unnoticed. Vincent van Gogh painted ordinary people that before had gone unnoticed or were deemed not worthy as subjects, and by doing so he helped us see the beauty in coal miners and potato pickers. Toni Morrison helps us begin to understand the terrible destructive forces of racism by telling the story of a little Black girl who wants blue eyes in *The Bluest Eye*.

We point to how things overlap with each other as another way to show relations. For example, we may begin to notice that our child has a low time of energy regularly which overlaps with dinnertime. At first we may not notice anything, but just find ourselves dealing with a crying, grumpy child just when we are looking forward to sitting down and enjoying a meal together. Often we hope these kinds of things are just stages children will outgrow, and we tolerate or cope with them the best we can. However, when time goes by and the same child is still grumpy at dinnertime, we might decide that this is a regular pattern and for this person these two events relate to each other. It just so happens that for this particular person dinnertime overlaps with being tired and irritable. For other people morning may be their low energy time, or later in the evening. For me it is the middle of the afternoon, which overlaps with the same time I used to put my children, and me, down for a nap.

When we tell a story about something that happened to us, we say we are relating our experiences. To relate is to give an account, a narrative. Often, if someone tells a story about an adventure or event, the person listening will tell a similar story that happened to them as a way of demonstrating that they understand the first person's narrative. Thus, similar narratives can be used to show that the listener "can relate" to the first person's account, and we find that not only does relate mean to give an account of something, it also means to feel sympathy. To be able to relate to someone else means I can feel with you, I have some understanding of what you may be going through. Your situation or story is similar to ones I have experienced and makes sense to me; I share a kinship type of bond with you because I have experienced something similar. I can relate.

To relate is to make reference to, as when a driver relates to a police officer how the driver came to be in the ditch along the side of the road, and the driver makes reference to all that took place in the chain of events that occurred. The officer finds out that there was a second driver who was passing the first driver in the passing lane, when a dog started to cross the road from the side of the road that only the passing driver could see. The passing driver swerved to avoid hitting the dog, and by doing so caused the first driver to run off the road and into a ditch in order to avoid hitting the swerving second driver. To relate what happened to the officer the driver in the accident makes reference to the events leading up to the accident. We also use relate to mean "to make reference to" when scholars publish the results of their research project and relate their results to other researchers' findings. Or, within the publication scholars will make reference to others' work as a way of establishing the need for their research project or describing their problem in relation to others' work.

For all of these different ways that we use the term 'relation' there is a common theme of *connection to others*, including other people, ideas, or even inanimate objects. I do not mean to emphasize just logical interaction and existential connection. The connection is not just accidental or incidental, in the sense that we do not just bounce off of each other like marbles when they hit each other in a shooting game. Dewey (1938/1965[1]) used the example of billard balls to describe this bouncing off of each other as an example of interaction, where there is no noticable change. I want to emphasize that relations are transactional in that we affect each other, dynamically and functionally, and each is changed as a result. As Martin Buber (1958) described this transactional quality, relations are mutual.

A relational (e)pistemology emphasizes the transactional nature of knowing in a variety of ways. Most important, it emphasizes the connections knowers have to the known and helps us understand that we are not spectators to Reality reporting on "it"; we are part of this world, this universe, affecting "it" as we experience "it." To describe ourselves as separate from each other and our world around us is really to miss all the ways we are connected and related, all the ways we are one with the universe, as a Buddhist might say. When we understand we are one with the universe, then we can begin to understand how connected we are, as knowers, not only to each other, but to our products as well, our knowledge. As Dewey (1938/1955) pointed out, it is really much more helpful to describe knowledge as knowing, as a verb, for 'knowing' helps remind us about the transactional nature of the relationship between knowers and the known. 'Knowing' emphasizes that this is an active process in which we are all engaged, 'we' meaning not just each other but also our wider world around us, in which we reside. Knowledge is made, by us, as products of this process of knowing.

I do not mean to sound mystical, but it is impossible to talk about relationality without sounding mystical and mysterious. The mystical, mysterious, poetic kinds of qualities that emerge in discussions on relationality are really more of a reflection of our Euro-western language and thoughts than on the concept of a relational (e)pistemology itself. Traditionally Euro-western language is used to classify and clarify. Our terms help us separate and straighten out our ideas. We use words to differentiate and distinguish, and what I am trying to do here is bring things together. I want to emphasize how things overlap, associate, integrate, refer, compare, connect, *relate* to each other, and in that relating, how things affect each other, and change each other. Our language tends to strive to create demarcations, either this or that, and I want to try to soften these marks and show how things are *both/and*, to unify. What I offer here is not a binary logic, or a triadic logic, but rather a unifying logic, like James's, that presents the universe as whole and open.

As indicated in the Introduction, I plan to explore the connection between individual knowers to other people, at a personal level (Chapter 4) and at a social level (Chapter 5). I also plan to develop connections between ourselves, as knowers, and our world around us, in terms of holistic and wholistic views as well as ecological views of nature in relation to human beings. I will turn to Eastern philosophy and Indigenous tribal views (Chapter 6) as well as Euro-western ecological philosophical views (Chapter 7), to help us understand the (e)pistemological connections between ourselves and the greater spiritual and material universe as well as the natural world with which we live in relation. I will consider mutual causality relationships and unifying, complementary, and dynamic connections when I explore the relational qualities of scientific ideas, in terms of relativity theory, quantum mechanics, general systems theory, co-evolution, and genetics in Chapter 8. I turn now to a further elaboration of each of these examples of relationality, in a general way, before I develop them more specifically within the following chapters. The following descriptions will serve as a map to help the reader find their way through the subsequent chapters.

Personal Relations

I begin an exploration of relationality at the micro level of personal relations, starting with the development of a baby within a mother's womb, and the birth of that child. Our first intimate relationships are with our biological mothers, who then become our adoptive mothers, or someone else adopts us, in the sense of electing to care for us (Ruddick, 1989). Our mothers, those who provide child care as a significant part of their daily work, help to preserve our lives, nurture us and foster our growth, and prepare us for life beyond our immediate homes. We cannot survive without the care of a mother; we begin our lives totally dependent on an other. In the womb we are literally attached to our biological mothers through our umbilical cord and it is not possible to mark the point where we end and our mothers begin. After birth and the cutting of our umbilical cord, we maintain an attachment to whoever feeds us, holds us, and keeps us warm and dry. Though our attachment is more tenuous, physically, it is still a very strong psychical connection, so strong that we do not consider ourselves separate from our adoptive mothers after birth; we do not have a sense of separate self yet, only of connection. Our relationship with our mothers begins as a very personal, intimate, private relationship, which becomes more public as we emerge into the larger social world.

Yet, at the same time, our mothers are immersed in their public, social world, and that social world affects their mothering behaviors, even before their child is born. We can see this in the variety of ways that different cultures respond to pregnant women, such as shunning them or isolating them from society, or not attending to them at all, or making them the center of attention. Pregnant women are fed different foods, served different liquids and potions (prenatal vitamins, coconut butter or aloe vera lotion, herbal teas), and made to endure invasive behavior by others in their culture due to their pregnancies (prenatal examinations). After a child emerges from the mother's womb, cultural influence on the adoptive mother's behavior does not dissipate, but continues as strongly as ever. Thus, we begin to understand that while starting an exploration of relationality from the micro level of personal relations helps us understand how we are intimately connected to others and highlights the primacy of interpersonal relations, we quickly come face-to-face with the public, social effects on that private relation at a macro level. The boundaries between private relations and social ones begin to dissolve.

Sara Ruddick (1989) explores the personal relationship between a mother and child predominantly from the perspective of the mother in her *Maternal Thinking*, and I rely on her description to help me consider mother/child relations as I make the case for our fundamental relationality. She will help us clearly see that a child's spirit unfolds through the intimate relationship with another. All knowers are social beings in-relation-to-others. Ruddick contrasts maternal thinking to rational thinking, maternal thinking being centered around human needs and the concrete, daily concerns for others, whereas rational thinking insists on objectivity and abstraction from the concrete. Maternal thinking requires an attentive love, where a mother is able to attend to the specific needs of her child, see her child's unique differences accurately, and dwell on his particular needs. Her effort to distinguish maternal thinking from rational thinking will help us understand what is lacking in the ideal of Reason, but I do not recommend we follow her dichotomous path. I suggest we use her maternal thinking to help us re-vision reasoning in a relational, wholistic manner. Ruddick's maternal thinking theory can be used to help make the case that *all* knowing is an activity that develops out of relational practices we participate in from the moment we are conceived. Maternal thinking and rational thinking represent different ways of relating to others, one being more personal and concrete and the other being more distant and detached, but they are both examples of our fundamental relationality.

Jane Flax (1983, 1990) helps us further understand the very intimate, personal relation children have with their mothers by considering the concept of relationality more from the standpoint of the child. I rely on Flax's psychoanalytic perspective, in particular her object relations theory, to further help me make the case that we develop a sense of self through powerful, intimate, affective relationships with other people, in particular our adoptive mothers. Flax describes how each of us develop a sense of self, an inner core as a potential knower, through the process of psychological birth, which takes place during the first three years of life after our physical births. Not only are we intimately related to our biological mothers within the womb in a very physical way, and then totally dependent on our adoptive mothers to care for our physical needs after we are born, we are also intimately related to our adoptive mothers during the early years of our lives in a strong psychological way. We are totally dependent on social relations with others in order for us to develop psychologically. Again, the social and interactive character of early childhood psychological development can be described in a very personal, intimate way, with one's mother. But Flax does not neglect the social context in which this intimate relation is embedded. She recognizes that child-care relations are affected by the more general social relations the childcare provider experiences.

Flax's contribution helps us heal the separation between the mind and the body that has existed in Euro-western philosophy since ancient Greece. Her emphasis on the primary social relatedness of infants-in-relation-to-their-care-providers supports the thesis that human relatedness is central to subjectivity. Flax helps us understand how we develop our own unique sense of self, what she calls our core identity, through powerful, intimate, affective relations with other people, in particular our primary caregivers, who are embedded within a larger social context. Even though our identity is shifting and changing as we experience different social forces, even though our sense of self is multifarious, contingent, and fractured, still, whatever sense of self we have develops from our relations with others.

Nel Noddings (1984) also contributes to a discussion of personal relations with her *Caring*. While Noddings's work is most often discussed in terms of ethics, I turn to Noddings for her description of a relational ontology. For Noddings, we are naturally in relation with others and our very individuality is defined in a set of relations. Relationality is a fundamental universal for all of us. Like Ruddick and Flax, Noddings describes relations in a personal, intimate way, with the mother/child relation serving as a basis for her. She describes personal relations in terms of the one-caring and the one-cared-for, underscoring that we are alive today because we have experienced caring relations with an other. She proposes that we all have a desire to be perceived as one-caring due to the caring relation we experienced with our mothers as infants. One of Noddings's unique contributions to a relational description is her emphasis on the reciprocity of the caring relations we experience, in terms of the one-cared-for receiving the caring offered by the one-caring. For Noddings the child in the mother/child relation has an active role to play, in responding to the mother's caring. By describing the one-cared-for as a participant in this personal relationship, as someone who willingly reveals himself to the one-caring, she establishes that our basic relationality is transactional; we affect our mothers through our relating to her.

While Noddings begins with the importance of the mother/child relation as fundamental to caring relations, she considers other examples of personal relations as well, such as the teacher/student relation. This is a controversial example for her to use since she resides in a culture that tries to maintain sharp boundaries between familial relations as intimate, personal relations, and teacher/student relations as examples of public, social relations that are not so intimate. In ancient Greece it was considered common for teachers to establish personal relationships with their students that were intimate, loving relationships, even to the point of physical intimacy as lovers.[3] Noddings's move beyond mother/child relations is an important one, though, for it underscores how we are fundamentally interdependent, relational beings, even outside of our family boundaries. Once establishing the importance of considering our early infantile experiences in establishing our relationality, I follow Noddings's lead and move beyond mother/child relations to consider interpersonal, adult relations with the help of Simone Weil (1977) and Martin Buber (1958).

Both Weil and Buber describe a very intimate, personal relationship between knowers and the known through their religious beliefs and the relationships they experience with God. Yet their descriptions are very different. Weil (1977) acknowledges that we start our lives as social beings and we develop our personalities through our relationships with others. However, Weil seeks to escape the influence others have on us by arousing ourselves out of our subdued existences and renouncing our personalities. Weil seeks to become impersonal and anonymous, for she argues that it is only through anonymity that we find God. We must escape our collectivity through total detachment in order to enter the realm of the sacred. She says there are two ways we can subdue our existences and become totally detached. One approach is through giving our attention to the joy of true beauty, and the other is through attending to the suffering of affliction. Both of these paths cause a state of nonbeing, the annihilation of the self. When we have totally detached from our self, then we are open and free to experience God's love.

Because Weil (1977) uses 'attention' as a means to losing one's soul and achieving impersonality, she becomes a vivid example of the kinds of concerns other feminists have expressed about Ruddick's (1989) 'attentive love' and Noddings's (1984) 'caring.' Therefore, I use Weil's position as a way of addressing these concerns. I make the case that attention, or what I call 'caring reasoning,' is what protects us from charges of determinism or relativism. Establishing caring relations with others not like us helps us gain a perspective on the influences of the collective, and helps us become aware of the taken-for-granted. Caring reasoning helps us gain a greater awareness of our own contexuality, at a macro and micro level, thus offering us a way to critique our contexuality, as well as offering us ways to imagine how things could be different. Weil acknowledges that we are fundamentally relational beings, but she wants to renounce our fundamental relationality at a personal level in order to establish an anonymous, impersonal relationship with her universal God. Martin Buber, on the other hand, says the only kind of relationship we can have with God is a personal, intimate one.

Buber (1958) describes our lives as beginning in relation, in terms of infancy, in agreement with Ruddick, Flax, and Noddings, as well as in terms of human spirituality, in agreement with Weil.[4] For Buber, our first relation is an intimate, personal one, which he descibes as an *I-Thou* relation. Our first word is *I-Thou*, before we ever say *I*. Buber describes an eternal *I-Thou* relation between ourselves and God, and he describes particular *I-Thou* relations with nature and with each other. Every particular *I-Thou* relation we participate in leads us to the eternal *I-Thou*. Our *I-Thou* relations are direct relations that are spoken with our whole beings. In contrast to *I-Thou* relations, we also experience *I-It* relations, but these are secondary relations that come with natural separation. First we are together with God, and in relation with our biological mothers and then our adoptive mothers, and then we become separated and experience the world of things (*It*). The *I* of *I-It* relations is an individual differentiated from other individuals. The *I* of *I-Thou* relations is a person in relation with others. So, we find that Buber does not recommend giving up the *I* of *I-Thou* relations. For him the personal, subjective *I* is indispensable in order for there to be *I-Thou* relations. However, he agrees with Weil that the *I* of individuality is dispensable, and that it gets in the way of our direct, intimate *I-Thou* relations. *I-Thou* relations are two-fold relations between *I* and *Thou*, they are transactional, similar to Noddings's description of caring relations. In fact, Noddings uses Buber's description of *I-Thou* relations as her model for her caring ethics theory. His relational ontology serves as an excellent source for a relational (e)pistemology as well. I consider relations in terms of social relations next.

Social Relations

While it is the case that we begin our lives in intimate, personal relations with our mothers and/or adoptive mothers, it has already been noted that our personal relations are located within larger social contexts. Our mothers live in social communities that affect their interpersonal relationships with us. As subjects, our mothers are accultured social beings, and we become acculturated too, through our personal relations with our careproviders. Our self-production is always a social enterprise. In my discussion of social relations we will find that shifting the focus from a personal, micro level to a social, macro level causes the boundaries between private relations and social ones to further blur. This blurring supports my effort to describe the transactional, relational qualities of knowers and knowing.

I turn to George Herbert Mead (1934) to set the tone for this discussion because of his highly influential social psychology behaviorist argument that we are first of all social beings who become individuals with minds out of our social relations with others. With Mead, the social is represented as the whole that is prior to the part, the individual. He traces social acts historically back to the stages that are prior to language in order to understand how we develop a mind and self. He suggests we start to develop a mind and a self with gestures, which initially are physical ones and then later become vocal gestures. When a gesture comes to mean a certain idea and my gesture arouses that same idea in you, then that gesture has become a significant symbol with a shared meaning, or what we call language. With the development of language, we are now able to think. A conversation of gestures is the beginning of communication. Mead reasons that in order for me to become aware of the meaning of my own gestures, I must be able to see myself as others see me. I must be able to take the attitude of the other towards myself. This reflective quality of language, this adjusted response, is the essential condition for the development of mind and self, according to Mead. By taking the attitude of the other toward myself, the self becomes an object to itself; it becomes self-conscious.

Mead (1934) illustrates how the development of the self occurs by considering how young children's role playing helps children develop the capacity to be an object in their own experience, and thus learn reflexivity. Later children learn how to play games, which are a more structured and more complex form of play for they involve agreed-upon rules and the ability to take on a variety of roles in order to play. The agreed-upon general rules of the game represent for Mead what he calls "the generalized other." The organized social group that our care providers belong to and we become initiated into is the generalized other. The generalized other is what supplies each of us with the general social attitudes of the community members. The generalized other gives us our sense of unity of self for it supplies the rules we need to know in order to live in this community. The generalized other supplies us with shared common meanings which make it possible for us to be self-conscious and self-reflective. Shared responses of the others socially validate the self. Yet, Mead acknowledges that our unified self is not just one personality; we all have multiple personalities depending on the various social communities to which we belong and the differing validations we receive. He also suggests that while the generalized other helps to initiate and shape who we become socially, we each have qualities which make us different from everyone else which we contribute to the changing of society and each other.

Mead (1934) assumes many dualisms in his description, between the mind/body, reasons/emotions, public "me"/private "I" for example, which create problems for him. He also describes the generalized other as being very strong in affecting our individual sense of a unified self, thereby raising the concern of social determinism. In addition, he relies heavily on certain concepts to carry his theory which need further discussion, such as his "shared responses," "vocal gestures," and "generalized other." John Dewey, a colleague and friend of Mead, offers a solution to the tension between individuation and socialization, to the self/society split, with his transactional theory. The split rests on an either/or logical approach, whereas Dewey proposes a both/and approach. I use *Democracy and Education* (1916) as an example of Dewey's emphasis on the interdependent nature of relationships, with his discussions of the individual and the community, the young and their elders, and varying methods of education, as well as various forms of associated living. Dewey agrees with Mead's position that individuals are first of all social beings, thereby escaping solipsism. But he also argues that individuals affect others, our social groups, right from the start, thereby avoiding social determinism. Dewey helps us understand that individuals are greatly affected by their social groups but social groups also are greatly affected by individuals and other social groups.

Once establishing that our social relations are transactional, that we are selves-in-relation-to-others, I consider in greater detail dangers involved in the socializing process of taking the attitude of the other and seeing ourselves as others see us, with the help of Peter Berger and Thomas Luckmann (1966). Berger and Luckmann further elaborate on Mead's description of the objectifying process and the role of the generalized other. They support Mead's position that the self is a social product, adding in greater detail how this process occurs, in a social world that we produce. Berger and Luckmann describe how "reality" is socially constructed, by actions becoming habituated and then typified, and eventually institutionalized. Social institutions are then passed on, via the educational process, as if they are given, unalterable, and self-evident. When we forget that social institutions are ones we have socially constructed and we can remake, we go beyond objectifying the world to reifying it as a fact, something that is fated. We develop a language, folktales, then theories offered by specialized personnel, and finally symbolic universes to explain why things are the way they are as part of the social legitimization process. However, symbolic universes are always problematic because they can never explain everything in a society and leave nothing in question, and as soon as there are any alternative explanations offered, the alternatives threaten the existing one by the sheer fact that they exist. Societies develop policing actions to help maintain their current symbolic universe. However, the social legitimating process can be changed by finding faults, cracks, and ruptures in the current symbolic universe and transforming the explanations.

I offer American Pragmatism, feminism, and postmodernism as examples of theories that currently play transformative roles in Philosophy. These theories help to raise our consciousness and our awareness of social relations. They play a critical kind of role by helping us critique the legitimization process. They offer us comparisons and contrasts so we can place what we take to be "reality" within a context and consider new possibilities. The responses these theories generate by traditional, Modernist Philosophers serve as examples of the policing activities that occur in legitimization, as described by Berger and Luckmann, to disarm the potential damage new theories can cause. The threatening theories are described as "naive," "unsophisticated," "contradictory," "illogical," and "obtuse," for example. The dangerous theorists are made fun of or ignored, and recommended for therapy, such as more education of the legitimate symbolic universe. Richard Rorty (1979, 1982, 1989), as a pragmatist, Dorothy Smith (1987, 1990) as a feminist, and Michel Foucault (1965, 1972, 1973, 1978, 1979, 1980, 1985) as a postmodernist, all serve as vivid examples of change agents in the roles of consciousness-raisers, as they point to the fissures and cracks in our socially constructed world and help to make visible what before was taken for granted and went unnoticed.

Each example I offer follows a similar technique of connecting theories back to practices and highlighting theorists connections to their larger society. Rorty uses historical analysis to contextualize Descartes's, Kant's, and Hegel's theories, for example. Smith treats the everyday world as problematic, people's activities that are prior to any conceptual expression, in order to help us problematize concepts we take for granted which shape our lives. Smith contributes to the deconstruction of her field of study, sociology, by showing the patriarchal role sociology has played, historically, and the consequences of excluding women from contributing to what becomes "culture." She wants sociology to validate 'others' by helping to subvert the process of institutionalizing, by getting back to experience and using that perspective to critique the legitimation process. Foucault follows the same technique that Berger and Luckmann, Rorty, and Smith follow, to help us see that unities we take for granted are socially constructed. Foucault applies an historical analysis to the field of historical knowledge in order to contextualize that theory, diversify themes of continuity, and restore specificity of occurrence. He is an archivist using a method he calls archaeology to look for ruptures and discontinuities. He finds these ruptures in the history of medicine, hospitals, asylums, and penal law, for example. Foucault develops a constitutive definition of power as a network of practices and institutions that shape and proliferate certain ways of being, similar to what Berger and Luckmann describe as the legitimating process for the social construction of "reality."

What we find in an exploration of social relations is that there is a direct transactional relation between our individual subjectivity and our general sociality. We are social beings who exist in relation to others at an intimate level as well as at a generalized level. I argue that there is a dialectic between social reality and individual existence. The split between personal relations and social relations is an artificial bifurcation that our discussion should help to dissipate. However, we know from the discussion of social relations that old habits die hard. This text is meant to serve as a catalyst for change. I explore this dialectic further in the following discussion of Buddhist and Indigenous relational views of knowing.

W/holistic Relations

In the discussion of personal relations, I emphasize a unity described between the knower and the known in intimate maternal, caring, I-Thou relationships. While we develop differentiated, objectified relations with others, we begin our lives as one with our mothers, our care providers, or as Buber describes this, our Spiritual Beings. We are connected materially and spiritually to a greater universe; our beginning experiences are undistinquished, wholistic experiences that become differentiated through our social interactions with others. As social beings, we develop language and concepts to help us bring order and meaning to our primal experiences. These concepts become our socially constructed "reality," helping us function on a daily basis, while at the same time limiting the range of our functioning. Our concepts are additions to our primal experiences; they do not take away from our inarticulated experience, but they cannot capture the flux and depth of pure, inarticulated experience. In fact, our concepts can deceive us and limit us by making us think they have captured all of our experiences when in reality our concepts function on a surface level while our primal experiences flow on below. We have to learn to get beyond our concepts, or one could say before our concepts or below our concepts, in order to help us tune in to our primal experiences of the universe as one.

While we have already discovered nondualistic thinkers in the Euro-west, such as James, Dewey, and Buber, they represent a minority of Euro-western philosophers, the vast majority having embraced various forms of dualisms. There are excellent sources for a wholistic view of the universe outside of the Euro-western tradition that can help us tune in to our primal experiences and further develop the concept of knowers as selves-in-relation-with-others, rather than some false notion of an autonomous, individual self to which the Euro-west so longingly clings. The concept of nonduality found fertile ground in the East and among Indigenous people, and sprouted in a variety of forms. I turn to Buddhism and Native American philosophy in particular for descriptions of nondualistic, unified approaches to knowing as I continue to dissolve the many dualisms the Euro-western philosophical traditions have built up, especially between the knower and the known.

Both Buddhists and Native Americans describe primal experience with a spiritual emphasis.[5] In fact, their spiritual emphasis is what helps them compensate for our tendency to describe the world in terms of dualisms. Their spirituality serves as their means to describing the universe in terms of holism. Thus, I will emphasize both wholism and holism (materially and spiritually), by writing the term in this manner, w/holism, as I describe Buddhist and Native American w/holistic relations. Since concepts cannot describe pure experience entirely, I will follow the Buddhist and Native American lead and rely on metaphors and stories to help me avoid the dualistic, surface trappings in which our concepts tend to contain and confuse us.

Buddhism relies on the ambiguous concept of nonduality as the basis for its view of w/holism. Buddhists do not deny a dualistic world of everyday experience, they just deny that this dualistic world is all there is. The dualistic world is superficial and relative; it is one we have socially created and this socially constructed "reality" causes us endless suffering for it is a world in which we have become severed from our source of life. Pure nondualistic experience is our source of life. Nonduality is the primal experience we all have had, yet it is very difficult for us to access this experience once we have been taught to relate to the world dualistically. Nonduality is not something we can understand conceptually or intuitively, it is something we must experience. For Buddhists the path to enlightenment where we are able to re-cognize our unity with the universe is necessarily arduous. It is a path that requires us to empty our minds of treasured concepts such as the concept of a self. Buddha presented several different dharmas (teachings) to help us re-experience nonduality.

One central Buddhist dharma is the dharma of dependent co-origination, or co-arising. This teaching suggests that all things are interconnected and interdependent. Buddhists suggest that it is ignorant to believe there exists a world of appearances that is separate, causally independent, and permanent. Appearances come into being through dependent co-origination, and they are neither existent nor non-existent. Yet we behave as if appearances are existent, separate, and permanent and it is this delusion that causes us great suffering. According to Buddhists, if we can eliminate our delusions we can eliminate our suffering. Buddha taught us how to eliminate our delusions by following the Eightfold Righteous Path of conduct: right view, right thinking, right speech, right action, right way of life, right endeavor, right mindfulness, and right meditation.

The dharma of emptiness teaches us that our original mind, big Mind, is an empty mind that is unobstructed. Our original mind sees things as they are, in a state of unity. Empty Mind means everything is always there, it includes everything. But our mind is also the basis for confusion, for our mind invents images, appearances, and identifies them as existing objects. The paradox about the mind is that just as our mind leads us away from our beginner's Mind by inventing appearances, our mind can lead us back to our original, empty/full Mind. Buddhists suggest that through the practice of meditation, we can learn to re-cognize our own minds, and dispel what our minds have invented, thus getting back to our original, nondualistic, big Mind. Buddhists renounce the world of appearances in the sense that they grow to recognize that the conditioned world is illusionary and devoid of truth. The biggest illusion our mind invents is the illusion of a separate self, the belief in the existence of a persistent, continuously existing, single, independent ego. The first step to enlightenment for a Buddhist is the relinquishing of a sense of self. The dharma of egolessness of self (anatman) teaches us that the self is nonsubstantial. If we understand the transitory and transparent nature of the world outside (which our mind projects), then we can understand that the ego is another such projection.

As with the mind, the paradox about the self is that the individual self leads us away from an awareness of the w/holeness of the universe, and yet we gain consciousness of the universal through the individual self. What distinguishes the different schools of Buddhism, Mahāyāna, Hināyāna, and Zen Buddhism are the paths they choose to follow to gain that consciousness. Southern Buddhists, Hināyāna Buddhists, believe the path we follow to enlightenment should be one where all individual desire is extinguished. They seek complete psychological detachment and annihilation of the 'self,' similar to Simone Weil's (1977) approach in her efforts to become one with God. Northern Buddhists, Mahāyāna Buddhists, also seek to master the individual self, however, not by extinction but instead by reorientation. They teach that the individual self can be expanded by following a path of limitless compassion. Mahāyāna Buddhism shares much in common with Martin Buber's (1955) approach to establishing a personal I/Thou relation with God and Noddings's (1984) caring relations. Zen Buddhists say that their way is both Hināyānistic and Mahāyānistic: they have Hināyāna practice with Mahāyāna spirit, rigid formal practice with informal mind. They seek to cut through the trappings of discursive thought by effortlessly practicing daily living. All Buddhists seek to return to the initial stage of bare perception, prior to conceptual influence. This is the stage of nonduality.

The Mahāyāna Buddhist dharma of compassion is a teaching I especially want to highlight, as it relates so directly with what I describe as caring reasoning. Because of their nondualistic ontology, and their sense of connectedness to the entire universe, Mahāyāna Buddhists embrace a spirit of compassion that is defined as total openness, or perfect kindness. They believe compassion is the way to achieve enlightenment, to re-experience pure experience beyond differentiation. We feel compassion when we overcome our sense of separation from the world and feel our togetherness (Khema, 1999). We learn to open ourselves up, and suspend ourselves, so that we can feel with others, and attend to others. In this opening up and attending to others with generosity and loving-kindness, we empty ourselves of any false sense of self-importance and become full in our awareness of our connectedness to the basic, primordial ground of pure experience.

While Buddhists rely on the concept of nonduality to describe their w/holistic views, Native American tribes living in North America rely on various organic terms to describe their concepts of spiritual w/holeness (e.g. Great Spirit, Holy Wind, Sacred Hoop). Unlike Buddhism, which has an enormous canonical literature to aid in understanding the Buddha's teachings, Native Americans have always relied on oral traditions that seek to protect their stories, songs, chants, and prayers from outsiders as well as some insiders in order to maintain their spirituality. In trying to represent Native American beliefs, I begin at great risk of misrepresenting them. Fortunately, I have access to several recent texts written by Native Americans themselves, as well as texts with direct translations of the original language included, to help protect me from misrepresentation. Even still, I proceed with great caution.

I share the story of Mabel McKay, a Pomo Indian from the Long Valley Cache Creek Pomo tribe, a Dreamer, healer, and basketweaver, as told by Greg Sarris (1993, 1994), a long-time family friend and the author of Mabel's biography. Mabel asked Greg to write her story. She shared with him many stories, and participated in innumerable conversations with him over the course of 30 years. Mabel modeled for Greg the Native American tribal practices that are communal, informal, experiential, sacred, and grounded in oral traditions and storytelling. Her stories interrupt and disrupt preconceived notions. She exposes chasms between various interpretive worlds, and implicates the listener, for her storytelling is an active, respondent activity. The dialoguing that goes on between the storyteller and the listener helps expose the limits and boundaries of each other's worlds.

Mabel McKay was guided in her healing, and basket weaving, as well as in her daily life, by Spirit, who talked to her and advised her in her Dreams. Spirit was her teacher. Spirit taught her songs and dances, and gave her the guidance and direction to make materials to give to the people of her tribe. She dialogued with Spirit in her Dreams, asking questions and sometimes getting answers. Her conversation with Spirit was like her conversation with Greg, open and interactive, relying on caring reasoning, as she attentively listened and tried to believe, in order to assure understanding. Mabel's storytelling, basket weaving, singing, praying, and dancing are all techniques she used to help her stay attuned to primal experience, to Spirit, for Spirit represents for her pure experience beyond differentiation. Mabel experienced an open, flowing universe and she shared that experience with Greg, who kept trying to order and differentiate it. Repeatedly she showed Sarris that concepts are only a small part of the whole material-spiritual universe. Finally, he did learn what she was trying to teach him, and he was able to write her story, their story, which was published in 1994, the year after Mabel died as the last Long Valley Cache Creek Pomo Indian.

I also turn to work concerning Navajo spirituality to guide me in exploration of w/holistic Indigenous descriptions of the universe. I use in particular the dissertation/texts of James McNeley (1981/1997) and John Farella (1984). These two works are significant because they attempt to maintain a w/holistic sense of Navajo spirituality rather than imposing Euro-western standards upon their studies that would allow them to meet Euro-western rigorous and restrictive methodological standards but render their detailed work void of any synthesis. McNeley centers his work around the Navajo concept, *nilch'i*, which he translates as Holy Wind. McNeley argues that Holy Wind is the concept that links the Navajo soul to the immanent powers of the universe and is thus central to Navajo thought. Like Mabel McKay's Spirit, "Holy Wind gives life, thought, speech, and the power of motion to all living things and serves as the means of communication between all elements of the living world" (McNeley, 1981/1997, p. 1). McNeley tells Navajo creation stories to help us understand how Holy Wind makes life possible and serves as a mentor and guide, talking to the Navajo people in the fold of their ears. All people are born with Holy Wind in them, but they have the choice whether to stay attuned to the voice of Holy Wind or not. If they choose not to listen to Holy Wind's advice, the Navajos believe the Wind weakens and eventually withdraws its guidance, thus assuring the person will die.

While the Navajos give Holy Wind various names, such as White Wind, Yellow Wind, based on different criteria, Holy Wind is a unitary being. Farella (1984) compares the Navajo concept of *sq'a nagháí bik'e hózhą́*, which he defines as "completeness" or "continuous generational animation," to McNeley's (1981/1997) air that animates all being, Holy Wind (*nilch'i*). Farella also refers to Navajo creation stories to help explain the concept *sq'a nagháí bik'e hózhą́*, as well as the concept *atkéé naa'aashii*. Like the Buddhist dharma of dependent co-origination, *sq'a nagháí bik'e hózhą́* dissolves boundaries, such as ego, and helps us understand our world in terms of wholeness. *sq'a nagháí bik'e hózhą́* is a concept that emphasizes how difference works together to achieve completeness and *atkéé naa'aashii* is a concept that emphasizes the flux and differentiation that exists in our world. *Atkéé naa'aashii* is a concept similar to the Buddhist dharma of emptiness which is also fullness, meaning cyclical, repeated creation. It can be used to describe any complementary phenomena. The Navajo claim that we started this world as a unity and we have gotten increasingly complex and diverse—however we are now becoming less diverse and eventually we will be unified again. This process of unification-diversification-reunification is an example of the concept *alkéé naa'aashii*. Our individual life cycles are another example that follows the same pattern. Farella (1984) demonstrates in the Navajo stories how contrasts such as good/evil, life/death, health/sickness, are bundled together and considered packages that are necessary in order to make a complete cycle, one whole. Because the Navajo spiritual philosophy emphasizes reanimation, their philosophy has served to revitalize the Navajo culture. Where there are around 1000 Pomo Indians alive today, there are 140,000–175,000 Navajos. Similar to Buddhists, Navajos emphasize an (e)pistemological shift, a reorientation changing the way we perceive the world, rather than a technological emphasis on altering the world. They serve as an excellent example of a nondualistic philosophy that describes the universe as connected and w/holistically related. I move on to consider ecological relations.

Ecological Relations

In my description of a relational (e)pistemology, we have learned that this (e)pistemological theory is supported by a nondualistic ontology which emphasizes that we are w/holistically connected with our greater universe, materially and spiritually. I argue that this connection is at a personal and social level, but I also argue that this connection is much wider, for I describe our primal experience as being one with the universe. Of course, such an expanded concept of relationality includes within it the natural world in which we live, our biosphere. The philosophical view I describe is consistent with an emphasis on ecological relations. In fact, I want to argue that such a view *must* include an emphasis on ecological relations. For a relational (e)pistemology and ontology, the natural world in which human beings live is one in which we are intimately connected. Consistent with Buddhist and Native American views about nature, I do not assume any separation between human beings and nature. I wish to describe human beings as one with nature.

This view of human beings as being one with nature is contradictory to the majority of positions Euro-westerns have historically taken, in philosophy, religion, and science. Philosophers, theologians, and scientists have all argued for separating humans from nature, thus creating a dualism, and they have given human beings a higher ontological status, thus creating a hierarchy. The next step has been the introduction of the "logic of domination" in order to explain and justify the subordination of nature to human beings (Warren, 1990). However, my view that human beings are one with nature is consistent with recent Euro-western developments in ecological feminism and science. I will describe scientific developments such as general systems theory, quantum mechanics, and relativity theory in the next section, but in this section I want to return to what Buddhists and Native Americans have to say about nature, and consider the deep ecology movement as well as ecological feminism (also referred to as ecofeminism).

From a Buddhist perspective, the dharma of co-origination, or co-arising breaks down any possibility of viewing humans as distinct and separate from nature. Co-origination teaches us that we are not separate entities, disconnected from each other. Human beings are not independent; rather we are mutually dependent and interconnected to the entire universe, including nature. We create boundaries and categories to distinguish ourselves from nature, but these are just human-made boundaries that do not really exist. The more we try to sharpen them and more clearly define them, the more the boundaries tend to fuzz and leak into each other. The dharma of co-origination denies a nature/human dualism. Consequently, it also denies a hierarchical approach to nature, with humans placed above nature. If there are not two separate categories to distinguish then there is nothing to rank in value as well. As a result, all of life in all of its multifarious forms takes on inherent value according to Buddhists. This is why we find in practice that most Buddhists are pacifists and vegetarians as they seek to avoid dominance over other living beings. They tend to live simple lives that do not require a lot of material resources. They live in harmony with the natural environment, considering themselves part of that natural environment, rather than striving to control and contain nature. Buddhists believe that nature and humanity are interrelated and their relationship with each other is one of mutual dependence, not opposition or exploitation. To oppose nature and try to assume dominion over nature, as the Euro-west has attempted to do, is to live a life that will only bring us more suffering in the end, for we are opposing ourselves.

The dharmas of emptiness, egolessness of self, and compassion mutually reinforce this w/holistic approach to nature. These dharmas encourage us to empty our minds of the false illusion that we are separate entities apart from nature, and to recognize these distinctions as mere appearances. With an empty mind we are full of appreciation of our interconnectedness with the alive, flowing world that surrounds us. When we let go of the idea that we exist as separate selves, we become open to cultivating our transactional relation with nature. We understand that human beings and nature are mutually dependent. With compassion, we open up and relate to nature in an intimate way that is mutually interpenetrating. Historically, people worldwide have found great peace and joy in their communions with nature, as well as great fear, awe, and reverence. Buddhists embrace an ecological view that encourages us to appreciate the intrinsic value of all phenomena.

I move on to describe Arne Naess's (1989) deep ecology movement, which helps further clarify the difference between a w/holistic ecological view and an ecological view based of a nature/human split. At a surface level, it appears that Naess's view is very similar to Buddhism. He wants to heal the split between human beings and nature, and his suggestion for how to do this is by reorientation through a new ontology that posits humanity as inseparable from nature. Naess embraces an ontology that emphasizes unity. This sounds very similar to the Buddhist dharma of co-arising. However, while Naess wants to encourage the concept of unity, he also worries about the need to support individuality and diversity. Naess's unity is not the same as Buddhism's nonduality. Naess does not embrace the Buddhist dharma of egolessness, choosing instead to describe his new ontology in terms of Self-realisation (his spelling). By Self-realisation he means the universal right to self-unfolding. He means the classical liberal sense of self-unfolding (self-sufficiency, self-determination, autonomy) expanded to include plants and animals as also deserving of this right to self-unfolding. Like many Euro-westerners, Naess misunderstands the Buddhist dharma of egolessness, or no-self, fearing the loss of self leads to determinism. The Buddhist dharma of egolessness gives up the idea of an independent, unique, individual self in favor of a relational sense of self that is transitory and multifarious. Thus, egolessness does not threaten the loss of diversity, it enhances it. But egolessness does undermine the Euro-western classical liberal idea of a separate, autonomous self. Naess does not give up the concept of 'self,' he just expands it to include nature, not just human beings, which is why he capitalizes Self.

Buddhists argue that self-sufficiency, self-determination, and autonomy are dangerous, illusionary concepts we develop out of fear in response to our initial experience of oneness. We go to great lengths to attempt to maintain these illusions. For Buddhists the self is impermanent and constantly changing, and does not exist as a solid entity. The impermanence of the self supports the Buddhist idea of co-arising, and mutual dependency. When Naess (1989) takes his classical liberal turn and describes his ontology in terms of Self-realisation, his position becomes an example of why the dharma of egolessness is so important to Buddhism. As long as we seek to maintain a strong sense of an individual self, even though we enlarge this concept to allow us to acknowledge that animals and plants are individuals too, we maintain a false sense of separation. This false sense of separation undermines the nondualistic ontology Buddhism represents and Naess seems to want to embrace.

Because Naess (1989) retains the concept of a separate self, even in its expanded form, we find in the end that he still maintains an ontological separation between human beings and nature. What distinguishes his view from other Euro-western views that assume a split between human beings and nature is the value Naess places on nature. Like other deep ecologists, he is strongly critical of Euro-western views that are anthropological in their approaches. However, Naess overcompensates for this anthropological tendency by valuing nature higher than human beings. For Naess, a state of nature is one that is devoid of human beings. Naess's (1989) deep ecology does not offer an ecological relational perspective that consistently maintains a w/holistic relationality. Still, he does point us in an ecological direction when he considers Buddhist ideas.

We have already found that Native Americans do maintain a w/holistic relational philosophy and so I turn to them as another example of an ecological relationality. When we speak of Nature within Native American philosophy, it is important that we capitalize the term to help remind us that Nature is a sacred, spiritual being for them. Not only do Native Americans serve well as another example of a nondualistic metaphysical approach to Nature, they also supply an important link to the ecofeminist focus on power issues in discussions of domination over Nature. This is because pre-contact Native Americans historically rejected patriarchy just as much as they rejected exploitation of Nature (Allen, 1986). They did not assume a dualism between Nature and humans, nor did they assume a split between men and women, so they never developed a hierarchical approach, placing humans over Nature and/or men over women, that could lead to domination over Nature and/or women.

We will find in the creation stories I present in Chapter 6 that Native Americans describe human and nonhuman beings as relatives. Humans are related to Nature as kin. The boundary between the spiritual world and human world is flexible, as is the boundary between Nature and humanity. Human beings are descendants of Spirits who are born from the Clouds, and all life is sustained by the Holy Wind. Native Americans describe themselves as one with Nature, and they lived and many continue to live in a manner that supports this ecological view. Their stories tell of how Animal kin advised them on hunting practices, so that people would understand how to balance between their eating of plants and animals in order to stay alive, and their replenishing of the land in order to help maintain animal and plant life. Native Americans consider Nature their teacher and they listen and observe, so they can learn. Not only did they learn how to hunt from Animal spirits, they learned much about the healing properties of Plants by watching Animals with Plants. Their knowledge of their local land is extensive because they have lived an intimate lifestyle in harmony with Nature for centuries and what they learned they passed on through oral traditions. However, it will require a fundamental (e)pistemological shift in order for the Euro-western scientific world to take Indigenous peoples' knowledge seriously. Still today scientists tend to discount Indigenous knowledge of Nature as superstition and childish ignorance. Indigenous knowledge of Nature is discounted until it is offered by White scholars, in White men's terms (Deloria, Jr., 1995). We need an (e)pistemological shift that recognizes humanity and nature as interconnected, interrelated, and alive. I hope this text serves to help stimulate such a shift.

I also want this text to serve a role in drawing our attentions to issues of power in connection to knowledge. We find these power issues in the racism White scholars express against Native Americans and other Indigenous people when they will not recognize their natural knowledge as a form of knowledge. We also find power issues when we explore the history of Euro-western views of nature in relation to women. Not only does Euro-western philosophy, religion, and science have a long history of offering theoretical arguments and 'evidence' to support human efforts to sever themselves from, devalue, and dominate over nature, they also have a similar history in regards to separating women from men in the category of human beings and linking women with nature. Again, the logic of domination is applied and men assume the right to suppress women just as they try to contain and control nature. The argument that usually is used to link women to nature is a biological one, based on women's reproductive role in society. Given women's socially constructed link to nature, ecofeminists argue that a discussion of ecological relations is not complete without drawing our attention to the role of patriarchy. They maintain "that there are important connections—historical, experiential, symbolic, theoretical—between the domination of women and the domination of nature" (Warren, 1990, p. 126).

Feminists agree that the dualism that splits men from women, the hierarchical valuing of men over women, and then the logic of domination that is used to justify subordinating women to men are wrong. Within that basic agreement, there are several different schools of feminism, some of whom embrace the split between human beings and nature (liberal feminists) and some of whom embrace the linking of women to nature (radical cultural feminists). Liberal feminists such as de Beauvoir (1952/1980/1989) want women to be classified with men in order to avoid devaluing, and they want to be separated from nature. They do not try to heal the split between human beings and nature, just the split between men and women. Radical cultural feminists want to underscore the connecting of women to nature but some of them do not want to heal the split between women-nature and men (Daly, 1978/1990). They agree that women are connected to nature, biologically, in ways that men are not.

Ecofeminists such as Ynestra King (1981, 1987, 1989, 1990), Karen Warren (1987, 1988, 1990), and Carol Merchant (1980, 1989, 1992) argue that the man/nature, culture/nature splits which link man with culture and women with nature and value man and culture over women and nature are historically sanctioned claims that are problematic. Warren contributes her analysis of the logic of domination to the discussion. Merchant presents important arguments for the historical connections between the domination of women and nature, particularly focusing on the history of Euro-western science. Daly (1978/1990) also presents important historical arguments, tracing the Judeo-Christian role in the domination of women and nature. King helps us see how to avoid sliding back into some form of natural determinism with her insightful criticisms. Ecofeminists help us reorient ourselves ontologically and (e)pistemologically, showing us how to re-conceive and re-vision our world, so that in our re-telling, re-writing, and re-weaving we can eliminate the logic of domination in all its forms and heal the dualistic splits the Euro-western world has embraced.

Scientific Relations

I end my discussion of various kinds of relationality by focusing on exciting changes occurring within Euro-western science. It is fitting that I end with science as science has usurped philosophy in status in this past century, just as philosophy usurped religion during the Age of Enlightenment. Today science enjoys highest status as the most respected, and most influential source of knowledge. Scientific knowledge is defined as warranted by empirical evidence which is viewed as factual and accurate, unlike philosophy, which is warranted by logical reasoning, and religion, which is warranted by personal faith, both of which warrants have been found to be fallible and biased and therefore lacking. Science is not suppose to be influenced by the personal biases of the scientist, and claims to have successfully achieved the severing of the knower from the known. Science claims to take everything as problematic and up for examination and questioning. Science claims that it does not matter who the knower is; with the use of the scientific method, the same result to inquiry should be achieved no matter who is doing the inquirying.

Yet, we already know from the previous two sections on w/holistic relations and ecological relations that it does matter who the scientific knowers are, as well as which methods are applied, using which standards and criteria. Buddhist, Indigenous, deep ecological, and ecofeminist scholars all reveal to us biases embedded within Euro-western science, such as the assumptions that nature is inert and passive, like a machine, and that we can better understand and control nature by dissecting her into smaller and smaller parts. In this chapter we will discover scientists within the Euro-western tradition who uncover many important scientific biases through their own research work, as they find themselves having to question and discard assumptions they took for granted. These scientists, and there are many more than I can possibly discuss in the space allotted, contribute significantly to a paradigm shift in science away from a reductionistic, mechanistic view of the universe toward a view of the universe as alive and multidimensional. What is offered here is a description of the universe as dynamic, transactional, and whole.

I begin an exploration of scientific relations with what Capra (1975) calls "the new physics," in particular relativity theory, quantum mechanics (also known as quantum theory), and particle physics. Einstein's work served as a stimulus for relativity theory as well as quantum mechanics, and so I turn to him to lead a discussion that emphasizes the continuity of the universe. We will discover that quantum theory, as developed by an international group of scientists, including Niels Bohr, Werner Heisenberg, and others, known as the Copenhagen interpretation of quantum theory, emphasizes the discontinuity of the universe. David Bohm (1980) will help us understand that both relativity theory and quantum theory work as complementary descriptions of the same, wholistic universe. Unfortunately, both Einstein and Bohr clung to some scientific assumptions from the classical mechanical description of science they inherited but helped to dismantle. Consequently, instead of being able to work together to enlarge their views, they fought against each other and eventually severed their relationships with each other. Einstein spent his later years trying to disprove quantum theory, as others became convinced it was correct.

Einstein's relativity theory shatters Newton's absolute, three-dimensional space and time model of the universe by describing space and time as intimately connected rather than as separate dimensions. According to Einstein, space and time form a fourth dimension he calls a 'space-time continuum.' Einstein proposed that people who move at different speeds see the same event in different ways, depending on their locations, thus elevating the speed of light to the level of a new principle of physics. This does not mean that we each experience a different universe or that we cannot come to agreement on the universe. What is does mean, though, is that matter and energy cannot be separated and divided up: they are in fact equivalent, contrary to earlier scientific assumptions. Einstein also discovered that gravity and acceleration are equivalent concepts too, rather than being separate, distinct concepts. Thirdly, Einstein realized that space is curved rather than flat as assumed. These discoveries caused Einstein to attempt to develop a "unified field theory" which shows that the universe is continuous and indivisible, a harmonious whole. He was not successful at achieving this theory, but his work has triggered others to continue contributing to his goal. Einstein's general theory of relativity revealed to scientists the mechanistic assumptions and biases embedded within Newton's classics physics and convinced us that Newton's concepts of absolute time and space are illusionary theoretical constructs of the world.

In Einstein's work with light, he successfully demonstrated that light is a particle, thus creating a paradox for physicists, for scientists had already successfully shown that light is a wave. How can light be both a particle and a wave? The paradox was solved when scientists realized they were assuming, à la Newton's classical physics, that matter is a substance made up of inert, solid particles called atoms. Scientists have discovered that atoms are not solid at all, but instead turn out to consist of vast regions of space. Quantum theory describes not only light as a wave and a particle, but also electrons as both waves and particles. What's more, the "uncertainty principle" in quantum theory, as developed by Heisenberg, shows that the equipment used to measure the positions of the electron in the atom will affect the electron and therefore affect the measurement. Heisenberg successfully demonstrated that the observer and the observer's equipment used for measuring atomic properties influence the results of the measuring. Scientists can never completely remove themselves, and thus their influence, from the scientific measurement. Quantum theory proves that scientists are implicated in their own experiments. So much for science lacking in biases and being objective and neutral!

Bohr took Heisenberg's "uncertainty principle" one step further by showing that Heisenberg was still assuming, à la Newton's physics, that electrons are 'things' with definite paths, when all we can really assume, at the subatomic level, is that electrons have "tendencies to exist," not that they are 'things.' Quantum theory demonstrates that we cannot assume that matter exists, only that it has a "tendency to exist," which can be expressed in terms of probability. With the influence of quantum theory, scientists have come to agree that they can never be sure that they can predict an atomic event with certainty. So much for science offering us more certainty than philosophy or religion! Scientists have learned that any property being measured is affected by/is the result of the act of measurement, at least to some extent. There are no separate, independent objects. Again we find that quantum theory comes to the same conclusion that general relativity theory comes to, that everything is an indissolvable whole. Quantum theory describes the universe as a complicated, complementary web of relations (Capra, 1975). Because Einstein clung to the idea that the laws of nature are objective, and Bohr insisted that no picture of the whole is possible, the two were never able to see how much in agreement their two theories are.

David Bohm (1980) is whom I turn to for help in understanding the complementary nature of relativity theory and quantum theory. In agreement with quantum theory, Bohm argues, much like Dewey and James, that factual knowledge we obtain is shaped by our theories. Bohm's arguments weave between solipsism and determinism, as my arguments do with personal relations and social relations in Chapters 4 and 5, and his arguments weave their way between relativism and absolutism, as my arguments do in Chapters 1 and 2. As I am, Bohm is critical of science's embracing of the Peircian Epistemological assumption that in the end of time scientists will all know and agree upon the final, fixed Answer. Bohm shows us that scientists must be as committed to qualified relativism as I argue philosophers must be, for knowledge must necessarily be flexible and adjustable to constantly changing circumstances. The universe is not fixed and final, but rather in a state of flux. The universe is a moving causal network that cannot be analyzed into parts but must be considered as an undivided whole. To help us intuitively understand *wholeness*, which he names as "the implicate order," Bohm turns to images of flowing streams with a vortex, holograms, drops of dye in a viscous liquid like glycerine, and fishtanks viewed with 2 cameras from different angles. Bohm's theory of wholeness emphasizes that underneath our theories and descriptions of the universe, "the explicate order," which serve as maps always making distinctions and separations, there is a flowing whole universe, "the implicate order," an enfolded-unfolding continuous "present." Bohm helps us understand how porous the boundaries between science and philosophy really are, as his physical argument becomes metaphysical. Bohm's implicate order is like James's pure experience, and Buddhism's No Mind or Big Mind. As Einstein linked space and time as a continuum, Bohm links mind and matter as a continuum, helping us understand how consciousness and matter are inextricably linked.

Once Bohm brings together relativity theory and quantum theory for us, and he brings together science and philosophy, I shift to considering two different examples of general systems theories, which explore how biological forms organize to sustain themselves in their environment. James Lovelock's (1979/1987, 1988) Gaia theory is my first example of a scientific general systems theory that represents science's current shift to a relational paradigm. Lovelock's work brings together chemistry, geology, and biology, in what he calls 'geophysiology,' meaning "the study of the planetary surface as an organismlike body" (Margulis, 1998, p. 118). Through Lovelock's study of the composition of the Earth's atmosphere, in comparison to other planets, as well as the Earth's surface temperature range, and amount of surface water as well as saline level in the Earth's oceans, he has come to the conclusion that the Earth, Gaia, is our largest living organism. By this he means that Gaia's quality of air, water, and temperature are actively maintained and regulated by life on the surface of the Earth, the biosphere, meaning the atmosphere, oceans, and soil. Gaia, which is an open system not in a state of equilibrium, is able to manage to remain relatively constant amidst apparent disorder. Gaia is a cybernetic system that uses feedback to adapt and maintain itself, as well as even transform itself, as it did when it had to adapt to the emergence of free oxygen in the atmosphere. Lynn Margulis (1997, 1998, 1999), a microbiologist, has collaborated with Lovelock on Gaia theory, for Gaia represents to her our largest example of symbiosis. By symbiosis Margulis means the living together of unlike organisms, without respect to outcome. She (1988) does not describe Gaia as a single living organism, but rather as "the series of interacting ecosystems that compose a single huge ecosystem at the Earth's surface. Period" (p. 120). The idea that the Earth is a single living ecosystem, or organism, of which we are a part, is in agreement with the Buddhist, Native American, and ecofeminist views described in the previous section on ecological relations. Gaia theory certainly represents another scientific theory that contributes to the shift in science from a mechanistic view of nature and the world toward a relational scientific description.

Margulis not only contributes to Lovelock's Gaia theory, an example of symbiosis at the macro level, but her work in microbiology serves as another vivid example of symbiosis at the micro level. Margulis studied the genetic systems residing in organelles outside the nucleus of cells, and realized their cell structures are very similar to free-living microbes. She (1988) developed an evolutionary theory she calls SET (*Serial Endosymbiosis Theory*) to describe how the organelles such as mitochodria and chloroplasts within plant and animal cells were once bacteria living freely and independently. Margulis suggests that inside each of our cells we have a microcommunity of what use to be four different bacteria that now live together in permanent symbiosis. These four independent and separate bacteria now supply our cells with energy, respiration, and cell movement. Margulis has been proven correct on three of these being former separate bacteria, there is only one that is still considered controversial: that cell movement comes from what used to be separate bacteria such as today's spirochetes. Even if Margulis is proven wrong on the fourth bacteria, her theory of symbiosis has already prevailed due to her correctness on the other three bacteria now living symbiotically within our cells. Our cells are communities of microorganisms living collaboratively together and they serve as another vivid example of how our world is connected, relationally, wholistically, and symbiotically.

I conclude this section with Evelyn Fox Keller's (1983) powerful description of Barbara McClintock's biogenetic work on corn cytogenetics. McClintock serves as a wonderful final example of a scientific relational approach to knowing, not just for her findings on genetic transposition, but also for her relational scientific methodology. McClintock approaches her work in a style very similar to Buddhist meditation practices, for she seeks to lose her 'self' in her work and rely on direct perception, intuition, to answer her questions. She uses caring reasoning and attempts to establish a relationship with the corn's genetic system. She gets to know the maize she plants intimately by relating to the corn like friends. She tries to listen carefully to what the plant tells her, and pay close attention to each corn plant. Her objects of study, the corn, become subjects to her, and her understanding of the plant's genes is based on a shared subjectivity. McClintock breaks down the split classical science assumes between the subject and object. As she studies the plant's genes, attending with care, the plant's chromosomes become larger and she becomes part of the plant's system, able to see the plant from within, as an insider, rather than as an outside. As an insider, she is able to see what the plant reveals to her.

McClintock began to see stable patterns of instability with the mutating genes of plants. She suggested that something was controlling the rate of mutation, and spent six years proving that she was right as well as over twenty years trying to help others understand the meaning of her findings. Genes change and adapt due to environmental influences, serving as another example of symbiotic feedback. Genes are not static entities, but rather complex structures in a state of dynamic equilibrium. Genes represent another example of dissipative systems that arise out of the flux and flow of macro and micro processes, that are able to bring order and structure to the chaos of changing forces by regulating and controlling their genetic mutations with the help of regulatory genes. Again we find another scientist's work that contributes to the realization of how things in our world are connected to each other. McClintock describes a wholistic, dynamic universe, not a reductionistic, mechanistic universe as she inherited from Newton's classic scientific theory. McClintock, Margulis, Lovelock, Bohm, Bohr, and Einstein all contribute to our understanding that the universe is indissolvably whole. They each found themselves questioning basic assumptions they inherited from their teachers, and reevaluating their employed criteria, standards, and methodology in order to solve the paradoxes their work created and make sense of their findings.

Conclusion

The description I offer above illustrates many ways of knowing and their relational qualities that I plan to explore in more depth in the rest of the text. This description should serve as a map for readers, helping them find their way and understand how the various discussions are connected together. I will also supply mapping within each chapter to help readers not get lost along the way. It is time to move on to the more developed discussions of the relational theories I sketched above. I will return to this general discussion in Chapter 9 when I connect the relational theories discussed within this text to implications in practices of education.

CHAPTER 4

Personal Relations

It is striking to me how infrequently infants are discussed in traditional Euro-western philosophical theories, in particular Epistemological theories. 'The Subject' (S) gets attention in 'S knows that p' statements, although many feminists argue she does not get enough attention (e.g. Code, 1993). But young children and babies are sadly neglected in particular, even though *all* of us begin our lives this way. Children are judged as unknowing, and therefore not important to theories of knowledge. The study of children has been delegated to psychology. Philosophy has denied and repressed early infantile experience. In typical epistemological discussions, knowers seem to have never been children, they are always only adults. It is as if we sprout out of the ground, like cabbages, and we are already complete, whole, functioning rational, autonomous, individual, unique human beings.

Childcare is something that historically has been relegated to the private, domestic world, and left unattended by philosophy. It is no accident that this private world which includes infant care has also been historically a woman's world, across all cultures. In fact, as Flax (1983) points out, there is no known culture in which men assume the primary responsibility for childcare of children under the age of six. Current anthropologists conclude that all contemporary societies are to some extent male-dominated; sexual asymmetry is presently a universal fact of life (Flax, 1983, ftnt 6). Feminists argue that the delegating of women to the domestic, private world, and then the subsequent neglect of the domestic, private world of women and children is an indication of patriarchy, and the sexist practice of encouraging individual male development at the expense of female development. Philosophy's neglect of the earliest period of individual history, infancy, is taken as an example of philosophy's misogynist tendencies. In seeking to bring infantile experience and women's activities as care providers to the forefront of philosophical (e)pistemological theory, I seek to reveal fundamental false assumptions and limitations in traditional Epistemological theories. Looking at Epistemological theories from the standpoints of those excluded will offer us means for critiquing these theories. However, we must remember that all of us have been raised since infants within this patriarchy, which means that women's experiences impose on them certain limitations as well.

In this chapter I seek to establish that all knowing develops out of relational practices we participate in from the moment of conception. I seek to make the case that knowers are fundamentally relational beings and that human relatedness is central to subjectivity. This chapter helps break down the splits between the mind and the body, knowers and the known (subject/object), as well as the personal and the social (private/public). I begin at the personal, micro level of children-in-relation-with-others, in particular children in relation to those who care for them physically and emotionally. This relational (e)pistemology starts with infants-in-relation-to-careproviders with the help of Sara Ruddick, Nel Noddings, and Jane Flax. I focus on their work because they draw our attention to children's experiences and adult's transactional relationships with them. They help to describe a relational ontology, and begin to explore the effects such an ontology has on (e)pistemology. I further extend their efforts. I then move to considering an intimate, personal view of knowers-in-relation-to-others as adults with the help of Simone Weil, and Martin Buber, both of whom contribute significantly to our understanding of interpersonal relations. Weil will help us explore the dangers of intimate relationships in her efforts to become impersonal and detached, and Buber will help underscore the mutuality of relations. I critique the focus on personal relations from a social, macro level with the help of other philosophers throughout the discussions. So, we begin at the beginning, with subjects as infants-in-relation-with-their caregivers.

Subject as Infant Cared-for

Noddings, and Ruddick have traveled individually over rough terrain to be able to address infants-in-relation-to-others in their philosophical work, and have this work taken seriously. Scholars in women's studies and education responded more receptively to their ideas initially than philosophers, and still today they generate a great deal of controversial discussion if they are fortunate enough to be addressed generously rather than just dismissed. Flax's field of study is psychology, which has a history of addressing infant development, and so her work has been more receptively received. However, it is certainly not without its own controversies since Flax points to the gender bias that exists within her own field of study. Sara Ruddick presents a relational ontology predominantly from a caregiver's perspective, Noddings looks at both sides of the relation, and Flax helps us understand more the infant's perspective. I will follow this order to begin to develop a full description of subjects as knowers-in-relation.

Ruddick(1989) begins *Maternal Thinking* by describing her life as shaped by a love affair with Reason, as a woman educated to be a philosopher in the Euro-western world, and the effects this love affair had on her in terms of personal alienation. Ruddick earned her Ph.D. in philosophy between 1957-1967, during a time when women's attempts to contribute to philosophy were generally met with contempt, scorn, and blatant discrimination. Ruddick (1989) tells us: "For a woman to love Reason was to risk both self-contempt and self-alienating misogyny" (p. 5). Not wishing to give up on the capacity to reason as a human good, yet finding the ideals of Reason (objectivity, self-control, and detachment) destructive, Ruddick set out to redescribe reason from a woman's perspective. Taking what she calls a practicalist view that argues thinking arises from and is tested against practices, Ruddick looked for what is a woman's practice. She chose mothering as the one activity that is central to many women's lives and indirectly affects the thinking of countless other women, as sisters, daughters, neighbors, and friends. Thus began the development of *Maternal Thinking* (1989).

Ruddick (1989) presents maternal thinking as one discipline among others, as she aims to articulate distinct ways of thinking about the world. Ruddick argues that distinctive thinking arises from the work of mothering, in contrast to rational thinking. This thinking, "maternal thinking," is centered around human needs (pleasure/pain) rather than a love of reasons (rationality). Maternal thinking is opposed to abstraction; it is involved in the 'dailiness' of care and concern for others. Ruddick does not present maternal thinking as the only way or the best way to reason, although she does consider how maternal thinking and practices are important resources for developing peace politics in the final part of her book.

Ruddick (1989) defines a "mother" as "a person who takes on responsibility for children's lives and for whom providing child care is a significant part of her or his working life" (p. 40). She uses the feminine pronoun for mothers because throughout history women have assumed disproportionally the responsibilities of childcare, but she does not limit mothering to women, nor does she think women are more capable at maternal work. Ruddick notes that men can do this as well, and more are sharing in childcare today. The demands of mothering work include preserving children's lives, fostering their growth, and teaching them how to be socially acceptable. "To be a mother is to be committed to meeting these demands by works of preservative love, nurturance, and training" (p. 17). The first two demands are based on the child's needs, but the third demand is made by the mother's social groups.

A "Father," on the other hand, is the one who historically has provided material support and protection for "mothers" so they can do child care. Whereas a mother earns her authority through care, a Father earns his authority from cultural demands, not children's needs. "They are suppose to represent the 'world'—its language, culture, work, and rule—and to be the arbiters of the child's acceptability in the world they represent" (Ruddick, 1989, p. 42). Ruddick capitalizes Father to protest the myth and practice of Fatherhood. Many women do maternal work without a Father, and many men do not have the resources or power to be Fathers. Others have questioned Ruddick on why she insists on maintaining a distinction between mothering and Fathering, thus reinforcing the stereotypical sexist notion that women are inherently better suited to parent (hooks, 1984; Grimshaw, 1986). Why not use the term 'parenting'? Ruddick responds that she hopes to see mother/Father roles combined; she wants mothering to be re-visioned as an activity "naturally" undertaken by men and women. However, she also wants to recognize and honor the fact that throughout history women have been the mothers. And she wants to make sure that shared parenting does not just mean bringing the authoritative Father and compliant mother both into the child's nursery.

Ruddick (1989) distinguishes a "mother" from a child's biological mother (birth-giver), in an effort to honor both. A "mother" chooses and commits to care for a child; to care for a child is not automatic. First there is the biological birthing of the child, and then there is the caring, which has an optional quality to it. For Ruddick, all "mothers" are "adoptive," choosing to respond to an infant's trust "that good and not evil will be done to him. . . . To adopt is to make a space, a 'peace' where the promise of birth can survive. All mothers-in-the-world, as adoptive persons, are peacemakers" (Ruddick, 1989, p. 218). Ruddick does not choose to use the term 'caring' to describe maternal work, because caring encompasses more than maternal work; caring labor includes housework (cooking, cleaning, mending), kin work (nursing sick and elderly family members), and much more. Maternal thinking is one central expression of a rationality of care, but not the whole of care. Ruddick recognizes that many caretakers do not choose to be mothers, and she also considers mothering to be a central human work worthy of its own close consideration.

Ruddick (1989) identifies "some of the specific metaphysical attitudes, cognitive capacities, and conceptions of virtue that arise from mothering," in regards to the three demands of protection, growth, and acceptability (p. 61). She treats each separately in order to highlight the conflict that arises between them. A mother's protective work involves an overwhelming obligation and commitment. "In protective work, feeling, thinking, and action are conceptually linked" (p. 70). The task of protecting is exhilarating and exhausting. Protection triggers thought-provoking ambivalence. Mothers are on the look-out, scrutinizing for dangers and striving to maintain control, while at the same time they are humbled by the realization that the world is beyond their control. "Nature" is their opponent, in the forms of diseases, poisons, fires, earthquakes, and "accidents," yet mothers cannot deny the natural and respectfully appreciate it, for their children are part of nature too. Protective mothering requires resilient good humor and cheerfulness, for cheerfulness is what helps mothers remain hopeful even though the world is not in their control. Cheerfulness increases and assists the power to act. And, protective mothering requires a fundamental attitude toward the vulnerable which Ruddick calls "holding," in the sense of minimizing risk and reconciling differences rather than sharply accentuating them (p. 79).

On the other hand, the mothering demand to foster growth in a child requires being able to look at and see a child accurately, without seeing yourself in the child. This accuracy depends on "attentive love," a concept we will find below in Simone Weil's work, as well as in Noddings's "care." Attention lets difference emerge. It is an act of dwelling upon the other, and letting otherness be. "To foster growth is to nurture a child's developing spirit..." (Ruddick, 1989, p. 82). It is an act of holding close while at the same time welcoming change. Mothers have a lot of experience with change. "The capacity to change with and through a child's changes requires an attitude that is, in traditional terms, a philosophical position. To understand her child, a mother needs to assume the existence of a partly conscious, continuous mind" (not separate from body or feelings) (Ruddick, 1989, p. 91). Mothers develop a cognitive capacity for concrete thinking, as opposed to abstract thinking. "The reflectiveness of concreteness must be developed through disciplined attentiveness and then expanded and tested through critical conversational challenge" (Ruddick, 1989, p. 98). Mothering expands a mother's intellectual life.

The third demand of mothers is one that directly addresses social norms, rather than individual children's needs, according to Ruddick. Mothers must teach their children how to be socially acceptable and able to abide by the social conventions of their cultural group. Mothers are "responsible for children's moral well-being..., helping them to become people who will be reliably moral when they are alone or among peers" (Ruddick, 1989, p. 108). In training their children, mothers become especially aware of the contradictions of maternal power. They need power in order to intervene and control their children's behavior, and yet at the same time they are expected to relinquish their power to the Father's public, cultural power. Mothers may even be treated with contempt in the public world, right before their children's eyes, thus rendering them powerless. It is here in this third demand that Ruddick particularly acknowledges culture's influence on mothering, and that caring decisions are not always made with just the children's needs in mind. The demand to teach children to be socially acceptable limits maternal power. To meet its demands requires abdication of maternal authority. Mothers find themselves having to concern themselves with "the gaze of others" in order to help protect their children from society's scorn and wrath.

Ruddick's (1989) efforts to distinguish maternal thinking from the public realm of cultural influences are defeated by a mother's responsibility to prepare her children for the public world. What Ruddick's distinctions point out is how culturally bound maternal thinking is, usually by gender, race, and social class. Her cultural description in the third mothering task makes us realize that culture is missing from the previous two descriptions. As Jean Grimshaw (1986) points out: "Ruddick's account tends to isolate mother and child as a self-contained unit of demand and response" (p. 247). It also maintains the myth of separate spheres with the mother and child occupying the private sphere and the Father residing in the public sphere. Yet mothering is embedded within other social relations and institutions such as church, state, and employment. It is a mistake to consider the social practices of mothers "apart from the context in which they exist" (Grimshaw, 1986, p. 257). Our conceptions of mothering have varied widely across time as well as cultures. Mothers have radical doubts about the nature of mothering and how it should be done. "Experts," such as religious leaders, scholars, and elders have always been involved in the naming and defining of mothering, and these "experts" have historically been men. Even activities that appear to just address a child's basic needs, such as sleeping and feeding habits, and holding/rocking/cuddling kinds of activities, vary greatly in different cultures and reveal ways in which the practices addressing basic needs are socially constructed.

Ruddick's efforts to distinguish maternal thinking from rational thinking so that maternal thinking can be valued and appreciated has the same dichotomous result that her mother/Father distinction has. While it is a beneficial distinction in terms of helping us understand what is lacking in the ideal of Reason as objective, detached, non-physical, and non-emotional, it is dangerous to "let Reason off the hook" by allowing it to continue to exist in its narrowed form, in contrast to maternal thinking. Glorifying mothers and their maternal thinking does not tackle the underlying dualistic assumptions that create these sharp dichotomies. We need to re-vision reasoning in a relational, wholistic manner rather than offering maternal thinking as an alternative kind of thinking based on a distinct field of work, thus reifying the very dualistic thinking that was so painful to Ruddick as a female student and new professor in philosophy.

We need to redescribe reason as embodied within physically active, concrete, historically located, emotionally feeling human beings, rather than letting reason stand for the mind separate from body and emotional feelings. We need to make the case that pleasure/pain cannot be separated from rationality. We need to insist that the context which is removed from abstract thinking be reinserted and remain, for decontextualized thinking is a dangerous illusion which pretends to be neutral while masking the power that exists in every reason offered for every problem considered worthy of attending. We need to underscore that when we reason, emotions, thinking, and action are conceptually linked, following the advise of classic pragmatists, feminists, and postmodernists.

Ruddick's (1989) description of "maternal thinking" clearly outlines the unfolding of a child's spirit as occurring through the intimate relationship with another. That other is the child's "mother." This is a significant contribution Ruddick makes to philosophy, for she takes the child seriously. For my purposes here, she helps me make the case for our fundamental relationality. She describes knowing as developing out of the relational practices we participate in with intimate others, our biological mothers prior to birth, and our adoptive mothers after birth.

106   Relational "(e)pistemologies"

In a more recent essay by Ruddick (1996), she offers some common characteristics of a relational (e)pistemology she labels "connected knowing," after the classic *Women's Ways of Knowing* study (1986). Her description of "connected knowing" is offered as an "instance of 'reason,'" as an "alternative epistemology." Ruddick still holds up impersonal procedural knowing as a contrast to connected knowing. Impersonal knowing "continuously separates knower from the known and the mind's knowing from its emotional, bodily, and social life" (Ruddick, 1996, p. 262). She says that connected knowing, as an alternative epistemology project, does not seek to eliminate impersonal knowing. "Impersonal knowing remains one way of knowing necessary for many projects and dominant in some" (Ruddick, 1996, p. 262).

Contrary to Ruddick, I am not trying to offer an alternative epistemology, rather I am trying to transform the way we think about (e)pistemology, and re-vision reason, in general. There are the seeds for this transformation in Ruddick's (1996) description of connected knowing, for she explains *all* knowing as an activity arising out of practices, not separate from emotional feelings. She recognizes that even in distant, detached, abstract knowing the knower has established a kind of *relationship* to ideas. She also describes *all* knowers as social beings in-relation-with-others, and therefore separation and detachment is now seen as a particular way of relating to others. She understands now that even our earliest, simplest relationships, with a single parent, are also embedded within other relationships so that we are relational selves at a personal, micro level, as well as at a general, macro level. Ruddick describes the fundamental relationality of each of us as preceding both knowing and gender. This concept of how we are fundamentally relational beings is developed further in Nel Noddings's work, so I would like to turn now to her for elaboration of this idea.

Nel Noddings came to philosophy by a different route than Ruddick. Noddings was first a math teacher and a parent before going on to study philosophy in the form of philosophy of education. She earned her Ph.D. in education in 1974, in a field much more strongly represented by women. Still, her work has caused quite a stir, and made a significant impact on philosophy. Noddings is influenced by existentialism, in particular Martin Buber (see below), as well as feminist theory, and pragmatism. While Noddings is mainly known for her contribution to the reshaping of the field of ethics, it is her relational ontology that I want to explore here, not her ethics. The relational ontology she relies on to support a caring ethic is the same ontology I rely on to support a relational (e)pistemology. I am arguing that 'relation' is ontologically basic and universal for all of us, in agreement with her.

In *Caring*, Noddings (1984) presents a relational view of self as a fundamental universality for all people. This view is in contrast to Carol Gilligan's (1982) work (*In a Different Voice*). Gilligan developed a concept of connected, relational self, as complementary to the Euro-western concept of individual, separate self. Noddings does not follow this dichotomous path. Noddings tells us relation is taken as ontologically basic for her, and the caring relation is taken as ethically basic. Noddings (1984) defines 'relation' as "a set of ordered pairs generated by some rule that describes the affect—or subjective experience—of the members" (pp. 3–4). By taking *relation* as an ontologically basic, she means "that we recognize human encounter and affective response as a basic fact of human existence" (p. 4). Noddings recognizes that we all start out our lives in a caring relationship, first with our biological mothers, and then with our caregivers, who may be the same person but not necessarily. "We are, by virtue of our mutual humanity, already and perpetually in potential relation" (Noddings, 1984, p. 86). We have all experienced caring relations in order for us to be alive today, although we have experienced caring in a variety of forms and to different levels/degrees. Even if our biological mothers gave us up at birth, we were dependent on her care to keep us alive until we were born. We have experienced natural caring. After we were born, keeping us alive required even more active caring, in terms of nurturing us and protecting us. We experienced more natural caring. Caring is what preserves the group and the individual.

As Noddings (1984) describes the self:

> I am not naturally alone. I am naturally in a relation from which I derive nourishment and guidance. When I am alone, either because I have detached myself or because circumstances have wrenched me free, I seek first and most naturally to reestablish my relatedness. My very individuality is defined in a set of relations. (p. 51)

As Noddings (1990) later explains, a relational ontology "posits the fundamental and creative role of relation" (p. 124).

> When we define human beings as relations, then, we see that—strictly speaking—we are not monadic; what we do for "others" we do, in part at least, for ourselves because "we" are products of relation, not mere constituent parts. . . . Caring rejects the notion of ontological otherness and invites us to participate in the creation of new relational "selves." (p. 124)

Let's explore this relational ontology more closely through Noddings's (1984) discussion of caring. She defines caring in a relational manner, giving names to the two parties involved, one-caring and one-cared-for, in order to ease her discussion as well as to maintain rigor. I will compare her two parties to Buber's (1958) I-Thou and I-It in the next section. In this discussion I follow Noddings's pattern and refer to the one-caring as she, the one-cared-for as he. For Noddings, both parties contribute to the caring relation, for the one-cared-for must somehow respond to the one-caring in order for the relationship to be called a caring one. The relationship is reciprocal, but not in the sense of being the same, or of being contractual. It is reciprocal in the sense that the one-cared-for receives the caring offered. He recognizes it and spontaneously responds. He does not necessarily respond in kind, nor even in words at all, but somehow he acknowledges the caring offered. His response is a gift to the caring relation that must be given freely. The cared-for's major contribution to the relation is the willing and unselfconscious revealing of himself. Thus we find in Noddings a way to acknowledge the infant's role in a caring relation, and not just focus on the caregiver's role. Noddings's (1984) description of the one-cared-for as needing to acknowledge and respond in order for a caring relationship to be established helps highlight that a relational ontology is transactional. It is not instrumental or deterministic, it is fluid and varied, and affects both the one-caring and the one-cared-for. Her description of relationality as mutually affective is an important contribution to a relational (e)pistemology.

Noddings (1984) tells us that to care, the one-caring must be responsive and receptive to the one-cared-for. The one-caring does not impose herself on the other, she must receive the other into herself. Her role is more sympathetic than empathetic for empathy tends to stress projection and sympathy is more receptive. She does not project her own thoughts, emotional feelings, and experiences on to the other; she attends to the other's thoughts, emotional feelings, and experiences (see Weil [1977] discussion below for more on attention). The one-caring feels with the other, thus creating a sense of duality, her own and the other's. All caring involves "engrossment," a term Noddings uses to emphasize that caring is a move away from self toward the one cared-for. She must be present to the other, and generously try to acquaint herself with the other. Caring is essentially nonrational in that it requires suspending rationality in order to generously attend to and receive the other. The one-caring does not critique the other in the act of caring.

In a caring relationship the one-cared-for responds to the presence of the one-caring. He feels acceptance and support due to the attending and receptivity the one-caring gives. Caring goes beyond acceptance to what Buber (1958) calls "confirmation" (see below). "The one-caring sees the best self in the cared-for and works with him to actualize that self" (Noddings, 1984, p. 64). An "attitude of warm acceptance and trust is important in all caring relationships" (Noddings, 1984, p. 65). When acceptance and trust are missing, the one-cared-for feels like an object. Noddings points out that not all caring relationships are on equal footing, as is often the case between a student-teacher, or parent-child. The one-caring may have more experience, skills, or abilites that she can offer to help the other, and these roles can often change. Yet, no matter how unequal the relationship, it still is a relationship that resembles friendship due to the engrossment on the one-caring's part and the sharing and responsiveness on the cared-for's part.

Noddings's (1984) ethic of care is based on the sentiment of natural caring and the need to maintain a caring attitude. Noddings (1984) tells us that the one universality her caring ethic rests upon is the *caring attitude*, "that attitude which expresses our earliest memories of being cared for and our growing store of memories of both caring and being cared for" (p. 5). This caring attitude is not unique to women, but is central to all people's lives, and their concepts of self. It is something we all have access to, for we have all experienced caring in our own lives. Given the fact that we are relational beings who have experienced natural caring, caring takes on the role of a moral imperative. Caring is a must, not an option, according to Noddings. We are obligated to do what is required to maintain and enhance a caring relation with the other in order to maintain a caring attitude. Our aim is to preserve and enhance caring in ourselves (as ones-caring) and in those with whom we come in contact.

We find that Noddings is not guilty of associating caring particularly with women, just as Ruddick does not associate mothering just with women, though both of them have been accused of this by readers. We also find that Ruddick is right: Noddings does use 'caring' to refer to more than just the maternal relationship Ruddick focuses on. Noddings often refers to student-teacher relations and she talks about caring for other living things such as plants and animals, as well as aesthetically caring for nonliving things (such as caring about ideas). Still, Noddings's focus for her relational ontology begins with the mother-child relationship and then expands to caregiver-child relationships, similar to Ruddick. Unlike Ruddick, though, Noddings does not make caring an option; it is a given. Her basic givens for a caring ethic are the assumption that caring is universally accessible and that we all desire to maintain a caring attitude, since we all have experienced being cared-for.

Noddings suffers from the same problem Ruddick does, in that she tends to talk about caring in a decontextualized way, without taking into consideration history, culture, race, class, etc. and their effects on caring. Noddings (1990) takes her critics advice to heart on this issue in agreeing she (we) "should pay far greater attention to historical context and social tradition" (p. 126). Noddings also tends to reinforce dichotomies, similar to Ruddick. For Noddings (1984) these splits appear in her discussion of caring as an ethic, in contrast to principled ethics, so that caring represents a particular, concrete form of moral orientation that relies on emotions (what she calls the mother's voice), while principled ethics represent a general, abstract, rational approach (the father's voice). My criticisms in regard to the reifying of dualities are the same for her as they are for Ruddick. Many have questioned Noddings's sharp distinction between principled and caring ethics, and she has replied by generously agreeing: "while I suspect my critics may be right that a concept of justice is needed, I think a great deal of work must be done on exactly what it contributes" (Noddings, 1990, p. 122). Noddings's contrasts help us value and appreciate what is lacking in a principled approach to ethics, but it is her relational ontology that supports efforts such as mine in (e)pistemology and hers in ethics, to re-vision these fields of study in a connected, wholistic manner.

Noddings's relational ontology is a significant contribution to philosophy in general and to a relational (e)pistemology in particular. Like Ruddick, Noddings takes seriously the infant's role in her philosophy. Noddings helps us understand that we are fundamentally interdependent, relational beings, not the separate, autonomous individuals that modern Enlightenment philosophy describes. We begin our lives in relation-with-others and we are alive today due to caring relations we share with ones who care-for us. Let's move on to Jane Flax's work, to help us further explore the infant-caregiver relationship, adding to our understanding of the infant's position.

In 1983, Jane Flax wrote a very powerful essay titled, "Political Philosophy and the Patriarchal Unconsciousness: A Psychoanalytic Perspective on Epistemology and Metaphysics," which she followed with *Thinking Fragments* in 1990. In *Thinking Fragments*, she tells us she juggles at least four identities and practices: therapist, philosopher, feminist, and political theorist. As a therapist, Flax works with patients suffering from "borderline syndrome." They are people who "lack a core self without which the registering of and pleasure in a variety of experiencing of ourselves, others, and the outer world are simply not possible." Her patients' selves are "in painful and disabling fragments" (Flax, 1983, p. 218). Her work contributes significantly to understanding ourselves as embedded and embodied relational human beings. Her goal is to contribute to the re/construction of concepts of the self that do justice to the full complexity of subjectivity.

Flax originally approached her work from within the intellectual frameworks of feminism, psychoanalysis, and critical theory, but postmodernism has disrupted those initial frameworks, replacing critical theory. *Thinking Fragments* is written in an effort to explore questions of "knowledge, gender, subjectivity, and power and their interrelations" from a postmodern perspective, that is "non-authoritarian, open-ended, and process-oriented" (Flax, 1990, p. 3). She uses a conversational mode that places these three theories in conversation with each other, not trying to resolve conflicts or synthesize their differences. She reaches no conclusion. For Flax (1990), while she has disagreements with particular aspects of postmodern thinking, "its self-analytic spirit . . . is one of its most important contributions. An integral and especially important aspect of postmodernist approaches is a refusal to avoid conflict and irresolvable differences or to synthesize these differences into a unitary, univocal whole" (p. 4).

Flax uses psychoanalytic theory, in particular object relations theory, in her discussions of epistemology, and that is what I want to explore here. I rely on her 1983 article for this task. Psychoanalytic theory presents persons as not fundamentally separate and isolated from each other, but rather literally constituted by the relations in which we participate. "The most basic tenet of object relations theory is that human beings are created in and through relations with other human beings" (p. 250). The term 'object' is used in object relations theory to symbolize other persons, so object relations theory is social relations theory. It is an unfortunate choice of terminology for a theory that seeks to break down subject/object dichotomies and seeks to underscore interconnectedness. Flax presents psychoanalytic theory as a crucial tool for feminists. It offers feminists a way to analyze the influence of patriarchy

Personal Relations

on the content and process of thought. "Its content represents a systematic attempt to understand human nature as the product of social relations in interaction with biology" (p. 249). However, Flax qualifies her psychoanalytic theory, through her use of object relations theory, for object relations theory questions Freud's "instinct theory," stresses the interaction of child and parents, and describes the first three years of life as the crucial period of psychodynamic development. Thus, object relations theory focuses on the mother-child relationship rather than the father-child one, which is traditional psychoanalytic theory's focus due to the argument that the child develops at a later age. Object relations theory describes reason as an innate potential capacity, rather than as "a fragile, tentative acquisition" (Flax, 1983, p. 249). The logic of object relations theory suggests that "human nature" changes as social relations change, while being limited on the range of changes by the extended time needed for biological change (thus avoiding determinism as well as vulgar relativism) (p. 250).

Object relations theory is based on seven basic tenets, according to Flax (1983):

1) that the psychological birth of the human infant takes around three years; it is a complex process (p. 250);

2) this "psychological birth" can only occur in and through social relations; there is a necessary social and interactive character to early human development (p. 251);

3) in the first three years of life, the most important tasks for infants are establishing a close relationship with their caregivers (symbiosis) and then moving to be able to separate and individuate themselves from their caregivers; by the end of three years we should each have a "core identity" (p. 251);

4) children's psychological development is a dialectic process played out in and through a changing relationship between caregivers and children (p. 251);

5) "(t)he social context of development includes not only the immediate child-caretaker(s) relation but also more general social relations which affect the child through its interactions with the caretakers" (p. 253);

6) "(t)his long period of development is unique to the human species" (p. 254);

7) the experiences we have during this time of development, as children, are intense, never to be repeated "except in psychosis and perhaps in altered states of consciousness such as religious or drug experiences;" it is prerational and preverbal and therefore difficult to screen, however these experiences are never lost (p. 254).

Flax (1983) shows how philosophy's repression of early infantile experience creates problems that are found reflected in different philosophical theories. "The character of the process [the psychological birth of infants] calls into question the simple separation of mind and body and any form of determinism built upon these distinctions such as mechanism (e.g. Hobbes), idealism (e.g. Plato or Husserl) or instinct theory (early Freud or utilitarianism).... The necessarily social and interactive character of early human development calls into question certain philosophies of mind and being, especially radical individualism and the 'monads' of Spinoza, early Sartre and others" (pp. 250-251).

Flax (1983) turns specifically to analyzing the theories of Plato, Descartes, Hobbes, and Rousseau using object relations theory as her tool to show the effects of repressing and denying early infantile experience on philosophy. The effects are reflected in how we view nature, our political life, our passions, our focus on domination and power, the separation of public and private, the inability to achieve true reciprocity and cooperation with others, and the translation of difference into inferiority and superiority (p. 255). Thus we find, for example, Plato separates the body from the mind and links women to the passions. Descartes's concern for certainty represents a desire for control of both nature and the body. The self which is constituted through thought is driven to master nature "because ultimately the self cannot deny its material qualities" (p. 260). The desire to know is linked to the desire to dominate, and nature is posited as the other that must be conquered. Both Plato and Descartes identify the body and passions with chaos and error.

Modern philosophers such as Hobbes and Rousseau seek to deny the primary social relatedness of infants-in-relation-to-their-care providers. "Natural man" is assumed to be solitary, seeking to avoid domination or submission by others. Culture and social institutions are represented as unnatural and corrupting. Flax (1983) argues that both Hobbes and Rousseau fear dependence. Hobbes's mechanistic model of human nature does not include the typical work women do, childrearing, as part of the human condition, and the qualities this work demands, such as relatedness, and nurturance, are not included as part of human nature (p. 268). Rousseau's natural man seems to have the choice of isolation or total engulfment. For both, women represent desire and the main cause of human misery. Their solutions to human misery are found in mastery and total domination. Their denial and repression of childhood experiences become justification for patriarchy, and relegating women to the private sphere. "Reciprocity, in the sense of mutual interdependence and independence is not possible" according to these philosophers (Flax, 1983, p. 267).

Flax (1983) recommends one of the tasks of feminist epistemology is to uncover patriarchy's effects on our concept of knowledge, as well as on the concrete content of bodies of knowledge (p. 269). I certainly hope my project is a feminist contribution to the effort to locate Epistemological theories within their social and historical context. She concludes by offering several theses as the beginning of a feminist theory of knowledge: that "all human knowledge serves (among others) a defensive function," and that "(a)n unhealthy self projects its own dilemmas on the world and posits them as the 'human condition'" (p. 269); "what is lacking [in philosophy] is an account of the earliest period of individual history, in which the self emerges within the context of a relationship with a woman (or women)" (p. 270). She recommends that feminists analyze the epistemologies of all bodies of knowledge, including emancipatory theories such as psychoanalysis and Marxism, by using dialectics as a method that is self-reflective and self-critical. Flax warns that 'women's experience' is not itself an adequate ground for theory, it is the other pole of the dualities and it must be incorporated and transcended. She suggests that feminist theory and practice must include a therapeutic, consciousness-raising aspect to help us demystify knowledge (pp. 269–271).

Are there any criticisms we can offer to Flax's psychoanalytic approach? Irigaray (1974, 1985) and Butler (1990a, 1990b) offer postmodern criticisms of psychoanalytic theory, for its tendency to form the self into the same representation. Psychoanalytic theory tends to describe all selves as the same, as "the self." With psychoanalytic theory, sameness is imposed at the level of the unconscious, in the depths of the psyche, in terms of self-development. Object relations theory offers feminists a tactic for destabilizing the subject and exposing masculine power, but the theory still becomes a normalizing developmental law that has the effect of essentializing gender acquisition. Object relations theorists shift the focus to a younger age and therefore place their relational focus on the mother-child relationship, as Ruddick did. Object relations theorists place more emphasis on parenting interactions, and are more open to change. Still, psychoanalytic theory, even as object relations theory, presents infantile develpment as resulting in a coherent female/male subject and such an image effectively closes off and limits the gender experience and falsely stabilizes the category of woman/man. Both Irigaray and Butler remind us that the very concept of subject is a male concept with woman in the othered role. They push for a loss of reification of gender relations and for more contingency.

Flax (1990) responds to this kind of criticism in *Thinking Fragments*, where she presents and critiques psychoanalytic, feminist, and postmodern theories. Here she shows that each theory is flawed in many ways. "Each unwittingly provides reasons for and proof of the inadequacy of some of the ideas it posits but cannot abandon" (p. 225). None of them can stand alone, but together they are mutually self-correcting though still limited. They fail to account for what they identify as problematic, and they "reflect the necessary incompleteness of all conversations about questions that matter to the ways people live" (p. 225). She agrees that psychoanalytic theory is overtly and subtly gender-bound and biased. But so is postmodern theory. Feminist theory is not free from the effects of gender either. She agrees that in many ways psychoanalytic thinking remains within the Enlightenment project, e.g., the self is viewed individualistically, and reason is emphasized as having liberatory power, in sharp contrast to the irrational demands of desire or authority. In contrast, feminist theories "displace unitary, essentialist, and asocial or ahistorical ideas of the self by analyzing the ways gender enters into and partially constitutes both the self and our ideas about it" (Flax, 1990, p. 229). Like object relations psychoanalysts, feminists stress the importance of sustained, intimate relations with other persons. "Unlike object relations theorists, however, feminists pay attention to the location of persons (and families) within wider contexts of social relations" (Flax, 1990, pp. 229–230). But feminists cannot fully abandon a concept of self either. And postmodern treatments of the self completely disregard intimate social relations in their efforts to abandon the self as "fictive." Flax (1990) wonders if certain postmodern deconstructions of the self are not just a new strategy for evading, denying, or repressing the importance of early childhood experiences (p. 232).

The feminist relational (e)pistemology I present rests on a relational ontology that locates the self in concrete social relations. Thus I am arguing that human relatedness is central to subjectivity. And the primary relationship we begin our lives in is the mother-child relationship. This caring relation shifts to other primary caregivers, but it always begins with our biological mothers. I am presenting the self as a social self that comes to be through powerful, intimate, affective relationships with other people (I will develop this further in Chapter 5). Out of these social relationships we develop a sense of self, our own unique voice (inner self, core identity). Our self is "simultaneously embodied, gendered, social, and unique" (Flax, 1990, p. 232). This self is not an overly differentiated and unitary self, the Euro-western conception of self following the masculine model: the mentalist, deeroticized, masterful, and oppositional self. Rather, it is a multifarious, fractured self that has had parts of it split off and disavowed due to the sexist, racist, classist, homophobic world in which we live. The repressive social forces we are all exposed to are too powerful and too pervasive for any individual self to overcome. Yet we do have a unique self that develops out of our relationships with others and which continues to exist in-relation-with-others. The alternative choice is no self, no core identity, no inner voice that has a basic cohesiveness and sense of continuity, and this choice leads us to psychosis (Flax, 1990).

We have found, by exploring the feminist work of Ruddick, Noddings, and Flax, that including an account of the earliest period of our development transforms philosophy. Including early infantile experiences and their caring relationships with their primary caregivers (usually women) in our discussions changes (e)pistemology. As Flax (1983) points out, feminism is revolutionary, for it offers for the first time the possibility for reciprocity to emerge as the basis of social relation (p. 270). It helps us understand the relational and contextual qualities of all concepts and how knowers cannot be separated from each other or their ideas (the known). Feminism helps us gain greater clarity and more humility, as we strive to be more self-reflective and self-critical. It encourages us to appreciate and graciously welcome multiple experiences and diverse perspectives, to help us become more aware of the limits of our own contextuality and relationality.

I move on now to consider the work of some philosophers who contribute to a relational ontology and its effects on a relational (e)pistemology mainly from an interpersonal, adult perspective. I choose to focus on Simone Weil's and Martin Buber's work because intersubjective relationality is central to their different philosophies. They both serve as excellent sources for a relational (e)pistemology. They will help me address questions with which a relational (e)pistemology must be concerned, in terms of fears of relativism or social determinism. Buber and Weil contribute philosophical perspectives that represent varying religious and existential perspectives. Martin Buber was devoutly Jewish, and Simone Weil was a nonpracticing Jew but devout Christian. I approach their work as an outsider to their religious perspectives who has a great deal of respect for them and interest in their ideas. I am not devoutly Jewish or Christian. I do not embrace a Transcendent God. I am not a devout participant in any particular church, though I am a practicing member of my local Unitarian Universalist Church, which welcomes and studies the beliefs of all major religions and many minor ones as well. I have participated in the studying of various religions throughout my lifetime, and I try to live a life that is caring and attentive to others, and the world in which I live. I have a wholistic, connected perspective, which places me in the realm of spirituality just as likely as in science or philosophy. However, I am a naturalist, not a supernaturalist. What I am interested in exploring in this next section are other examples of intimate, personal views of knowers-in-relation-to-others, and the examples I offer describe an intimate, personal relationship between themselves and God (capitalized to symbolize again transcendence).

I/Thou Relationships

With their differing views on their relationships with God, Martin Buber and Simone Weil offer us alternative ways to consider the very personal relationship between knowers and the known beyond the boundaries of the mother/child. Both philosophers describe a very intimate, connected, personal relationship between knowers and the known which help to soften the boundaries between the two. I begin with Weil because her work is less known and has been less influential, though it is becoming more so. Weil's life was cut short and as a result her work was not given the opportunity to develop to its fullest extent. She died of starvation and pulmonary tuberculosis at the age of 34, in 1943. Her starvation was a political act as well as a religious one. She was restricting her diet to what was available for her compatriots in German-occupied France. She also chose to follow the moral doctrine of Catharism, which she saw as the embodiment of Christian Platonism, and committed suicide by starvation. She offers us greater insight into caring as attention, similar to Ruddick's 'disciplined attentiveness' and Noddings's 'engrossment,' which I want to further explore. I will then move on to consider Buber's relational theory and we will find many comparisons between his I-Thou relationship and Noddings's one-caring/one-cared-for.

Even with her short lifetime and serious health problems, Simone Weil was a prolific writer who left behind much for us to ponder. Her work can be found in a comprehensive collection that exposes the reader to the essential contributions she makes, *The Simone Weil Reader*, edited by George Panichas (1977). I rely on this collection for my discussion. She is considered by many to be a great spiritual writer. She writes as a religious philosopher, not as a theologian, and she represents a personal, intuitive, meditative style of writing. Philosophically, Weil comes from a Christian, French, Greek tradition, not a Hebraic one, for her parents were nonpracticing Jews. She is critical of Judaism, and in particular of the Old Testament of the Bible. However, she is critical of the Catholic church too, and places herself as a religious Outsider. Weil (1977) defines a genuinely Catholic church as one that is inclusive, impartial, universal (p. 9). She tells us: "The love of those things that are outside visible Christianity keeps me outside the Church" (p. 111). Panichas (Weil, 1977) describes Weil as: "(t)eacher, classical scholar, intellectual par excellence, and French-Jewish genuis; political and religious nonconformist, Spanish Civil War participant, Free French movement worker; factory and farm laborer; poet, visionary, mystic, suffering 'friend of God,' religious thinker and philosopher precariously situated at 'the intersection of Christianity and everything that is not Christianity' (to quote her own words): Simone Weil combined brilliantly, enigmatically, all of these roles as no other twentieth-century religious thinker has done" (pp. xvii–xviii).

There are several key themes in Weil's (1977) writing, which overlap and affect each other. Let me begin to describe her views through her discussion of personality. Weil thinks there is something sacred in every person, but it is not what many might think, our unique qualities, our individual personalities. For Weil, what is sacred is our impersonalities. Truth and beauty dwell at the level of the impersonal, the anonymous. We start out our lives as members of a collective, and we develop our personalities out of that collective. We can only escape the collective by raising above the personal to the impersonal. It is as though the collective represents an acculturation process that subdues us and numbs us. Rather than striving for independence and the development of our own personality, Weil wants us to renounce our independence, renounce our personality, out of love for God.

There are two ways we can arouse ourselves out of our subdued existences, or as Weil (1977) puts it, "pierce our soul." Beauty and affliction are the only things that can arouse us. "I am convinced that affliction on the one hand, and on the other hand joy, when it is a complete and pure commitment to perfect beauty, are the only two keys which give entry to the realm of purity, where one can breathe: the home of the real" (p. 92). How does Weil describe beauty? Beauty is good in itself; it has no end in view. "Beauty is the harmony of chance and the good" (p. 377).

Beauty of the world is the co-operation of divine wisdom in creation. When we have real, direct, and immediate contact with the beauty of the world, we have contact that is of the nature of a sacrament. True beauty is the real presence of God in matter (p. 380).

Affliction is also a sacrament. However, it is not something we can desire or seek, it must be suffered unwillingly. It is wrong and perverse to desire affliction, yet the possibility of affliction is always there. Affliction is a state of extreme and total humiliation. It is an unrooting of life, socially, psychologically, and physically. Contempt, revulsion, and hatred penetrate to the center of the soul when one is afflicted. It causes a state of nonbeing, the death of the soul (Weil, 1977, p. 332). It is anonymous, indifferent, by chance. It is ridiculous. It deprives its victims of their personality and turns them into things, objectifying them. Weil believes the only way into Truth is through one's own annihilation. Affliction is necessary so we can un-create ourselves. All the acculturation we learn through our communities, and the personality we develop, gets in our way of knowing Truth. The only way we can know Truth is by getting rid of that personality that acts as a barrier. Affliction forces us to let go. Affliction destroys the personality, strips away humanity, deprives us of all human relationship, and pulverizes the soul. We have to face affliction with steady attention and let the soul die. When affliction is consented to, it leads to baptism and the state of perfection. Affliction makes us inert and mute. For Weil (1977), only God can set us free. Affliction is the surest sign that God wishes to be loved by us, the most precious evidence of his tenderness. Total detachment is the condition for God's love. His love is completely anonymous, impartial, universal love, thus we understand the need to become impersonal and annihilate the soul. We experience love of God through obedience to him and a giving up of our selves. Through joy the beauty of the world penetrates our soul, and through suffering, affliction, it penetrates our body.

The "steady attention" Weil (1977) describes is similar to Noddings's (1984) 'care' and Ruddick's (1989) 'attentive love,' yet it differs in significant ways as well. Weil describes attention as something that requires great effort, but a negative sort of effort. Attention is a waiting, a watching, not a searching. Attention is scarcely possible when we become tired, unless we have already had a good deal of practice at attending (Weil, 1977, p. 48). It is better to stop working altogether, seek some relaxation, and come back to the task of attending later. "Attention consists of suspending our thought, leaving it detached, empty, and ready to be penetrated by the object" (Weil, 1977, p. 49). Weil talks about how studying helps increase the power of attention, with a view to prayer. Prayer is the highest form of attention, which makes contact with God. But schools can help us develop a lower type of attention that will help us increase our powers of attention, which we can then use for prayers as well. Thus we find, for Weil (1977), that: "Every school exercise, thought of this way, is like a sacrament" (p. 50). We have to desire to attend to the work, and wish to do it correctly. "The intelligence can only be led by desire.... There must be pleasure and joy in the work" (p. 48). Then, after completing the work, we must look carefully at where we have failed, and what we have gotten wrong. This will help us acquire the virtue of humility, as we contemplate our stupidity. Weil wants us to gain a sense of our own mediocrity. "The soul empties itself of all its own contents in order to receive into itself the being it is looking at, just as he is, in all his (T)ruth. Only he who is capable of attention can do this" (Weil, 1977, p. 51).

For Weil (1977), attention leads to loss of one's soul, to impersonality, which opens us up to God's love. By giving up our soul through attention, we escape false illusions. For Noddings (1984), remember, the one-caring must listen and attend to the one-cared-for. She must be receptive and responsive. Caring is a passive mode of engrossment, where the one-caring does not try to impose her self on the other. Caring opens us up to generously receiving the other to make sure the other is heard and understood. For Ruddick (1989), attentive love is an act of dwelling upon the other, and letting otherness be so that difference can emerge. For all three of them, caring and attention are passive, a waiting and watching and listening, an opening up. However, caring does not require us to lose ourselves. In fact, Noddings talks about how the one-caring must care for her self, in order to be able to care for others. Caring requires us to suspend ourselves as much as possible for the moment, so that we can listen and really hear the other, but it is always with the understanding that we will regain ourselves. Our selves could be changed as a result of our caring encounters, and likely are changed, but so are the ones-cared-for due to having someone validate them. We do not annihilate our selves in order to be totally receptive to the one-cared-for. We must have a sense of self in order to care for others. We must have a memory of having been cared for our selves, and want to sustain that memory through our caring attitude toward others. Also, for Noddings and Ruddick one does not treat the one cared-for indifferently, as a universal object, but rather as a unique person worthy of attention.

Weil (1977) wants to annihilate the self (the personality) and achieve impersonality, anonymity. She recognizes our lives as developing through relationships with others, but she seeks to escape our collectivity through total detachment and enter the realm of the sacred, where Truth, Beauty, Justice, and Goodness dwell, where God dwells. In the end, Weil's innate pessimism, her denial and alienation from life, and her despair and self-hatred cause her to seek to escape nature and society. Panichas credits Buber with saying, "Reality ... had become intolerable to her, and for her, God was the power which led her away from it" (Weil, 1977, xxii).

Weil (1977) represents the beauty of caring-as-attention, as well as its dangers. Many feminists have written essays in response to Noddings's (1984) *Caring* and Ruddick's (1989) *Maternal Thinking* in which they point to the dangers of caring. These dangers are even more vividly highlighted in Weil's description of 'attention' than in Noddings's 'care' or Ruddick's 'attentive love,' for Weil's 'attention' strives for self-annihilation, whereas Noddings's caring and Ruddick's attentive love affirm the self.[1] Several feminists, such as Grimshaw (1986), warn us about the idea of associating *caring* particularly with women as that association can be used oppressively against women, as it has in the past. Women, as the one's "naturally" good at caring, become the ones assigned to child care and domestic care, assigned to the private sphere of the home and barred from public life. Other critics express concern about the "dangers of valorizing relationships in which carers are seriously abused" (Card, 1990, p. 101), "that the unidirectional nature of the analysis of one-caring reinforces oppressive institutions" (Hoagland, 1990, p. 109), and "that if the one-caring sees her moral worth as wholly dependent upon her capacity to care for others, or contingent upon being in relation, then she may opt to remain in relations which are harmful to her" (Houston, 1990, p. 117). In general, they warn that "caring cannot be insular, and it cannot ignore the political reality, material conditions, and social structure of the world" (Hoagland, 1990, p. 113).

Noddings (1984, 1990) resists justifications for caring in terms of trying to distinguish genuine caring from false forms of caring, due to a concern that to try to offer epistemological justifications for caring risks too narrowly defining caring, as well as giving it an absolute status. However, Noddings's fears are based on the traditional transcendental definition of Epistemology as absolutist rather than a qualified relativist view of (e)pistemology such as the one I offer here. Her resistance to offer epistemological justifications for caring maintains a false separation between epistemological concerns of justification and ethical concerns. Noddings counts on caring to be self-justifying, that the one-caring/cared-for dyad will identify genuine caring. As Alison Jaggar (1995) points out, care is treated as a "success" concept, in that I am successful at caring for another if I am able to assess another's situation accurately, the one-cared-for recognizes and responds to my care, and I am self-authenticated as a result of the caring. Yet, this is not a warranted assumption. There are too many examples of abuse and harm done in the name of caring, even willingly received on the part of the one-cared-for, that history has later judged to be morally wrong: footbinding, clitorectomies, incest, abuse, neglect, or overindulgence ("discipline" and "spoiling"). One can argue that Weil's death is a vivid example of the abuse and harm that is done in the name of caring. How does caring avoid being paternalistic, authoritarian, and/or dogmatic (Pagano, 1999)? It is dangerous to avoid epistemological justification, for fear it will limit and essentialize caring. Without justification we are left with vulgar relativism (anything goes).

I want to argue that caring not only plays a vital role in moral orientation, as Noddings and others describe, but it also is vital to a nontranscendent (e)pistemology. It is possible to describe caring in a way that addresses context, offers justification, and avoids dangerous results for the one-caring and/or one-cared-for, and yet helps us understand caring's indispensable role in good reasoning. Caring is actually able to function in a critical capacity as *caring reasoning*. Caring reasoning is like what Dewey (1960) called "sympathetic understanding." The first step in understanding another is noticing the other. We must first have our attention drawn to another, we must decide that we value the other enough to notice it and try to understand it. We must show interest in the other; we must recognize the other. The act of showing interest or recognition is an act of care, for all interest is selected interest. I am interested in this and not that; I cannot be interested in everything at once. When I select something to attend to I also, at the same time, reject something else which I decide not to notice. "There is care, concern, implicated in every act of thought" (Dewey, 1960, p. 101).

Dewey (1938) says that all inquiry starts with a felt need, and all interest is an expression of felt desires. It is not the case that reason is in opposition to emotions. Such a view of reason is impoverished, for reason and emotions are really very closely intertwined. Our emotions stir us and move us to act; they are expressions of doubt and concern, love, hate, fear, and surprise, for example. Caring reasoning is what we use to recognize and select what interests us about our qualitative experiences (Thayer-Bacon, 2000, Chapter 8). Once we recognize and select a particular experience to attend to—say there is someone we want to talk to—we must use our care reasoning again, in order to help us understand the other. This act of attending to the other in order to gain understanding is an act of care. However, it is also important to consider the manner in which we attend to the other. A cursory glance will not do. Caring reasoning commits us to attending to the other in a generous manner. We must listen intently and suspend our own doubts long enough to make sure we have heard correctly. We must be fair and sympathetic in our listening and not move to critiquing what we hear, yet. We must be open to the other.

Dewey's sympathetic understanding and definition of the inquiry process, Weil's attention, Ruddick's attentive love, and Noddings's engrossment serve as examples of what I mean by *caring reasoning*. What protects caring, as a moral orientation, from charges of determinism or relativism is the same thing that protects a relational (e)pistemology from similar charges, the enlarging of our view through interactions with others not like us. Other individuals help us gain a better perspective on our own situation, thus affording us a way to critique our own personal situations, at a micro level. Others, as social groups outside of our own, also help us critique our own social institutions, at a macro level. Others help us imagine possibilities beyond our own limited experiences, and help make us aware of (bring to the foreground) what was in the background of our consciousness, what we have been assuming as taken-for-granted reality. We use caring reasoning in order to understand others, at a micro and macro level.

Let's look at the critical role caring reasoning plays in this process. Barbara Houston (1990) is concerned about women's inability to resist physical and sexual abuse, and worries that a misplaced sense of responsibility for "the moral goodness of those who abuse us, exploit us, harm us" (p. 116) is what supports women's inability to resist.

Could it be that abused women lack a comparison of their situation to others? It certainly is the case that when women are offered comparisons, and are able to gain a greater contextual perspective on their own experiences, reports of abuse increase dramatically. One of the significant results of the public broadcast of the O. J. Simpson trial in the USA was a sharp increase of women reporting spousal abuse. Hearing Nicole Simpson's story helped many women recognize their own, and assured them that if it could happen to her, it could happen to anyone.

The powerful way that caring reasoning functions to help us critique can be seen in support groups. In the USA there are support groups for alcoholics, and their families, for cancer victims, people with AIDS, incest survivors, just to name a few. Support groups offer an incest survivor a safe place to go where people are committed to listening to her with care. The support group's role is to allow the victim to speak, and for them to attentively listen to make sure they have understood. Individuals who attend support groups find tremendous relief and affirmation, knowing others hear their voices generously, that others notice them, value them, and feel sympathy for them. They also attain an outsider's perspective of their own situation, because they hear others share their own stories. The individuals attending are recognized as unique individuals, but they also are often surprised to find out how much they share in common with others. Caring reasoning is vital to helping us enlarge our views and place our own situation within a wider context, thus giving us a way to compare and critique.

Claudia Card (1990) is concerned with how caring, with its particular, personal focus, can help us resist complicity in evil-doing that strangers commit (e.g. racism in a society). Her worry is similar to Jaggar's (1995) worry that care emphasizes the quality of individual relations at the expense of addressing "structural oppositions between the interests of social groups that make caring difficult or unlikely between members of those groups" (Card, 1990, pp. 196–197). For example, how does caring reasoning help us address worker exploitation? Caring reasoning works in the same way at the macro level that it does at the micro level. Caring reasoning helps us name the evil that stangers commit as evil, by offering us a way to first notice the act, become aware of it, and then inquire about it in a way that helps us understand it, so that we are able to critique it and fight back. For example, when Rosa Parks refused to give up her seat on the bus and stand in the back, she made us notice racism. Because she was someone people could identify with, the effort to generously consider her situation was not so difficult; many were moved to critique the public transportation's racist policy for what it was.

Karl Marx (1848, 1964) used caring reasoning to help him understand workers as people who were being exploited by capitalism and the Industrial Revolution. (Simone Weil [1977] writes about factory workers as well in "Factory Work"). He had to use caring reasoning to first notice the workers' plight. He had to selectively choose to attend to their needs. He had to talk to the workers and compare their stories to his own, with an effort to being receptive and generous in his listening to their voices. Marx turned to history to give him an even larger comparison between the current worker's plight and previous laboring conditions. This historical comparison gave him an even greater enlarged view, in order to be able to critique the current times. And then he shared that larger view with the local workers, in order to offer them a way to compare as well. The current workers would not listen to him if he was unable to show sympathetic understanding of their experiences. He had to be able to recognize them in their concreteness, and then he offered them a way to recognize their commonality as well, their generalness.

Carol Gilligan's (1982) work on moral development has structurally impacted the field of psychology. Psychology is changed as a result of her caring reasoning. Gilligan had to notice that women were being judged consistently as morally inferior in Kohlberg's moral development theory. She went back through the transcripts of what women had to say and listened to them with generosity. She attempted to believe them, prior to judging them, and in doing so she began to notice a pattern. She sought interviews with other women, from a variety of backgrounds, in order to compare what she noticed to what others had to say. The pattern she noticed was confirmed, and so she reported on her work, and in doing so enlarged all of our comparisons, and thus enhanced our abilities to critique. The same can be said for other feminist contributions. Caring reasoning offers us a way to gain greater awareness of our contextual surroundings, at a personal level as well as at a social institutional level, and that awareness is what enables us to be able to critique our current situation as well as help us imagine how things could be different. Paradoxically, we must use caring reasoning in order to help us better understand "it" and find ways to justify "it."

Let us explore one more vivid example of a relational ontology and (e)pistemology at a very personal level, Martin Buber's (1958) position in *I and Thou*, which is quite different from Weil's. Whereas Weil helped me address concerns in regards to loss of 'self' in personal relationality, Buber will help me consider further the transactional nature of selves-in-relation-with-others, what he calls "mutual relation." Recall that Weil's relational ontology is anonymous, impartial, and universal. We experience God by giving up, annihilating our personal souls. Buber's relational ontology is personal, intimate, and spoken with the whole being. Weil wants us to give up and renounce ourselves in order to experience God's love, but for Buber if we give up ourselves the saying of *Thou* ceases for there is no more two-fold relation. If the *I* is swallowed up by *Thou*, then *Thou* is alone, thus consuming the relation.[2]

Martin Buber is a Jewish scholar and an existential philosopher from Germany who later made Israel his homeland. Levinas (1994) credits Buber with showing "the Western world that Judaism exists in a contemporary form of life and thought," and of teaching "Judaism itself that it was again visibly exposed to the outside world" (p. 5).[3] Buber's *I and Thou* (*Ich und Du*) was first published in German in

1923, and in English in 1937. I have the second edition, which was published in 1958 with an added Postscript from Buber. *I and Thou* is written like a poem, spiraling back on the same topics, sometimes even repeating the same lines. Buber tells us in the Postscript that when he wrote the first draft of the book it was based on a vision that had come to him again and again since he was a child, and finally reached such a state of clarity that he felt he needed to write it down. He has written additions to the book to further clarify points and respond to criticisms and comparisons to others' work, but these appear in other forms, leaving the original *I and Thou* intact.

Buber (1958) starts *I and Thou* (1958) with a duality, declaring humans have a dualistic attitude. The duality is linked to the primary words humans speak, *I-Thou* and *I-It*. These primary words do not signify things, but they intimate relations. "Primary words are spoken from the being" (p. 3). Buber considers how we begin in relation, in terms of the spiritual history of primitive human beings, as well as in terms of infancy. Already in the original relational event human beings speak the primary word *I-Thou* before we recognize ourselves as an *I* (p. 22). If we look at the development of every child, we find children begin with the effort to establish relation, *I-Thou*, and *I-It* comes with natural separation (this is in agreement with Flax's object relations theory, above) (p. 24). "In the beginning is relation—as category of being, readiness, grasping form, mould for the soul; it is the *a priori* of relation, *the inborn Thou*" (p. 27). Even if we look at how community is built, we find that community is built first of all through a living Centre, the eternal *Thou*, and then second of all, through individual reciprocal relations with each other, particular *Thou's*. According to Buber (1958), "(t)he true community does not arise through people having feelings for one another (though indeed not without it), but through, first, their taking their stand in living mutual relation with a living Centre, and, second, their being in living mutual relation with one another" (p. 45).

I-Thou establishes the world of relation. According to Buber (1958), there are three spheres to the world of relation: our life with nature, our life with other people, and our life with spiritual beings. We can have particular *I-Thou* relations with nature, other people, and spiritual beings. However, we have an eternal *I-Thou* relation only with God. The world we experience as objects is the world of *It*, and things establish the realm of *It* (*He* or *She*), and bind it. *I-It* is an objectified relation. But, *Thou* has no bounds and is not closed. *I-Thou* is a direct relation, whereas the objectified relation of *I-It* is indirect and irrelevant. *I-Thou* can only be spoken with the whole being. We can only meet *Thou* in silence, for every response binds up the *Thou* in the world of *It*. *I-Thou* is present, now, whereas *I-It* has no present, only the past (p. 12). We can experience a thing in a variety of ways. Buber uses a tree as his famous example to show that we can perceive it, classify it, dissipate it, all of which are *I-It* experiences, and we can also be bound up in relation to it (*I-Thou*). We do not give up the other experiences in *I-Thou* relations; we unite them.

Buber (1958) tells us, the *Thou* meets us through grace; it is not found by seeking. We do not experience *Thou*, yet every one of us has awareness of *Thou*. The *Thou* confronts us individually, but we, as *I*'s, step into direct relation with it. The relation means being chosen and choosing, suffering and action in one (p. 76). "Every real relation with a being or life in the world is exclusive. Its *Thou* is freed, steps forth, is single, and confronts you. It fills the heavens" (p. 78). When a baby is born, she confronts her mother in her uniqueness. An *I-Thou* relation rests on individuation; this is its joy. Every real relation in the world is consummated in the interchange of actual and potential being. "(I)n pure relation potential being is simply actual being as it draws breath, and in it the *Thou* remains present" (p. 100).

However, the melancholy of our fate is that every particular *Thou* must become an *It*, except the one eternal *Thou*, which can never become an *It*. People swing between particular *Thous* and *Its*; we must leave *Thou* again and again, for we are not able to remain in *Thou*. "The particular *Thou*, after the relational event has run its course, is *bound* to become an *It*. The particular *It*, by entering the relational event, *may* become a *Thou*" (Buber, 1958, p. 33, emphasis in original). It is not possible to live in the bare present, without *It* we cannot live. This is because we can only organize our lives with the help of the past (*It*). Yet, it is possible to live only in the past, to fill each moment only with experiencing and using. Buber (1958) warns us though: "But he who lives with *It* alone is not a man" (p. 34). For us, every particular *Thou* serves as a glimpse of the eternal *Thou*. The extended lines of relation (particular *I-Thou's*) meet in the eternal *Thou*, in the Centre.

We learn from Buber (1958) that the history of the individual and of the human race is a progressive augmentation of the world of *It*. Each generation has a more extensive world of objects, in general. *I-It* is a connection of *experiencing* and *using*. The world of causality has unlimited reign in the world of *I-It*. *I-Thou* is the world of relations. As we develop the function of experiencing and using we decrease our power to enter into relation (p. 43). The world of *It* is set in the context of space and time. *Thou* appears in space and time, but cannot be arranged and ordered: only *It* can. *Thou* is not causally linked to a chain of causes, it is in relation of mutual action with the *I*.

Buber (1958) says: "Through the *Thou* a man becomes *I*" (p. 28). He goes on to explain that the *I* that is formed of *I-Thou* is a different *I* then the *I* of *I-It*. The *I* of *I-It* is individuality, being differentiated from other individualities. The *I* of *I-Thou* is a person, subjectivity, in relation with others. "The one is the spiritual form of natural detachment, the other the spiritual form of natural solidarity of connexion" (p. 62). Just as particular *Thous* are destined to become *Its*, no *I* is pure individuality and no *I* is pure person, "(e)very man lives in a twofold *I*" (p. 65). *I-It* is not evil, but it can rob us of our person, our *I* of *I-Thou*, if we let it have mastery over us. For Buber, the *I-Thou* relation does not mean giving up the *I*, as Simone Weil recommends. The *I* is indispensable to this relation, as it is to every relation. But Buber's distinction between a personal *I* and an individual *I*, helps us appreciate there is a giving up of *I*, in the sense of individuality, in order for the subjective, personal *I* to enter into an *I-Thou* relation.

Buber (1958) also disagrees with Weil in terms of renouncing the world. The eternal *Thou* is unconditionally inclusive and exclusive. All else lives in *Thou*'s light, and yet for each of us *Thou* confronts us singularly. Buber (1958) says, "For to step into pure relation is not to disregard everything but to see everything in the *Thou*, not to renounce the world but to establish it on its true basis" (pp. 78–79). According to Buber, we do not need to seek God, for there is no place where, no thing in which, He can not be found. God is the 'wholly Other' but he is also the wholly Same, the wholly Present (p. 79).

If we compare Buber (1958) to Noddings (1984), we find that the one-caring and the one-cared-for in a caring relation are similar to the *I* and *Thou* in a particular *I-Thou* relation. Both Buber and Noddings describe the relation as one that effects both participants, as being a sharing responsiveness, equally 'between.' Noddings talks about how a caring relation must be reciprocal, in that it must be willingly received and acknowledged somehow by the one-cared-for. Buber describes reciprocity in terms of "mutual relation." "My *Thou* affects me as I affect it" (p. 15). The relation is not in the *I* or in the *Thou*, but between the two. As in marriage, love is between *I* and *Thou*, it is an *I-Thou* relation, it is not in either of the *I*s. The *I-Thou* relation is neither one of full dependence or full absorption; both of these abolish relation. With dependence the saying of *Thou* ceases for the *I* is swallowed up by the *Thou*, and there is no more two-fold being. With absorption, the *I* is identified with the *Thou*, the divine exists in the Self, and there is no more two-fold being there either. One consumes relation, the other treats relation as a delusion to be overcome (p. 84). For Buber, Spirit exists with humans; we are mutually included. God comprises but is not the universe. God comprises but is not my Self.

Conclusion

To sum up what I have established in this chapter, a relational (e)pistemology considers subjects as knowers-in-relation-with-others. Thus a relational (e)pistemology is supported by a relational ontology. Together they form the netting that catches up concepts and shapes their meanings with a wholistic, connected focus. Our fundamental relationality precedes both knowing and gender. I have argued, in Levinas's language, for the phenomenological irreducibility of human relations.[3] These relations are between; they are mutual and reciprocal, in the sense of mutual interdependence and independence. Their transactional nature insures the alerity of the other as well as prevents the I from being reduced or subsumed by the other (or Thou).

In the discussion on the self-in-relation-to-others I presented our selves as embodied, social, and unique. Our selves are multifarious, contingent, and fractured, not stabilized or the same. However, there is a basic cohesiveness and sense of continuity to the self, which is necessary in order for each of us to develop our unique, individual voices. This description of selves is meant to displace unitary, essentialist, and asocial or ahistorical ideas of the self while at the same time emphasizing the importance of sustained, intimate relations with other persons.

Contrary to traditional Philosophy and its tendency to ignore infantile experience and women's activities as careproviders, I have presented our lives as beginning in concrete relations, with our biological mothers and our adoptive parents (who can be the same person), those who take on the responsibility of caring for us. Bringing children-in-relation-to-their-careproviders to the foreground helps us reveal Philosophical false assumptions and offers us a way to critique Philosophy's androcentric theories. It locates Epistemological theories within their social and historical context. I discussed this infant-parent relation in terms of Ruddick's maternal thinking, Noddings's caring, and Flax's object relations theory, and critiqued each of their theories from a more social, macro level that pays attention to the location of persons (and families) within the wider contexts of social relations. This level of critique points us in the direction of the next chapter, where my focus will shift from an intimate, personal view of concrete relations with others to relations with generalized others. The shift between concrete and general levels of contextuality will occur throughout this text, as I strive to consider a topic from a variety of angles.

I have also worked to describe caring, in terms of attention, and its role in reasoning. I have made the case that we can only be sure of understanding the other with the help of caring reasoning. Caring reasoning requires us to generously attempt to believe an other, before moving to critiquing the other. With caring reasoning we must try to suspend our own doubts long enough to make sure we have heard fairly the other's voice. Not only does caring have an important role to play in ethics, but it is essential to (e)pistemology as well. This is because we need others to help us gain a better perspective on our own situations. Others help us become more aware of our own background assumptions and what we take for granted. Others draw our attention to more varied selected interests and help us imagine new possibilities. Others, first as our very intimate Thou, our parent(s), our childcare provider(s), help us develop our unique voices, and teach us how to contribute our voices to the conversation, through their loving attention, their care, for each one of us. I move on to Chapter 5, and a consideration of a relational (e)pistemology in terms of more general social relations.

CHAPTER 5

Social Relations

I began Chapter 4 by pointing to a tension that continues to persist in philosophy between the individual, in the private sphere, and others, in the public sphere. I claimed that infants and mothers historically have been relegated to the home, as the private sphere, and thus dismissed to "the ontological basement."[1] One finds this dismissal occurs with significant philosophers such as: Aristotle, Descartes, Kant, Hume, and Rousseau.[2] Only when the infant grows up and enters the public sphere, does he tend to become a subject in philosophical discussions. Girls, who grow up to be women traditionally remaining in the private sphere of home, have therefore not been the usual subject of philosophical discussions. A significant exception to this rule is Plato (1979), who introduced women into philosophical discussions by proposing they be released from the private sphere so that they could be guardians for the *Republic*. Notice, though, that he did not attempt to dissolve the boundaries that separate the two spheres. Plato proposed that people (women) who were good at childcare should be the ones to attend to infants, thus freeing some women from that task so that they could exercise their talents in the public realm. In Chapter 4 I argued that Ruddick, Noddings, and Flax contribute significantly to the raising of women's status in the private sphere, by drawing our attention to the importance of the infant-mother relation. However, their work still tends to maintain a dichotomy between the private and public spheres.

Amongst current postmodern and pragmatist philosophers, we also can find a sharp distinction maintained between the private and public spheres, although the private sphere is described in important terms of creativity, autonomy, and self-development, not in terms of babies, laundry, and dirty dishes. Richard Rorty (1989) presents an example of a split between the public/private realms, with the separation he maintains between "the private ironist" and "the public liberalist" in *Contingency, Irony, and Solidarity*. Here we find that the private realm has high status as the place where I develop and exercise my personal voice, where I long for autonomy. The private sphere is the place where I can be radical and free, where I can be concerned with my personal development, with self-creation. The private is "the part of life in which we carry out duties to ourselves, and do not worry about the effects of our actions on others" (Rorty, 1996, p. 74). Rorty points to Hegel, Nietzsche, Heidegger, Sartre, Foucault, and Derrida as examples of philosophers who focus on the private sphere, as private ironists. In contrast, the public sphere is where I do worry about the effects of my actions on others. According to Rorty's private/public distinctions, he links what he calls "ironists" with the private realm, and "liberalists" with the public realm. An ironist is someone who recognizes the contingency of language, self, and community. A liberalist is someone who wants to avoid cruelty and achieve solidarity with others not like me (Rorty, 1989). Thus, Rorty upholds a strong distinction between the personal (relegated to the private sphere) and the political (assigned to the public sphere).

There are feminists working hard to dissolve the private/public split in its various forms (e.g. domestic/foreign, internal/external, psychical/physical, personal/political, individual/social), and my work here is meant to be a contribution to that effort. An original insight of the women's movement is that the personal is political, and the political is also personal. Feminists argue "that there is a direct relation, however complex it may be, between sociality and subjectivity, between language and consciousness, or between institutions and individuals" (de Lauretis, 1986, p. 5). This chapter will support that argument. It will bring out the voices that were critical in the previous chapter, those that insist we must represent personal relations as embedded and embodied within larger social contexts. Whereas in the previous chapter I described potential knowers as subjects who begin their lives in intimate, interpersonal relations with an other, in this chapter I locate those personal relations within the larger context of social relations.

In Chapter 4 we found that psychologists pay more attention to infants as subjects than philosophers (individuals-in-relation-with-one's caring), and here we will find that sociologists pay closer attention to individuals-in-relation-with-others than philosophers. In Chapter 4 I credited feminists, psychologists, and religious philosophers with bringing intimate, interpersonal relations to the foreground of philosophical discussions. In this chapter I turn to sociologists, feminists, and postmodernists to help me further make the case that as individuals-in-relation-with-others, the relationships we experience are transactional relations which are embedded within larger social contexts. I will begin by exploring the theme of subjects as acculturated social beings in section one. I turn to sociologist George Herbert Mead to position personal relations within general social relations because he is a central person responsible for this sociological positioning to which others then respond. I then highlight particular problems with Mead's theory, and let Dewey show us a way out of these problems with his transactional theory. I argue, in agreement with Mead, that individuals are first of all social beings—we begin our lives in relation with an other who lives in relation with many others—but individuals also affect and change their social relations right from the start. This transactional point is the significant contribution Dewey makes to help us avoid solipsism as well as social determinism.

I will then further consider the limits of a socially constructed view through the theme of power and cultural issues. The sociologists Peter Berger and Thomas Luckmann lead off this second section by describing the socializing process in greater detail, thus helping us further consider the dangers involved. I then discuss vivid examples of individual theorists serving as change agents and consciousness raisers within their larger social communities by exploring the work of Richard Rorty, Dorothy Smith, and Michel Foucault. These particular, socially situated voices will help us confront what it means to be embedded and embodied within a socially constructed reality. I am working to point us beyond an either/or logical structure to a both/and structure. My hope is that the conversation in this Chapter will help further break down the private/public dichotomy that makes it so difficult for us to appreciate the transactional, relational qualities of knowers and knowing.

Subject as Accultured Social Being

George Herbert Mead was a philosopher and a scientist, a psychologist and a sociologist during a time when those fields of study still had fuzzy boundaries (interestingly enough, after efforts to draw sharp distinctions, the social sciences are leaking into each other again). Mead described his theory as social behaviorism in his famous Social Psychology class, which he taught at the University of Chicago for thirty years (1900-1930). Mead never put his thoughts on this topic into a comprehensive book form, although he published many papers. His genius was best expressed through his lectures, which he gave without using any notes. Mead's dedicated students, who often attended his class several times, took extensive notes of his class lectures and even hired a stenographer to take verbatim notes of his class (1927). They did this in order to record Mead's genius and transfer his ideas into a comprehensive book format. The result of these efforts, along with the contribution of Charles Morris as editor, is Mead's *Mind, Self, and Society*, published posthumously in 1934, not written by Mead but delivered by him through lectures. I rely on this text for my discussion on his work.

Mead (1934) argues that we become individual selves with minds out of our social relations with others, thus turning upside-down psychology's focus on individuals *qua* individuals. He also turns upside down the philosophical classical liberal view of the individual subject as separate and autonomous from society who is born with a mind and begins life already a self. Mead abandons "the conception of a substantive soul endowed with the self of the individual at birth," and argues we are first of all social beings, who then become individuals (p. 1). Contrary to psychology, with its focus on the individual, social psychology views the whole, society, as prior to the part, the individual. Social psychology looks at experience from the standpoint of society. Mead describes his point of view as social behaviorism because of his social focus and his claim that the act is his fundamental datum. His theory is behaviorist because his fundamental approach is through conduct. However, he is anxious to distinguish his behaviorism from others such as John B. Watson's, who declares there is no subjective, no imagery, no consciousness. Mead admits the existence of mind or consciousness in his theory. As Mead defines behaviorism, "(b)ehaviorism in this wider sense is simply an approach to the study of the experience of the individual from the point of view of his conduct, particularly, but not exclusively, the conduct as it is observable by others" (p. 2).

Mead (1934) tries to go back to the early stages of social acts preceding symbols and deliberate communication, apart from some form of consciousness, in order to understand how we develop a "mind" and "self." Going back to the early stages of social acts as a methodology means looking historically at early human beings' conduct, as well as looking at infants' experiences, both as they are prior to language. We find in Mead's methodology comparisons of human behavior to animal behavior (e.g. dogs fighting and birds talking), as well as discussions concerning the development of the first vocal gestures of human beings. Mead argues that we must assume individuals are brought into essential relation with the social process before communication so that contact with the minds of other individuals is possible. If we assume selves are antecedent to the social process, this leads us to solipsism. For, if one argues that the individual develops language as a private language prior to communicating with others, that leads us to the conclusion that we would not be able to communicate with anyone else for we would each have our own private languages. Mead's significant point is that first we have experiences within a context; we have the conduct of the individual to the environment. This environment is a social one. It is through communication by a conversation of gestures in a social process that our consciousness develops, our mind arises, and we develop a self.

Mead (1934) suggests we start to develop a mind, and a self, with gestures. Gestures are our first means of communication, they are "these beginnings of social acts which are stimuli for the response of other forms" (p. 43). Gestures are "those phases of the act which bring about the adjustment of the response of the other form" (p. 45). Our first gestures are physical ones, such as a facial grimace or a hand reaching out for another, though for human beings they quickly become vocal gestures as well, e.g. when a baby cries. One gesture does not necessarily result in a similar response. Mead explores dog fights, boxing, fencing and parent/child crying as examples of one gesture stimulating a different response. An animal attacks, another animal responds by fleeing instead of attacking back. A baby cries, the parent picks up the child and makes shushing noises to sooth the cries. The response is different, yet it is clear that the crying gesture has triggered the shushing gesture. A baby cries to arouse in another the effort to attend to the baby's needs. When a gesture means an idea and it arouses that idea in the other individual, then we have a significant symbol. A significant symbol signifies a certain meaning, and we call this language (p. 46). With language there is a universality, or generality, to the response and the meaning, against the particularity of the stimulus that evoked it. When our gestures have shared meaning and become significant symbols, then we are able to think. According to Mead, thinking always takes place in terms of symbols, and our symbols are universal, in the sense that they share common social meanings; they call out the same response in another as they call out in us. Mead defines thinking as "simply an internalized or implicit conversation of the individual with himself by means of such gestures" (p. 47).

Mead (1934) explains that in order for an individual to become conscious of the meaning of her own gesture, she must be able to take the attitude of the second individual toward that gesture, and respond to it in the same way (p. 47). As we are able to take the attitude of the other toward our own gestures, our consciousness evolves. So that, the mind, or intelligence, is defined by Mead as "the taking of the attitude of the other toward one's self, or toward one's own behavior" (p. 48). This "taking the attitude of the other" is not the same thing as imitation, for although imitation of vocal gestures is the origin of language, imitation can be unconscious and have no meaning, as it does with talking birds. What is essential in order for consciousness to evolve is what Mead calls "a co-operative activity," so that the gesture of one form calls out the proper response to others. When our gesture calls out the same response in the other and ourselves, then we are more or less unconsciously seeing ourselves as others see us. "We are unconsciously putting ourselves in the place of others and acting as others act" (p. 69). When a gesture indicates to another the same that it indicates to the individual, then it has meaning. This is why Mead says that meaning is a social act. Meaning need not be conscious at all; in fact meaning is not conscious until significant symbols having shared meaning are evolved in the process of human social experience. So we find that for Mead there is a three-fold relation to meaning. The logical structure involves: (1) one organism gestures to another, (2) the second organism responds to the first organism's gesture, and (3) the second organism indicates the completion of the given social act initiated by the gesture of the first individual (pp. 76–77). We have the gesture, the adjusted response, and the result. The "adjusted response" is the reflexive quality in the relation that is "the essential condition, within the social process, for the development of mind" (p. 134). The mind is simply the interplay of gestures in the form of symbols.

Mead (1934) describes the vocal gesture as being more important than any other gesture (and for people who are deaf, it is hand gestures), for with vocal gestures we hear ourselves talking and what we say has the same impact on us that it has on others. When our gestures call out the same response in the other and ourselves, then we are unconsciously seeing ourselves as others see us. We can see ourselves through the vocal gesture in ways we cannot see our facial and other bodily gestures without a mirror, for we can never see all of our body. Vocal gestures allow us reflexivity, the ability to turn-back our own experiences upon ourselves. When we ask someone else to do something, we are always replying to ourselves just as other people reply. Mead claims "it is only the vocal gesture to which one responds or tends to respond as another person tends to respond to it" (p. 67). The conversation of gestures is the beginning of communication. Conscious communication arises when gestures become signs, with definite meanings or signification in terms of the subsequent behavior of the individuals making them. In order for language to exist one has to understand what she is saying; it has to affect her as it affects others (p. 75). Conscious communication makes mutual adjustment possible, for the individual is able to take the attitude of the other toward herself, and therefore adjust herself to the process, and modify the results.

For Mead (1934), the self is not there at birth, but develops in the process of social experience and activity by becoming an object to itself. He emphasizes the temporal and logical pre-existence of the social process to the self-conscious individual that arises in it. Mead assumes a sharp distinction between the self and the body, arguing that we cannot get an experience of our whole body, but we can get a whole experience of our self. Psychology's essential problem, according to Mead, is explaining self-consciousness: how can the self get outside of itself to become an object to itself? The answer to this problem is that the self becomes an object to itself by taking the attitudes of other individuals toward her within the social environment (p. 138). The language process is essential for the development of the self, for communication provides a form of behavior in which the individual may become an object to herself. Mead defines self-consciousness as when reason takes an impersonal, objective, non-affective attitude toward itself. Self-consciousness is essentially a cognitive rather than an emotional phenomenon (p. 173). Thus we find that not only does Mead assume a sharp distinction between the self and the body, he also embraces a dualistic view of reason in contrast to emotions.

Mead (1934) explains the development of the self in terms of children's play, and games. Through play, children role play and take on the role of the other (e.g. a sibling, parent, doctor, police, or fire fighter). By taking on these varied roles, children develop the capacity to be an object in their own experience, which requires the reflexivity which is at the core of self-consciousness. This stage helps the child organize particular attitudes of other individuals toward him or herself and toward one another in the specific social acts in which s/he participates. Children who go with their parents/childcare providers to the grocery store or market will come home and act out what happens there. They will play the role of the cashier, grocer or shopper and try on these varied roles to help them gain a better understanding of the different attitudes expressed in the social act of shopping.

Games differ from play because they are more formalized in their rules and structure. Each role has a definite relation to the others, and the child must be able to take on all the roles, and understand all the rules, in order to play the game. Mead (1934) uses the example of baseball to show how the batter has to understand the pitcher's role, as well as the fielders, and that when s/he hits the ball s/he must run to first base and try to get there ahead of the ball, etc. The rules of the game supply the organization, and without agreement on the rules, it is not possible to play the game successfully. This stage helps the self unify in terms of the general social attitudes of the others in the social group to which s/he belongs. The organized community or social group gives the individual her unity of self. Mead calls this organized community the "generalized other." The child does not start out in life with an organized, definite character; we have no specific personality, according to Mead (p. 159). The metaphor of the game helps us understand how an organized personality arises. After a person has developed a self through a social structure and social experiences, then it is possible for a self to be alone, and not risk losing itself. Once we have taken on the attitudes of our organized social group we can be placed in solitary confinement and still maintain a self. Mead also explains that we do not have just one personality, contrary to what his "unity self" suggests. We all have multiple personalities, with lines of cleavage running through us. We can be different selves to different communities.

Mead (1934) tells us: "The attitude of the generalized other is the attitude of the whole community" (p. 154). The individual must take the attitudes of the organized social group to which s/he belongs in order to develop a complete self. The individual must be able to take the attitude of the generalized other toward herself in order to think, as well. For thinking always takes place in terms of symbols, and our symbols are universal, in the sense that they share common social meanings; they call out the same response in another as they call out in us. The generalized other, the community structure of rules, supplies the self with shared common meanings, which makes it possible to be self-conscious, and self-reflective. Mead relates habits to the unconscious, and defines consciousness as referring to the field of experience, whereas "self-consciousness refers to the ability to call out in ourselves a set of definite responses which belong to the others of the group" (p. 163).

The different attitudes we take on exercise a definite control over us. Although, Mead (1934) assures us that "(o)f course we are not only what is common to all: each one of the selves is different from everyone else" (p. 163). He also tells us, "selves can only exist in definite relationships to other selves" (p. 164). What Mead suggests is that the self has a social structure that is entirely separable from its subjective experience. The self's subjective experience is memory, and imagination, which is accessible only to the individual. Mead calls the social structure of the self, the "me." The "me" stands for convention; it is the self I am aware of for it is the organized attitudes of others based on the past. Mead calls the subjective self, the "I." The "I" is unpredictable and uncertain for it exists in the now, the present. The "I" is that moment into the future, and it is unknowable; I can only become aware of it when it is past. The "I" is the self's action over and against the social situation. It is the self that gives us a sense of freedom, of initiative. The social "me" represents the responsible side of the self and the "I" represents the novel side of the self. Together they form one self, which adjusts to others' attitudes and at the same time changes others' attitudes (p. 179).

Notice that Mead creates a public/private split between the "me"/"I" in order to solve the problem of social determinism. He does try to show us how the two can become one again. There are times in our lives when the "I" and "me" can fuse together, during certain social activities like religious, patriotic, and team experiences. When this happens there arises in us a sense of exhilaration and we experience intense emotions. This sense of exhilaration cannot be maintained continually but it can return. Mead calls this fusion of the "I" and "me" the successful completion of the social process (p. 275). It is a feeling of complete identification of the self with the other. One wants to give, and one's interest is the interest of all. One feels acceptance of everyone as belonging to the same group. The fusion of the "I" and "me" takes place in the act itself.

As Mead (1934) describes the development of a self, and mind, it is clear that the "me" gives the form to the "I." The "me" acts like a censor, setting the limits of the self through social control. The response of the "I" involves adaption. Assuredly, we are situated beings located within specific social communities which help to shape whom we become. The social self must be recognized by others to be validated. Our self-respect depends on others' recognition of our selves. Does this shaping mean our selves are socially determined? How do communities change? Mead says that all of us are molded by society, and yet all of us contribute to the changing of society and each other. Our social origin does not contradict our ability to be individuals, for each of us has our own peculiar standpoint. We each reflect the social pattern from our own unique position (p. 201). We continually react back against our society. Individuals continually change communities through their interactions, exchanges, and communications. It is because we can think that change is possible. Individuals can use reason to get a voice that is more than the voice of the community (p. 168). Geniuses and leaders change their society in profound ways, but all of us contribute changes, though most of them are minor changes that are hard to detect, except by looking back. It is like George Bailey in the classic movie, "It's a Wonderful Life" who wishes he was never born, and then has the opportunity to find out what life would be like if he had never lived. He discovers that one person does have a significant impact on his social community.

Now that I have described Mead's basic social behavioristic theory on the development of mind and self (I have left out much of what he says in his society section), I would like to further explicate his theory through a critical discussion of points within his theory that come under question. There are several issues we need to address, most of which I have already pointed to but would like to sum up here.

Mead says repeatedly in his lectures that he wants to avoid metaphysics, just prior to introducing a basic category that takes on a metaphysical influence. For example, Mead assumes a mind/body split in his discussion on the mind and self, as well as a reasons/emotions split in his discussion on thinking and self-reflection. He also assumes a public/private split (the social "me" and the qualitatively unique "I"). He uses his public/private split to try to avoid social determinism, while at the same time describing the generalized other in incredibly powerful terms. How does an individual gain a unified self when s/he is othered in the social community, when she is a girl in a misogynist community, a Black in a racist community, a homosexual in a homophobic community? For Mead, the individual must take the attitudes of the organized social group to which s/he is a member in order to develop a complete self, but if the social group's attitudes are sexist, racist, and/or homophobic and you are a female, Black, and/or gay, and you adopt their attitude, such adoption will diminish your sense of self. Mead says that our self-respect depends on the recognition of ourselves by others, but again, this is a problem for oppressed minorities who are not recognized and treated with respect and dignity by the generalized other. Mead does not discuss the concerns of outsiders to particular social communities. Nor does he discuss the alterity of the other.[3] Mead's reflexive theory of the self depends heavily on certain concepts that need further discussion in order for them to be able to carry the weight he places on them (such as "shared responses," "vocal gestures," and "generalized other").[4] I turn to John Dewey, as a contemporary of Mead's, to offer us a way out of Mead's dualisms.

John Dewey and George Mead were good friends and colleagues, even neighbors in Chicago. Dewey hired Mead at the University of Michigan, and then brought Mead to the University of Chicago when Dewey was hired there. They greatly influenced each other, as they were both developing their individual theories during the time they worked together. Not only did they work together in Michigan and Chicago, but they also lived side-by-side as neighbors in Chicago. Like Mead, Dewey holds a social behaviorist view of meaning. However, Mead's individual tends to be subsumed by the generalized other (the social 'me' disciplines and censors the 'I'), whereas Dewey's individual actively interacts with and changes general society. There are several texts that can serve as ways into Dewey's position, for he was a prolific writer who lived a long, full life. His *Human Nature and Conduct* (1922) describes his psychology with a social emphasis (habits) based on an evolutionary framework (impulses). Here Dewey describes habits as constituting the self and mind, and we discover that habits serve the regulatory role for him that the generalized other serves for Mead, yet with greater potential for flux and adjustability due to impulses. Habits, which are acquired, are affections; they are demands for certain kinds of activities. How do we acquire habits? Habits are enforced upon us from the day we are born, by the very fact that we are social beings who cannot survive without the help of others. As soon as others begin to care for us they begin to affect us and enforce habits upon us. Thus habits come from our social environment and are imposed on us through social custom. Yet habits are acquired and secondary, not native to us as impulses are. Impulses are what give us flexibility and diversity and habits are what give our impulses direction and shape.

I want to turn to a different text, though, to consider a significant contribution Dewey makes to this relational (e)pistemology, the concept of transactional relations. Although Dewey (1949) wrote about transactions in a much later published book focused on logic, titled *Knowing and the Known*, which he published with his co-author, Arthur Bentley, I want to turn to a text that Dewey wrote during the years he was working with Mead in Chicago. It is not a text that focuses on social psychology or logic, but rather one that focuses on education. However, Dewey's (1916/1944/1966) classic, *Democracy and Education*, offers insight into how to heal the self/society split. It serves us well for this discussion.

Dewey (1916) begins *Democracy and Education* with a discussion of what distinguishes living and inanimate things, that distinction being that living things maintain themselves through renewal. Dewey defines this renewal process as continually readapting the environment to the needs of living organisms (p. 2). He also calls this renewal process the "continuity of life," and he asserts that human beings achieve continuity of life by means of *education*. "Education, in its broadest sense, is the means of this social continuity of life" (p. 2). Thus we discover education is a social need, for every society needs to renew itself. This renewal process includes for humans re-creation of beliefs, ideals, hopes, happiness, misery, and practices.

Dewey (1916) describes people as living in communities, based on what they have in common, "and communication is the way in which they come to possess things in common" (p. 4). To be a community, people have to share purposes and have a communication of interests. Thus, we learn that a social life is one based on communication and all communication is educative, for it enlarges and changes experience. This is because, in order to formulate an experience so that it can be communicated, the one communicating must step outside of the experience and see it from the outside as the other would see it. The one communicating must try to consider how to connect their experience to the other's experiences so that the other will understand. The one communicating must find some way of establishing shared meaning with the other, so that the other can appreciate what's being communicated and receive it. And, the one receiving the communication must be able to "step outside" as well in order to understand what is being offered to her. In order to be able to successfully communicate, both the communicator and the one receiving the communication will have enlarged views as a result of their experiences of looking from the outside. "Except in dealing with commonplaces and catch phrases one has to assimilate, imaginatively, something of another's experience in order to tell him intelligently of one's own experience. All communication is like art" (p. 6). So, we find that for Dewey, in order to be able to communicate with others we must be able to get outside of our own point of view. Language requires meaning in order for us to be able to communicate with others, and meaning depends on connection with a shared experience. Certainly Dewey's theory has much in common with Mead.

In *Democracy and Education*, Dewey (1916) considers how a society educates its young as a means of renewing itself, and maintaining social continuity. Education serves a social function. With a simple society, the renewal process is very informally communicated as the young share experiences with their elders. The more complex the society is, the more lengthy and formal the education process develops. As society's become more complex, we begin to find schools. The role of schools in a society are to simplify and order the environment, weed out what is undesirable, and create for its young a new and broader environment, a wider and better balanced environment (p. 22). More enlightened society's realize that they should not transmit *all* of their existing achievements to their young, but only those that will make for a better future society.

For all levels of education, Dewey (1916) tells us we educate "by means of the action of the environment in calling out certain responses" (p. 11). Education can not be pounded into the young, or poured into their heads, it must be done indirectly, through the environment. "(T)he environment consists of those conditions that promote or hinder, stimulate or inhibit, the *characteristic* activities of a living being" (p. 11, emphasis in original). Given that we are social beings who associate with others, this means we have a social environment. We cannot perform our own activities without taking others into consideration, for they are indispensable to the conditions for realizing our own tendencies. "When [s/he] moves [s/he] stirs them and reciprocally" (p. 12). Our social environment is "educative in its effect in the degree in which an individual shares or participates in some conjoint activity" (p. 22). With these qualifications in mind, Dewey proceeds throughout the rest of his book to describe the conditions that help to nurture the immature members of a society.

Dewey (1916) often refers to the young as the "immature" members of society, as opposed to the "mature" members of the group. Each of us is "born immature, helpless, without language, beliefs, ideas, or social standards" (p. 2). Still, each individual is their society's future representative. When Dewey uses the term 'immature' he does not mean this in the detrimental sense that we often use the term today, to mean behaving in an inferior or less than adult-like manner. For Dewey, 'immaturity' is the primary condition of growth (p. 41). Growth is the "cumulative movement of action toward a later result" (p. 41), and immaturity designates the *power* to grow (p. 42, emphasis in original). So, when Dewey describes the young in society as 'immature' he does so to highlight their plasticity, their ability to learn from experience and grow (p. 44). The immature are less encumbered by habits and more open to their impulses.

It is also important to note that Dewey (1916) describes children as physically helpless, but socially powerful. They are totally dependent on others for their survival and would not survive for an hour based on their own physical strength. Yet they do survive, and their survival is testimony to their ability to compensate for their physical incapacity with their social capacity. "(C)hildren are themselves marvelously endowed with *power* to enlist the coöperative attention of others. . . . (C)hildren are gifted with an equipment of the first order for social intercourse" (p. 43, emphasis in original). They are incredibly sensitive and attentive to the attitudes and doings of the people around them. They are intensely interested in their social surroundings, much more so than their physical surroundings, though they are interested in those as well. "From a social standpoint, dependence denotes a power rather than a weakness; it involves interdependence" (p. 44). What Dewey describes in terms of the youngs' interdependent relationship to their elders is something he later in his career calls a "transactional" relationship. Yet, the seeds for this transactional description are right in *Democracy and Education*. Dewey distinguishes his views from Mead's by creating a transactional model that describes social groups affecting individuals *and* individuals affecting social groups. The young, immature, affect the mature *and* the mature affect the young.

We can find another example of Dewey's (1916) transactional relational model in his discussion about democracy within the same text, *Democracy and Education*. In his Chapter 7, "The Democratic Conception of Education," Dewey offers a description of a democratic community that recognizes the interactive, interrelational, interdependent qualities of individuals in relation to others. He begins this chapter by reminding us that education is "a social function, securing direction and development in the immature through their participation in the life of the group to which they belong" (p. 81). This means that education will vary with the quality of life that prevails in a group. Given that people associate together in many different ways and for many different purposes, Dewey offers us a way to measure the worth of any given mode of social life. The criteria he offers are based on the interdependent qualities of individuals in relation to others. How much are the interests of the group shared by all of its members? And, how full and free are the group's interactions with other groups? These two criteria help us recognize and attend to the transactional nature of social relationships. The first criteria signifies the importance of "more numerous and more varied points of shared common interest" [as well as] "the recognition of mutual interests as a factor in social control" (p. 86). The second criteria highlights not only the importance of freer interaction between social groups but also why freed interaction is important in terms of "change in social habit—its continuous readjustment through meeting the new situations produced by varied intercourse" (pp. 86–87). For Dewey, these two criteria point to a democracy as more than a form of government: "it is primarily a mode of associated living, of conjoint communicated experience" (p. 87). For our purposes here, these two criteria help us understand that individuals are greatly affected by their social groups but social groups are greatly affected by their individuals as well. And, social groups are affected by other social groups as well. Because we are social beings, we are always affected by this transactional nature of relations at the micro level of individual relations as well as at the macro level of social relations.

Dewey's transactional description helps us find our way out of the either/or tension between solipsism and social determinism. We find, in agreement with Mead, that individuals are first of all social beings. We are immature young who are born into particular social groupings. Even if we are born on a deserted island, where we have been shipwrecked, we at least have our mother to relate to and help form our social community. And our mother brings with her the influence of the social community in which she grew up and the affects of the father who contributed to our conception. We escape solipsism because we do not start out life with a self; we develop a sense of self out of our social interaction with others. Still, we affect our 'others' right from the start, and I place that start as being even prior to birth. Before we have even been introduced to our social group, once our presence is know by the mother, and then the social group (this is usually the order of awareness but not always), we cause changes within the social group. Will we be received or rejected? How does our mother's role in her society change as a result of having us? Who will care for us as well as our mother during the final stage of gestation and the recovery time after birth? And, what about our extended need for care; who will meet that need? In fact, at the individual level the mother-to-be will begin to experience dramatic physical changes before she is even aware of her child's presence. Certainly, every parent as well as every society is affected by the birth of a child, in terms of its reception, care, and induction into that society. Each of us represents the potential future of our society and we begin to affect and change our social environment right from the start. This transactional nature of social relations is how we escape social determinism. It is guaranteed that we will be greatly affected by our social surroundings, but it is also guaranteed that our social surroundings will be affected by us. The logical structure here is not an either/or structure, but a both/and structure.

At this point I want to move on to further explore the power associated with Mead's concept of the generalized other. I want to consider in greater detail the socializing process, with the help of Berger and Luckmann, and begin to explore how others who are marginally recognized and oppressed in a social community gain a sense of self and are able to affect changes in the attitudes of their social communities. I want to consider more the negative effects lack of care has on us, in terms of lack of validation, recognition, and generous, loving attention, at an individual and social level, given that we are selves-in-relation-with-others.

Power and Culture Issues

Remember that for Mead, we gain a mind and a self by being able to become objects to ourselves, by taking the attitude of the other and seeing ourselves as others see us. This reflective process places our self identity in the hands of others, our social community. Peter Berger and Thomas Luckmann (1966), who wrote *The Social Construction of Reality*, another classic text in the field of sociology, credit Mead as one of their influences, along with Marx, Durkheim, Weber, and others. In their text, they further elaborate on Mead's description of the objectifying process and the role of the generalized other, as they explore "the process of becoming a man" and how this process takes place in an interrelationship with an environment.[5]

According to Berger and Luckmann (1966), man's instinctual organization is underdeveloped compared to other higher mammals. "Humanness is socio-culturally variable" (p. 49). They do not deny that it is possible to say the man has a nature in the sense of anthropological constraints, though they do deny that there is human nature "in the sense of a biologically fixed substratum determining the variability of socio-cultural formations" (p. 49). Given the plasticity of humans and their susceptibility to socially determined influence, it is more significant to describe man as constructing his own nature, "or more simply, that man produces himself" (p. 49). At the same time that the human organism is developing his interrelationship with his environment, the self is also being formed. Berger and Luckmann say that we each are born with genetic presuppositions, but the self is a social product, since we produce our social world (p. 50). In agreement with Mead and Dewey, they argue that our self-production is always a social enterprise (p. 51).

In *The Social Construction of Reality*, Berger and Luckmann (1966) alert us to the dangers of this social enterprise through their description of how our social world is constructed. They describe the institutionalization process of our human activities, as our actions become habituated and then typified as they are subsumed under social control. Human actions then become predictable, and human beings begin to fulfill certain roles. "Institutionalization occurs whenever there is a reciprocal typification of habitualized actions by types of actors" (p. 54). Institutions become "crystallized" when they are experienced as having a reality of their own and they appear as given, unalterable, and self-evident (p. 59). Parents transmit social institutions to their children as an objective reality through their education.

However, according to Berger and Luckmann (1966), institutions, and society in general, do not "acquire an ontological status apart from the human activity that produced [them]" (pp. 60-61). We have a tendency to forget that our world is socially constructed and that it can be remade. We tend to treat human phenomena as if they were things, in non-human or supra-human terms (such as facts of nature, results of cosmic laws, or manifestations of divine will). When we do this we reify the social world. To reify the world is to dehumanize the world. Reification of the social world is an extreme version of objectification of the world. "The objectivity of the social world means that it confronts man as something outside of himself" (p. 89). Reification is when we lose sight of the fact that objectifying the world is a human enterprise and we understand the world as a "non-human, non-humanizable, inert facticity" (p. 89). When our world becomes reified, we begin to describe the world in terms of "necessity and fate," to consider ourselves as having no choices, and to see ourselves as acting only due to our particular position or role. Our identities become reified, as Jewish or Catholic, as man or woman, as Black or Latino, as heterosexual or homosexual.

Berger and Luckmann (1966) suggest that the analysis of reification is important because it serves as a means of correcting the reification tendency of theoretical thought in general, and sociological thought in particular. They recommend that we need to note the social circumstances that favor dereification, but they consider this task as being beyond the scope of their project (p. 92). I will explore this reification tendency further with the help of select feminist and postmodern scholars. Before we move on to their contributions, though, Berger and Luckmann actually offer significant contributions to our understanding of this dereification process themselves, with their description of the social legitimation process.

According to Berger and Luckmann (1966), legitimation is the process we develop to explain and justify to the next generation what seems self-evident to us, by means of our own recollection and habituation. The process of legitimation allows us to take our "first order objectifications" which have been institutionalized, and make them objectively available and subjectively plausible to a new generation (p. 92). Legitimation "explains" the institutional order, by giving reasons for why things are the way they are and why we should perform this action and not another. Legitimation also functions to "maintain" our socially constructed reality.

Berger and Luckmann (1966) describe how the first level of legitimation is pre-theoretical, and "is present as soon as a system of linguistic objectifications of human experience is transmitted" (p. 94). It occurs through the meanings attached to words that we are taught. The second level of legitimation occurs through the beginnings of theories, in terms of highly pragmatic moral maxims, wise sayings, and folktales. The third level of legitimation moves beyond pragmatic application and becomes "pure theory." Here complex theories are developed and administered, usually by specialized personnel who have received some kind of formalized initiation procedure. "With this step, the sphere of legitimations begins to attain a measure of autonomy *vis-à-vis* the legitimated institutions and eventually may generate its own institutional processes" [e.g., higher education institutions, commonly known as universities, with professors as legitimizers] (p. 95). The fourth level of legitimation is constituted by "symbolic universes," which are products of human consciousness that present themselves as "full-blown and inevitable totalities" (p. 97). Symbolic universes are "bodies of theoretical tradition that integrate different provinces of meaning and encompass the institutional order in a symbolic totality" (with symbolic referring to "realities other than those of everyday experience") (p. 95). Symbolic universes claim that *all* reality is humanly meaningful, and they represent the furthest reaches of man's effort to externalize himself (p. 104). Legitimation at this level transcends pragmatic application once and for all, for it cannot be experienced at the level of everyday life experiences (p. 95). Symbolic universes "set the limits of what is relevant in terms of social interaction" (p. 102). They are self-maintaining and self-legitimating by the sheer fact of their objective existence in the society (logic plays this role in Euro-western philosophy).

Berger and Luckmann (1966) warn us that every symbolic universe is incipiently problematic because no society is totally taken for granted since all social phenomena are *constructions* produced historically through human action. Kuhn (1962/1970) describes in his *The Structure of Scientific Revolutions* how science develops theory to explain the world a certain way. This theory becomes a paradigm (symbolic universe) which continues to develop as it continues to strive to answer questions and solve problems that present themselves to the theory. When there are enough problems that cannot be solved, there is a "paradigm shift" and a new scientific theory is presented. Anytime an alternative symbolic universe appears, it poses as a threat to the existing one, "because its very existence demonstrates empirically that one's own universe is less than inevitable" (Berger & Luckmann, 1966, p. 108). We find policing actions to help maintain the present symbolic universe, such as declaring the other theory irrational, and those that hold it as incompetent, or worse, as insane or criminal. We assign deviations from the official definitions of reality to therapy. "The threat to the social definitions of reality is neutralized by assigning an inferior ontological status, and thereby a not-to-be-taken-seriously cognitive status, to all definitions existing outside the symbolic universe" (Berger & Luckmann, 1966, p. 115).

Berger and Luckmann (1966) do offer us hope for transforming our socially constructed reality. Their own theory serves the function of placing all theories within the context of living individuals, who have concrete social locations and concrete social interests. They remind us: "(C)hange is brought about by the concrete actions of human beings" (p. 116). They suggest that alterations in our socially constructed reality, transformations, require a process of re-socialization. This process needs identification with significant others who are guides to the new reality (like saints, gurus, teachers). Because our primary socialization takes place through our main careproviders under circumstances that are highly emotionally charged (see Chapter 4), this kind of change is not easy. In fact, it is usually traumatic and very difficult. However, it is possible. Change requires reinterpretation of the past. The very people who serve as legitimators of symbolic universes, such as religious leaders, philosophers, teachers, poets, and scientists, can also serve as change-agents.

American Pragmatism has played a transformative role for philosophy, as has feminism, and postmodernism. There are many forms and shapes that the philosophical perspective of pragmatism can take. However, in all its variety of forms, pragmatism is always a form of philosophy that stresses the relation of theory to practice. Charlene Haddock Seigfried (1996) offers a summarizing definition of pragmatism in her *Pragmatism and Feminism*. "Pragmatism . . . takes the continuity of experience and nature as revealed through the outcome of directed action as the starting point for reflection" (p. 6). Pragmatists are fallibilists (believing in the impossibility of attaining knowledge that is certain) and pluralists (believing in the impossibility of attaining knowledge that is universal). Pragmatists reject the central problems of modern philosophy as presupposing dichotomies (e.g. mind/body, reason/will, thought/purpose, intellect/emotion, self/others, belief/action, theory/practice) which they argue are false, in favor of a radical empiricist description which emphasizes a primal, integral, relational unity. Pragmatists believe that human action can improve the human condition, and that the results of inquiry are the measure of theory. Pragmatists describe individuals as embedded and embodied selves who are constituted by and in their social relations with others (Seigfried, 1996, pp. 7–8).[6]

If we compare this definition of pragmatism to Berger and Luckmann's (1966) discussion of legitimation levels, we can see that pragmatism seeks to lower the level of abstraction of philosophical theory. It seeks to highlight "the centrality of contingent and revisable social practices in acquiring knowledge" (West, 1989, p. 45). For Peirce (1958), we cannot separate our ideas from our experiences, knowers from knowledge, for there is an inseparable connection between rational cognition and rational purpose, between thought and action, or thinking and doing. Remember, "(a) belief is 'that upon which a man is prepared to act'" (Peirce, 1958, "The Fixation of Belief," p. 92, see Chapter 1 and 2). We already know from our earlier discussion of pragmatism that Peirce (1958) strongly connects concepts to their effects with his Pragmatic Maxim: "(C)onsider what effects, which might conceivably have practical bearings, we conceive the object of our conception to have. Then, our conception of these effects is the whole of our conception of the object" (p. 124). Peirce (1958) deconstructs "modern philosophy" in terms of its symbolic universe through his devastating criticism of Descartes, and he shifts the level of legitimation back to level 3, with an insistence that even at level 3, we should not lose sight of theory's connection to experience, and theorists' connection to their larger society. According to Peirce we cannot universally doubt, as Descartes attempted to do, for doubting presupposes something to doubt; therefore this means we must have prior beliefs. We also cannot find the answer to our doubts in our own individual consciousness, as Descartes argued, for this "leads toward a full-fledged subjectivism, an imprisonment in the veil of ideas with no reliable bridge between ideas and things, consciousness and reality, subject and object" (West, 1989, p. 44).

Finally, we cannot ignore the relatedness of ideas to other ideas, as Descartes's philosophical method of inference attempts to do. In the end, Descartes relies on God to account for the self and the world. For Peirce, having recourse to God leads to a result that is inexplicable. For Berger and Luckmann, relying on God is an example of the legitimation process reified.

More examples of pragmatism's transformative changes to Philosophy can be found by considering Dewey's efforts to contextualize philosophy in general, and logic in particular, as well as James's efforts to delegitimize "Truth" as a concept, and enhance the value of "experience" (see Chapters 1 and 2). Clearly, Mead's theory of how we develop a self has resulted in offering serious criticism to classical liberal philosophy and in shifting political philosophy in a more communitarian direction. However, we do not need to look further than the present to find a vivid example of pragmatism's efforts to change Philosophy, with Richard Rorty's (1979) work. His publication of *Philosophy and the Mirror of Nature*, with its searing criticism of Descartes in particular and modern, Enlightenment Philosophy in general, sent major shock waves through Philosophy departments around the world, from which they are still trying to recover.

How other philosophers have responded to Rorty's work also serves as a vivid example of the policing activities that occur in legitimation, and the threats that an alternative theory will create for the majority symbolic universe. Many have responded by declaring Rorty's work ontologically inferior, therefore neutralizing its threat. Logic is applied to point out inconsistencies and faulty arguments, as we found in Chapter 1, with Siegel's treatment of Rorty's ideas. In fact, Siegel (1997) tends to reference others' criticisms of Rorty rather than indulge himself in a serious attempt to generously consider Rorty's ideas, and the articles he references are also guilty of not taking Rorty's arguments seriously. For example, Siegel references an article written by Rosenberg (1993), which he describes as "hilarious and hardhitting" (1997, ftnt 21, p. 215). Rosenberg's (1993) article is meant to be a review of Rorty's *Contingency, Irony, and Solidarity*, but instead it is basically a parody of Rorty's work that refuses to take it seriously. Rosenberg's article begins by comparing the changes in Rorty's author pictures, from an earlier photograph where he is wearing a suit and tie (as can be found in *The Michigan Quarterly Review*, 1991), to the photograph on the cover of *Contingency, Irony, and Solidarity* (1989), where he is dressed casually, without tie, and with a natural setting in the background. This is a common ploy feminists are well aware of, when the scholars of the legitimate symbolic universe shift our attention away from our theory, which is critical of theirs, to our physical appearance, and thereby place the audiences' focus on our bodies (which are rated as inferior in value) instead of our minds (which might actually be offering something that is a challenging threat to the status quo). Rosenberg's article, which Siegel finds hilarious, I find offensive. It is a policing action to disarm the potential damage Rorty's theory can do to Philosophy.

The reader may have already recognized the Introduction, and Chapters 1 and 2 of this text are written in anticipation of policing actions my work will likely initiate, assuming it is taken seriously at all by Epistemologists (as scholars of the legitimate symbolic universe). What often happens with feminist scholarship is that it is just dismissed as inferior, and therapy is suggested for the writer (more education). Dorothy Smith (1990) offers us a vivid example of this, with her efforts to rewrite sociological theory from a feminist perspective. She begins *The Conceptual Practices of Power* by sharing with the reader her own participation in psychiatric therapy in order to try to figure out what was wrong with her, why she was "discontented and difficult in [her] marriage," so that her marriage could be saved (p. 5). She talks about "someone's need to act out of desperation, fear, or rage and the social invalidation . . . that progressively denies the possibility of socially coordinated and hence socially effective courses of action" (p. 5). Smith reassures us she has never been diagnosed as mentally ill, but she acknowledges that she knows enough about it as an insider to write about it. We learn that in her text that she relies heavily on analysis of the ideological practices of psychiatry, because of her earlier specialization in psychiatry as a sociologist, as well as psychiatry's distinctive political significance for women, and because of her personal experiences. After analyzing the alienating practices of psychiatry at a theoretical level, she analyzes their practices in different sites of psychiatry: the statistics on women and mental illness; the textual accounts of suicide; and the specific textual account of Virginia Woolf's suicide. Psychiatry's policing action serves to control and contain 'others,' including women, by labeling 'others' mentally ill. One devastating way to resist such labeling is suicide. Another way to resist is to reject the therapy, as did Smith. Smith takes another giant proactive step by finding a way to critique the therapy. Smith builds on what she learned in breaking up the alienating practices of sociology for her analysis of the alienating practices of psychiatry.

Smith (1987) contributes to the transformation of sociology in her *The Everyday World as Problematic*. Here we find that, like Mead, Smith's focus is social and the act is her fundamental datum. Her theory is behaviorist because her fundamental approach is through conduct, through what she calls "the actualities of our . . . everyday/everynight worlds" (p. 393). Smith (1997) uses "actual" to point to "you are here," to point to "where we live and where discourse happens and does its constituting of reality" (p. 393). Smith's work is inspired by the women's movement and her discovery that we (women) are living in a world from whose making we were almost entirely excluded. The women's movement served the powerful role of validating women's experiences in a world that treated women as inferior outsiders. This validation process is an expression of care. Smith wants sociology to serve this same kind of validating role for 'others' by helping to disclose "the relations of ruling" and subvert the process of institutionalizing. She wants sociology to help raise our consciousness, our awareness of social relations, just as the women's movement helped women raise their consciousness as they struggled for language and the naming of issues by sharing their particular, unique stories and discovering what they held in common. She wants sociology to get back to experience, to the particular and local stories of people, and use that perspective to critique the legitimation process. She wants sociology to connect up concepts and theories with the actualities of peoples' lives and help create "a way of seeing, from where we actually live, into the powers, processes, and relations that organize and determine the everyday context of that seeing" (Smith, 1987, p. 9). In order for sociology to be able to play this critical, consciousness-raising kind of role, though, the role it has come to play must be deconstructed.

Smith (1987) examines the properties of a patriarchal sociology from the standpoint of women's experiences, at the point of ruptures, the fault lines, where women's experiences break away from the discourses mediated by texts. She demonstrates the gender subtext of the rational and the impersonal, and how women are confined to the subjective, the local, the particular, the private. Our ideological practices constrain women to be treated as objects. This issue is more than one of bias. Sociologists have sought an Archimedian point external to any particular position in society in order to try to achieve detachment, impersonality, total anonymity. Smith explores the history of women's exclusion from the making of ideology, of knowledge, and shows how women's private world has been produced, defined, and shaped by men's public world. She makes the argument that our culture does not arise spontaneously, it is manufactured, and many people do not participate in the manufacturing of culture. Forms of thought have been made for women and not by women. One standpoint (the male's) has come to represent the general, the universal (all). Smith lays out the history of women's exclusion and talks about the consequences of excluding women from a full share of what becomes "culture." "The institutional practices of excluding women from the ideological work of society are the reason we have a history constructed largely from the perspective of men, and largely about men" (p. 35). Women are outside the frame, unable to suggest themes and topics to the discourse of sociology.

Smith (1987) tells us her fault line, her point of rupture that became a place for her to start deconstruction, was the rupture between her academic work and her childcare work. Disjunctures, bifurcations of consciousness, occur between experience and the forms in which experiences are socially expressed. Smith realized that everyday experiences can serve as the starting places outside the relations of ruling, to help us become more aware of these relations, and find ways to address them. She uses 'relations of ruling' to mean a complex of organized practices, including government, law, business, finance, professional and educational institutions "as well as the discourses in texts that interpenetrate the multiple sites of power" (p. 3). Smith uses 'discourse' as Foucault uses the term, to stand for the conversation mediated by texts that is not a matter of statements alone but of actual ongoing practices and sites of practices (see below, *The Archaelogy of Knowledge*). "Texts are the medium of a knowledge that is a property of organization rather than of individual" (p. 212). Her central claim is that "(w)e are ruled by forms of organization vested in and mediated by texts and documents, and constituted externally to particular individuals and their personal and familial relationships" (p. 3).

Besides the women's movement, another important source for Smith (1987, 1990) is Marx and Engels, particularly their *The German Ideology* (1848, 1947, 1970). Smith credits Marx, in particular, as offering her another way to conceive of ideology. She discovered Marx was not doing with 'ideology' what established sociology was doing. Marx was struggling to connect up concepts and theories with the actualities of people's lives. He treated ideology as practices or methods of reasoning, not as meaning, sense, or signification. To think ideologically, as established sociology defined 'ideology,' is to think at a conceptual level divorced from the ground, the actual ordering of what living people do. Marx is Smith's (1990) source for defining ideology as "practices that design how actualities are inscribed in the texts of sociological discourse" (p. 35). As Smith strives for a sociology that exists only in particular people's activities in definite places and times, she finds Marx's 'ideology' helps move us back to a lower level of legitimation, back to experiences.

Given that we, women, live in a world mediated by texts that describe us as 'other,' Smith (1987) advises that we have to begin from a site outside and prior to institutional rulings mediated by texts. We need to learn how to do research differently, how to inquire from the standpoint of women. According to Smith (1987), a feminist sociology does not mean a sociology exclusively for women, it means a sociology that addresses society and social relations from the standpoint of women situated *outside* the relations of ruling. The standpoint of women is the world of the actual, the practical, everyday/everynight world. We begin where we are in the world, treating this everyday world as problematic. It is necessarily local, and historical. Smith does not treat the actual, everyday world as if it was a phenomenon. Phenomenons are treated as objects of sociological inquiry and are isolated. She treats the everyday world as problematic, which means to constitute the everyday world as that in which questions arise. Because people's activities are prior to any conceptual expression, they can function as problematic for concepts we take for granted which shape our lives. Yet, the everyday world is not fully understandable to us within its own scope. We are not fully aware of our everyday activities.

Smith (1987) does not want to just add women's experiences to sociology and stir, or just be critical, she wants to change the field of discipline. She wants to preserve the subject as active and competent, as the knower of inquiry, the knower to whom our texts should speak (p. 142). Beginning from the subjects, from their experiences, safeguards the presence of the subject and their differences. It allows for multiple perspectives. And, it reminds us that the sociologist is also, already, always a situated insider whose only route to a faithful telling is to commit herself to a method of inquiry that is allegiant to the actualities of the world and does not let the categories and concepts of ideologies substitute for actual relations, practices, processes, and forms of practical knowledge. Smith wants sociology to be able to play the role of "continually opening up." With her studies on single parenting, and mother-child-school partnerships, she describes "methods of inquiry *and of writing sociology* that organize the relation between the text and those of whom the text speaks as 'cosubjects' in a world we make—and destroy—together" (p. 141, emphasis in original).

Dorothy Smith makes a significant contribution to sociological theory by analyzing its androcentric bias and critiquing its reified methodology. She reminds us very powerfully that our world is socially constructed and it can be remade. She helps us understand the harmful effects of finding yourself *not* reflected in the dominant theories, and she points to the need to find validation by some community in order to thrive at an individual level. The women's movement served as Smith's community which was able to give her the loving attention and affirmation a caring community gives, so that she was able to feel healthy and whole, and find a way to critique the socially constructed sociological "reality" that surrounded her. Other minorities, such as people who are deaf, homosexual, or hold particular religious views, form Deaf communities, Gay communities, or Amish communities that become their cultural base of support, where they can find themselves reflected in the group as one of the norms instead of being a stranger, and they can feel cared for and valued. With that kind of support, an individual can thrive and gain a critical perspective on the "norm." Without it we are silenced, shunned, and we feel unhealthy, crazy, criminal, even suicidal.

It is ironic that, in reading Smith's work, the reader will discover her language is very academic and abstract, quite a contrast from the proposals for sociology she makes. At times she lets her voice be heard, as the researcher, but not often. When her personal voice is heard, the details of her actuality are not shared with the reader. She peeks out from within the protection of her text, only to disappear into it again. So, on the one hand, one of her main criticisms of sociology is its assumption of a privileged standpoint for the external observer, yet on the other hand she lets her voice become a privileged voice as well. She tells us she studies single parenting partly due to her own experiences as a single parent, and yet there is very little the reader learns about her actual, everyday experiences as a single parent to help make her very abstract ideas more concrete and contextualized. We found, above, that Smith (1990) calls on her experience in therapy to help credit her work in sociological psychiatry in *The Conceptual Practice of Power*, yet she does not share that experience with the reader. There is a performance contradiction between Smith's recommendations for sociology and her own writing style, for she encourages sociologists to expose their perspectives as well as maintain the presence of the subject so that the two are co-authors, and yet she only discloses a few spartan pieces of information about herself, preferring to allow her voice to remain abstract and hidden. As a philosopher, I struggle with being vulnerable to the same criticism.

Smith is critical of Foucault's theory as being part of "the law of the father," while at the same time relying on his concept of 'discourse,' yet, she is forgiving of Marx's androcentric perspective, given her reliance on his concept of 'ideology.' She forgives Marx even though she is aware of other feminists' criticisms of Marx's theory as representing "the law of the father" as well. With Smith's argument that the male standpoint has come to represent the general, and women have historically been excluded from an education and the chance to contribute to theory development, we can assume *any* scholar she would have found as a resource would represent "the law of the father," including Marx and Foucault. Again we find inconsistencies in her project.

A final tension I want to point to in Smith's work has to do with her arguments for the value of local and particular subjectivity, and her fear of the relativism to which this might lead. She recognizes the importance of representing multiple perspectives, yet worries about being able to speak with confidence, "truthfully and faithfully." She wants us to take seriously the qualitatively unique, individual perspectives "we" represent, yet at the same time Smith speaks repeatedly about "women's experiences" without seriously addressing racial and ethnic differences, for example (she does talk about class some). The result of this contradictary practice is that Smith generalizes women's experiences, and whitewashes out their distinctive differences, a common criticism that has been placed on middle class, White, educated feminists by Chicana, Black, Indigenous, Third World, and lesbian women, for example. Also, her suggested methodology for the sociologist and her subject is all the assurance she will ever find as a researcher, and all she should need in order to be able to speak with confidence. Anything more than the qualified relativism her transformed sociology offers steps beyond the boundaries she has so carefully defined and defended, and risks becoming essentializing.

Michel Foucault's work also contributes to our understanding of the legitimization process and its validating as well as destructive qualities. His project is very similar to Berger and Luckmann's, and Smith's, applied to history instead of sociology. He wants us to see that unities we take for granted are socially constructed. Foucault employs a method of historical analysis to help uncover the principles and consequences of a transformation taking place in the field of historical knowledge. He calls this method *archaeology*. He looks at the phenomena of rupture, of discontinuity, rather than stable structures, unities. He attempts to diversify the theme of continuity and restore specificity of occurrence. He analyzes rarities, rather than searching for totalities.

150   Relational "(e)pistemologies"

In *The Archaeology of Knowledge* (1971, 1972), Foucault claims that his archaeological analysis is different from the history of ideas in four ways: the attribution of innovation, the analysis of contradictions, comparative descriptions, and the mapping of transformations. Archaeology describes spaces of dissention. The comparisons are always limited, regional, and they are not intended to reduce diversity. Archaeology's aim is not to overcome differences but to analyze them, to differentiate them. In order to analyze changes (ruptures), which are always discontinuities, we must analyze transformations.

Thus we find in *The Archaeology of Knowledge* (1971, 1972), Foucault attempts to be an archivist trying to describe the relations between statements, which are prior to concepts. He looks for the conditions necessary for an appearance of an object of discourse, and he explores the strategies for how concepts are changed. He discovers discourse involves a system of real or primary relations, reflective or secondary relations, and discursive relations. He then looks at statements, which appear to be the atoms of discourse. His purpose in applying an archaelogical analysis is to describe discourses themselves, not the thoughts in discourse. His analysis is not interpretative; it is specific, differential analysis. It is the systematic description of a discourse-object. Its purpose is to maintain discourse in all its many irregularities.

In *The Birth of the Clinic* (1973) and *Madness and Civilization* (1965, 1967) Foucault applies his archaeological methodology to a study of the history of medicine, hospitals, and asylums from the 17th century to the present. In *Discipline and Punishment* (1977, 1979), Foucault becomes a cartographer diagramming penal law and the history of prisons, then *The History of Sexuality* (1978, 1984), and later still he becomes a topographer, mapping out the terrain of thought in *The Use of Pleasure* (1985, 1986). In all this work, Foucault helps us become more aware of the social construction of reality as he develops a new conception of power. For Foucault, power is a relation that is part of the social situation. Power is a strategy that is exercised. It is the set of possible relations between forces. It is not a property or privilege that can be possessed. It has no essence. Nor is it homogeneous, but rather it can only be defined by the particular points through which it passes (Deleuze, 1988, pp. 25, 27). Power is the thought of the outside. Each of Foucault's topics represent different sites of power, that have changed dramatically over time, and have tremendous effects on people's lives. To be labeled sick, insane, or a criminal is to be labeled an outsider. By exploring these ruptures, and their changes and transformations in society, Foucault exposes their power relations. He helps us understand their discontinuities and he localizes them within specific occurrences.

Of course, Foucault also experiences policing actions to his work for it presents an alternative symbolic universe that challenges Modernity. He suffers less from the charge of irrationality and contradiction that Rorty receives, and more from charges of incoherence, and extreme density, due to the meticulous detail he applies to his work. He is said to offer no social hope, and to show no human feelings (Rorty,

1996). Feminists wonder about his neglect of gender in his analysis. However, at the same time Foucault has become an important source for others who want to analyze power relations in a socially constructed reality.[7]

Conclusion

Recall that Berger and Luckmann (1966) suggest the analysis of the reification tendency of theoretical thought in general, and sociological thought in particular is so important as a way of correcting reification. Smith, and Foucault serve as examples of the important role analysis plays in effecting changes in our socially constructed universe. Still, in the end, it is our daily actions that change things, our regular resistant work that withstands oppression and opens up choices and new possibilities. The theorists in this chapter serve as change-agents in helping us understand that our world is of someone's making rather than given. They serve in a consciousness-raising capacity, and encourage us not to take our society for granted. They offer us comparisons and contrasts, so that we can begin to gain an outsider perspective and be better able to critique what we mistook for "reality." In particular, the theorists in this last section work hard to help us reinterpret our history so that voices that were not allowed to contribute to the conversation and be a part of the history are now included. I sincerely hope that this text contributes to their transformative efforts, as I work to redescribe (e)pistemology in a nontranscendent and relational manner.

Chapter 4 seeks to dissolve the private/public split from the private angle of personal relations, and Chapter 5 dissipates this bifurcation from the public angle of social relations. Together, the two chapters argue that there is a dialectic between social reality and individual existence. Individuals exist in relation to others, at an intimate level, as well as at a generalized level. There is a direct relation between our individual subjectivity and our general sociality, for personal relations are embedded and embodied within larger social contexts. We develop our individual voices from within a society that teaches us what is "reality" as they have socially constructed it. And, we learn to gain a critical perspective on that "reality" with the help of others as well. Others support and validate us as individuals, and also remain as strangers to us, due to their otherness. With the use of imagination, and other tools available to us, such as our emotions, intuition, and reason, we are able to try to take the viewpoint of the other, and better understand ourselves as a result. Others reflect our selves to us, and they enlarge our view. Yet they also inhibit our view, for they only reflect their partial, limited, locally situated perspectives. Others socially validate us as well as threaten to socially determine us. And we, as others, stimulate changes in our society. We, as individuals, are shaped by our social communities due to our immaturity, yet our immaturity also makes us flexible and open to changes, thus stimulating our more mature community members, as habituated selves, to change. The relationship between individuals and others is a transactional relationship relying on a both/and logic that describes individuals affecting their social groups and social groups affecting their individuals, for we are all selves-in-relation-with-others. I have argued that there is a dialectic relation between individuals and others. In Chapter 6 I turn to philosophies outside of the Euro-western traditions to help me further explore relational theories of knowing.

CHAPTER 6

W/holistic Relations

With this chapter I shift our focus beyond the boundaries of Euro-western thinking, to include Eastern and Indigenous thinking, in particular Buddhist and Native American views.[1] We have learned that the best way to become aware of our own socially constructed "reality" and what we count as "knowledge" is to listen to others' voices that are outsiders to our own views. So far I mainly have presented outsider views that are within Euro-western boundaries with my discussion of pragmatism, feminism, and postmodernism in order to help me develop a relational theory of knowing in contrast to individualistic theories. Now I step outside of Euro-western boundaries, and by doing so I become an outsider to their views.

I am very humbled by the task of trying to represent some of these views fairly and generously, knowing that I am an outsider who cannot claim fluency and expertise in these views. I feel this way even though I have spent much time studying Buddhist and Native American views. The more I learn the more I realize I have yet to learn. These views, which Euro-westerners consider 'alternative views,' have a tremendous history (2,500 years for Buddhism, thousands of years more for Native Americans) and a great depth and breadth of scholarship applied to them. They are complex and diverse and no scholar can claim expertise in all areas of Buddhism or Native American views. I know enough about Buddhism and Native American views to know that it is very difficult to represent them and discuss them in a theoretical way, binding them to an English language that is fundamentally dualistic and seeks to distinguish and classify, when they seek to bring together what the English language keeps trying to pull apart. Both Buddhist and Native American beliefs are spiritual-material beliefs that are best understood through the daily practice of living them. For me to try to explain them and theorize about them risks taking the life out of them, even though it may give them greater legitimation status for Euro-western scholars. For all of these reasons, I must begin by reminding the reader of my location as an Euro-westerner exploring views to which I am an outsider. I apologize now for my lack of insider knowledge or expertise, while at the same time knowing that this is not a simple insider/outsider problem. No scholar has a perfect view into the lives of others, regardless of cultural and historical affiliations. I take heart in knowing the ideas I present here are powerful enough to stand on their own, without help from me and regardless of the harm I may unwittingly cause them.

It is very striking to me to realize that when we step outside of Euro-western thinking, we find ourselves in a world that mainly describes knowers in relation to the known, and represents a variety of relational (e)pistemologies. I have already been very selective to limit my discussion to Buddhist and Native American views, and I will have to be even more selective in my presentation of particular Buddhist and Native American views in order to stay within a one-chapter boundary. Some of the ideas discussed here will spill into the next chapter, for Buddhists and Native Americans have holistic views that include nature, and they could be described as ecological views as well. Separating these views from the next chapter's is an artificial boundary that we will find is very porous. Like the personal relations and social relations chapters, these next two chapters work in a dialectic relation together.

In this chapter I have chosen to present particular representatives of Buddhism and Native American philosophy who are highly respected and commonly cited sources among scholars in these fields of study. I will consider Mahāyāna Buddhism, in particular Tibetan Mahāyāna Buddhism as presented by Chögyam Trungpa, Japanese Mahāyāna Buddhism as presented by Daisaku Ikeda, and Zen Mahāyāna Buddhism as presented by Shunryu Suzuki. Others will help me along the way. For the Native American section, I will consider Navajo philosophy as presented by James McNeley and John Farella, and Mabel MaKay's Pomo Indian insights as presented by her student, Gary Sarris. Others will contribute to that discussion as well. As a feminist, it is striking to notice that the vast majority of Buddhist scholars I have reference to are men, whereas many of the Native American scholars are women. In fact, in the *Ajitasena Sūtra* the message is clear: the old beggar woman is told she will not be born in the future as a woman or a pauper, so that she can realize her status as a Bodhisattva (a person who works to achieve enlightenment for the benefit of all sentient beings). Historically, Buddhists have believed that it is necessary that a female becomes a male before she can be enlightened. Wise women and girls are traditionally given the role of interlocutors of the Buddha, but the religion that teaches nonduality and emphasizes the need to rid ourselves of false, relative concepts we create in our minds, has historically embraced a gendered model that disfavors females in favor of males. While this gender bias seems to be changing, it has done so very slowly.

In contrast, there are numerous examples of women as wise spiritual leaders in Native American tribes, such as Mabel McKay (Sarris, 1993, 1994), Essie Parrish (Sarris, 1993, 1994), Paula Gunn Allen (1986), and Beverly Hungry Wolf's grandmothers, including her adopted mother, Paula Weasel Head (Wolf, 1980).

Women's role in spiritual/material development of their people dates back to origination stories. For example, in Navajo philosophy gender is a highly valued construct used to describe our origins, with First Man and First Woman, as well as help to maintain central philosophical ideas, such as the importance of encouraging growth, change, and readaptation, with First Man and First Woman's daughter/granddaughter, Changing Woman. As a Laguna Pueblo/Sioux, Paula Gunn Allen (1986) makes the argument "that for millennia American Indians have based their social systems, however diverse, on ritual, spirit-centered, woman-focused worldviews" and she connects the more recent Euro-western physical and cultural genocide of North American Indian tribes to a patriarchal fear of gynocracy (pp. 2–3).

Buddhists tell stories, or *sūtras* to illustrate an idea and make a point (in Zen Buddhism, they tell *koans*). The *sūtras* are "read" by chanting aloud, and they are intended to be mnemonic devises that provide the scaffolding for their beliefs. The meanings of the *sūtras* have changed over time. Deep philosophical analysis is not offered because Buddhists believe that concepts do not lead us to wisdom; instead they delude us and distract us from enlightenment. Buddhists also rely on meditation to help them spiritually develop, for meditation cuts through our conceptual delusions. Native Americans also rely on stories and the use of metaphor to teach a lesson. Their practice includes chanting, singing, dancing, and basket-weaving, as well as the use of sweat lodges and herbal or plant stimulants to cleanse the body-mind. These styles of relating ideas will affect my style of writing, for I will try to maintain some of the flavor of the traditions to help me represent the ideas as generously as I can, as I rely on caring reasoning to help me.

In describing a relational knowing that relies on a unifying logic rather than a binary or triadic logic, I am dissolving dualities created in Euro-western philosophy such as the mind/body, subject/object, knower/known. This unifying logic does not mean that the universe is one, and there is no room for plurality and diversity. The nondualistic universe I describe is a fluxual, open universe that has infinite possibilities for making connections and transactions, as it is not based on "real existents" that are external, permanent, and independent of human thought. Rather, the universe is a unity in the sense that James (1912/1976) describes it, as "primal stuff" or "pure experience," or we will find in this chapter, as Buddhists describe it as "big Mind," "beginner Mind," or *prajñā*, and Native Americans describe as Spirit, Dreams, the Sacred Hoop, and Holy Wind, pure experience beyond differentiation.

First we have immediate experience, the mere *thatness* of experience. Then we create concepts to try to give meaning to our experiences. Concepts function to try to shape, organize, and describe this open, flowing universe, while the universe continually escapes beyond our artificial boundaries, like a fishing net trying to scope up the ocean's waters, catching some of the ocean life while much falls through and back into the ocean. Concepts need to be understood as an addition to pure experience; they cannot take away from pure experience. They can bring meaning and continuity to our universe, but they also distract, deceive, and confuse us, so that we no longer notice discontinuities and what our concepts do not catch up in their net. We become "out of tune" with our awareness of what is primal stuff. All concepts are limiting for they are unable to penetrate and capture the flux and depth of pure experience; they serve to fix the universe in a particular way, into a particular description. The use of techniques such as meditation, prayer, singing, and chanting help us become more "in tune" with the universe, to "dive back into the flux itself," and listen to the spirits (attunement is a Buddhist concept, the second is James, the third is Native American). These techniques serve to help remind us that thoughts deal only with a small part of the universe: no thought includes everything. They help remind us that not only are knowers in relation with each other, as personally connected at a micro level and socially connected at a macro level, but that these relations are plurally related to the whole of a universe that is loosely connected and nonrational.

Nonduality

I begin the discussion of Buddhist ideas by considering what nonduality means. In his book, *Nonduality: A study of comparative philosophy*, David Loy (1988) tells us, "(n)o concept is more important in Asian philosophical and religious thought than *nonduality* (Sanskrit *advaya* and *advaita*, Tibetan *gÑis-med*, Chinese *pu-erh*, Japanese *fun-ni*), and none is more ambiguous" (p. 17). Loy explores this very ambiguous concept and the variety of ways it is used. Nonduality is used to mean "the negation of dualistic thinking, the nonplurality of the world, and the nondifference of subject and object" (the third meaning is what he focuses on), as well as "the identity of phenomena and Absolute, or the Mahāyāna equation of *samsara* and *nirvana*, which can also be expressed as 'the nonduality of duality and nonduality,'... and "the possibility of a mystical unity between God and (people)" (Loy, 1988, p. 17). We have already encountered individual mystical unity with God in Weil's and Buber's work in Chapter 4. We will encounter these other examples of nonduality in the doctrines of Mahāyāna Buddhism discussed below. There are connections between these different uses of nonduality, they overlap and relate to each other, for Buddhists suggest that "it is because of our dualistic ways of thinking that we perceive the world pluralistically" (meaning in parts instead of as a whole), and we mistakenly think there is a self that is distinct from what is perceived (Loy, 1988, p. 25). As extraordinary and counterintuitive as this concept of nonduality may be, it is the basis for many Eastern views, and of some Euro-western views.

Loy (1988) points to Plotinus, Spinoza, Schelling, Hegel, Schopenhauer, Bergson, and Whitehead from the past, and more recently Nietzsche, Heidegger, and perhaps Wittgenstein, as a few examples of nondualistic thinkers in Euro-western philosophy (p. 1). I point to William James's radical empiricism in Chapter 2 and John Dewey's theory of transaction in Chapter 5 as examples of Euro-western philosophers who describe a unifying logic. Loy acknowledges that the seeds of nonduality have never found fertile ground in the Euro-west because it is too contrary to Plato's and Aristotle's dualistic metaphysical influence which has taken such a strong hold and sprouted into modern science and technology. Interestingly enough, we will find in Chapter 8 many examples to support the claim that currently science is moving in a nondualistic direction.

In the East the seeds of nonduality found very fertile ground and have sprouted into a variety of philosophical views that have been very influential, especially Buddhism, Vedānta, and Taoism. It is not the case that these Eastern views deny a dualistic world of everyday experience, it is that they suggest that dualistic world is superficial and relative, and there is another mode of experience that is deeply significant and lasting that is w/holistic. The East does not claim that the nondual nature of reality is revealed to us automatically as intuitive and it cannot be understood conceptually. Nonduality is an experience that is only accessible to those who are willing to follow the necessarily rigorous path to enlightenment, or liberation. The experience of nonduality transcends philosophy and its dualistic ontological and epistemological categories, dissolving, for example, the separation between knowers and the known. Nonduality is not supported by argumentation, but by our own actual experiences or the testimony of others' experiences whom we trust and accept. By realizing our nonduality with the world, we overcome the delusions of dualistic views and end our suffering and alienation caused by these delusions. Of the Eastern views Loy (1988) discusses, I want to look at Mahāyāna Buddhism.

Paul Williams (1989) is an excellent source for the doctrinal foundations of Mahāyāna Buddhism, as well as the historical context within which Mahāyāna Buddhism developed. Williams helps us understand the impossibility of the task of claiming expertise in a religion that has: over 2,500 years of teaching development; no popes, central councils, central leaders or hierarchical structure (Buddha refused to appoint a successor when he died); no attempt to impose a doctrine, let alone a uniform doctrine; a relative flexibility in the rules of the discipline in which adaption is seen as a virtue of the *dharma* (meaning the discipline or Buddhist teachings); and widespread adoption across Central, South, South-east, and East Asia. Buddhism is readily accessible to foreigners for it does not try to compete with or replace other religions, and Buddhists prefer to teach the dharma in local languages. All of this contributes to the diversity of Buddhism, and actually encourages it. Buddhism stresses the importance of appreciating diversity of views and it critiques others as creating an essentialist doctrine if they try to limit the teachings of Buddha. Buddhism is naturally open and flexible.

On top of all the complexity of Buddhism, Mahāyāna Buddhism is not a unitary phenomenon, sect, or school either. Williams (1989) refers to it as "a spiritual movement"

(p. 3). There is a canonical literature, the Mahāyāna *sūtras*, but it is enormous. Mahāyāna Buddhism developed over a number of centuries and this development occurred centuries after Buddha died, and much dharma change and geographic dispersion had already taken place. There's no historical evidence to identify Mahāyāna Buddhism with one particular pre-Mahāyāna school. Buddhism spread along trade routes, most likely, and the Buddhist monks were natural missionaries, as their lives were semi-nomadic. It is rumored that Mahāyāna Buddhism developed under lay influence and involvement, in close relation with the monks. However, Williams seriously doubts this suggestion, mainly because the monks were the teachers of the *sūtras* and they had the time to initiate religious change, while the lay were occupied with survival efforts. The Mahāyāna *sūtras* are clearly the products of monks (Williams, 1989, p. 23). Other non-Mahāyāna Buddhist traditions consider the Mahāyāna *sūtras* to not be the words of Buddha, but rather the work of poets. They take issue with what counts as an authentic spiritual text. However, Mahāyāna Buddhists argue that Buddha described the dharma as whatever leads to enlightenment, whatever is spiritually helpful. To argue that the Mahāyāna *sūtras* are not the word of Buddha is to miss the point of Buddha's teaching.

Mahāyāna is not a rival school of Buddhism; it is possible to be a member of any Buddhist school or tradition and still embrace Mahāyāna (Williams, 1989). Mahāyāna Buddhists were very much in the minority within Indian Buddhism, but this has changed. Today there are mainly two schools of Buddhism: Mahāyāna, meaning the large vehicle, and Hīnāyāna, meaning the small vehicle. Both Tibetan Buddhism and Zen Buddhism come under the broad umbrella of Mahāyāna Buddhism, which is also referred to as Northern Buddhism, in contrast to Southern Buddhism. All Buddhists embrace the dharma of dependent origination (*pratītya samutpāda*), emptiness (*śunyata*), egolessness of self (*anatman*), and Buddha nature (*tathagata-garbha*), which I will discuss below. All Buddhists rely on the canonical texts called "the three baskets" [the *vinaya* (*vinayapitaka*), the *sutra* (*sutrapitaka*), and the *abhidharma* (*abhidharmapitaka*)].

What distinguishes Mahāyāna Buddhism from other schools of Buddhism is the idea that the Bodhisattva path is the ultimate aspiration for all (Williams, 1989, p. 25). Rather than attaining self-enlightenment to Buddhahood by renouncing the world and becoming a monk, Mahāyāna Buddhists are committed to helping all sentient beings (experiencing feeling or sensation) attain Buddhahood (full enlightenment). Contrary to popular myth, it is not the case that Bodhisattvas (enlightened ones) refuse to achieve full enlightenment, Buddhahood, until all others have attained this goal. That would deny the value of becoming a Buddha. Rather, Mahāyāna Buddhists reject other nirvanas for the full nirvana of Buddha, and the full nirvana of Buddha is obtained by following the Bodhisattva path (Williams, 1989, pp. 53–54; Trungpa, 1973, pp. 106–124). As Bodhisattvas, they take a vow to have concern for the welfare of all beings, not just a specific group or themselves, and this compassion for others causes them to be politically and socially actively involved in the world, rather than removed from their surroundings. Within this context, lay people gain in importance. Deep spiritual compassion for all sentient beings seems to be a common characteristic of Mahāyāna Buddhists.

I turn now to a basic description of each of the basic teachings common to all Buddhists, as well as a further exploration of the Mahāyāna Buddhist development of the concept of compassion. As I broach these different tenets, I will also present common misunderstandings and criticisms of Buddhist views, and how Buddhists respond to these criticisms.

The Dharma of Dependent Co-origination (Pratītya Samutpāda or Paticca Samuppāda)

A fundamental belief of all Buddhists is the dharma of dependent co-origination, or co-arising *(pratītya samutpāda)*, a teaching "that all things exist because of their relations with other things" (Ikeda in Galtung and Ikeda, 1995, p. 31). For Buddhists, the world of phenomena or appearances, and this includes the self, is a relative world empty of inherent existence. Appearances come into being through dependent co-origination, and they are neither existent nor non-existent. We perceive and behave as though things were existent in their own right, therefore casually independent and thus permanent. But this perception of permanence is what leads to our suffering due to our ignorance. Beyond this relative world of appearances there is the Truth that all beings arise only in interdependence, a dependent co-arising. "(E)verything arises through mutual conditioning in reciprocal interaction" (Macy, 1991, xi). Buddhists see a unity of relative truth and ultimate Truth that is free from the dogmatic extremes of nihilism, belief in the nonexistence of phenomena, and eternalism, belief in lasting and True existence (Kongtrül, 1992). They believe nothing can exist in absolute independence of other things or arise on its own accord. All things are connected and interlinked, all things are interdependent. Their view represents the middle way between existence and nonexistence, between pain and pleasure, between eternity and annihilation. It is a dharma of mutual causality (Macy, 1991).

Because Buddhists believe in the interconnectedness of all things, they believe in compassionate caring for life in all life's forms (which includes nature). Buddhists consider nature and people to be interrelated, and they teach that the relationship between people and nature is not one of opposition but of mutual dependence. They are not monotheists, and they argue that monotheism has dispelled the original respect and awe people use to have for their environment. Monotheists no longer consider the environment divine, only God is divine (Toynbee and Ikeda, 1989). Buddhists argue "that we cannot be satisfied with any religion that elevates a God above his creation without seeing the Infinite in all things. If spirit is anything other than the true nature of this world, then the world is devalued, and we too insofar as we are of it" (Loy, 1988, p. 303).

All Buddhists embrace the four Noble Truths: the truth of suffering, the origin of suffering, the cessation of suffering, and the path to the cessation of suffering. The path to the cessation of suffering is the Eightfold Path: right view, right thinking, right speech, right action, right way of life, right endeavor, right mindfulness, and right meditation. The four Noble Truths are often misinterpreted as being fatalistic, due to their focus on suffering, and Buddhism in general is perceived as pessimistic and defeatist. However, all sects of Buddhism agree we must begin by seeing the experience of life as it is, birth, aging, illness, and death, all perceived as suffering. Buddhists consider their realism to be hopeful and joyful for they know how to end suffering. They believe that "the cause of suffering is delusion; eliminating delusion is eliminating suffering; and the way to eliminate delusion is set forth in the Eightfold Righteous Path of conduct" (Galtung and Ikeda, 1995, pp. 86–87). Eliminating suffering leads to exhilaration and liberation.

The Dharma of Emptiness (S̀sünyata)

All Buddhists believe that appearances arise from the mind, what Suzuki (1970) calls "big mind" or "mind-only" or "essence of mind" or oneness. Our original mind is empty, a ready mind, a nondualistic mind, with no thought of achievement and no thought of self. It is the beginner's mind, the mind of compassion which is boundless (Suzuki, 1970, p. 22). We are free from extremes when we realize that emptiness and dependent co-origination are one and do not contradict each other. "This thingness of things as they are is what is called 'emptiness,' s̀ünyata, the actual isness quality of things" (Trunga, 1978, p. 37, my italics). The mind is empty *and* luminous, meaning unobstructed. It is nonthought, nonconcept, the state of unity. David Loy (1988) helps us further understand the concept of s̀ünyata: S̀ü "means 'to swell' in two senses: hollow or empty, and also full, like the womb of a pregnant woman. Both are implied in the Mahāyāna usage: the first denies any fixed self-nature to anything, the second implies that this is also fullness and limitless possibility, for lack of any fixed characteristics allows the infinite diversity of impermanent phenomena" (p. 50). Our English translation only captures the first sense, empty, and it misses the fullness sense of s̀ünyata: S̀ünyata means that the true nature of the world is empty of all description and predication, and entails the nonexistence of any self-sustaining object "behind" a percept (Loy, 1988, p. 51).

Not only is the mind empty and full, the mind is also the basis for confusion (*samsara*), for all appearances, phenomena, arise from the mind. Phenomena do not really exist as independent, permanently existing objects. Objects are merely mental images, projections of the mind, which identifies them as one thing or another

(Kongtrül, 1992, p. 72). The mind is the basis for confusion (samsara) and liberation, enlightenment (nirvana) (Kongtrül, 1992, p. 22). Achieving enlightenment means recognizing one's own mind. This is difficult to do and takes time, because of the habits and patterns we have developed that we need to get rid of, the concepts we have invented such as I/other, body/mind, good/bad, which represent our socially constructed reality. Buddhism explains that people are fundamentally responsible for their own fate, for they are the inventors of appearances and they can dispel what they invent.

All sects of Buddhism practice meditation, as a way to help people dispel what they have invented. Meditation is inner-dialogue, whereas conversation with others is outer-dialogue (Ikeda in Galtung and Ikeda, 1995). Meditation helps us be realistic and acknowledge that we are fools. Meditation is meant to create a space where we can expose and undo our socially constructed reality. Meditation is necessary to help us get rid of our habits. It is a space for doing nothing. It requires mindfulness and awareness. Mindfulness is like a microscope, clearly and precisely presenting what is there, and awareness is seeing the discovery of mindfulness. They work together to help cut through our thoughts and accept living situations as they are. The idea is to be present, right here, now. Nothing new is created, nothing is changed, nothing is judged. There is no arising or achievement of anything. There is no special technique and no particular goal. Meditators just try to be mindful of what is happening. They try to be composed and aware. Most Buddhists sit in a lotus position to meditate, and try to become aware of their bodily movements, especially their breathing. Many chant or recite a memorized song. But once a person has developed the habit of meditating, meditation can be practiced throughout one's day, in one's daily practice. Buddhists aim to see things as they are, to develop "transcendental common sense," with the help of meditation (Trungpa, 1988, p. 5).

People misunderstand that renouncing samsara means giving up everything. From a Buddhist perspective: "What renunciation really means is developing the certainty that the conditioned world of samsara is devoid of true value, . . . that everything is transitory" (Kongtrül, 1992, p. 43). People also mistakenly perceive Buddhism's emphasis on meditative techniques as resulting in an anti-intellectualism view. Buddhism is perceived as being limited to fruitless, passive meditation that becomes ritualistic. According to Buddhists, however, mediation is our vehicle to nondual thinking, and the nondual intellect is our most creative faculty. They point to many examples of writers, artists, musicians, and even scientists who describe their original inspirations as not being theirs. The idea just came to them, whole, with no sense of a directing ego. These creative people talk about trying not to direct their thoughts, but just letting them arise spontaneously and independently, trying to let their mind go and lose itself, and then nondualistic thinking comes, original thoughts, or what Loy (1988) describes as "genius."

Relational "(e)pistemologies"

The Dharma of Egolessness of Self (Anatman)

All Buddhists believe that the first step toward developing transcendental common sense is the surrendering of the ego, ceasing to believe in the existence of a persistent, continuously existing, single, independent part of ourselves. We/I must become the lowest of the low, a grain of sand, simple, with no expectations (Trungpa, 1988, p. 9). Buddhists believe there is no eternal and unchanging substance in the ego (Toynbee and Ikeda, 1989, p. 335). All phenomena, including the self, come into and go out of being as a consequence of mutual dependence. The term 'self' signifies a relation rather than an entity. Our ignorance stems from our efforts to fixate on the self as a subject/object. We want to believe that our self is continuous, solid, and permanent, instead of impermanent and constantly changing. The continuous vicious cycle of confirmation of existence is called *samsara*, meaning continual circle, ocean of confusion. Recall that *samsara*, confusion, is quite interdependent with *nirvana*. "If there were no confusion, there would be no wisdom" (Trungpa, 1988, p. 68). The concept *tat tvam asi* (thou art that), a belief that the essence of the individual self is identical with ultimate spiritual reality, is a concept central to both Buddhism and Hinduism. The dharma of impermanence, emptiness, and the non-substantiality of the self is the way to enlightenment.[2]

The paradox about the self is that our consciousness of the universal self, and access to it, is through the individual self, yet the individual self also leads us in revolt against the universal self. What distinguishes Mahāyāna Buddhism from Hīnāyāna Buddhism has to do more with the focus of their practice then their basic beliefs. Southern Buddhists, Hīnāyāna Buddhists, believe the path we follow to enlightenment should be one where all individual desire is extinguished. Hīnāyāna Buddhism seeks complete psychological detachment, destruction of the individual self to effect ultimate communion, similar to Simone Weil's (1977) approach to try to establish a personal relation with God (see Chapter 4). Hīnāyāna Buddhism tries to merge the individual self with the universal self by rejecting and destroying the individual self (Ikeda, in Toynbee and Ikeda, 1989, pp. 295-296).

Northern Buddhists, Mahāyāna Buddhists, do not advocate the extinction of all desire or the destruction of the self. They seek to master the individual self, but not by extinction, instead by reorientation. They teach that entering into nirvana is to enter into limitless compassion, not a void. Desire can be overcome by changing greedy desire to altruistic desire (Ikeda, in Toynbee and Ikeda, 1989, pp. 295-296, pp. 334-335). The individual self can be expanded through altruistic acts. Northern Buddhists attempt to dedicate themselves totally to compassion, to what we call 'love' (Ikeda, in Toynbee and Ikeda, 1989, p. 346). Mahāyāna Buddhists stress that we master the self and become enlightened by following a path of limitless compassion. They direct love towards all humankind and all other life on earth, based on an unbounded respect for the dignity of life (Toynbee and Ikeda, 1989). Mahāyāna Buddhism shares much in common with Martin Buber's (1955) approach to establishing a personal I/Thou relation with God and Noddings's (1984) caring relations (See Chapter 4).

Zen Buddhists say that their way is both Hināyānistic and Mahāyānistic, they have Hināyāna practice with Mahāyāna spirit, rigid formal practice with informal mind (Suzuki, 1970/1985, pp. 90–91). The goal of Zen Buddhists' practice is to have right practice, and right attitude, which will lead to right understanding. Always, with Zen Buddhism, they come back to their practice. There is a direct, wordless nature to their teaching, as an effort to cut through the trappings of discursive thought. Zen Buddhists sit in the lotus position to meditate, with right posture, to emphasize two and one, mind and body as two sides of the same coin. They breathe, and count their breathing. They concentrate on inhaling and exhaling. "The true purpose is to see things as they are, to observe things as they are, and to let everything go as it goes. This is to put everything under control in its widest sense" (Suzuki, 1970/1985, p. 33). In breathing, Zen Buddhists try to let their throat be like a swinging door that lets the inside out and the outside in. "When we become truly ourselves, we just become a swinging door, and we are purely independent of, and at the same time, dependent upon everything" (Suzuki, 1970/1985, p. 31). After meditating, Zen Buddhists bow to the floor nine times. By bowing, they give up their selves, giving up their dualistic ideas. Bowing helps to eliminate their self-centered ways. Zen Buddhists believe that the practice of Zen is enough, that there is no nirvana outside of their practice. "Zen practice is the direct expression of our true nature" (Suzuki, 1970/1985, p. 47). Suzuki (1970/1985) advises, just practice Zen and don't think about anything else, and our true nature will resume itself.

For a Zen Buddhist (Suzuki, 1970/1985), right attitude means that when we do something we should be very observant, careful, and alert. Zen is concentration on our usual daily routine. Zen advises us to try to remain joyful and calm, constant, ordinary, not excited, for everyday life itself is enlightenment. Zen recommends that we just do whatever it is we are doing, without any effort. Just do it! Hināyāna Buddhism classifies practice in four ways or stages: have no thinking and no curiosity in your practice, have physical and mental joy, have physical joy in your practice, and just do it (Suzuki, 1970/1985, p. 73). Zen practice is for everyone, and everyone has to find their own way of practicing. "The best way is just to practice without saying anything" (Suzuki, 1970/1985, p. 90). In terms of right understanding, Zen is not concerned with philosophical understandings, they emphasize practice. If we practice sincerely, with right effort, our best effort in each moment, we will understand. For Zen, the understanding is the practice itself. Zen tries to help us houseclean our mind, and achieve emptiness in our activity. As we know, emptiness means everything is always there. "No mind" is Zen mind, which includes everything. There is no gap between you and I. "We must have beginner's mind, free from possessing anything, a mind that knows everything is in flowing change" (Suzuki, 1970/1985, p. 138). Zen is stable awareness without a watcher.

People falsely accuse Buddhists of saying we need to do away with all sense-perception. Buddhism does not reject all sense-perception, rather it rejects compound perceptions (*savikalpa*) for "bare" percepts (*nirvikalpa*), which do not provide some knowledge to someone about something (Loy, 1988, p. 50). Buddhism recommends that we should return to the initial stage of perception, prior to conceptual influence. "Bare" perception is nondualistic, where there is no seer to see and nothing to see. It is empty (*śūnyata*). Nondual perception escapes the main problem of Euro-western theories of perception: how can I even have knowledge of things if those things are separate from my mind? Nondual perception is prior to the bifurcation of mind and matter.

Some people criticize Buddhism for embracing a form of tolerance that extends even to the acceptance of political violence, acquiescence of economic structural violences, isolation of the clergy from society, and ingratiation of themselves with authorities promising advantages (Galtung in Galtung and Ikeda, 1995). They think that Buddhism lacks energy to confront social reality. The absence of self can lead to nihilism (Galtung in Galtung and Ikeda, 1995, pp. 79–80). However, as we have found, Hināyāna Buddhism is more isolated, retreating, and stresses more meditaton and being more withdrawn. It is more fatalistic. Zen Buddhism also tends to be more isolating, due to its Hināyāna practice, but it is more compassionate due to its Mahāyāna spirit. Mahāyāna Buddhism focuses its energies outward, on society and its well-being. It stresses the outward external expression of the inner self. It equates Buddha Law with life in actual society and it is free of fatalism.

The Dharma of Compassion, the Buddha Nature (Tathagata-garbha)

Buddhists believe that buddha nature, which can be defined as simply unconditioned awareness of the nature of mind (big Mind), is inherent in the mind of all beings. This unconditioned awareness is our basic nature and it is always already there. It is primordial, it is prior to and so free from all relative reference points. It is not that all sentient beings *have* buddha nature, "it is that 'sentient being' refers to everything, and everything *is* the Buddha-nature" (Williams, 1989, p. 114). Buddha nature transcends conceptual mind. Achieving enlightenment means recognizing one's own mind as unobstructed, perfect emptiness and fullness, already containing all the Buddha qualities (Kongtrül, 1992, p. 80). Buddha nature is inherent in every sentient being and is the most precious of all things (Ikeda, in Galtung and Ikeda, 1995, p. 77). Buddha-nature is not a seed that has to grow; it is already the flower. Beings are already Buddhas, in reality there is nothing to be attained. "The Buddhist faith may be described as a discipline for putting oneself in agreement—establishing life resonance—with the universal Buddha nature" (Ikeda, in Galtung and Ikeda, 1995, p. 75).

This belief in buddha nature causes Mahāyāna Buddhists to have a strong emphasis on nonviolence, and a nonexploitative approach to the natural world, as well as a spirit of compassion free of sophistry (Galtung, in Galtung and Ikeda, 1995, p. 95). Compassion is defined as total openness. It is perfect kindness, which is equated with perfect wisdom *(prajñā)*, a state of consciousness which understands emptiness and fullness (*śūnyata*). Prajñā is pure experience beyond differentiation. It is liberation. Mahāyāna Buddhists believe that if we are one with the world, we cannot be fully enlightened unless all others are as well. Love, compassion, is the way to achieve enlightenment. They teach us that "compassion arises and manifests itself naturally when we have overcome our sense of separation from the world" (Loy, 1988, p. 297).

Ayya Khema (1999), a present-day Buddhist nun, can add to our understanding of compassion. Khema tells us in *Be an Island*, that in order to live skillfully we have to pay attention to others and feel our togetherness (p. 41). We need to learn how to be skillful communicators (right speech), including learning how to be easy to speak to. "This means being ready to give up our own point of view and accept the other person's" (Khema, 1999, p. 47). It does not mean we must not have a view, just that we must be willing to question it. Skillful communicators are good listeners. They listen with total attention.

> Listening means being empty of self-importance and reacting to what we hear with empathy. It is an art and a skill, just as speaking is. It requires really being with the other person. Just listening with total attention to what is being said . . . is part of compassion. It is also loving-kindness (Khema, 1999, p. 48).

Compassionate people, as good communicators, are sparing with their words and deliberate with their speech. They learn to be watchful of others and make sure they offer their words at the right time, "when we are completely calm and the other person is attentive, at ease, and ready to listen" (Khema, 1999, p. 49). They learn to lovingly offer words with the right motivation, which is one of kindness. They also learn to be very watchful of themselves, to check again and again for their own motivations.

Compassion involves learning to accept and love ourselves in a wholesome manner, where we do not blame ourselves or others for our problems, but instead realize that all of us have the same kinds of problems and the same faculties to deal with them. We need to give ourselves loving care, by paying attention to ourselves, being kind, accepting, and forgiving of ourselves. With the help of a good sense of humor, we can learn to recognize our problems, accept them, and then change our lives. Khema reminds us that the heart's real work is to love generously. "The heart is our center" (Khema, 1999, p. 96). If we can learn to relate to ourselves, and be content, satisfied, and grateful, then we can learn to be at peace with ourselves and with others. "Knowing ourselves in a caring and realistic way opens our heart and brings buoyancy to our introspection" (Khema, 1999, p. 56). Khema's description of compassion should remind the reader of Ruddick's (1989) "maternal thinking" and Noddings's (1984) "caring relations." Her description of compassion is like the caring reasoning I described in Chapter 4. If we can use our compassion to recognize we are buddha nature, we will have transcended our conceptual minds, and tuned into the our basic primordial nature, and achieved enlightenment.

I hope it is clear to the reader how entertwined the concepts of dependent co-origination (*pratītya samutpāda*), emptiness (*śūnyata*), egolessness of self (*anatman*), and buddha nature (*tathagata-garbha*) are. It is very difficult to attempt to separate them in order to explain them, for, of course, such an act is contrary to the basic concept of interdependence being presented here. No matter where one starts to tell the story of Buddhism, one is quickly enmeshed in all of these concepts. The effort to explain these four central dharmas demonstrates the very interconnectedness that Buddhism describes. I have attempted to model the relationality of these concepts in my description as well as offer enough individual attention to allow the reader to understand these central Buddhist ideas, which may be foreign and new. Strangest to Euro-western thinking may be the idea of no-self, which we now know is really an idea of no independent, unique, autonomous, separate self, as an entity, in favor of a relational sense of self (or big Mind) that expresses itself in transitory, multifarious ways. When we explain the doctrine of no-self in this manner, the concept begins to sound similar to what some pragmatists, radical feminists, and post-modernists are saying as well (as we found in previous chapters), and we discover that these ideas are not so strange or alternative after all. They have already been finding some form of expression among the Euro-west, with the East serving as a source on inspiration.

Also strange to the Euro-western mind is the doctrine of dependent co-origination. The Euro-west has perceived causality in a linear, uni-directional manner since the days of ancient Greece, when Plato sided with Parmenides and embraced a view of reality as stable, permanent, and unchanging (Plato's Forms), instead of embracing Heraclitus's dynamic view of reality as being in process, always changing (Macy, 1991). In the Euro-west, modern science incorporated this one-way causality model. However, recently a mutual casual paradigm is emerging in Euro-western science; a shift is occurring toward a dynamic, systemic, process view of reality (Macy, 1991). We will discover in Chapter 8 "general systems theory," a scientific interdisciplinary approach (including the areas of philosophy, psychology, political science, ecology, computer science, and organizational management, for example), which relies on an understanding of mutual causality. Words like *synergy, feedback, causal loops, symbiosis* are now becoming part of our language as our thinking is changing dramatically. We will also discover this mutual casual paradigm in Chapter 7's discussion of "deep ecology."

Buddhism certainly models an approach to knowing that is nondualistic, and relies on a unifying logic. Many misunderstand Buddhism to be limiting, nihilistic, anti-intellectual, detached and removed, when actually what it offers is a suggested way for cutting through the misconceptions and delusions we continue to create through our socially constructed reality. It offers us a way to gain a clearer vision of our own embeddedness and to help us find a way to take responsibility for that embeddedness, and change our views. In previous chapters we have learned that outer-dialogue with others helps us gain a perspective on our own limitations; here I have introduced another means of gaining perspective on our own thoughts, inner-dialogue, through meditation (in Chapter 4 Weil used prayer as her form of meditation). Inner-dialogue also helps us become aware of our own concepts and how they shape our views. It is important, though, that meditation does not become a way for us to remove ourselves from society or that we use meditation to delude us into thinking we can become enlightened all by ourselves as solitary knowers. All schools of Buddhism stress that students work with teachers, and even that they meditate in community settings. The different sects vary on how they perceive teachers, the Hīnāyāna view their teacher as a parental figure, the Mahāyānas view their teacher as a spiritual friend (Trungpa, 1988, p. 132), but they do not disagree on the need for others to help us become aware of our own deceptions and ignorance.

Ayya Khema was part of the first generation of Euro-western women teachers of Buddhism. She was born to Jewish parents in Berlin in 1923, and she became an ordained Buddhist nun in Sri Lanka in 1979. She wrote over 25 books on Buddhism, which have been translated into over seven languages, and she founded several Buddhist monasteries in places like Australia and Germany. As an example of her work, *Be an Island* (1999) is based on 24 talks Khema gave concerning one particular Buddhist sutra. Khema became a social activist for the cause of Buddhist nuns, due to the hardships they, and she, experienced as a result of being treated as second-class citizens by many sects of Buddhists who still today embrace male supremacy beliefs. Khema helped found the International Association of Buddhist Women. Ayya Khema died of cancer Nov. 2, 1997, never knowing she received, in 1998, full ordination in the nun's lineage at the Chinese Hsi Lai Temple in Los Angeles. It was the only full ordination available to her, one that was not accepted by her own tradition of Theravada monks, which officially neglected her. Ayya Khema's life work serves as a reminder than even a dharma such as Buddhism that offers hope for taking action to end our delusions, can still have practicing members who clearly continue to struggle with their own delusions, such as the gender bias they vividly demonstrate. Buddhism is an example of a relational approach that offers room for great diversity and flexibility, but it needs people like Ayya Khema to help its followers become aware of their own delusions and open up their hearts even more.

I move on to consider the particular Native American perspectives of Pomos, Navajos, and others, as we continue to explore non-Euro-western descriptions of w/holistic relational theories of knowing. We will find the Pomos and Navajos offer us more examples of nondualistic, connected approaches to knowing based on a unifying logic such as I rely on to describe a relational (e)pistemology.

Great Spirit, Dreams, and Holy Wind

There is tremendous variety in the diverse Native American tribes living in North America. Still, there are some common threads to their diverse views. In general, Native American philosophy is based on a sense of connectedness between individuals and the world around them. They use different organic terms to describe this concept of spiritual w/holeness. Navajos talk about the Holy Wind, the Pomo talk about the Spirit as Dreams, the Keres of Laguna Pueblo talk about the Sacred Hoop, and the Dakota talk about Skan, "the Great Spirit," as they all strive to capture a sense of indispensable interrelatedness. For Native Americans, the world in which we live is considered alive, and we are intimately a part of this life. They do not view themselves as autonomous, separate individuals in the traditional Euro-western classical liberal sense, but rather have contextual, communal views of themselves as individuals-in-relation-with-others (Bredin, 1999). Native Americans do not separate spheres of knowledge into different compartments, as we have done in the Euro-west, rather they describe spheres of knowledge as being integrated and antihierarchical. Thus we find they consistently do not drawn sharp distinctions between science, philosophy, and spirituality, for example (Hytten, 1999). In general, Native American sense of time is non-linear and is more accurately described as cyclical, as co-occurring synchronously, in contrast to the Euro-western linear, causal approach (Farella, 1984). Also of importance, Native American languages are historically oral and it is only in this past century that their languages have been translated into written forms.

Unlike Buddhism, which is translated into a variety of languages and has an enormous canonical literature to aid in understanding the Buddha's teachings, Native American languages are unique to their tribes, not easily translated into English, and rooted in an oral tradition that seeks to maintain the spirituality of their teachings by treating the teachings like special property to be handled with care.[3] Concepts that are central to various Native American tribes, which are learned through oral traditions of stories, songs, chants, and prayers, are considered sacred and are protected from sharing with outsiders, as well as with all insiders. These concepts are often only shared with the most educated within their tribe. Added to the exclusive quality of Native American spirituality is a lack of willingness to share their teachings with Whites in particular, due to their experiences of having White translators treat their ideas as artifacts, as Whites appropriate and reshape the teachings Native Americans have shared. Native Americans' mistrust of Whites is based on the very real fact of colonization, which all Native Americans share in common, across their diversity. All of these factors increase the chances of misunderstanding Native American philosophy. A White scholar, such as myself, attempting to write about Native American philosophy, must be critically aware of my own situatedness, not only as an outsider to the particular cultures, but also as someone from a culture guilty of colonizing them. I also have the problem of speaking a different language that is presented in a different form, which risks changing the meaning of the ideas expressed.

The history of anthropological studies of Native Americans is a history of fieldworkers not respecting their interviewees' world views, and asking them to break taboos (Sarris, 1993). For example, Pomos are very private people who are forbidden to tell Coyote stories in the summer. Yet, anthropological fieldworkers do almost all of their fieldwork in the summer, when it is taboo for these private people to tell stories that explain their philosophies. Native Americans participate in the fieldworkers' interviews in order to earn needed money, but interviews collected in the summer are edited by the Native Americans and shaped in certain ways to adjust for their taboos. They give the fieldworkers what one Pomo woman calls "pieceworks," pieces of this and that, but never the whole picture (Sarris, 1993, p. 105).

Pomo language structure is different from English; Pomos seldom use pronouns and frequently start their sentences with a verb, also using much repetition (Sarris, 1993). They move back and forth in time and place in their narratives, using the past to comment on the present and vice versa (p. 99). They name places as a way to give action in a story a theme, and they use repetition to underscore their theme. Yet, written texts of Pomo stories do not reflect the Pomo language, but instead reflect the structure of the English language. Most autobiographies of Native Americans are actually narrated autobiographies, with the Native American recorded and their language transcribed by a recorder-editor. Sarris (1993) tells us that 83% of the more than 600 published Native American texts are narrated, 43% of these collected by anthropologists and 40% collected by other non-Indians (footnote, p. 84). The recorder-editors rearrange the narratives, changing the structure of the sentences, and adding words judged to be missing. A narrated autobiography of a Native American is actually an account of an account, an interpretative text rather than "facts" as usually presented. Historically the editor remains hidden, absent from the text, and the text is presented as if it is the actual words of the interviewees. Also, the editing work that is done by the recorder-editor is not usually approved by the interviewees, they are not seen and not consulted. "The Indians are absent or they are strategically removed from the territory, made safe, intelligible on the colonizer's terms" (Sarris, 1993, p. 90). Scholars of narrated autobiographies have not historically acknowledged the limits of their work or its consequences, in a historical or political realm (Sarris, 1993, p. 88). They have not taken responsibility for their contribution to the text and made themselves present in the text.

Added to the complexity of the subjectivity of the text is the subjectivity of the reader. Readers are also tied to particular locations, embedded with particular historical and political contexts. "(R)egardless of the reader's cultural and historical affiliations, he or she is not a perfect lens into the life and circumstances of either the non-Indian recorder-editor or the Indian narrator" (Sarris, 1993, p. 91). Sarris (1993) recommends that where the tensions are felt in the text and with the reader, that is the place to start to open up dialogue with the Indian and non-Indian narrator. Such a dialogue needs to validate and respect the subjectivities of text and reader. Texts are representations of interaction and the occasion for interaction. They can help us become aware of the chasms between our different experiences and world views, challenging our assumptions and improving our awareness of ourselves. They can help us expose problems, not solve them.

The Pomos

The problems I point to are poignantly demonstrated with Greg Sarris's (1994) efforts to write Mabel McKay's story, at her request. Mabel knew Greg needed a dissertation topic, and she wanted to help him figure out his own story too so she asked him to write her biography. Sarris was part of Mabel's Dream. Mabel McKay is a Pomo Indian from the Long Valley Cache Creek Pomo tribe. When she was born in 1907 there were only 6 members of her tribe left alive, and when she died in 1993 she was the last member. As a Pomo Dreamer, healer, and basketweaver, Mabel was adopted, when she was in her 40's, into the Kashaya Pomo tribe by her friend and fellow Pomo Dreamer and healer, Essie Parrish. Sarris got to know Mabel when he was a child and a friend of her son, Marshall. He ended up knowing her for over 30 years, recording her stories, and befriending her adopted family, only to find out later that he is in fact directly related to the Parrish family himself. Sarris was adopted as a baby, and discovered as an adult that his natural father was a mixed blood, half Filipino and half Miwok and Pomo Indian. It turns out that his great-great-grandfather was married to Essie Parrish's grandmother.

When Greg Sarris agreed to take on the task of writing Mabel's story, he planned on this as his dissertation. However, Sarris (1993) tells us he ended up writing his dissertation on Indian autobiographies, as he struggled with problems related to being the recorder-editor of Mabel's autobiography (Sarris, 1989). Mabel McKay's autobiography became Sarris's and her story woven together, published in 1994, after Mabel's death, and after Sarris learned what Mabel tried to teach him about storytelling and about life. The learning process for Native Americans tends to be communal, informal, experiential, sacred, and it is grounded in oral traditions and storytelling. Mabel reasserted these tribal practices through her teachings with Sarris (Bredin, 1999). Sarris (1993) escorted Mabel McKay to many of her presentations and talks, and he learned from her a verbal art. Mabel engaged her audience in a dialogue and challenged their assumptions. She forced "her interlocutors to examine presuppositions that shaped and are embedded in their questions" (Sarris, 1993, p. 19). She would not let herself be recorded at invited talks, not wanting to be absent from any discussion of her world. Her talk points to what constitutes difference. She "makes the interlocutor immediately aware of the present context and of the ways the interlocutor may be framing her world, which does not close the discourse but exposes the chasms between two interpretive worlds over which the discourse must continue" (Sarris, 1993, p. 23). Mabel calls for dialogue that interrupts and disrupts preconceived notions. Her talk resists closure.

In his effort to write Mabel's autobiography, Sarris kept trying to order Mabel's stories into a linear fashion, and remove himself from the text, following Euro-western standards about biographies. Mabel told Greg her story had nothing to do with dates, it has to do with the everlasting. Mabel kept trying to implicate Sarris as a listener. Sarris learned that storytelling is an active, respondent activity. Mabel expected him to ask questions, respond, agree, disagree, take up the story in different contexts and innovate and renovate it (Bredin, 1999). Sarris ended up writing her stories as a dialogue between the two of them, a continuing conversation that is the story of his hearing her stories (1993, p. 4). He explains to us that he uses a dialogical methodology to help "expose boundaries that shape and constitute cultural and personal worlds" (1993, p. 4). He learned from Mabel that there are multiple voices in a written text, and they call for reflexivity. Sarris writes in a style that emphasizes a process, an on-going conversation. His writing is a dialogue with the text and the reader, as he collapses the dichotomy between personal narrative and scholarly argument and uses these different methods to communicate with and inform each other (1993, p. 7).

The history of Pomo Indians is devastating (Sarris, 1993). The Pomos are from California, north of San Francisco, and north of the Coast Miwok tribe, which first had contact with Europeans. The Pomo and Miwok tribes in the southern area closest to San Francisco experienced more exposure to disease, enslavement, and cultural disruption then the northern Pomo tribes experienced. Padres forced Miwok and southern Pomo tribes into Spanish missions, and then when the missions were taken over by the Mexicans, the Indian tribes were raided and the people were traded as slaves. The northern Pomo tribes were also enslaved, but by the Russians instead, at Ft. Ross (1812). The Russians did not try to convert the Pomos and they protected them from the Spanish and Mexicans, thus making it possible for them to retain their culture. As a result, today there are many Pomos who still speak their native language, whereas there are no Coast Miwoks who know their native language and none have danced in 50 years. Sarris informs us that by 1900, disease, slave raiding, and starvation had just about wiped out the Pomo and Miwok people. In 1838, smallpox alone killed over 90% of them. Today there are around 1000 Pomos and around 100 of them are permanent residents on the Kashaya Reservation.

The Pomo resisted cultural domination and retained their culture and language. They have continued their traditions of storytelling, dancing, singing, and basket weaving. Yet, due to their oral tradition, there is no record of their pre-contact culture. Around 1871-1872 they revived their culture with the Bole Maru (Dream Dance), also called the Bole Hesi in the east (Sarris, 1994, p. 8). They have had strong leaders who helped them maintain a national pride, and separation from White influence. Their Dreamers were predominantly women who, though not called chiefs, assumed the role of tribal leaders. Annie Jarvis was a leader from 1912-1943, and Essie Parrish was the last Kashaya Pomo Dream leader, from 1943-1979. Mabel McKay, as an adopted Kashaya Pomo Dream leader, helped continue Essie's teachings until her death in 1993. However, the Pomos are currently splintered, due to forces they have experienced since the 1950's. Many Pomos converted to the Mormon and Pentecostal religions, while others maintain the traditional teachings (Sarris, 1993, p. 9-10). While at first the Mormons appeared to be tolerant and accepting of the Pomo traditional teachings, after establishing followers on the reservation, they began to teach the Indian traditions are satanic, devil worshipping, and they encourgaged the Pomos to reject their spiritual leaders, Essie, and Mabel. When Essie died in 1979, her tribe was deeply divided. Essie directed Mabel to close and lock the Roundhouse, which is the Pomo place of traditional ceremonies. It is customary that when a Pomo Dream leader dies, her songs, dances, and materials made by her, given to the people through Spirit's directions and guidance, are no longer used unless the leader gave special permission to do so before her death. The Pomos wait for the arrival of another Dreamer to guide them, and administer to them.

As a young child, Mabel McKay had no one to teach her how to be a leader in her tribe (Sarris, 1994). She was trained directly by the Spirit, who spoke to her in her Dreams. She started having Dreams when she was around three years old. She would sleep restlessly, crying and humming in her sleep, and during the day she would glaze off with long, full stares. Because of the intensity and frequency of her Dreams, Mabel was a tired, fragile, undernourished child. Her immediate family, Sarah Taylor, her grandmother who raised her, understood about Dreams, but Sarah was not a Dreamer, and she often wished she had her brother or Old Taylor to consult and help her with the raising and care for Mabel. Sarah's brother, Richard Taylor, was a Dreamer, as was Sarah's grandfather or great-grandfather, Old Taylor. Richard was the last Dreamer to live at Long Valley Cache Creek, and when he died he was buried in the Roundhouse, and the door was locked. While Sarah understood Mabel's special gift and tried to help her and protect her, most of the rest of her neighboring Indian tribal members were fearful of Mabel. They knew Mabel was different even when she was a child, but they thought she might be poisoned, and would maybe poison their children if they played with her. Mabel grew up feeling isolated from Whites and Native Americans.

Sarah took Mabel to the Wintun reservation in Cortina, and they lived with Sarah's son, Andrew and his wife Rosie. The Wintun had an active Roundhouse and participated in ceremonies and dancing, etc. But staying there did not work, again because people feared Mabel's spiritual power. When Mabel was twelve her mother tried to take her away, but Sarah was able to prevent this by asking the neighboring White lady, Mrs. Spencer, to take Mabel in. Mabel spent the next four years living with a White woman, only seeing her family for two weeks in the fall. She continued to Dream, but was forbidden by Spirit to tell Mrs. Spencer about the Dream work. Mrs. Spencer did get Mabel's physical strength up to the level where she was able to attend school. She attended a White school for only two years, long enough to learn the alphabet, how to write her name, and some basic mathematics. She had a hard time concentrating because she was exhausted from constant Dreaming. She learned she was very different from the other White children, and after two years of school she quit.

Beyond that formal schooling, Mabel's learning was through direct experience, with Spirit as her teacher. Spirit put things to her, taught her about good and bad, and she had to sort them out. Spirit advised her and made predictions to her about things that were going to happen to her. Spirit predicted she would meet Essie Parrish 20 years before she actually did. Spirit told her she would someday teach at colleges and universities. Mabel dialogued with Spirit in her dreams. She asked questions, and sometimes she got answers, sometimes not. Like Mabel's dialogues with Greg Sarris, her conversations with Spirit were interactive and open. Spirit predicted things and guided her, but she had the choice of listening or not. Mabel chose to listen, just as Greg chose to listen to her. To listen with care in order to really understand means trying to believe that which is being said is true. It is what I call *caring reasoning*.

Spirit taught Mabel McKay how to weave beautiful coiled baskets, using willow rod, sedge, and redbud, and how to be a doctor (Sarris, 1994). The baskets were for doctoring, for her patients to help them heal. Spirit fixed Mabel's throat for sucking out diseases. Mabel became a sucking doctor and she would suck out the diseases of her patients and spit them into a particular basket Spirit directed her to make for that purpose. However, Mabel did not begin doctoring until Spirit told her it was time to do so. As a teen-ager, she worked washing lettuce, traveling with a carnival, in a Japanese restaurant in San Francisco, and she met many different people. Then she returned to Sarah Taylor's home, and began to doctor patients, after a final initiation and further instructions from Spirit. She was officially announced and welcomed as a Pomo tribal doctor and patients began to seek her out. When they would come, Mabel would pray and sing, and Spirit would guide her on what to do.

Now Mabel McKay's baskets are on permanent display in the Smithsonian and other museums, for she is a world reknown basket weaver (Sarris, 1994). However, Mabel only made baskets after praying to Spirit and asking for Spirit's guidance.

According to Spirit, each basket has a purpose and a rule, and they need to be cared for, watered and fed and blessed, for they are living. Mabel performed many healing miracles and became a famous medicine woman and spiritual leader. She was asked to speak often at colleges and universities, and other famous spiritual leaders, such as the Pope, sought an audience with her. California Governor Jerry Brown appointed her to the first Indian Heritage Commission. Sarris (1994) tells us, "(h)ers was a life that gave, a life only in the Dream" (p. 164). When she died in 1993 she was buried next to Essie Parrish in the Kashaya Pomo cemetery, the last two Pomo Dreamers. It rained and thundered the day each of them was buried.

Mabel McKay's life, as a mirror of traditional Pomo philosophy, is an example of a life lived by a unifying logic. Throughout her life, Spirit guided her through her Dreams, and she was able to tune in and listen, enabling her to stay aware of pure experience beyond differentiation. Mabel worked for thirty years to get Greg Sarris to let go of the concepts he kept trying to use to shape and order the open, flowing universe she experienced and continued to describe to him. Mabel repeatedly showed Greg what his concepts could not "catch up" in his net, what they missed and let fall through. Her basket weaving, singing, praying, and dancing were all techniques Mabel used to help her become more attuned with primal experience, with Spirit, and stay attuned, as well as expressions of that experience. Her stories and talk, in all their forms, helped to continually remind him, and others, that thoughts deal only with a small part of the universe, no thought includes everything. The story that Greg Sarris shares with us of Mabel McKay's life, and Essie Parrish's, reminds us that not only are knowers in relation with each other, personally and socially, but that these relations are plurally related to the whole of a material-spiritual universe.

Navajo's Holy Wind or Main Stalk

My two sources for Navajo philosophy are dissertations written into published texts, James McNeley's (1981/1997) *Holy Wind in Navajo Philosophy*, which was his dissertation, originally written in 1973, and John Farella's (1984) *The Main Stalk: A Synthesis of Navajo Philosophy*. Farella tells us, "The Navajos are probably the most studied group of people in the world" (p. 3). There are hundreds of volumes devoted to their religion, the formal rituals and symbolism of the Navajos, published in Navajo and English. Father Berard Haile alone spent over 50 years living in the Navajo nation and he took very detailed and precise ethnographic notes. The Navajo have a history of not being very good materialistically but they have been good with ideas, and good at adaption. When they returned home from the "Long Walk" to their lands from Ft. Sumner in 1868, there were 5,000–7,000 Navajos. Today the population is 140,000–175,000, contrary to the Pomo, who currently number around 1,000.

McNeley's (1981/1997) text is based on field interviews with ten Navajo informants, nine of whom spoke only Navajo, six being between the ages of 75–94. Aware of the problems of being a recorder-editor, McNeley sought to preserve and faithfully to present the Navajo point of view (half of his text is a presentation of his informants' native voices, recorded in their own language). He sought out people who were least influenced by Euro-western acculturation. All of his informants lacked any significant formal education in White schools and all lived in the Navajo nation. A Navajo informant is a receiver of a particular variation of the Navajo sacred lore, which is customarily learned from an elder relative or singer with whom one is apprenticed. What the informant learns is not shared commonly with others, but instead is treated like valuable property to be guarded and protected. McNeley's research also involves extensive library research and was aided by his work as a social worker on the Navajo reservation where he later became a teacher. His presentation is based around the Navajo concept of *niłch'i*, which McNeley translates as the Holy Wind.

Farella's (1984) own dissertation work on the Navajos was influenced by McNeley's work, for it caused Farella to realize that what he originally set out to do is considered irrelevant and trivial from a Navajo perspective. Rather than try to hold his study to a rigorous and restrictive methodology which was again going to render lots of details on Navajos but make no sense of the whole philosophy, Farella decided to "open up" his study and turn it into an effort to offer a synthesis of Navajo philosophy, centered around the Navajo concept of 'whole,' *sq'a nagháí bik'e hózhą́*. Farella relied on five primary teachers, four Navajo men and Father Haile's data, and three years of fieldwork in the Navajo nation, for his study. He also made use of the extensive literature available on Navajos.

Both Farella (1984) and McNeley (1981/1997) are aware that Navajos, Dineh, have been studied from outsider's perspectives, with the researcher's methodology used as the measuring stick by which to measure Navajo views. Navajo philosophy has been presented as "religion," "beliefs," of "world views," which are outside of the Euro-western norm. Their ideas are treated as "artifacts." Researchers bring their biases into their reports, as they portray Navajos as fundamentalists, and they translate their views as literal interpretations. Farella and McNeley, in their individual, separate projects, both make a concerted effort to present Navajo philosophy as the way the world is, and to let Navajos critique misrepresentations of their philosophy. Though they approach their work from different angles, in the end, Farella and McNeley together offer an important synthesis of Navajo philosophy, which is why I turn to them in this chapter.

I begin with McNeley's (1981/1997) work because his text preceded Farella's (1984) and contributed to the synthesis Farella offers. McNeley's text is centered around a concept that is not generally described as having a primary role in Navajo philosophy, and is often translated in contradictory, misleading ways. McNeley argues that the Holy Wind, *niłch'i*, is the concept which links the Navajo soul to the immanent powers of the universe and is thus central to Navajo thought. *Niłch'i* has been commonly translated as 'wind,' but McNeley tells us 'wind' is an inadequate translation, for "*niłch'i* refers to the air or atmosphere in its entirety, including such air when in motion, conceived as having a holy quality and powers not acknowledged in [Euro-]Western culture" (p.xviii). Therefore, he uses the term 'Holy Wind.' He cautions us that "traditional Navajos do not conceive of the Wind within one as being immutable or discrete from that existing everywhere," so "the Wind within one" serves better to describe their meaning than the usual translation of "in-standing" or "in-dwelling Wind Soul" (p. xviii). McNeley's central claim is: "Holy Wind gives life, thought, speech, and the power of motion to all living things and serves as the means of communication between all elements of the living world. As such, it is central to Navajo philosophy and world view" (p. 1).

McNeley (1981/1997) begins his explanation of this central, key concept of Holy Wind with the Navajo creation story.[4] A mist, or cloud of light became the source of the Wind, and Wind made life possible, first in the underworlds with the deities (Holy People), by providing a means of breathing as well as providing guidance and protection, serving as a mentor and guide. First Man and First Woman create the Holy People, such as Dawn Man and Dawn Woman, Sky Blue Man and Sky Blue Woman, Twilight Man and Twilight Woman, and Darkness Man and Darkness Woman. The Wind is thought to have emerged from below, the underworld, with the Holy People when they emerged from below. The Wind has diverse names because of various criteria, but Wind is a unitary being. The cardinal directions (north, south, east, west), which in the Navajo world are marked by four mountains, mark off the boundaries of the Navajo world, and mark the four different kinds of Wind, White Wind (from the east, representing dawn), Blue Wind (from the south, representing day), Yellow Wind (from the west, representing twilight), and Dark Wind (from the north, representing night). These Winds are also described in gender categories, although which one is female or male is debated in the various texts (Farella, 1984). For all reports, however, there are an equal number of female and male Winds. The Winds lie on one another, and through the reproductive process Earth People are born.

According to McNeley (1981/1997), for Navajos, Holy Wind is believed to be in the individual from the moment of conception, producing movement and growth. Wind from the four cardinal directions is within each person, as different aspects of a single Wind that suffuses all living things. The Holy People have a primary role of governing human thought and behavior, as humans participate directly with the deities. The Holy People send messages by way of Messenger Winds to our earfold, giving warning and advice to us. The Wind talks to people, through a corner of their ear. Wind is closely associated with word and language. Natural phenomena, because they are endowed with inner forms and Holy Wind, are also able to think and live. They are able to provide guidance and instruction to the Navajo too. Although the Navajo believe that all people are born with Holy Wind within them, they also believe that there are evil Winds that can cause wrong conduct. If the Holy Wind is weak within us, then we are more susceptible to evil Winds. The evil Winds are called ghosts for they are the breath, the departed Winds of those who have died too young. A person can counteract the effects of weak Wind by petitioning the Messenger Winds and asking for their Holy Wind to be strengthened. The Winds provide forewarnings of harmful influences and they can be petitioned for help (p. 49). However, Navajos believe people are responsible and accountable for their own conduct. They have the option to listen to the Holy Wind's advice, and, if they choose not to heed the advice of the Wind, the Wind weakens, and eventually withdraws its advice. When the Holy Wind withdraws its guidance from a person, that person will eventually die.

We understand, from McNeley (1981/1997), that the Holy Wind is a unitary being that is the source of all life, movement, and behavior (p. 50-51). The Navajos have subcategorized the Wind (White Wind, Blue Wind, Yellow Wind, and Dark Wind), but this should not be translated as different separate Winds. The Holy Wind is an omnipresent entity in which living beings participate. A unitary Holy Wind "envelopes the individual throughout life" (p. 52). Navajos describe individuals as directly participating in the primary source of all beneficial power. A healthy individual is one who heeds the advice of the Wind, living a life of proper relationship to one's environment, a life of beauty, harmony, order, and well-being (hózhą́). McNeley (1981/1997) compares the Navajo Wind concept to the Dakota concept of Skan, "the Great Spirit" (p. 61). Farella (1984) compares the Navajo concept of sq'q naghái bik'e hózhą́, which he defines as "completeness" or "continuous generational animation," to McNeley's air that animates all being, the Holy Wind (p. 151).

For Farella (1984), sq'q naghái bik'e hózhą́ (SNBH) means completeness, that which is whole. He tells us that the source of sq'q naghái bik'e hózhą́ is First Man's magic bundle, full of the reproductive fluids, flesh and life forces, that reanimate us. To understand Farella's offered synthesis, in terms of sq'q naghái bik'e hózhą́, we must return again to the Navajo creation story. Farella begins with diyin dine'é—"the experience of being part of something larger and grander than oneself, the direct experience of oneness, something quite profound" (p. 23). The Navajo believe they descended directly from diyinii (gods, divinity, what McNeley (1981/1997) calls "the Holy People"), and that the boundary between gods and people is flexible. All diyinii are sq'q naghái bik'e hózhą́ (whole). However, diyinii are often translated as "benevolent holy people" and are descibed as representing only "goodness" in contrast to hóchxó, which represents "evil." Farella is greatly troubled by the dualism this kind of translation creates, which he claims is a misrepresentation of Navajo philosophy. He argues that diyinii is instead a concept of becoming and of process, a relationship, it is not an attribute inherent in a certain class or set of being (p. 31). Again we find translators have glossed the concept and reduced it to something more reflective of Euro-western thought.

One cannot list Navajo gods (the Holy People) from the most to the least powerful, for they are too complex and it depends on the context (Farella, 1984). Diyinii are on a power continuum, and all power, for Navajo, is based on knowledge. Mistakes and misfortunes are due to lack of knowledge. First Man was born from the place where Black Cloud (night) and White Cloud (dawn) meet, in the East; First Woman was born from the place where Blue Cloud (day) and Yellow Cloud (twilight) meet, in the West. The Navajo include gender as a primal universal quality, for the overriding theme of their religion is creation, and including gender assures creation. Gender is needed for reproduction, for birth, and the Navajo refer to intercourse, though usually overtly, as the source of creation. All creation is sexual or reproductive. These acts of creation are achieved ritually, through performance, even with the diyinii. Sexual fluid, semen, represents new life. First Man's medicine, his "bundle" or "basket," is the source of all beings. The magic bundle includes hide and stones (flesh and bones) and reproductive fluids.

In the dualistic translations, First Man is regarded as evil, and First Woman is good, but this is not the case for Navajos (Farella, 1984). One is not evil, the other good. For them, First Man is omniscient; he is the creator; and he wanted to create *just* what he created. He is "neither fumbling or ignorant. His actions were purposeful and carried out with the knowledge of their ultimate result" (p. 49). For example, First Man created "packages" or "bundles," "sets of entities" that were necessary to the Navajo, even if they embodied both good and evil. These bundles create the preconditions that make the creation of current conditions possible. For example, death was introduced to help make it possible for births, as death and birth together make a complete cycle, one whole. Poverty and hunger were introduced to remind us to continue to work hard for our food so that we can have abundance. The negative state is there to assure the positive will occur. These packages that describe any two phenomena that are in an on-going, permanent relationship of opposition to each other are called *ałkéé naa´aashii*.

First Man ordered Coyote, his agent, to kidnap the water buffalo's children so that she would flood the underworld, where all the diyinii lived, in her efforts to find her children (Farella, 1984). This flood was needed to cause the diyinii to have to leave the underworld and come to the earth's surface. The movement to the earth's surface was necessary because the underworld was getting too crowded, and the diyinii did not have enough space to live in peace. The Holy People were unwilling to move away from what they knew to the unknown; instead they voted to stay below. Therefore, First Man had to trick them into moving. As a result of Coyote's kidnapping of the water buffalo's children, not only was First Man able to get the Holy

People to move up to the earth's surface, but we also now have thunder and lightning on the earth's surface (the water buffalo's maternal anger), as well as rain, which is necessary for life on the earth's surface.

Another example of First Man and First Woman making plans for the world which are not necessarily perceived for their value at the time is the story of Changing Woman (Farella, 1984). Changing Woman is equated with White Shell Woman and Earth Woman. She is the nurturer, the provider, and the giver. She created the earth-people and what they need to survive. She has "responsibility for all those giving birth" on the earth's surface, which is almost everything for the Navajo (sheep, corn, plants). Changing Woman is whom the Navajo now sing too, as she is the daughter of the sky (father) and the earth (mother). She it is who supplied the Navajo with sheep for their livelihood. First Man and First Woman are her grandparents, as they created earth and sky. First Man and First Woman foresaw a need to rid the earth's surface of suffering *(nayéé)*, so First Man taught Changing Woman everything he knew, and gradually relinquished control over to Changing Woman. He manipulated, behind the scenes again, and arranged for Sun to have intercourse with Changing Woman, planning a union of which she was ignorant. And Sun, who did what he was ordered by First Man, did not know that the purpose of this intercourse was so Changing Woman would have twins, whose purpose were to slay *nayéé*, suffering. Suffering includes jealousy, fear, worry, as well as old age, poverty, and disease: anything that gets in the way of a person living her life (p. 51).

Similar to the Buddhist view of how one eliminates suffering, First Man and First Woman teach us, through Changing Woman and Sun's twins, that to get rid of *nayéé*, first you describe it and objectify it, then there is a battle, and then a celebration of what is basically a new way of looking at the world (Farella, 1984, p. 52). These are metaphorical, heuristic devises that simplify a very difficult and complex process (p. 53). Even though First Man and First Woman arrange the marriage of Changing Woman to Sun, they are saddened and angered by her move to live with Sun in the West, leaving them behind, deprived of their grand/daughter and the services of their son-in-law.[5] The all-powerful creators are separated from the conditions they created. This is a key to Navajo philosophy, for again we find that they believe in free will. Holy People can guide us and try to give us advice, but what we decide to do is up to us. The teacher has to relinquish control over the student and let her decide for herself, just as First Man must relinquish control over Changing Woman, and loses her to Sun, his arranged union to rid the world of suffering.

A final example of First Man's purposeful actions that can appear to some as signs of fumbling or ignorance is the story of First Man's bundle and his "forgetting" of it (Farella, 1984). We know that First Man's "bundle" is the source of all beings, so it is not something one would want to forget and leave behind. But, when the diyinii move to the earth's surface from the underworld, First Man leaves his bundle behind by "accident" and must send one of the birds back to the underworld to fetch the bundle. However, First Man does nothing by accident; his act of forgetting his bundle is done as a kind of instruction to earth people. This is a lesson to show Navajos how to place or entice a part of a victim to the underworld, and bring that part back to the surface, making him whole again (p. 81). With this action, First Man demonstrates how others can be harmed, but also how a cure could be effected.

Navajos have a concept that is similar to the Buddhist idea of nothingness, *samsara*, which we found to mean both emptiness and fullness. This Navajo concept is *ałkéé naa'aashii*, which we already ran into above in the description of First Man's packaged bundles of necessary good and evil, e.g. death/birth, poverty/wealth, hunger/abundance (Farella, 1984, p. 95). Farella defines *ałkéé naa'aashii* as meaning cyclical, repeated creation. With this concept the Navajos even predict their own demise, for they predict that all life started this world as a unity, and then things got increasingly complex and differentiated, and now the process has reversed and things are entrophying and becoming more unified, back to primal stillness. Each of our own life cycles also models this process, for we start out our lives indistinct within the womb, adolescence is when we reach the height of distinction, and by old age we are indistinct again. Navajos view this process as one of reanimation or renewal. *Ałkéé naa'aashii* is a central feature of Navajo philosophy, meaning "increase with no decrease" (p. 99), generational increase or boundlessness, the continuance and immortality of life itself, the non-egoistic perpetuation of process (p. 100).

Farella (1984) tells us a Navajo initially comes into contact with the concept of reanimation with "the cardinal phenomena" (dawn, blue sky, twilight, darkness). The cardinal phenomena serve to summarize and to bring about the entire pattern of Navajo life (patterns of behavior and thought, larger temporal units, such as the seasons, associated with certain activities and thoughts), and they summarize qualitative difference (such as dawn and twilight being seen as good, in terms of safety, and day and night as bad, in terms of dangers). Dawn (white) serves to stir, to awaken (if we rise early and make plans, this leads to attainment of wealth), daytime (skyblue) is the time to carry out the activities one has planned (it is also a time of danger and death), twilight (yellow) is when people come together and activity ceases as we reflect on the day, and night (black) is the time of rest, as well as death and birth.

For Navajos difference is needed for it is essential for existence and growth (Farella, 1984). Continuation can only be assured if changes are embraced. Differentiation is the process that pervades all entities; it is identical with being. This concept, *ałkéé naa'aashii*, deemphasizes "thingness" and emphasizes process, it breaks down boundaries and emphasizes relative (but not exclusive) boundlessness. "*Ałkéé naa'aashii* is a concept that can describe *any* two phenomena that are in an ongoing, permanent relationship of opposition to each other" (p. 121, emphasis in original). Completeness results from a combination of the two. So, for a Navajo, gender difference, and sexual desire, assures that animation will occur through births. They describe males as providing strength and power and females as providing stability and safety, and it is the two together that result in completeness. The two pairs of most notable animators are the Sun/Moon and the Earth/Changing Woman. *Ałkéé naa´aashii* describes the process of continuation, and, like Zen Buddhists, Navajos encourage us to be aware of this process and accept it with indifference. Navajos call people who try to use the process of reanimation to benefit themselves witches, who represent people caught up in the false illusion of egoism. Navajos embrace a concept of no-self which is similar to the Buddhist concept of *anatman*.

The concept of reanimation (*ałkéé naa´aashii*) emphasizes the flux and differentiation that exists in our world. *Sq'q naghái bik'e hózhą́* emphasizes how difference works together to achieve completeness. It dissolves boundaries, such as ego, and helps us understand our world in terms of wholeness. "*Sq'q naghái bik'e hózhą́*, then is completeness, but its source is the lack of completeness of the individual" (Farella, 1984, p. 181). *Sq'q naghái bik'e hózhą́* is continuous generational animation, the Holy Wind that animates all beings (McNeley, 1981/1997). Paradoxically, the Navajo philosophy of reanimation serves as a revitalization of the Navajo culture, through its emphasis on growth, adaption, and change. Their strategy is one of inclusiveness and relabeling, similar to Buddhism, but unlike many other Native American philosophies, such as the Laguna Pueblos or Pomos, who have become more secretive and exclusive about their cultural teachings. Navajos emphasize an epistemological shift, changing the way we perceive the world, rather than a technological emphasis on altering the world. They have known how to use paradox. They have changed and adapted, but these changes have helped them thrive and stay the same, in terms of their philosophy. Certainly their philosophy serves as an example of a unifying view of the universe as connected and whole. Theirs is a philosophy that describes the universe as in flux, alive and continually in the process of renewal.

Pre-contact Indigenous population is estimated at being between 20–45 million, while the 1980 consensus revealed there were 1 million Indigenous people alive currently in the United States, less than 1/2 of 1% of the more than 200 million U.S. citizens today (Allen, 1986). Many tribes face extinction, as Mabel McKay's life vividly illustrates (Sarris, 1994). Native Americans struggle today for physical survival as well as cultural survival. Part of their struggle is one of reclaiming their stories and myths, and rewriting them so that they reflect their philosophies and not their colonizers' views. We learned from Sarris (1993) how the reshaping of Native American narrations takes place. We found in the presentation of the Navajo creation stories, that Farella (1984) accuses Euro-westerners of misshaping their stories into a good/evil dualism and McNeley (1981/1997) highlights a central concept of Navajo philosophy, the Holy Wind, that translators have mistranslated in contradictory, misleading ways and ignored in terms of its primary role. Fortunately, Indigenous people are regaining control of their ritual memories and redescribing their heritage. They are listening to the Holy Wind and it is getting stronger inside of them, guiding them, healing them, and making them whole again.

Conclusion

In this chapter I have explored Mahāyāna Buddhism and the Native American philosophies of the Pomos and Navajos for they offer excellent examples of nondualistic philosophies which describe the universe relationally. These differing views have much in common, for they all seek to dissolve sharp distinctions and dualisms, emphasizing instead how the universe and individuals are connected, spiritually and materially. Their knowing relies on a unifying logic that describes the universe as whole, as well as holy. I have discussed this concept of w/holistic relationality, nonduality, in terms of dependent co-origination, no-self, nothinginess that is full and empty, of unconditioned awareness of oneness (Buddha-nature). And, I have discussed w/holistic relationality (Spirit, Dreams, Sacred Hoop, and Holy Wind) in terms of continuous generational reanimation, a becoming, a process of renewal. I offer Buddhism and Native American philosophy as non-Euro-western sources that can help us understand how a relational (e)pistemology is supported by a nondualistic ontology which emphasizes that we are w/holistically connected with our greater universe, materially and spiritually. Buddhism and Native American philosophy teach us how to tune into our primal experiences and they further help us develop the concept of knowers as selves-in-relation-with-others. The mistranslations of their nondualistic philosophy teach us how language not only attempts to add meaning to our primal experiences but also how language confuses, misrepresents, limits, and fixes our primal experiences, while the universe flows on below the net of language. My description of Buddhist and Native American philosophies is meant to help us understand that not only are we related to each other personally, as Chapter 4 argued, and socially, as Chapter 5 argued, but that we are related to a whole universe, materially and spiritually, stretching beyond the artificial boundaries of human beings. This universe includes the natural world, and so it is time to move on and consider this philosophy from the perspective of our biosphere, and explore more how a w/holistic relationality affects our sense of connectedness with the living world that surrounds us.

CHAPTER 7

Ecological Relations

Historically, Euro-westerners have embraced an ontology that separates humans from nature. The dualisms of mind/matter, man/nature, soul/body can be traced back to ancient Greece and Plato's ontological categories of the Forms. For Plato (*Meno*, 1970; *Republic*, 1979), our soul is not of this material world and therefore mortal, as our body is, but instead our soul is immortal and one with the Forms. The Forms are the material world Idealized and made Transcendent. The material world of nature which our body inhabits is a world that is temporary and particular, a world that distracts us and deceives us. Since our soul is immortal and has experienced all, it knows all Truth. We are able to tune in to what our immortal soul already knows by separating our mind from our body, from matter, from nature, and using our mind to recollect the Truth we already know.

The ancient Greek anthropocentric dualisms are reinforced by the religious views of the Judeo-Christians. From a Judeo-Christian perspective, God created the world, and placed humans in the world as his descendents, with nature there to serve humans. Humans are commanded to subdue nature and multiply themselves. There is a strict ontological hierarchy with God in the transcendent role, humans following, and nature following humans. Christianity is based on the belief that the end of history is coming, and then humans will leave Earth, which is an evil place of pain and suffering, for Heaven, which is a glorious place of only goodness (Deloria, Jr., 1995). Since the Age of Enlightenment and the dawning of the Scientific Revolution, philosophers and scientists in the 16th to 17th centuries further codified the ancient Greek anthropocentric dualisms by defining nature like a machine, a system of dead, inert particles moved by external forces, which needs to be controlled and shaped for the benefit of human beings (Merchant, 1980). Thus, historically we find that in Euro-western philosophy, religion, *and* science 'nature' is placed in an "Other" category, in contrast and opposition to humans.

Buddhists and Native Americans have never embraced such views about nature. For them, the world in which we live is alive and intimately connected to us. Buddhists believe that people and nature are mutually dependent on each other and equally valued, and so it is vital that we care for all of life's forms; doing so is how we care for ourselves. Native Americans say the planet is our mother, Grandmother Earth, and she "is *physical* and therefore a spiritual, mental, and emotional being. Planets are alive, as are all their by-products or expressions, such as animals, vegetables, minerals, climatic and meteorological phenomena" (Allen, 1990, p. 52, emphasis in original). We gain knowledge and understanding of this world by participating in events, and observing all of nature around us, the birds, animals, rivers, and mountains (Deloria, Jr., 1995, p. 56). Native Americans consider themselves, still today, part of the Sacred Hoop of nature, of the same value as other living things, not of higher status and worth, as Euro-western Judeo-Christians seem to believe (Allen, 1986).

There are several different theoretical perspectives offered as to why the split between humans and nature exists in the Euro-western world and various recommendations are offered concerning what we need to do to heal this split. Much evidence is offered from a variety of theorists and activists to demonstrate the destructive results this split continues to cause today: depletion and erosion of soil; air pollution, ozone depletion, and the resulting greenhouse effect; water pollution and acid rain; human overpopulation and starvation and disease; the extinction of one fourth of the earth's species of plants, animals, microbes, and fungi; the cutting down of the Rain Forests, causing loss of homeland, more extinction, and loss of oxygen. Buddhism blames the split between humans and nature on false illusions we create and learn through our social cultures that we must unlearn. We create the appearance of a self that is separate from others and we must empty ourselves of that delusion so that we can be aware of the Truth that all things, including ourselves, are interdependent and exist in relation with each other. Environmental philosophers point to Judeo-Christianity, rationalism, mechanistic science and technology, colonialism, and capitalism for causing the split between humans and nature (Callicott & Ames, 1989). Euro-western ecofeminists blame the split on patriarchy, making it clear that man has always been placed higher on the hierarchy than woman, with woman identified with nature (Daly, 1978/1990; King, 1990; Merchant, 1980; Warren, 1990). Native Americans point to the same culprits that environmental philosophers and ecofeminists point to (Allen, 1986; Deloria, Jr. 1995). Allen (1990) suggests our planet is entering upon a great initiation, a passage where she is becoming someone else, she has gone coyote, *heyoka*. "She is giving birth to her new consciousness of herself and her relationship to the other vast intelligences, other holy beings in her universe" (p. 54).

This chapter will explore some key ecological theories offered in efforts to heal the Euro-western split between nature, man, and woman. I am arguing that a relational (e)pistemology, supported by a relational ontology, *must* include an emphasis on ecological relations for the natural world is a world in which human beings are intimately connected. Again, I must be very selective about which theories I choose to discuss, due to limitations of space and time, but I hope that my exploration will cause the reader to want to seek others' views as well. I have narrowed my focus sharply by choosing to discuss only one or two representatives of the major positions presented so that I can consider their work in more depth. What I offer just begins to scratch the surface in ecological relational approaches, a fact I find very exciting and heartening. While the field of ecological philosophy is relatively new (since the early 1970's), natural relational approaches to knowing date back to the beginning of time. Indigenous people have persevered a vital storehouse of environmental wisdom based on over 40,000 years of continual relationships with special environments (Cajete, 1994). As a result of recent efforts to record this knowing in printed form, there is a wealth of text available for reading.

I have divided this chapter into two basic sections: one considers the human/nonhuman nature split mainly from a metaphysical angle, and the second section looks at the human/nonhuman split more with a focus of power issues, introducing patriarchy into discussions of domination over nature. The first section will continue the discussion introduced in Chapter 6 of Buddhist and Native American spiritual beliefs concerning nature, as well as present Arne Naess's *deep ecology* view. Environmental philosophers, ecological feminists, and social ecologists will serve as critics of these views. The second section will present the ecofeminist perspectives of Mary Daly, Carol Merchant, Ynestra King, and Karen Warren, with various feminists serving as critics of these views. In this way a dialogue should emerge, and from this dialogue we should be able to discover tensions as well as key themes and central ideas held in common that will help us further develop a relational (e)pistemology.

Ecological theories seek to describe humanity and nature in an inclusive, biological manner as biocentrically connected. They emphasize principles of w/holistic unity and systematic integration, internalistic life-movements, and organic balance. Ecological theories serve as another example of an ontological and (e)pistemological shift away from metaphysical dualisms and absolutism, toward a transactional model of organism-environment. The shift is away from a model emphasizing rationality and quantitative calculations toward a model that is more reflective of concrete experiences of life in their fullest dimensions. As theories, ecology breaks the artificial boundaries of philosophy, religion, and science, offering examples of w/holistic theories based on a relational ontology and (e)pistemology. We will find in Chapter 8 that there are examples of current Euro-western scientists in fields as diverse as physics, chemistry, and geology making similar shifts away from metaphysical dualisms and absolutism, toward a relational ontology and (e)pistemology. General systems theory, quantum mechanics, and cybernetics are based on a mutual causality similar to classic pragmatism, Buddhism, Native American, and ecofeminist philosophy, with their emphases on transactional relationships, change and process, complexity, contextuality, and interconnectedness.

Human/nonhuman Nature

Environmental philosophy began in the early 1970's, as a product of the 1960's, according to Callicott and Ames (1989). From its beginning, Euro-western environmental philosophers have assumed that we can find ecological wisdom in the East, as well as among Indigenous cultures such as the Native Americans. The assumption is that while the Asian or Indigenous cultures cannot offer us better scientific understanding of nature, they can offer us different ontological perspectives. Studying these alternative philosophies will provide an outsider standpoint, which will help Euro-westerners be better able to critique themselves as they become more aware of their own deep-level, background assumptions. These alternative cultures can offer Euro-westerners new metaphors that will help us imagine new ways of articulating our world. They can help us reach the goals of cultural redirection and environmental rehabilitation (Callicot and Ames, 1989).

At the same time that Euro-western environmental philosophers have pointed to the values of studying Native American and Asian philosophy for their environmental wisdom, Euro-western authors have pointed to ecologically destructive practices in these same cultures. Based on fossil evidence that predates European contact on the North/South American continent, Native Americans are accused of hastening the extinction of animals such as the buffalo by driving herds of buffalo off cliffs (Callicot and Ames, 1989). The East is accused of mass slaughtering of animals such as whales, severely polluting their water, ruthlessly exploiting the rain forests of southeast Asia, gross overpopulation, and massive soil erosion. It is argued that there are glaring inconsistencies that exist between professed ideals and actual practice (Callicot and Ames, 1989). In defense of Native American practice, we will find below that Vine Deloria, Jr. (1995) questions the fossil dating techniques of Euro-western scientists and other methodologies used to establish the Pleistocene overkill theory. Deloria, Jr. effectively calls into question this theory, and others, based on flawed evidence. As for much of the evidence currently held against sound Asian ecological practices, many of these practices can be shown to be a direct result of Euro-western imperialism and industrialization. Tragically, the current trend in Asian countries is to adopt Euro-western practices, which are perceived to offer great technological advances that will make life easier and more comfortable, as Euro-westerners are now beginning to realize the threat technology creates for our natural environment (Callicot and Ames, 1989).

Given the supposition that Asian philosophies can offer the Euro-west an ecological wisdom, it is surprising to discover that Asian philosophers have not participated much in conversations with Euro-western philosophers on this topic. That is, it is surprising until we uncover Euro-western philosophical biases that have precluded such serious philosophical discussions. Euro-western philosophers historically have defined philosophy in terms of certainty, objectivity, rationality, and logic, and then used that definition to exclude the East from philosophical discussions due to its not meeting the West's criteria. The East has been judged by the West to not have any strong philosophical positions, and the East's views have instead been classified as religious. However, recent developments in Euro-western philosophy by pragmatists, feminists, and postmodernists have caused the Euro-west to abandon certainty, objectivity, dualism, and determinism. Now Eastern views, which represent worldviews that are nondualistic, w/holistic, relational, and organic, can meet the new criteria and have risen in status.

Still, most of the Euro-western philosophical conversations about Eastern philosophies have taken place by Euro-westerners who study Eastern philosophies as outsiders. Even in a text such as *Nature in Asian Traditions of Thought: Essays in Environmental Philosophy* (Callicott and Ames, 1989), which had the explicit aim of encouraging more conversation between the East and the West, Asians are conspicuously missing, representing a small minority of the authors included in the anthology. Within many of the essays included, it is still difficult to find serious presentations of Asian views; what are most often presented are in-depth discussions of Euro-western philosophical influences, in contrast to Eastern ones. And nature, which is suppose to be the main topic of the entire text, is barely included in many of the essays, often finally appearing in the concluding remarks of the authors, as an afterthought. Unfortunately, this text represents the rationalistic Euro-western criteria its authors and editors are critically aware of and yet still model in their own practice.

At this point I would like to explore the Euro-western supposition that Asian philosophies can offer the Euro-west an ecological wisdom by taking another look at the Mahāyānā Buddhism we considered at some depth in Chapter 6. It is important to remind the reader that Eastern philosophies are complex and diverse and cannot be reduced to one view. There is no one "Eastern" view—there are many—each representing unique perspectives with significant histories and intricate developments. In Chapter 6 several key ideas of the Buddhist doctrine were presented, the dharmas of dependent co-origination, emptiness, egolessness of self, and compassion. These fundamental beliefs are central to understanding Buddhism's ecological philosophy.

Recall that the dharma of dependent co-origination, or co-arising, is a metaphysical position that subverts the concept of ontologically independent *entities*. Buddhists claim that all beings are mutually dependent and interconnected. While it is possible to maintain distinctions and differences among different forms of nature, dependent co-origination reminds us how porous and fluid these distinctions really are. Nature is perceived w/holistically as a structured, differentiated whole. Dependent co-origination also subverts the idea of individual life forms having higher or lower status, thus undermining a hierarchical approach to nature. In believing that all life forms are interconnected and mutually dependent, Buddhism helps us understand that all life forms are interrelated. All life forms participate equally in a dynamic cosmos. This means that all life forms have intrinsic value and they all affect each other. Buddhists do not place different forms of nature, e.g. plants, animals, human beings, on a hierarchical scale and rate them according to varying importance, worth, or value. Humans are not ontologically privileged. To a Buddhist, that kind of thinking is dangerously deceptive and arrogant. All life in all its forms are valuable and important; all of the natural world has intrinsic value. This philosophy maintains an ecocentric view of nature rather than an anthropocentric one. As Francis Cook (1989) points out, if we compare historically the art in our museums, we find the European art reveals a strong anthropocentric bias, for the subject of its art is people, represented mainly by portraits. Nature serves as an unobtrusive backdrop for the human foreground. However, the main subject of Asian art is landscapes, with people represented in the visual display, but barely visible in scale to the land. "Nature here is not a background for man; man and nature are blended together harmoniously" (p. 218).

In Chapter 6 we learned that emptiness and dependent co-origination are one and the same concept for Buddhists. The dharma of emptiness teaches us that our original mind is empty of false illusions of separate entities and full of limitless possibilities. Our original mind understands that things exist *only* interdependently, thus again undermining the concept of separate entities, including the concept of a separate self. The concept of mutual dependence applies to all phenomena. Our self, as a separate entity, is only an illusion. Buddhists embrace a process concept of self, which they describe as 'no self' (anatman). We are impermanent and nonsubstantial, lacking any self-essence. We are in process, in a state of becoming, always in flux. The term 'self' signifies a relation. The dharma of emptiness helps us understand that if we empty our minds of the false illusions we have built up, we will be able to see nature as undistorted, and understand that we are nature.

For the Mahäyanä Buddhist, the way we destroy the illusion of a self is not by extinction of all desire, but rather by reorientation. We overcome our greedy desires to contain and control nature by changing greedy desires to altruistic desires to help us fully participate *with* nature. We develop our compassion and love, our total openness. We relate to nature with care, and develop a deep emotional affinity with nature. We listen and attend to nature, and begin to establish communication. We begin to understand that nature is not dead at all, but is most vital and alive. We realize that nature is endowed with divine presence, and that while we, as sentient beings, must seek Buddhahood, nonsentient beings already have Buddhahood. We cultivate an intimate relation with nature that is mutually interpenetrating, an intersubjective experience, an authentic experience of nature, an "awareness untainted by the habits of conceptualization" (Shaner, 1989, p. 171). We overcome our sense of separation from the world. "The epistemic mode of experience to be cultivated is therefore a dynamic process; it is primarily an attitude, a becoming that occasions an intimacy with the whole of dynamic nature" (Shaner, 1989, p. 168).

Mahāyanā Buddhists strongly emphasize nonviolence, and nonexploitation of the natural world in their ecocentric philosophy. They experience profound feelings of gratitude and respect for all of life. There is much they can teach us about how to live in peace with each other, including our natural surroundings. The Euro-western supposition that Asian philosophies can offer the Euro-west an ecological wisdom is sound, and we will find their influence in the deep ecology movement described below. This is not to say that Mahāyanā Buddhists have been able to avoid the environmental disasters the Euro-west has embraced. However, their ecological view that all things live in interdependence and are interrelated offers important insight and hope for all of us. This view emphasizes the intrinsic value of all phenomena.

Cook (1989) refers us to the metaphor of "the jewel net of Indra" to help us understand. Imagine an infinite net that is stretched over the entire world. At each eye of the net there is a single glittering jewel, and since the net is infinite, there are an infinite number of jewels. When we look at one jewel, we discover that all the other jewels are reflected in that one jewel, and this is true for each individual jewel, "so that there is an infinite reflecting process occurring." This image "symbolizes a cosmos in which there is an infinitely repeated interrelationship among all the members of the cosmos" (Cook, 1989, p. 214). The jewels represent simultaneous relationships of mutual identity and mutual intercausality. For Buddhists, the cosmos is a nonteleological, self-creating, self-maintaining, and self-defining organism. It is a universe in which everything counts, and we all share our destinies.

I move on to consider the deep ecology movement. We will not be leaving Buddhism completely behind though, for Buddhism has influenced various people involved in the ecological movement, in particular the view I wish to explore here of Arne Naess. Naess does not often directly cite Buddhism as a source for his ideas, but he is influenced by Spinoza and Gandhi, and thus we can trace his Buddhist influence through them. Naess is a Norwegian philosopher, who is credited with introducing the term 'deep ecology' into ecological discussions in 1973 in an article titled "The shallow and the deep, long-range ecology movements." Naess worked for over thirty years as a professor in philosophy, contributing to work in semantics, philosophy of science, and analysis of the philosophy of Spinoza and Gandhi. He resigned his academic position in 1969 in order to become a social activist in the ecological movement, believing philosophy can help guide our actions as we seek to heal the split between humanity and nature. In 1976 Naess published a book, *Økologi, samfunn, og livsstil*, which was not published in English until 1989, as *Ecology, community and lifestyle*.[1] He has also published several articles (1984, 1985, 1986). As he is considered an important thinker in the deep ecology tradition, I turn to his work to help us understand what has become a movement in the last 20–25 years.

Naess (1986) describes deep ecology as a religion and a philosophy, and he suggests that deep ecologists come from various religious backgrounds, including Christian, Buddhist, and Taoist. Naess (1985) uses the term 'deep' "to suggest explication of fundamental presuppositions of valuation as well as of facts and hypotheses" (p. 256). He wants us to question the foundational normative and descriptive premises of ecological philosophy. Naess suggests that the way to heal the split between humanity and nature is by changing our consciousness through an inward transformation. He offers a new ontology that posits humanity as inseparable from nature. The methodology he relies on to help him develop this new ontology is phenomenology, using his intuition to develop his concept of Self-realization (Naess's spelling). Naess suggests the term 'ecosophy' to describe philosophy inspired by the deep ecology movement that is a synthesis of theory and practice. He prefers to refer to ecological philosophy as an ecological movement, to highlight the fact that artists and poets are contributing to this movement, not just philosophers, and to emphasize the important of social action, not just philosophical theory development, in order to help us change our conditions. Naess describes his own particular philosophy in regards to ecology and philosophy as 'Ecosophy T.' He does this to suggest that his is not the only one; there are many others, A, B, C, etc.

For deep ecologists, the argument that we should take care of the Earth so humans can survive is a weak argument. The stronger argument is to insist that all non-human life on Earth has intrinsic worth, just as human beings do. Naess rejects a view of man-in-environment in favor of a relational, total-field image that emphasizes biospherical egalitarianism in principle. In "A defense of the deep ecology movement," Naess (Fall 1984) described the basic tenets of the deep ecology movement, which he says he developed with the help of George Sessions. In 1985 he further adjusted these tenets, and in his 1989 book publication they are further altered to the following:

> (1) The flourishing of human non-human life on Earth has intrinsic value. The value of non-human life forms is independent of the usefulness these may have for narrow human purposes. (2) Richness and diversity of life forms are values in themselves and contribute to the flourishing of human and non-human life on Earth. (3) Humans have no right to reduce this richness and diversity except to satisfy vital needs. (4) Present human interference with the non-human world is excessive, and the situation is rapidly worsening. (5) The flourishing of human life and cultures is compatible with a substantial decrease of the human population. The flourishing of non-human life requires such a decrease. (6) Significant change of life conditions for the better requires change in policies. These affect basic economic, technological, and ideological structures. (7) The ideological change is mainly that of appreciating life quality (dwelling in situations of intrinsic value) rather than adhering to a high standard of living. There will be a profound awareness of the difference

between big and great. (8) Those who subscribe to the foregoing points have an obligation directly or indirectly to participate in the attempt to implement the necessary changes. (p. 29, emphasis in original)

In his various discussions of these tenets, we find that Naess (1989) realizes there are vague terms such as "vital needs" within the tenets that need further clarification, but he purposely uses these terms to encourage us to engage in conversations concerning the concepts and "to allow for considerable latitude in judgment" (p. 30). His hope is that these conversations will point us to the metaphysical assumptions on which our different world views are based. Naess (1989) does not do more than sketch his own Ecosophy T in *Ecology, community, and lifestyle* for the same reason. His aim in the text is to encourage his readers to clarify their own views. Consequently, Murray Bookchin's (1988) criticism of Naess's theory for being vague is a fair criticism, but it mainly points to the differences in their two philosophical positions. Naess's (1989) position is that completeness is impossible, and even meaningless while Bookchin, as a social ecologist, counts on the human species evolving reasoning ability to give humans the clarity of understanding necessary to intervene and change nature, by way of society.

Naess's (1989) Ecosophy T begins with a basic axiom or postulate he describes as "Self-realization!" (N1). He uses explanation points with his normative statements to emphasis that these are calls to action. Self-realization is a concept that Naess employs to try to connect unity with diversity, individuality with the whole. Self-realization is the universal right to self-unfolding, to live and blossom. Naess does not mean self-realization in terms of just individual human self development, as the classical liberalists use the term. He calls this the narrow self, the ego. Self-realization is the realization of the comprehensive Self, not the cultivation of the ego. Yet, Naess does mean individual self-development in a classical liberal sense of self-sufficiency, self-determination, autonomy; he just wants to expand this concept so that it includes other forms of nature, not just human beings. Apparently, the expanded Self is a gender-neutral concept of self (Kheel, 1990), although Naess does not specifically address women in his text at all. For Naess, plants and animals have the right to self-unfolding too. This is why Naess uses the capital S in Self-realization, to emphasize a large concept of Self which includes all of nature. While he includes all of nature in his concept of Self-realization, and he wants to emphasize we are part of the ecosphere as much as we are part of society, he does not want to dissolve the individual self either. Naess points toward the East and their mysticism, but moves in the end to reinstating the central position of the existential individual, for fear of determinism.

There is a tension in Naess's (1989) philosophy between wholism and existentialism. Naess means Self-realization is a process, a way to live one's life. He talks about identification with greater wholes and the need for us to more toward I/Thou relationships. However, he does not recognize, as Buber (1923, 1937, 1958) suggests, that we begin our lives in I/Thou relationships that become I/It. Naess (1989) describes individual selves in terms of diversity, and as intimately interconnected. He uses a both/and logic, referring to this as a *gestalt* understanding of the piece *as a whole*, with whole and part internally related (p. 57, emphasis in original). He insists there are no completely separate objects, just objects in relation with each other (similar to Buddhism's dependent co-origination, or co-arising). However, while he refers to the Buddhist concept of no-self (anatman), he does not completely embrace anatman in his own philosophy, for he wants to maintain a separate, individual self while we already know that Buddhists argue such a concept is an illusion we socially construct to ward off our fears of the absence of self.

Naess (1989) includes the norms of self-sufficiency, decentralisation, and autonomy as his second-level principles in his Ecosophy T (N6–8), thus further revealing his leanings toward classical liberal norms which undermine his wholism. Deep ecology seems to represent an expanded self that is an enlargement and an extension of egoism. The assumption still seems to be that human nature is egoistic and that the alternative to egoism is self-sacrifice (Plumwood, 1991). Buddhists argue that self-sufficiency and autonomy are illusions we create which cause us a great deal of suffering. The concept of autonomy depends on the belief that the self is a continuous, independent subject. For Buddhists, the 'self' represents a relation, not a solid entity, and all phenomena, including the self, are impermanent and constantly changing. The 'self' comes in and out of being as a consequence of mutual dependence. Naess recognizes this mutual dependence when he says that complete Self-realization requires the realization of all (similar to the Buddhist idea of all attaining Buddhahood). However, for Naess (1989) the realization of all is never reached but is an Ideal worth striving for. Self-realization is a kind of perfection. It is a process as well as an ultimate goal. "The term includes personal and community self-realization, but is conceived also to refer to an unfolding of reality as a totality" (p. 84). Naess wants to embrace a concept of self that includes others, but his concept of separate self hinders the relational approach he seeks to take.

Naess's (1989) underlying illusion of separate selves undermines his response to the human/nature divide as well. He wants to dissolve the split between humans and nature. He argues for an egalitarian position that does not set human beings apart from nature and higher in value than nature. He describes all of nature as having intrinsic worth, including all living species. He opposes the historical Euro-western tendency to place humans at the center of the moral universe (to be anthropocentric), and to assume that nonhuman nature has no value in itself. He wants humanity to be for nature instead of against it, to care for it and nurture it, mainly by leaving it alone as much as possible. Naess argues for self-realization for all living beings, and for the importance of making room for nature to diversify and develop in complexity, in order to continue the evolutionary process (N2-4). Diversity and complexity are necessary to increase Self-realization potentials.

For Naess (1989), making room for nature to diversify and develop in complexity means allowing for large, open spaces of land that have no human contact. The state of nature is one that is undisturbed by human beings. Thus, we discover that Naess still maintains a split between humans/nature, for he assumes a state of nature is one that does not include human beings. He describes humans as against nature, rather than as part of nature. As Watson (1983) explains:

> if we view the state of nature or Nature as being natural, undisturbed, and unperturbed only when human beings are *not* present, or only when human beings are curbing their natural behavior, then we are assuming that human beings are apart from, separate from, different from, removed from, or above nature. (p. 252, emphasis in original)

Deep ecology is based on a position that sets humans apart from nature, even though deep ecologists' most fundamental position is their opposition to the historical Euro-western propensity to place humans at the center of the moral universe (to be anthropocentric). What deep ecologists accomplish is the abstract negation of the original dualism between man/nature (King, 1991) and nature/culture (King, 1987, Warren, 1990).

Naess's (1989) Ecosophy T assumes the importance of: no exploitation, no subjugation, equal rights, no class societies, and self-determination (N9-13). He is opposed to a hierarchical view in regards to humanity and nature. He wants us to identify with our ecosystem and other species by widening our concept of the self. Strong identification with the whole of nature in its diversity and interdependence of parts is what will motivate us to actively participate in the deep ecological movement. Naess wants us to recognize that our ecosystem and other species have their own intrinsic value independent of our valuation. Identification with nature is a source of belief in intrinsic values. How do we widen identifications? By widening our perspectives, deepening our experiences, and reaching higher levels of activeness (Naess references Spinoza's "self-preservation" concept, p. 85). Increase of identification will help us achieve what moralizing cannot, beautiful actions that are the result of "acting more consistently from oneself *as a whole*" (Naess references Kant's "beautiful actions," p. 86, emphasis in original). Unfortunately, Naess's altruism calls for an impersonal love of the cosmos. Plumwood (1991) criticizes his wide identification for beings as indiscriminate and intent on denying particular meanings. This kind of love is very different from the love of their land that Indigenous people express, which is very specific and local, as we will discover below. Others worry that deep ecology's description relies too much on logic and language, causing nature to become a disconnected abstraction (Cheney, 1987).

Deep ecologists such as Naess are criticized for failing to supply an adequate historical perspective or an adequate challenge to the human/nature dualism (Plumwood, 1991, Bookchin, 1988). Some criticize deep ecologists for still relying on a rationalist-inspired account of the self (Plumwood, 1991), while others criticize them for not relying enough on man's reason to solve our ecological problems (Bookchin, 1988, Watson, 1983). We will find out below that ecofeminists criticize deep ecologists for ignoring the role of androcentric thinking. Robert Sessions (1991) informs us that the controversy between deep ecology and ecofeminism has been going on since 1980. "Some deep ecologists have accused ecofeminism of shallowness, anthropocentricism, short sightedness, and environmental naivete, while various ecofeminists have called their accusers sexist, shallow, ahistorical, stoical, and even fascist" (Sessions, 1991, p. 91). Ynestra King (1991) describes deep ecologists as "Daniel Boones in ecological drag." It does not go unnoticed by ecofeminists that most deep ecologists (and ecological philosophers, and social ecologists, for that matter) are White males.

We will discover below that ecofeminists do not disagree with deep ecology's anthropocentrism. They argue that anthropocentrism relies on the same either/or logic as androcentrism. However, they insist that anthropocentrism is deeply embedded within androcentrism. Deep ecologists agree that ecofeminists such as Warren (1990) have successfully shown that the logic of androcentrism is parallel to the logic of anthropomorphism. They agree men are far more implicated than women, as are certain cultures and classes, in the exploitation of nature. They agree that egalitarian attitudes should apply to all humans too. For Warren (1990), deep ecology must be feminist at its core for nature and women are parts of a whole. Failure to notice the connections between nature and women *is* male-gender bias (Warren, 1990, p. 144, emphasis in original). Deep ecologists are not androcentric, but they are guilty of complicity by not recognizing sexism and naturism. What we have discovered with Naess's ecosophy in particular is that he has not successfully made the ontological transformation to which he points. He has not succeeded in dissolving the Euro-western human/nature split himself, but rather has recommended a philosophy that shifts the value from humans to nature. Still, his consideration of Buddhist ideas and process ideas such as *gestalt*, point us in an ecological relational direction.

I return now to a discussion of Native American ecological views. Native Americans do not embrace a human/nonhuman split, thus eliminating the need to create a hierarchy between humans and nonhumans. For them, human beings are part of Nature, and Nature is part of us. This is a transactional relationship that cannot be separated. "(H)umans not only live in relationship to the natural world; we are the natural world" (Cajete, 1994, p. 80). For Native Americans, spirit and matter are one and the same, and Nature is a sacred, spiritual being. They describe humans and nonhumans as relatives, interrelated and connected to each other, part of one whole which is the planet Grandmother Earth. Paula Gunn Allen (1990) describes Nature as relatives of womankind and mankind.

> I am speaking of all our relatives, the four-leggeds, the wingeds, the crawlers; of the plants and seasons, the winds, thunders, and rains, the rivers, lakes, and streams, the pebbles, rocks, and mountains, the spirits, the holy people, and the Gods and Goddesses—of all the intelligences, all the beings. I am speaking even of the tiniest, those no one can see; and of the vastest, the planets and stars. (p. 55)

We learned from the Navajo creation stories shared in Chapter 6 that while humans are described as descending from dyinii (gods), the boundary between the spiritual world of gods and humans is flexible and fluid. The Navajo experience themselves as being part of something larger than themselves, linked to the immanent powers of the universe in a profound oneness. They are the Holy People themselves. We also learned that people were described, First Man, First Woman, as being born from Nature, from Black Cloud and White Cloud, from Blue Cloud and Yellow Cloud. Nature is described in spiritual terms, as imminent, and the boundary between Nature and humans is again a flexible and fluid one. Not only are the Holy People descended from Nature, but Nature serves as a teacher and mentor for the Holy People and helps guide them in their lives. Nature advises people through the Holy Wind talking to them, whispering in their ears. The Holy Wind gives people life, animates them, and directs them. The Holy Wind is Spirit. Even though Mabel McKay, as a Pomo Indian, described Spirit in different terms, she still described a similar connected relationship with Spirit and Nature, in unified and w/holistic terms, with Spirit advising her and giving her life, speaking to her in her Dreams instead of in her ear, teaching her how to heal others and make them whole again.

Native Americans did not place themselves above animals, plants, and the land, but instead described themselves as one with Nature. We can see the results of their connectedness to Nature in how they chose to live their lives, historically, and continue to do so today. Native Americans did not clear the forests and erect fences, trying to claim the land as theirs, and tame it. They tried to maintain a harmonious relationship with the land.

> Indian people lived with as little impact on the natural state of the land as possible. They allowed the land to be, taking from it only the resources necessary for their survival, but always remembering that it was given to them as a gift. (Cajete, 1994, p. 77)

They did not view themselves as property owners of the land they lived on; that is an Euro-western idea they had to adjust to in order to have any remaining land on which to live. Rather, Native Americans viewed the land as alive and helping them be alive, and they continue to relate to Nature in this way. They literally view themselves as having been born from the land. They view it their sacred responsibility to maintain a harmonious, sustainable relationship with the land. They regularly give thanks to the land's spirit for supporting their lives. Land is sacred to Native Americans, indeed, all Indigenous people. "Indigenous means being so completely identified with a place that you reflect its very entrails, its soul" (Cajete, 1994, p. 87). Loss of land for Indigenous people means more than loss of a home. It means loss of a way of life, loss of meaning and identity, for their culture is tied so intimately to the land.

Native Americans do not try to amass wealth by accumulating more of Nature than they need to survive. Animals, as kin, are often described as transforming into human shapes in tribal stories, and then offering their human relatives advice on such things as hunting, so that they do not risk offending the Animal Spirits. In general, Native Americans have historically only killed what animals they needed for survival, and when they did kill an animal, they apologized for doing so and gave thanks for the gift of life the Animal's Spirit gave them. They promised to offer their human body back to the plants and animals and the land in order to help sustain those lives as well. It was very important that the hunter have a good heart, for his actions represented his community to the Animal Spiritual world. The hunter's journey is a spiritual journey toward completeness, as he participates in the "great dance of life" (Cajete, 1994, p. 54). Native Americans also try to show their gratitude by not being wasteful of Nature so that, for example, they use the animal's body as thoroughly as they can so as not to need to kill more than a necessary number of animals. They have a history of sharing what they have with others in their tribe, so that everyone has enough to survive.

To Native Americans, plants are the hair of Mother Earth. They are sacred too, and must be used with care and gratitude. Plants not only supply people with a source of food, they serve as material for making clothing, housing, and for artistic expression, for example. Plants also serve as sources of medicine. Indigenous people have tremendous knowledge about plants and their uses for healing. They are healers, and herbalists, naturalists, botanists, and ecologists. They view illness as a sign of loss of dynamic balance and displeasure of the Holy Ones. Shamans and healers try to diagnose what is wrong and apply a treatment so that balance and harmony can be restored. Illness is due to disrespect, dishonor, disturbance, misuse or misconduct, and ignorance. From a Native American perspective, the current condition of our Earth, with its unprecedented exploitation of human and natural resources, and profound alienation, is a tremendous sign of our lack of balance and harmony with Nature, and the displeasure of the Holy Ones.

As we know from the previous chapter, Native Americans have historically relied on an oral tradition to pass on their cultural wealth to the next generation. Deloria, Jr. (1995) tells us that the reliance on oral tradition is still true today, and that only 10% of the information Indians possess is printed and available for discussion. Many of their stories are witness stories or scouting reports of such things as geological events that occurred a long time ago, yet Euro-western scientists treat oral tradition as if it is not true. This disrespect for oral tradition is in spite of the Native American claim that their elders are like scientists, for as storytellers they specialize in particular stories and treat storytelling as a precise art. The people who often became the tribe's great storytellers were scouts, who had to be good observers and analyzers, and had to be trusted for telling the truth.

As a Dakota Sioux Indian, Deloria, Jr. (1995) offers powerful criticisms of Euro-western science's view, since Descartes, of Nature as an inert object. He points out practical examples of science gone mad, and the impact of scientific doctrine on the status of Indians in American society. The Indian explanation of Nature is always cast aside as superstition, and childish ignorance. Euro-western science does not respect non-western traditions. Racism is inherent in Euro-western academia and in scientific circles, and the evidence is seen in how information offered by a Native American scholar is discounted, and will only become valid when it is offered by a White scholar recognized by the academic establishment (p. 49). Deloria, Jr. (1995) points to many examples of Euro-western scientific frauds (e.g. Medel, Pasteur) and he points to subjects that are prohibited because they call into question long-standing beliefs. He describes how Euro-western science tenaciously holds on to its beliefs and how prestigious personalities dominate a field, creating a scientific folklore.

Given that background defense, Deloria, Jr. (1995) offers a Native American account of North American history. He looks at the scientific fields of anthropology, geology, and biology to call into question geological time scales, the Pleistocene overkill theory, and the Bering Strait theory. He helps us understand that Native Americans possess tremendous knowledge of Nature because they treat Nature as alive, and consider it a knowledgeable teacher, offering them countless lessons. They study mammals and birds to learn the use of medicinal plants, for example, and have always done so. However, Euro-western science does not recognize that knowledge as authentic until it is "westernized," as can be seen by the 1992 announcement, at the annual meeting of the American Association for the Advancement of Science, of a new field of study—"zoopharmacognosy"—studying the use of medicinal plants by animals (Deloria, Jr., 1995, p. 58). Deloria, Jr. suggests that in order for the Euro-western scientific world to take Indian knowledge seriously, a fundamental (e)pistemological shift must occur, one that recognizes humanity and nature as interconnected, interrelated, and alive.

Paula Gunn Allen (1986) connects Euro-western judgment of Native American philosophy-religion-science to patriarchy. She presents the case that Native Americans embraced gynocentric creation stories pre-contact by Euro-westerners by pointing to many examples of various tribal creation stories where women play central roles. Allen's case draws our attention to a strong connection for Native

Americans between females and nature. She describes how women have always held honored, respected roles within Native American tribes as spiritual leaders due to their intimate connection with Nature. Allen argues that Euro-western colonizers sought actively to replace the gynocentric focus of Native American views with patriarchal Euro-western models. One of the major ways this reshaping and remodeling occurred was through severing the Native American connection to Nature.

Euro-westerners pushed the Indigenous people of North America off their lands. By doing so, Native Americans were separated from not only their physical livelihoods, but also their source of knowledge, and their spiritual strength. With the loss of their land, they lost their sense of connected wholeness and their sense of direction. Native Americans lost control of not only their land, but their heritage as well. They have fought in every way imaginable to them to regain and maintain their connection to Nature, even resorting to allowing their gynocentric focus to be replaced with a patriarchal one. The results of these battles between Native American and Euro-western views have been devastating for Native Americans. Only recently have they begun to regain control of their heritage and heal the split between human beings and nature, between man and woman, forced upon them by Euro-westerners.

Allen's (1986) connection of Native Americans relationality with Nature to Native American ways of relating to women is a very important connection. While Buddhists and deep ecologists describe a strong relationality between human beings and nature, they do not address woman's role in this relationality. They deny the necessity of specifically addressing 'women' as a category. For Buddhists this specificity is not necessary for women can evolve to the higher spiritual category of men, as they continue their spiritual journey to Buddhahood. It is argued by deep ecologists that 'women' are subsumed under the general ontological category of 'human being.' However, feminists argue that history belies that assumption. 'Man' is assumed under the category of 'human being,' and 'woman' falls below man in the hierarchy, associated more with nature than with man (Merchant, 1980).

For a long time feminists have been trying to make explicit the connection between women and nature, and the destructive oppression that results to women *and* nature, due to a patriarchal hierarchy that devalues both of them. More recently this connection has been strongly drawn, and feminists working on this project have been labeled *ecofeminists*.[2] The efforts of ecofeminists make an important contribution to our understanding of ecological relations. They expand the metaphysical arguments for ecological relations to include political issues of power and domination. They help us understand that in order for us to begin to rethink environmental problems we must begin to reshape the power relations in the world. They argue that ecology remains an abstraction that is incomplete without making the connection between misogyny and hatred of nature (King, 1989). While deep ecologists argue against anthropomorphism, ecofeminists argue against anthropomorphism *and* androcentrism. With that distinction in mind, I turn now to a closer examination of women's relation to nature, and how this relation effects our ecological relations.

Woman and Nature

Feminists have been aware for a long time of the socially determining efforts of various cultures to link women to nature. In *The Second Sex*, Simone de Beauvoir (1952/1980/1989) described women and nature as the original "others." Women are defined in contrast to men and nature is defined in contrast to human beings and culture. Predominantly, women are linked conceptually to nature through biological arguments that focus on women's reproductive role. In the Euro-western world, where nature is described in contrast to human beings and is viewed as a force to dominate and control, linking women to nature places women in a dominated role as well. Linking women to nature also means women are defined in contrast to culture. The effort to link women to nature has been an argument for biological determinism. It has also been an argument for women's inferiority, and for harmful female sex-gender stereotypes used to justify women's subordination. It is an argument that is socially constructed so that "(w)omen's oppression becomes neither strictly historical nor strictly biological. It is both" (King, 1981, p. 15).

Ecofeminists such as Karen Warren (1987, 1988, 1990) and Ynestra King (1981, 1987, 1989, 1990) help us consider more closely the connection between the sexist treatment of women and ecological devastation. They suggest that these problems may have the same root, patriarchy. Ecofeminists insist that analysis of the human/nonhuman split must be grounded in an understanding of power and social reproduction. King, one of the earlier feminists contributing to the ecology movement, has been actively participating in ecological issues since the early 1970's, prior to the coining of the term 'ecofeminist.' King has contributed significantly to the development of ecofeminism as a concept and as a movement, publishing articles and teaching classes on ecofeminism at the Institute for Social Ecology in Vermont. She has helped organize conferences, and she has participated in direct action protests against war, nuclear energy, and toxic waste dumps, and in support of clean water, and organic farming, for example. She (1989) defines ecofeminism's basic principles as:

1) Western civilization is built around the subjugation of nature and women, who are believed to be closer to nature.
2) "Life on earth is an interconnected web, not a hierarchy" (p. 19). Ecofeminism seeks to show the connections between all forms of domination. Ecofeminism practice is necessarily anti-hierarchical.

3) "A healthy, balanced ecosystem, including human and nonhuman inhabitants, must maintain diversity" (p. 20).

4) We need a renewed understanding of our relationship to nature, one that challenges the dualism of nature/culture (pp. 19–20).

King (1981) argues that the nature/culture split is the primary contradiction of our time, and it is also the split that weds feminism to ecology. "Without an ecological perspective which asserts the interdependence of living things, feminism is disembodied" (King, 1981, p. 15). As King (1990) describes the task of ecofeminism, it is antidualistic, dialectical, involving theory and praxis. "Ecological feminism is about reconciliation and conscious mediation, about recognition of the underside of history and all the invisible voiceless activities of women over millennia. It is about connectedness and wholeness of theory and practice" (King, 1981, p. 15). She calls for a reenchantment of human beings with nature. I will come back to this call later in this section.

Warren (1990) carefully defines ecological feminism as "the position that there are important connections—historical, experiential, symbolic, theoretical—between the domination of women and the domination of nature" (p. 126). Warren argues that the connection between women and nature is a conceptual one that has been socially constructed. However, she rightfully points out that connecting women to nature does not lead automatically to oppression. We have already found this to be true, for Native American spiritual views connect women and men to Nature, as Spirit, and even emphasize women's biological role of reproductive mothering, and yet this connection did not lead to the domination and oppression of women. Instead, the connection of women to Nature led to Native Americans honoring and valuing women's role in creation. Women earned roles as spiritual leaders and healers in their tribes due to their relationship with Nature (Allen, 1986).

We have to introduce what Warren (1990) calls the "logic of domination" in order to explain and justify the subordination of women and nature to men and culture. Even if we consider socially constructed realities that are based on hierarchies and dualisms, hierarchies and dualisms are not inherently problematic either, according to Warren. She points to taxonomies and biological nomenclature as examples of hierarchical thinking that are important for classifying, organizing, and comparing material, and yet they do not make judgments concerning the value of that which is classified. We can even make value judgments and still not be guilty of oppression. It is what we do with our judgments, the way we use them to establish inferiority and then to argue that inferiority justifies subordination, that causes problems. The logic of domination is the step where subordination is applied. Without the establishment of moral superiority and that superiority justifies subordination, all we have established is that there are some differences (between man and woman, between man and nature, between culture and nature).

Warren (1990) carefully diagrams the ecofeminist argument, by first laying out the argument for patriarchy as argument B:

(B1) Women are identified with nature and the realm of the physical; men are identified with the 'human' and the realm of the mental.

(B2) Whatever is identified with nature and the realm of the physical is inferior to ('below') whatever is identified with the 'human' and the realm of the mental; or, conversely, the latter is superior to ('above') the former.

(B3) Thus, women are inferior to ('below') men; or conversely, men are superior to ('above') women.

(B4) For any X and Y, if X is superior to Y, then X is justified in subordinating Y.

(B5) Thus, men are justified in subordinating women (p. 130).

Notice that step B1 establishes an assumption of dualism, and step B2 establishes an assumption of hierarchy. We will find out below that some ecofeminists, such as social ecofeminists like Carol Merchant (1980, 1989, 1990, 1992), deny B1 as being true, biologically, while other ecofeminists, such as radical cultural ecofeminists like Mary Daly (1978/1990) claim that women are connected to nature, biologically, in ways that men are not. Some liberal feminists, such as de Beauvoir (1952/1980/1989), argue the truth of B2 is the reason for insisting on the severing of the dualism in B1, separating women from nature. No matter whether feminists agree on the truth of B1 and B2, all feminists oppose the logic of domination, step B4, and all feminists agree that it is a historical fact that B1 and B2 have been assumed to be true in the dominant Euro-western philosophical tradition. Ecofeminists argue that although B1 and B2 are historically sanctioned claims, they are problematic claims. "(T)hey are problematic precisely because of the way they have functioned historically in a patriarchal conceptual framework and culture to sanction the dominations of women and nature" (Warren, 1990, p. 131).

We found in the section above that Buddhists, deep ecologists, and Native Americans all deny the truth of B2, although they do not deny that B2 is a historically accurate description of Euro-western views of nature. Ecofeminists also deny the truth of B2. Deep ecologists are working to overturn the human sense of superiority over nonhuman nature. Buddhists and Native Americans deny the dualistic split in B1 between humans and nature.

Warren (1990) argues that "ecofeminism is necessary to *any* feminist critique of patriarchy, and hence, necessary to feminism" (p. 131, emphasis in original). This is because ecofeminism clarifies why a logic of domination must be abolished. "Feminism *must* embrace ecological feminism if it is to end the domination of women because the domination of women is tied conceptually and historically to the domination of nature.... A responsible environmental ethic also *must* embrace feminism" (pp. 143 and 144, emphasis in original). Warren does not present the arguments for the historical connections between the domination of women and nature. Instead, she points to others' work where that argument has already been made—one of the others being the feminist historical scholar, Carolyn Merchant (1980, 1989). Merchant serves as an excellent resource in this manner, for although she is not a philosopher and consequently her philosophical analysis is lacking, she is a historian of science and her historical analysis is strong. I turn to her as my source to help make the case for the historical sanctioning of nature and women as connected and inferior, by Euro-western philosophers, and scientists. Following Merchant, Mary Daly (1978/1990) will be my source to add to deep ecologists' case for the domination of women and nature by Christian theologians. This historical sanctioning by Euro-western philosophers, scientists, and theologians justified the subordination of nature and women to men and their cultures. I will return to Warren at the end of this section, for her argument for loving perception directly relates to my argument for caring reasoning.

As a historian of science, Merchant's (1980, 1989) focus is more on the contextual social and intellectual factors involved in the changes in science, than on the actual content of science itself. Merchant (1980) is interested in the overlapping values expressed by both feminism and ecology, as expressed by sharp criticism "of the costs of competition, aggression, and domination arising from the market econom(y), [and] the consequences of uncontrolled growth, [as well as by their efforts to] restore the balance of nature, . . . [and] live within the cycles of nature" (pp. xvi and xvii). She (1980) examines "the values associated with the images of women and nature as they relate to the formation of our modern world and their implications for our lives today," in an effort to liberate women and nature from anthropomorphic and androcentric views (p. xvii). In *Death of Nature*, Merchant (1980) traces the changes in European views of nature and women from ancient Greece through the work of the founding fathers of modern science: Francis Bacon, William Harvey, René Descartes, Thomas Hobbes, and Isaac Newton. In *Ecological Revolutions*, she (1989) traces the ecological history of North America, in particular New England, by looking at colonial America during the time frame of 1600–1860. She chooses to focus on New England because changes in its ecology and society were rapid and revolutionary. What took Europe 2500 years of development, the USA did in 1/10th the time.

In both books Merchant's (1980, 1989) themes are the same: the roots of the environmental crisis, the roles of women in history, the change from nature as mother to nature as machine, and the place of science in the creation of the modern world. She analyzes reproduction in relation to production, and science within the broader context of human consciousness. She looks at different ways of knowing nature, and how they change over time. Merchant (1989) tells us:

> My thesis is that ecological revolutions are major transformations in human relations with nonhuman nature. They arise from changes, tensions, and contradictions that develop between a society's mode of production and its ecology, and between its modes of production and reproduction. These dynamics in turn support the acceptance of new forms of consciousness, ideas, images, and worldviews. (pp. 2–3)

For Merchant (1980, 1989), science and history are both social constructs. She (1989) argues that nonhuman nature is an active complex that participates in change over time and responds to human-induced change. "Nature is a whole of which humans are only one part" (p. 8). The human-nonhuman relationship is reciprocal. Merchant describes an ecological paradigm as one that takes relations, context, and networks into consideration, and asserts the primacy of process in the natural world.

Merchant (1980, 1989) concludes that in 1500 the cosmos was bound together as a living organism. By 1700 it had become a machine. These two views have existed in underlying tension throughout time. The mechanistic view of nature assumes that nature can be divided into parts, the parts can be rearranged, and facts can be extracted and tested and verified by resubmitting to nature. The mechanistic view of nature assumes that science offers us objective, value-free and context-free knowledge of the external world. It attempts to reduce human behavior to statistical probabilities and conditioning (e.g. Skinner). Replacing the mechanistic paradigm is going to take a global social and economic revolution. According to Merchant (1989), this revolution will require getting rid of capitalism and patriarchy. If we can reintegrate nature with culture, mind with body, male with female, we can make the transition to a sustainable earth.

Ecological thinking rests on different assumptions about nature:

> (1) everything is connected to everything else in an integrated web; (2) the whole is greater than the sum of the parts; (3) nonhuman nature is active, dynamic, and responsive to human actions; (4) process, not parts, is primary; and (5) people and nature are a unified whole. (Merchant, 1989, p. 263)

Merchant (1989) points to new work in science: Gregory Bateson's ecology of mind; David Bohm's physics; James Lovelock's Gaia hypothesis; and chaos theory, as examples of changes that are taking place, moving us toward an ecological paradigm shift. I will turn to some of these examples in Chapter 8, for they do indicate a shift in science's focus to cyclical processes, the interconnectedness of all things, the essential role of every part of an ecosystem, and the leveling of hierarchies.

Merchant (1990, 1992) classifies her analysis of ecology and feminism as representing a socialist ecofeminist perspective. Social feminists place their focus on issues concerning social justice and domination, and offer a critique of capitalist patriarchy.

Social feminists describe nature in terms of how it functions as a material basis of life, supplying food, shelter, clothing, and energy. Nature is described as being socially and historically constructed (not biologically). The focus of their analysis is on the transformation of nature by production and reproduction. In general, social feminists have not paid too much attention to ecological issues, but rather place their focus on class, gender, and race issues. Merchant is an exception to the case, for as a social feminist, Merchant is the main scholar who has placed ecology on the socialist agenda. King (1981) compliments Merchant for focusing ecofeminists' attention on material conditions. But she criticizes Merchant for not including a spiritual focus. Social feminists do not place their attention on spirituality, preferring to focus on materiality as the force driving social change. They do not offer a utopian vision of how the world could be and a strong cultural foundation, and King (1981) suggests this is a lack, for it is vision and spirituality that drive a revolution.

King (1981) attempts to align Merchant's social feminism with liberal feminism, but this is an unfair representation of Merchant's work. Let me show why. Simone de Beauvoir (1952, 1980, 1989) is an excellent representative of a liberal feminist. De Beauvoir's position is that feminists must sever the woman-nature connection in order for women to achieve liberation. As long as women are tied to nature they will be devalued by society. She suggests that it is a sexist ploy to define women as being closer to nature than men. This liberal position does not seek to question the dualistic split between nature and man, or nature and culture, but rather seeks to place woman on the same side of the split as man, separated and disconnected from nature, and higher in value. Liberalism assumes the anthropocentric notion that humanity should dominate nature and that the domination of nonhuman nature is a precondition for human freedom. Because of this, as King (1981) rightly points out, liberal feminism is unwittingly anti-ecological. Merchant (1990, 1992) compares the liberal position to reform environmentalism, in contrast to radical ecology. Reform environmentalism seeks to improve our natural conditions and change human relations with nature through the passage of new laws and regulations. Their belief is that better science and better laws will solve our environmental problems. Liberalism's roots reside in the Enlightenment Euro-western philosophical-scientific analysis of nature as composed of atoms moved by external forces, and humans as individual rational agents who are motivated by self-interest.

Clearly, Merchant (1990) does not represent a liberal feminist position, such as de Beauvoir represents, for liberal feminism maintains its roots in the very mechanistic science Merchant argues against. Unlike liberal feminists such as de Beauvoir, Merchant does challenge the culture/nature split and she strongly maintains an ecological view of science. However, King's (1981) criticism that Merchant's socialist feminism lacks spirituality is a fair criticism. Merchant does focus on materiality at the expense of spirituality. Merchant (1990, 1992) labels the spiritual position that connects women to nature "radical ecofeminism." King (1981, 1990) labels the same position "radical cultural feminists," which is the term I will use as it more specifically describes the view. As we will find next, with a discussion of Mary Daly's *Gyn/Ecology* (1978, 1990), radical cultural feminists argue that women are closer to nature than men, and they celebrate women's biology and nature as sources of female power. Radical cultural feminists, such as the Native American, Paula Allen (1986), emphasize spiritual connections between women and nature, and consider spirituality to be the driving force for social change.

Merchant (1990, 1992) tells us that she worries that radical cultural feminism, "in emphasizing the female, body, and nature components of the dualities male/female, mind/body, culture/nature, . . . runs the risk of perpetuating the very hierarchies it seeks to overthrow" (1990, p. 102). However, there are many different examples of radical cultural feminists, some of whom are more dualistic in their perspectives than others, so to reduce them to one position is an unfair and inaccurate description. Paula Allen (1986) has a different perspective from Mary Daly (1978, 1990), or Susan Griffin (1978), and both Allen and Griffin avoid the dualisms Daly seems to want to embrace. Also, in her expressed concern, Merchant conflates dualities with hierarchies, yet Warren (1990) has demonstrated for us logically that dualisms and hierarchies are not one and the same thing. Warren also shows us that logically either one or even both together do not necessarily lead to oppression without the logic of domination.

Still, I share Merchant's concern about dualisms and hierarchies, for even though logically they do not necessarily lead to domination, historically they have tended to do so. Like King (1989, 1990), I think ecofeminism must be anti-hierarchical and anti-dualistic in its philosophy in order to have a chance of changing views on nature and women in a wholistic direction. We need to embrace a both/and logic. We must recognize the existence of differences and their vital importance in helping us gain perspective on our own views and in stimulating growth and change and at the same time we need to emphasize connections. I hope this text helps us recognize the interconnectedness of all things, as in a web, and their essential role in our ecosystem. In dualistic thinking the emphasis is on differences at the expense of connections. Before we know it, hierarchical values are placed on the differences, and one is valued more than the other. Then the logic of domination is applied easily to one side or the other of the dualistic split, and the result is oppression.

Native Americans stand as a strong example of cultural groups that maintain Nature is Spirit, and recognize that women have a strong connection to Nature, and yet Native Americans value women and honor them because of this connection, rather than devalue them and treat them in a subordinated role. Men are not disfavored in their cultures either. Yet, we will discover with Mary Daly's position, below, that Daly inverts the male/female, mind/body, culture/nature dualisms and embraces a hierarchical value in favor of the female, body, and nature components of the dualities, against the male side of the dualism. Her position threatens to reintroduce the logic of domination as she names males the enemy, and she refuses to teach male students in her classes.[4] In spite of Daly's radical stance, she does help us understand how to dissolve the very dualisms she seems to want to reify. And, she offers an important, strong analysis of Judeo-Christian theology's role in historically sanctioning the domination of women and nature.

Before turning to Daly's analysis, there is another criticism of Merchant's work that I would like to offer. It is also a criticism that will apply to Daly's work, below. Both authors contribute significantly to our understanding of the dominant Euro-western influence of philosophy, science, and theology on our present ecological condition. But, in the process they both neglect minority views and race as a category, so that the dominant influences, which are White, become totalizing and essentializing. Their arguments neglect an important form of domination and risk being reductionistic, as a result. The general criticism of neglecting minority views is a criticism that all feminists are guilty of to varying degrees.

As to the neglect of race as a category, this is a problem feminists such as Merchant and Daly have learned from and have sought to alleviate in their subsequent work. Because all feminists are opposed to the logic of domination, as Warren (1990) explains, they are easily able to include race as a category, once it is brought to their attention. Racism depends on the same logic of domination as sexism. Neither Merchant, nor Daly, intentionally neglected race and for both of them their analysis can easily be expanded to include race as a category as well as specific minority ethnic perspectives in their discussions. Merchant (1989) does expand her own historical analysis in *Ecological Revolutions* to include more minority perspectives, in particular Native American cultures. She offers a new synthesis—how different cultures occupied the same space with different effects on the environment. Daly addresses this issue in her newer introduction written for the 1990 printing of *Gyn/Ecology*, pointing out that she does cite women of color often in her original text, for example Adrienne Rich, and she thanked Audrey Lorde in the original Preface for her encouragement. She means her book to be an "Open Book." She apologizes for any pain her unintended omissions may have caused others, especially women of color. "The writing of *Gyn/Ecology* was for me an act of Biophilic Bonding with women of all races and classes, under all the varying oppressions of patriarchy" (p. xxxi). Let us move on to a discussion of Daly's (1978/1990) *Gyn/Ecology* specifically.

Mary Daly (1978/1990) represents an excellent example of a radical cultural feminist. Rather than trying to sever women from nature, as liberal feminists tend to do, radical cultural feminists delve deeply into the woman/nature connection and celebrate the relationship between women and nature. Rather than focusing on material conditions, as socialist feminists tend to do, they embrace a spiritual focus. Theirs is a deeply women-identified position that celebrates spirituality. Allen

(1986) serves as another excellent example of a radical cultural feminist whom we have already come across. Allen (1986) turns back to pre-contact Native American creation stories to highlight women's connection to nature. We find in *Gyn/Ecology* that Daly (1978/1990) looks to prehistory (pre-Greeks) for examples of Goddesses (Ishtar, Isis, Demeter and Persephone, Shekinah) to highlight women's connection to nature.

Daly (1978/1990) is a philosopher and theologian, holding Ph.D.'s in both fields of study. She is a professor of theology and her approach to the women/nature issue emphasizes her theological background, in particular her Christian background. *Gyn/Ecology* is Daly's powerful deconstruction of Christianity's hatred of women and nature, and her own celebrative embracement of the women/nature connection. As Daly describes her task, she is exorcising christianity, as noxious gases, and spinning anew. As I shift into Daly's language, it is important to point out that Daly plays with language a great deal in her text, similarly to other postmodern philosophers. Her use of language is very consciously done, to draw our attention to the meaning of words, and to actively work to change that meaning. For example, Daly does not capitalize words we commonly capitalize, such as 'christianity,' and she does capitalize words that are not normally capitalized, such as 'Lesbian.' *Gyn/Ecology* is written in a non-scholarly style that draws the reader's attention to words and language, and invents new words as well as recreates old ones. Many of Daly's references are to the dictionary and the etymology of words. Notice that even in her title, she takes the standard term for the medical science of women's diseases and severs the term, and reappropriates it. When the title is displayed visually, we discover that the '/' used to split 'gyn' from 'ecology' is the double-axe of the Amazons, the Labrys, which Daly uses to cut through double-binds and double-binding words.

Daly (1978/1990) seeks to emphasize that her view is a woman's view, a wild woman's view. Her sources are women's experiences, thus the reason for 'gyn' in her title. She describes a Journey, a Voyage for the Lesbian imagination in All Women, for the Hag/Crone/Spinster in every *living* woman. She uses 'ecology' to point to the complex web of interrelationships between organisms and their environment. Daly is concerned with what she calls pollutions of the mind/body/spirit inflected through patriarchal myth and language on all levels. Thus, besides focusing on language, Daly focuses on myths and symbols that are direct sources of christian myths.

One of Daly's (1978/1990) very important contributions to feminist scholarship is the distinction she makes between foreground (which is the male, patriarchal world) and deep Background (which is the feminist world). We discovered in Chapters 1 and 2 that Dewey and James make a similar distinction between foreground and background. Background is pure experience and foreground is the meanings we give to that pure experience. Foreground experiences are always in addition to pure experiences; they do not take away from pure experience. But foreground draws our attention to noticing certain of our experiences and not others, causing us to lose awareness of much of our pure experience, all that is not caught in the ontological net of categories our foreground uses. I also discussed this idea in Chapter 5, with Berger and Luckmann's description of a socially constructed reality as foreground.

Daly (1978/1990) makes a metaphysical distinction between pure experience in its fullness, undifferentiated, as background, and experience that is categorized and socially constructed, as foreground. For Daly, the foreground we all experience is patriarchy, and she means *all*, for she describes patriarchy as the prevailing religion of the entire planet. Here is an example of the tendency to reductionism I pointed to earlier, for we know from Chapter 6 that Native American cultures did not embrace patriarchy in their creation myth stories. According to Allen (1986), patriarchy was imposed on Native American spirituality by the White colonizers of America, when they brought their christian myths to America and insisted that Native Americans must convert to christianity. In *Gyn/Ecology*, Daly (1978/1990) tries to uncover the language and myths that hide the background of women's experiences. For Daly, every woman is a battered woman, at a psychic level, from the start, due to the patriarchical foreground that surrounds her.

Part I is an uncovering of the master's maze in christianity, a charting of deadly deception and dismemberment (Processions). Daly (1978/1990) focuses on the all male Trinity (Father, Son, and Holy Ghost) and its circular pattern for muted existence. She also considers christian myths, pointing to Apollo as "the personification of anti-matriarchy, the opponent of Earth deities" (p. 62), and Dionysus as the other face of the same god. Dionysus's mother is already dead long before he is born, as his father, Zeus, "dispenses with the woman and bears his own son" (p. 65). Daly describes Sadomasochism and male methods of mystification: erasure of women, reversal, false polarization, and divide and conquer techniques (p. 8). She contrasts the christian trinity as the paradigm of processions to triple Goddesses of early mythology, such as Athena (Greece), Neith (Libya), Hera-Demeter-Korê (pre-Hellenic), and Eire-Fodhla-Banbha (Irish), for example. The basic pattern represents Maiden, Nymph, and Crone, or Maiden, Mother, and Moon (p. 76). The Goddesses represent the Tree of Life, but with christianity, the tree becomes the symbol of the torturing cross, and "Christ assimilates/devours the Goddess," as he becomes the symbol of life (p. 81). The cauldron, which was a symbol associated with the Mother Goddess, identified as women's transforming power, is stolen by christian myth and becomes the chalice, "a symbol of the alleged transforming power of an all male priesthood" (p. 82). Daly's point is that "(i)n christendom as well as in postchristian secular society, the words/expressions of female spirit are raped, twisted, tortured, dismembered" (p. 93).

Part II is a study of various Sado-Ritual Syndromes, the Re-enactment of Goddess Murder. In particular, Daly shows us how the female spirit is "raped, twisted, tortured, dismembered" through the vivid examples of: India-Suttee (widows ceremoniously burned alive on the funeral pyres of their husbands); Chinese footbinding

(binding a young girl's feet so they will remain small, thus crippling her); African genital mutilation (the circumcision and then sewing up of much of the young girl's exterior genital area, to insure virginity at marriage); European witchburning; American gynecology; and Nazi medicine and American gynecology compared.

Part III is Daly's (1978/1990) positive vision, Gyn/Ecology, which she describes as: Spooking (positive paranoia, unpainting, re-membering, enspiriting the self, bonding with daughters, learning to hear and respond to the call of the wild), Sparking (Female Friendship, in contrast to war's comrades), and Spinning (weaving tapestry's of our own creation, spiraling, whirling). Daly affirms in Gyn/Ecology that everything is connected with everything else. Creativity is spinning in the sense of dis-covering the lost thread of connectedness, repairing the web, spiraling, whirling. Spinning as amphibious/multibious be-ings, spinning as spiders. "Genuine Spinning is spiraling, which takes us over, under, around the baffle gates of godfathers into the Background" (p. 405). It's a holistic process of knowing. "The metapatriarchal journey begins with hearing the dissonent voices of the foreground and dis-spelling them" (p. 405). This is the function Part I and II have in Daly's text, to hear the dissonent voices of the foreground (patriarchy) and dis-spell them. She seeks to re-claim life-loving female energy, and argues that males' very existence depends on stolen female energy. "If patriarchal males loved life, the planet would be different" (p. 352). Daly describes the State of Patriarchy as the State of War (rape).

Daly (1978/1990) argues that males fear female bonding as a much bigger threat then infidelity. This is because Sisterhood is an affirmation of freedom. Sisterhood does not result in loss of self-identity but rather encourages the expression of it, discovery of it, creation of it. Sisterhood encourages self-acceptance. Female Friendship does not result in merging, tokenism, or self-sacrificing. Since we begin our lives in patriarchy, we begin in an injured state, not a state of innocence. Our Voyage is not to regain lost innocence, but is to learn innocence, to increase innocence. "Powerful innocence is seeking and naming the deep mysteries of interconnectedness" (414). Crones are constantly weaving and unweaving. "Unweaving involves undoing our conditioning in femininity" (p. 409). Daly's Part I and Part II are examples of unweaving. Part III is her weaving. She is Spinning so she can survive. "Ceasing to Spin is subviving" (p. 410). Daly affirms that gyn/ecologists have "a deep communion with our natural environment" (p. 409).

The reader can easily see that Merchant (1990) is right to be concerned that Daly's position is one that reifies the very dualities she seeks to overthrow. Daly (1978/1990) vividly portrays the logic of domination as it has been used in Christianity to oppress women and nature, so vividly that it is painful to read. Her focus is on the logic of domination as patriarchy, and its effects on women. She does not discuss how patriarchy harms males as well. Consequently, she maintains a sharp split between women and men, and romanticizes women as good in contrast to evil men. In doing so she also essentializes women, not adequately addressing the real diversity of womens' lives and histories across race, class, and national boundaries. As King (1981) points out with radical socialist feminism (Merchant) and radical cultural feminism (Daly): "The problem with both analyses, however, is that gender identity is neither fully natural nor fully cultural. And it is neither inherently oppressive nor inherently liberating" (p. 13).

Daly's (1978, 1990) painful, powerful analysis of Christianity's patriarchy and its harm to women and nature can work to help us become aware of the acculturation, the conditioning we have *all* experienced (not just females). Her methodology of carefully examining the symbols, myths, and language upon which our ideas rest, similar to Allen's and Merchant's, helps us understand how to critique our own acculturation. Daly's historical tracing of myths back to origins helps us find ways to undo the harm our myths created, through the wrong-headed directions our myths took. She shows us how to contrast our myths and symbols to others, not like ours, so we can better critique our own by gaining an outsider's perspective. We can retrace our steps and learn where we went wrong, re-conceive and re-vision our world, then re-tell our myths, re-write them, re-weave them. In that re-telling, it is vital that we eliminate the logic of domination, in all its forms, and create "a world in which *difference does not breed domination*" (Warren, 1990, p. 145, emphasis in original). This section should make it vividly clear to Buddhists and deep ecologists that focusing on nature's domination without addressing women's domination will not lead to the end of oppression for either nature or women, as both are supported by patriarchy. The voices of socialist feminists should remind us we must address material issues as well, and work to solve the oppression of poverty. The voices of Native American scholars and other minority scholars represented here should also make it clear to White scholars, male and female, that we will not end the oppression of nature until we address racism as well. These same voices, and those of radical cultural feminists such as Daly, should remind us of the importance of addressing our spiritual needs.

King (1990) contrasts ecofeminism to liberal, social, and cultural feminism, arguing that they all make contributions to help us find our ways, but they all surrender to some form of natural determinism that ecofeminism does not surrender to (p. 130). She points to a need for a dynamic developmental theory of the person, a need for mystery (spirituality) and attention to personal alienation. She calls for "rational reenchantment," which she means as a healing of the heart/mind split, a healing of the split between the political and the spiritual, between the spiritual and material, between being and knowing. This is the project of ecofeminism, "the moment where women recognize ourselves as agents of history—yes, even as unique agents—and knowingly bridge the classic dualisms between spirit and matter, art and politics, reason and intuition" (King, 1990, pp. 120–121).

As King (1987) points out, ecofeminists do not think we should abolish science, but rather that we should do science as Barbara McClintock (Keller, 1983) and Rachel Carson (1962) have done, with compassion, by connecting loving and knowing

(p. 731). I will discuss McClintock's work in Chapter 8. This connection between loving and knowing, between the heart and the mind, is what I refer to as caring reasoning (see Chapter 4). Caring reasoning is not practiced just with other human beings, as part of the larger natural world, but with all others that make up the natural world. Caring reasoning is the art of generously and attentively listening to the other, presuming and maintaining differences (pluralism), recognizing the importance of valuing and respecting the other, while at the same time acknowledging and appreciating our commonalities and our interconnectedness with each other. Caring reasoning highlights how we are separate and distinct and how we are connected. Caring reasoning allows us to use our hearts and our minds, to openly embrace others as well as critique others. We cannot fairly critique until we have lovingly perceived the other. By other, I do mean all others in the cosmos, as related kin.

With an ecological relationality we do not need to draw our attentions to social justice at the expense of spirituality or vice versa, for a w/holistic relational ontology insists the two cannot be separated. Our metaphysical assumptions and our epistemological assumptions exist in a transactional relationship with each other. Issues of power, as we have found with our discussion of patriarchy, are very connected to spirituality issues, as we discovered with our discussion of transcendental theology. A relational (e)pistemology, which is supported by a relational ontology, helps us focus our attention on our interrelatedness, and our interdependence with each other and our greater surroundings. It helps us become more aware of our foreground so that we can critique it. A relational (e)pistemology is contextually situated and in process. It is critically deconstructive as well as creatively reconstructive. It helps us dive back into our inarticulate primal experience, as a whole, not separate from nature or each other, but one with all of life. I move on now to consider recent changes in scientific ideas, which depend on a paradigm shift away from atomism and individuality, away from mechanism and dead, inert nature, toward an alive, compassionate, connected, relational approach.

CHAPTER 8

Scientific Relations

In Chapter 1, I began with the difficult task of describing Epistemology within the context of Philosophy, as historically defined in the Euro-western world. I did so to help point to assumptions and biases that are embedded within the study of Philosophy, as defined. We learned that a hierarchy of value and importance has developed toward the various fields of study within Philosophy and that this hierarchy reflects embedded biases, such as the valuing of abstraction over practice. Thus we found that Metaphysics and Epistemology enjoy higher status in Philosophy, due to their increased level of abstraction and removal from the world of practice, whereas ethical and political theory are treated more as applied fields of study in Philosophy and have lower status. We also learned, in Chapter 1, that feminists began their contributions to Philosophy from the margins, from the realms of ethical and political theory. They have worked their way into the core fields of study in Philosophy, Metaphysics and Epistemology, by challenging the basic assumptions and biases upon which these fields of study are based. Feminists challenge the Philosophical premise that a neutral, inclusive, general account of knowledge is possible. Philosophy's will to transcendent power and its desire to embrace dualisms such as theory/practice, mind/body, knower/known, subject/object are also called into question.

It should not be surprising to discover that Euro-western scientists, in their efforts to break away from Philosophy and carve out their own field of study, brought with them their own set of assumptions and biases which have shaped science's defining.[1] We have already run into many of these assumptions and biases, in particular in Chapter 7, with Carol Merchant's (1980) description of the history of science in regards to its view of nature. Historians of science name Francis Bacon, William Harvey, René Descartes, Thomas Hobbes, and Isaac Newton as the founding fathers of modern science and they describe the Scientific Revolution as occurring during the 16th and 17th centuries. The formation of the Royal Society in England in 1660 is used as a way to mark the beginning of science as we know it today. We learned in Chapter 7 that the modern definition of science that became dominant is based on a mechanistic (and patriarchal) view of nature that describes the world as a machine that is passive and inert (and nature as a woman who should be forced to reveal herself, and who should be subdued and controlled).

Modern science's mechanistic view is reflected in the basic scientific assumption that the universe is fundamentally made up of smaller and smaller parts (scientific reductionism). These parts are the building blocks for the machine, the smallest parts being labeled 'atoms,' which are assumed to be elementary solid particles. This reductionistic, mechanistic view of the universe describes matter as being inert, like billiard balls, which bounce off of each other. The force that acts between particles is gravity. Scientists assumed a strictly causal and determinate nature of physical phenomena. Science also embraced assumptions it inherited from Euro-western Philosophy, such as the idea that subjects can be separated from their objects of study, that there exists an independence between observers and what they observe, as well as the idea that the measurements we use to test out and answer our questions are neutral. Scientists assumed they could offer an objective description of nature and this assumption is still with us today, even though relativity theory and quantum theory both insist that an objective description of nature is no longer valid, that the observer is included in the complicated web of relations between the various parts of the whole, and that scientists can only offer theories that are approximations of a universe that is multidimensional, creative, alive, and flowing.

It is not surprising that science is structured hierarchically, similarly to Philosophy, based on its built-in assumptions and biases. Scientists do not describe themselves in a hierarchical fashion, however, but in terms of fundamental levels. Physics is considered the most fundamental science for it strives to describe the universe at the most basic level, the movement of the simplest parts of particles. Chemistry follows physics, and biology follows chemistry, in terms of levels of fundamentality. Is it just a coincidence that we find, as we found in Chapter 1 with Philosophy, that women scientists make their contributions to science mainly in the field of biology and related areas? Or, is it similar to Philosophy, that women scientists start on the margins of biology, as they work their way in toward the core field of physics? In all the reading I have done (which I do not claim to be comprehensive, but it is substantial), I have only read about one woman physicist, Marie Curie, yet I have read about many women biologists.

We find many who rush to give scientists accolades for the tremendous leaps of knowledge they have achieved in the last 300 plus years as scientists seek to master and tame nature. Great achievements are pointed to, such as electrical lighting, refrigeration, and central heating, the train, automobile, and airplane, the radio, telephone, television, and computers, and medical advances such as vaccines, organ transplants, and laser surgery. Science is pointed to as the prime example of how we are getting closer and closer to Truth, following Peirce's linear theory of knowledge described in Chapter 2. It cannot be denied, significant contributions have been made by scientists, and continue to be made, to improve the qualities of our lives and as a result people are living longer lives. However, many others are quick to point out the destruction that has resulted from scientific "advancements" as well. Examples of destruction include the extinction of a large number of plants and animals, environmental pollution (air, water, and land), overpopulation and resulting starvation, and an increase in violent crimes and death due to advanced forms of killing machines (guns, bombs, missiles). The mounting evidence of the adverse consequences of science to the qualities of our lives can also not be denied.

Most important for my discussion in this chapter is the argument that the image of life/nonlife that science has held since ancient Greece is useful in some contexts, but inaccurate as a description. There is an exciting paradigm shift, to use Kuhn's (1962, 1970) terminology, occurring in science that is leaving the reductionistic, mechanistic, neutrally objective assumptions of science behind. The shift is toward a wholistic and intrinsically dynamic conception of the universe (Capra, 1982). Scientists are beginning to recognize that everything in the universe is alive, even the soil, similar to Native American views described in Chapter 7. Scientists are beginning to describe the universe as nondualistic and complementary, similar to the Buddhist idea of the unity of all things described in Chapters 6. While present-day physicists may disagree with the concepts I emphasize here, they all agree that physics has gone through a paradigm shift and has transcended the mechanistic view of the world for which Descartes and Newton are often cited.[2]

Once again I find myself in the difficult, and humbling position of writing about a field of study from the perspective of an outsider to that field. I am not a scientist, but a philosopher who is interested in scientific relational ideas. When the discussion of scientific theories slides into mathematical formulas, as it often does, I am lost in a foreign, highly technical language. Still, there are many who are writing about the current paradigm shift that science is going through in lay terms that nonscientists can understand, and they serve as invaluable sources for me. In particular I will rely on John Briggs and David Peat (1984, 1989), and Fritjof Capra (1975, 1982) to help me not get lost along the way. Again I find myself in the difficult and very encouraging position of feeling like I have opened Pandora's box and discovered incredible possibilities to choose from for this chapter on scientific relations. There is so much exciting work going on in science today that is contributing to this paradigm shift! Once again I must be very selective in order to do justice to anyone's particular contributions, and I must encourage the interested reader to seek further readings.

Because the foundational structure of science has had such an impact on the shaping of this field of study, I will follow it and allow physics to lead the way in dismantling its own foundational status. I will begin with a discussion of relativity theory and quantum theory, and consider the directions this work is moving toward with a discussion of solid state and particle physics, through the work of David Bohm.

However, I plan to discuss these theories in conjunction with the Eastern comparisons of Fritjof Capra (1975), who highlights in his work the same themes I have already developed in Chapters 6 and 7. As examples of systems theory, I will turn to the chemist, J. E. Lovelock (1979/1987, 1988), and his Gaia theory, which describes the earth as a self-regulating single living organism. Lynn Margulis (1997, 1999), a microbiologist, has contributed significantly as a co-author to Lovelock's Gaia theory and I will include her contributions as well as her (1982, 1998) co-evolutionary theory based on collaboration. I will end with a discussion of Barbara McClintock's (1983) biological work in plant genetics and her theory of transposition. In this way, we will find that while the men start this recent scientific revolution toward a transactional relational view of the universe, women scientists are contributing their own influences, as some of them rely on compassionate methodologies (similar to the Buddhist dharma of compassion) to describe a universe that is transactional and collaborative.

The scientists we will study in this chapter are all people who began their very promising careers within the standards and guidelines of their fields of study. However, for all of them, as they became more and more immersed within their prospective fields, they came across questions and paradoxes that they perceived could only be solved by taking a larger, more wholistic perspective. Their various insights within their fields of study caused them to shift their focuses beyond the boundaries in which they were trained. These scientists have been viewed as mavericks in their own times, often placed in outsider roles, but their ideas have grudgingly come to be recognized as being very important and correct. Several of them are Nobel laureates in their fields of science. All have contributed significantly to a paradigm shift in science from a particular, separate view of nature that is mechanical and inert, to a wholistic view of a universe as unified, complementary, dynamic, and compassionate.

We will find in this chapter that the boundary between science and philosophy has become very porous and at times as I describe physics the reader will think I am referring to metaphysics. Again we will find powerful examples of scholars who have to address the Philosophical assumptions of transcendent Epistemological standards which science has embraced, in order for them to call into question science's will to transcendental power so that their theories are considered seriously and generously. Scientists are aided by mathematics in their efforts to translate their perceptions and insights, their direct experience, into a proof that others will understand and accept. But still, they must translate their mathematical proofs into a theoretical explanation that uses common language and relies on common sensorial experiences that can be very deceiving indeed. The scientists in this chapter have learned that the assumptions they make and the theories they develop affect what they see. They have learned that science is not neutral, objective, and universal, all the transcendent qualities Philosophy and Religion have already tried to claim. They have discovered that science is socially constructed and that it is impossible to separate the observable from the observer. There is no reality that exists separate from you and I. The scientists in this chapter have discovered that criteria and standards can be in error and must be corrigible in order to help us compensate for social influences on criteria and standards and what we define as "reality." The scientists I present have come to the realization that we live in a world that is dynamic and alive, a world that is unified, complementary, and connected, and that the way to understand it is through compassion, co-operation, and humility, with the help of a relational (e)pistemology.

The Universe as Unified, Complementary, and Dynamic

Capra (1975) begins *The Tao of Physics* with comparisons between what he calls Eastern mysticism (in which he includes Buddhism, Hinduism, Chinese thought, Taoism, and Zen) and the new physics. He points out that 'physics' means "the endeavour of seeing the essential nature of all things," which is also the central aim of all mystics (p. 20). Capra includes separate quotes by the famous scientists, Robert Oppenheimer, Neils Bohr, and Werner Heisenberg, in which they each draw parallel comparisons between the new physics and the traditions of the Far East. Relativity theory and quantum mechanics are causing scientists to radically revise basic concepts such as space, time, matter, energy, cause, and effect. The new physics is shifting its view of the world from a mechanical view to one that is organic, describing the universe as unified and mutually interrelational, as well as intrinsically dynamic. These are basic concepts that are very much in harmony with Buddhism's dharma of dependent co-origination discussed in Chapter 6.

Relativity Theory

What is it that physicists discovered that shook their basic concepts at such a foundational level and caused them to develop a more subtle, wholistic, and organic view of nature? The journey into transcending the limits of our sensory imagination begins in the world of the infinitely small, in atomic physics, but also turns toward the infinitely large. At the age of 26, Albert Einstein published two articles in 1905 that had a tremendous impact on physics and earned him the Nobel prize in physics in 1921. One article drastically changed our concepts of space and time and became the basis for his theory of relativity. Einstein spent the next 10 years almost single-handed developing his general theory of relativity. The other article was on electromagnetic radiation, which was to become the basis for quantum theory and took 20 years and an international team of scientists to work out. That team of scientists includes: Niels Bohr from Denmark, Louis de Broglie from France, Erwin Schrödinger and Wolfgang Pauli from Austria, Werner Heisenberg from Germany, and Paul Dirac from England (Capra, 1975). Bohr won the Nobel prize in physics in 1922, de Broglie in 1929, Heisenberg in 1932, Dirac and Schrödinger in 1933, and Pauli in 1945. Before describing what is known as the Copenhagen interpretation of quantum theory, which was developed by Bohr and Heisenberg in the late 1920's, and then contrasting that view to David Bohm's (1980) interpretation, I would like to follow Einstein's path further, to trace his significant contributions to physics in relativity theory.

It is interesting to note at the beginning of our discussion of relativity theory and quantum theory that while Einstein's ideas on electromagnetic radiation showed that energy possesses a particle-like nature, which became the basis for quantum theory, indeed Einstein even gave quantum theory its name by calling the energy that is emitted in packets rather than continuously, 'quanta,' Einstein did not agree with quantum theory's description of nature as discontinuous (Capra, 1975). Relativity is based on the idea of continuous fields. Both Einstein's and Bohr's separate theories led to the same conclusion, "that there was a wholeness to the universe, but the theories that led to this insight contradicted one another" (Briggs and Peat, 1984, p. 67). Einstein spent his later years trying to prove quantum theory was wrong, and he severed his relationship with Bohr. While Einstein was revered for his early work, he found himself criticized by his colleagues later in his life for not being willing to accept quantum theory as the new science (Briggs and Peats, 1984, say he was "pitied," p. 73). Today we have the insight to see that both scientists were still clinging to biases and assumptions from the classical mechanistic description of science, and we understand now how the two theories work together as complementary descriptions of a wholistic universe. Relativity theory emphasizes the order in the universe and quantum theory emphasizes the disorder, and we know now that the two are "dynamically and mysteriously intertwined" (Briggs and Peat, 1989).

According to Briggs and Peat (1989), Einstein strongly believed in nature's inherent harmony, and he sought a unified foundation of physics. He believed that there is an existent real world separate and independent of you and I (realism). For Einstein, the universe had to be objective and deterministic. His theory was founded on what he called 'observables.' He took as his starting point only things that could be measured and observed, and he threw everything else out in his effort to get rid of metaphysics. He criticized quantum theory for being incomplete, meaning that it lacked a clear cause-effect picture, for quantum theory describes the world in terms of probability. Einstein did not recognize that his criteria of clarity and cause-effect are based on metaphysical assumptions. Einstein assumed that the observed is separate from the observer. Because of his insistence on objectivity, which we will discover below quantum theory proves is impossible, Einstein did not allow himself to completely let go of modern science's paradigm, and shift into the wholistic paradigm we find today, which his own theories triggered. He certainly gave physicists a push in the direction of a wholistic view of the universe, even if he was not able to follow that direction completely himself. We will find below that Bohr also clung to some assumptions of his own, namely that the universe is made up of parts, discrete or separate units, and no picture of wholeness is possible. Einstein's and Bohr's stories serve as two examples of how paradigms are like maps that help permit vision, but they also limit it. Today physicists accept both relativity theory and quantum theory as true and they are making rapid advances in unifying the two theories (Briggs and Peat, 1984). We will look at some of those advances through David Bohm's (1980) "implicate order."

Newton's classical physics was based on a model of absolute, three-dimensional space and time which is supported by Euclidean geometry, dating back to ancient Greece. Geometry was believed to be inherent in nature, rather than a model that human beings have created and imposed upon nature. Newton's three-dimensional model treats space as independent of the material objects it contains, and treats time as a separate dimension which flows at the same, even rate absolutely, again independent of material objects (Capra, 1975). Newton described movement as absolute movement, arguing that any movement could be measured and compared to any other movement. "The problem was that Newton admitted that scientists might never be able to show by experiment that absolute motion really existed" (Briggs and Peat, 1984, p. 56). Using his methodology of excluding what could not be observed as an example of metaphysics, Einstein recommended that the theory of absolute motion be dropped (as well as the theory of ether which was proposed to be the material that filled empty space but was also unobservable).

Einstein's relativity theory describes space as not being three-dimensional and time as not being a separate entity. He argued that space and time are intimately connected and form what he called a 'space-time continuum,' a fourth dimension. Einstein elevated the speed of light to the level of a new principle of physics. He suggested that observers who moved at different speeds would see events in different ways. Because light needs time to travel from an event to the observer, what might look like a single event to one observer may appear as two distinct events to another, depending on the observers' positions in relation to the event. Others misunderstood Einstein's theory of relativity to be saying that the universe is relative, that each of us sees a different universe, but this was not Einstein's claim. "The act of observation in no way affected Einstein's universe" (Briggs and Peat, 1984, p. 59). For Einstein, the universe is real, objective, and independent of the observer. The laws of nature supply the invariant objectivity necessary to guarantee us that no matter how observers move, and experience different phenomena, and make different measurements of the same event, we will be able to translate these differences and come to an agreement. Einstein's metaphysical and epistemological assumptions seem to be very much in agreement with Pierce's (1933–58, see Chapter 2).

Einstein's theory of relativity demonstrated that matter (mass) and energy can not be separated. Einstein found that matter and energy are equivalent, that whether something is considered matter or energy depends on the frame of reference. "Relativity theory showed that mass has nothing to do with any substance, but is a form of energy" (Capra, 1975, p. 77). Thus we have Einstein's famous equation: $E = mc^2$, energy equals mass multiplied by the speed of light, squared. The speed of light (c) is the constant that is fundamentally important for the theory of relativity. With relativity, new notions of structure are implied which emphasize events and processes rather than conceiving of matter in terms of the idea of a rigid body. Particles are now described as "bundles of energy" rather than as consisting of basic "stuff," and "the implication is that the nature of subatomic particles is intrinsically dynamic" (Capra, 1975, p. 202-203). Particles are understood as four-dimensional entities in space-time.

In 1915 Einstein expanded what is now referred to as the 'special theory of relativity' to include gravity and this expanded theory is known as the 'general theory of relativity' (Capra, 1975). He found that his original theory did not account for acceleration, and that without solving the problem of acceleration his special relativity theory was only half a theory. "(A)cceleration appeared to suggest there is an absolute background against which things move" (Briggs and Peat, 1984, p, 63). However, Einstein conceived one day in 1907 that a man falling from a roof would not experience gravity and that if he was carrying a brief case as he was falling and he let go of the brief case, "the brief case wouldn't fall but would remain where it was relative to him, though of course both man and brief-case would be falling relative to the ground" (Briggs and Peat, 1984, p, 63). This must mean that gravity and acceleration are indissolubly tied together. Einstein realized that gravity and acceleration are mathematically equivalent, which then caused him to conclude that since acceleration is a geometric concept, gravity must be too.

> But if gravity and acceleration can be considered the same thing, Einstein reasoned, what looks like the force of gravity pulling things in curves (or orbits) around planets is actually acceleration. Therefore, if things accelerate in curves, he realized, it must be because space itself is curved. He called these curves in space-time 'geodesics.' (Briggs and Peat, 1984, p, 64)

Einstein's general theory of relativity has been expanded to include ideas such as "black holes" in our curved space, and his theory has been confirmed and is considered well established today, thanks to accurate atomic clocks, artificial satellites, and laser distance determinators, for example. Einstein spent the rest of his life trying to develop a "unified field theory" which supported his vision of the universe as a harmonious whole, where "everything is ultimately equivalent to and transforms into everything else" (Briggs and Peat, 1984, p. 67). He was not able to achieve this theory, but others, such as David Bohm (1980), have contributed further to this goal. Einstein was able to help change the way science perceived the universe. He revealed a world for us where concepts that seemed entirely different, such as space and time, have been unified. He saw a universe that is continuous and indivisible. Doesn't this sound similar to Buddhism's dharma of dependent co-origination, or co-arising, the idea that all things are connected and interlinked, that all things are interdependent?

Recall, Buddhism stresses the unity and mutual interrelation of all things and events. Buddhism teaches us that our divisions are abstractions that we have created which are illusionary. Physicists are discovering the same insight—"that the constituents of matter and the basic phenomena involving them are all interconnected, interrelated and interdependent; that they cannot be understood as isolated entities, but only as integrated parts of the whole" (Capra, 1975, p. 131). Einstein's general theory of relativity helped to highlight assumptions and biases embedded within Newton's classics physics, and convince us these were illusionary theoretical constructs of the world that did not describe the world as it is. According to Bohm (1980), the theory of relativity was the first theory to seriously question classical physics's mechanistic assumptions. Einstein convinced us that the notion of absolute time and space is wrong, as well as the notion that matter is substance made up of inert particles. I turn now to quantum theory, also known as quantum mechanics, which developed out of Einstein's idea that matter is a form of energy. We leave the journey into the world of the infinitely large behind and travel now into the world of the infinitely small, in atomic physics.

Quantum Theory

Quantum theory is the theory of atomic phenomena. Capra (1975) informs us: "The mathematical framework of quantum theory has passed countless successful tests and is now universally accepted as a consistent and accurate description of all atomic phenomena" (p. 132). However, the description of that mathematical framework in common language is not so easily in general agreement. According to Capra (1975) and Briggs and Peat (1984, 1989), the most accepted description is one developed by Bohr and Heisenberg in the late 1920's, known as the Copenhagen interpretation—therefore that is the one I will now present, with David Bohm (1980) then offering critique of this interpretation. The story of quantum theory seems to begin with Niels Bohr's suggestion of an atomic model that differed from the planetary model proposed by Ernest Rutherford. "Rutherford said the atom was like a tiny solar system, with a massive central core surrounded by lighter orbiting electrons" (Briggs and Peat, 1984, p. 35). Bohr was attracted to this model, but realized that when the laws of classical physics were applied to the model, calculations said that the atom would collapse, thus suggesting that all atoms should collapse, and the universe should have no stability. Since we do have a universe that is able to maintain form, something must be wrong with the model and/or the laws of classical physics.

Bohr was also attracted to Max Planck's idea "that light energy can be emitted and absorbed in discrete or separate units he called 'quanta'" (Briggs and Peat, 1984, p. 38). Physicists were wresting with a paradox that had developed at the time, because light had been demonstrated in the early 1800's to be a wave, and Einstein showed that light, as Planck suggested, is a particle. How could light behave like a wave and a particle? Bohr proposed a model for the atom that integrated the new insights of Planck and Einstein on the discontinuous quantum nature of energy with Rutherford's framework of the atom as orbits around a central body, which is based on classical Newtonian physics, suggesting:

> that the possible energy levels for an atom are 'quantized,' that is, they are fixed and discrete. An electron can move only in certain separate orbits, almost like a set of grooves drawn around the nucleus. An electron can't lose or gain energy in a continuous way, spiraling to higher or lower orbits; it takes in or throws off a packet (quantum) of energy and leaps from one groove to the other. . . . (Briggs and Peat, 1984, p. 39)

As Bohr was being congratulated for his exciting new model of the atom, others such as Heisenberg and Pauli, graduate students at the time, were unsatisfied with the compromise Bohr suggested with his hybrid model of new quantum ideas and older planetary orbit ideas. Heisenberg attended a lecture of Bohr's and stood up and made objections to his model, after which Bohr talked with him further and invited him to Copenhagen for a visit. Before Heisenberg got to Copenhagen, though, he was able to develop on his own mathematical quantum mechanics to explain the atom.

Heisenberg used Einstein's methodology of "observables," taking only what could be measured and observed as his starting point, and he dropped all else as unnecessary metaphysically baggage, including the idea of planetary orbits. This technique helped him let go of the paradigm of mechanical physics he was taught in Germany. Thus clearing his mind, he began with the observable facts of the atomic spectra, the fingerprint lines that form when the light produced from an atom is passed through a prism. Heisenberg studied the distances between the lines and the thickness of the lines of the spectra (his observables), and translated them into numbers, and then arranged these numbers into patterns, treating the whole pattern like an algebraic symbol. The result was what is known as quantum mechanics.

Shortly after Heisenberg achieved success with his quantum mechanics, de Broglie proposed a new theory of "wave mechanics," suggesting that an electron "could at times behave like a wave and at other times like a particle" (Briggs and Peat, 1984, p. 45). Though de Broglie's theory did not seem to attract a lot of attention, it got the attention of Einstein, who sent the thesis on to a colleague from his home town of Zurich, Erwin Schrödinger. Schrödinger was able to show that electron energy levels could be wave patterns: they assume the same frequency as waves as they do in Bohr's model, or Heisenberg's calculations. It was determined that Heisenberg's and Schrödinger's theories solve the same problem and are mathematically equivalent, even though they are conceptually different. Still, at the time many physicists preferred Schrödinger's wave mechanics to Heisenberg's quantum mechanics because of its greater intuitive clarity. Schrödinger offered physicists a physical picture of the atom whereas Heisenberg offered them mathematical equations.

In 1927 Heisenberg rented an apartment in Copenhagen and Bohr and he began to work out the Copenhagen interpretation of quantum theory. Quantum behavior challenged all the cherished ideas of physics as well as common sense. Physicists had discovered that light is both a wave and a particle, and electrons are both waves and particles (Briggs and Peats, 1984). How could they make sense of this? Heisenberg followed Einstein's advice again, which was suggested when Heisenberg shared with Einstein that he had used his observables methodology to successfully develop quantum mechanics. Einstein told him that even though he had worked that way once, "'It's nonsense all the same.' Einstein ... explained that it was pointless to attempt to build theories on observables, for, after all, it was the theory itself which told physicists what could, and could not be observed in nature" (Briggs and Peat, 1984, p. 45). Heisenberg wondered if his quantum mechanical theory already gave the answer to his questions, that there was no answer. What he arrived at is now known as "the Heisenberg uncertainty principle."

Like Einstein's thought experiments, Heisenberg used the same technique and imagined a microscope experiment where he wanted to find out how an electron moves from point A to point B (Briggs and Peat, 1984, p. 49–51). Because the electron is very small, a gamma-ray microscope must be used to be able to pin down the position of the electron at point A. Then one has to measure the electron's speed and direction multiplied by its mass, its momemtum, in order to predict its arrival at point B. But the equipment used to measure the position of the electron, the gamma-ray microscope, will affect the electron by striking it with a particle of light (a photon) and therefore speeding it up and knocking it off its path. Heisenberg realized that:

> When the values of certain observables are measured, others become uncertain. The closer we try to measure the position of a quantum object, the more uncertain becomes its momentum.... Heisenberg's uncertainty principle showed that the actual properties of objects could no longer be separated from the act of measurement and *thus from the measurer himself.* (Briggs and Peat, 1984, p. 51, emphasis in original)

Heisenberg's "uncertainty principle" shattered the classical scientific belief that scientists (observers) could objectively separate themselves from their observations, and that they could continually refine their experiments to get rid of all external influences to their results. He found that scientists could never predict an atomic event with certainty.

According to Briggs and Peat (1984), Bohr reacted very strongly and negatively to Heisenberg's microscope thought experiment. He agreed with Heisenberg's point that the closer one gets to measuring the position of an electron the further one gets from measuring its momentum, but he suggested that in his experiment, Heisenberg was assuming that an electron has a path and momentum that is continuous which is disturbed by the observation. Bohr argued that an electron is not a 'thing' that has a definite path and definite independent properties. He claimed that view is still a hold-over from the old Newtonian paradigm. Bohr suggested that at the smallest level, we no longer find "things" but "tendencies to exist" (Briggs and Peat, 1984, p. 54).

> (W)e can correctly calculate probabilities and patterns of what we find at B, but that's all; we cannot even say for sure that the particles detected at B were the same ones emitted at A, and we certainly can't say what path they took to get there. We can't even know what arrived at B, either. We have tracks on our equipment. But what they really are is uncertain. (Briggs and Peat, 1984, p. 55)

Matter does not exist with certainty, but rather shows "tendencies to exist" which are expressed as probabilities. For Bohr, "Isolated material particles are abstractions, their properties being definable and observable only through their interaction with other systems" (Capra, 1975, p. 137). Quantum scientists discovered that they could very accurately predict group particle behavior but not individual particle behavior. This probability position is considered a "given" in quantum physics now. The physical world is divided into an observed system and an observing system and the observed system is described in terms of probability.

In the end, Bohr and Heisenberg agreed:

> (A)ny property is, to some extent, a result of the act of measurement. . . . There are no separate, independent objects. At the quantum level the world cannot be divided into independent parts, each exerting cause-and-effect relationships on the other, because, at the atomic level, everything is an indissolvable whole. (Briggs and Peat, 1984, p. 54)

Notice, we have come to the same conclusion with quantum physics that we came to with relativity theory, that there is a wholeness to the universe. We have again described a theory that ends up sounding very much like Buddhism's dharma of dependent co-origination, or co-arising. Just as Buddhism teaches, physicists have discovered that we impose our own artificial descriptions of the world upon the world and create theories to explain how the world is, only to find ourselves mistaking our illusionary descriptions for the world as it is. Einstein, Bohr, and Heisenberg went through the struggles of trying to let go of the illusions they had been taught so they could see the essential nature of all things. This "letting go" of past teachings is a long and difficult path, as described by philosophers, mystics, or scientists. For most people, it requires many years of training. It is a letting go of what Mead (1934) calls 'the generalized other' and Berger and Luckmann (1966) describe as our 'socially constructed reality,' in order to become aware of what James (1912/1976) refers to as 'pure experience.'

As Capra (1975) explains, "(q)uantum theory forces us to see the universe not as a collection of physical objects, but rather as a complicated web of relations between the various parts of a unified whole" (p. 138). Quantum theory shatters the Newtonian idea of solid particles, for atoms turn out to consist of vast regions of space and not to be solid at all. Quantum theory also demolishes the Newtonian idea of particles existing as isolated entities, for it shows that nature is not made up of isolated building blocks, but rather appears "as an interconnected web of physical and mental relations whose parts are only defined through their connections to the whole" (Capra, 1975, p. 142). Entities can only be understood as interconnections between the preparation of the experiment and the following measurement, which always includes the observer in an essential way. Thus, quantum theory destroys the Newtonian idea of certainty, the idea of strictly deterministic laws of nature, for matter turns out to not exist with certainty but rather to show a "tendency to exist" which can only be expressed as probabilities. And, quantum theory shatters the Newtonian ideal of an objective description of nature, for the scientist cannot play the role of a detached objective observer (Capra, 1975, pp. 61–62).

Just as relativity theory dissolves the distinction between space and time, and matter and energy, quantum theory reveals a world that is destructible and indestructible, matter that is continuous (waves) and discontinuous (particles). We now know that these concepts are not opposites, but rather complementary descriptions of the same reality, each being only partly correct and having a limited range of application. Capra (1975) tells us that Niels Bohr introduced the idea of complementarity in physics. It is certainly a concept that he shared in common with the Eastern concept of yin/yang. Because Einstein continued to insist that the laws of nature are objective and Bohr continued to insist that no picture of the wholeness of the universe is possible, the two were never able to see how close they were on their discoveries of wholeness. It takes another perspective, the wholistic perspective of David Bohm, to help us bring relativity theory and quantum theory together and understand their complementary qualities. I move on to a discussion of Bohm's solid state and particle physics.

Particle Physics

At the beginning of quantum theory Niels Bohr asked "why is matter stable?" David Bohm's answer is, matter is not stable, it is only relatively stable and separate. Bohm (1980) developed "a theory of quantum physics which treats the totality of existence, including matter and consciousness, as an unbroken whole" (from the back book cover of *Wholeness and the Implicate Order*). My sources for understanding Bohm's ideas come from Briggs and Peat (1984) who have written extensively about his work, as well as from Bohm's (1980) own book, *Wholeness and the Implicate Order*, which is well written and accessible to a nonscientist such as myself. Indeed, *Wholeness and the Implicate Order* succeeds in blurring the boundaries between science and philosophy.

David Bohm is a world-reknowned solid state and particle physicist who was born in Wilkes-Barre, Pennsylvania, USA, was educated at Pennsylvania State College and University of California at Berkeley (one source says UCS), studying with Robert Oppenheimer, and served a post-doctoral position at Princeton University, where he met Einstein. While at Princeton, Bohm (1951) wrote a text on quantum theory to help him better understand the theory himself. This text, *Quantum Theory*, received high praise for its clarity, including from Pauli and Einstein, who complimented Bohm for being the one to completely explain the theory to him (Einstein) finally. Bohm's *Quantum Theory* is now considered a classic in the field of physics. Bohm discovered that the more he knew quantum theory the more he didn't understand, and he became convinced that there was some deep confusion in quantum theory. He found he agreed with Einstein that quantum theory had achieved spectacular success, but it was not the complete theory for microscopic processes it claimed to be. He also found that when he began to criticize quantum theory, his approach was misinterpreted as trying to reintroduce classical determinism when what he was trying to do was open the door for more satisfactory theories. Like Einstein, Bohm became classified as a maverick, a brilliant scientist unwilling to embrace the Copenhagen interpretation of quantum physics (Briggs and Peat, 1984). He was Professor of Theoretical Physics at Birkbeck College, London when he retired.

Bohm realized that the pursuit of an ultimate particle, the ultimate quantum, or the ultimate force, is based on an assumption that the universe is made of parts. Yet, quantum concepts imply that the world acts more like a single indivisible unit (individual parts relationally connected). In his first major research, Bohm studied the collective motion of the astronomical number of electrons that make up a metal and showed how collective effects (now called "plasmons") "reflected the behavior of every electron in the metal. [And conversely,] . . . how orders of collective motion could be concealed or implied in individual explicit movements" (Briggs and

Peat, 1984, pp. 95–96). Bohm says he had a sense that the electron sea was "alive," which became a deep insight he was able to use in his later theory. "Bohm discovered that deeper orders are hidden in the movements that appear superficially random and that at these deeper levels structures are enfolded and spread out in novel ways" (Briggs and Peat, 1984, p. 96).

In his second book, *Causality and Chance in Modern Physics*, Bohm (1957) took on science's views of causality, and argued that "the cause for any one thing is everything else." He suggested that "insufficienct thought had been given to the implications of the fact that the universe as a whole is a moving causal network" (Briggs and Peat, 1984, p. 96). Bohm changed the whole idea of causality so that it no longer represents a chain of events, but now is described as an interweaving of complex effects and causes. In 1965 Bohm wrote another book titled, *The Special Theory of Relativity*. Here he stressed the role of perception in science. He argued that scientific theories are maps that guide how and what things are seen, in agreement with Kuhn (1962/1970). Bohm insisted this does not imply solipsism. It implies there is more in the world than what we perceive and know. Notice that Bohm is trying to weave his way between solipsism and determinism, much like my discussion of personal and social relations in Chapters 4 and 5 of this text. Bohm's arguments attack the premise "that nature can be analyzed into parts. . . . [Instead] he proposes to consider the universe an undivided whole" (Briggs and Peat, 1984, p. 98).

Bohm's arguments also try to weave their way between absolutism and relativism, as I did in Chapter 1 and 2. He criticizes science for embracing the Epistemological assumption that there is a final, fixed answer scientists will come to know and upon which they will universally agree (Peirce's theory, see Chapter 2). Bohm describes knowledge as necessarily needing to be flexible and adjustable to constantly changing circumstances. Bohm wants to construct a theory of physics that will provide "insight" and not just knowledge. He defines "insight" as "an act or angle of perception. . . . The insight finds a relationship among moving elements which makes sense. . . . Insights involve recognition that there are aspects going on that are beyond analysis" (Briggs and Peat, 1984, p. 99). Bohm argues that when science shifted its focus from insight to "knowledge," scientists shifted their focus away from the whole to parts. Bohm wants to shift science's focus back to wholeness. However, by emphasizing wholeness, he does not propose to get rid of differences and distinctions. He argues that without understanding wholeness we will confuse parts for the whole; "we will not only divide what can't be divided, *we'll try to unite what can't be united*" (Briggs and Peat, 1984, p. 104, emphasis in original).

Bohm (1980) believes that the factual knowledge we obtain is shaped by our theories. Our theories provide us with a means for organizing our factual knowledge, and our overall experience is shaped this way. 'Facts' should not be viewed as independently existent objects that we find or pick up. Bohm (1980) points out that the Latin root of the word 'facere' means 'what has been made' (p. 142). Like

James and Dewey, Bohm says we begin with immediate perceptions. We develop the fact by giving it further order, form, and structure with the aid of our theoretical concepts. Bohm's description of science's process for establishing facts is what we discovered in Chapter 5 as socially constructed realities. Bohm describes scientific theory as a point of view which makes contact with nature. But the universe extends beyond any map, equation, definition, or theory. Like James (1909/1975a, 1909/1977), Bohm is not a mystic but a thoroughgoing realist. "It's just that, as he sees it, the problems now require a new order of insight into nature—an insight which is clear about wholeness" (Briggs and Peat, 1984, p. 105). Like Dewey (c. 1934/1958), with philosophy, Bohm (1980) wants science to be more like art, and seek original and creative acts of perception. He suggests perception should be interwoven continually with activities aimed at accommodation. "(T)hought with totality as its content has to be considered as an art form, like poetry, whose function is primarily to give rise to a new perception, and to action that is implicit in this perception, rather than to communicate reflective knowledge of 'how everything is'" (Bohm, 1980, p. 63).

Following a technique similarly used in Buddhist teachings, Bohm (1980) resorts to images and examples to help us understand *wholeness*, for it can only be grasped implicitly. For example, the image of a flowing stream with a vortex is a favorite image of his. The whirlpool and the stream appear to be two different "things," but when we get closer we realize we cannot tell where the stream stops and the vortex begins. What seemed easy enough to separate is not so easy after all. Bohm (1980) also experiments with a new language, the rheomode, which is a variation on verbs, thus emphasizing flowing movement rather than separation—noun-verb-direct object fragmentation. Bohm seeks to find a way to communicate his ideas in a language that emphasizes wholeness, similar to Dewey's (1949/1960) emphasis on 'knowing' instead of knowledge. With his rheomode, Bohm draws our attention to language's role in bringing about fragmentation of thought. He recognizes that we are doomed to map and talk, and in doing so we define and distinguish the whole into parts. However, he does not want us to misinterpret the content of our thoughts and regard them as in direct correspondence with objective reality. He calls for an *integration* of thought.

Bohm (1980) understands quantum theory and relativity theory to offer assistance for his integrative project, for they both contain deep implications that spell the end for a mechanistic paradigm and lead us toward an organic wholeness. Einstein's relativity theory forces us to abandon the idea of a rigid body, and thus the idea of separate particles. Quantum theory shows us that the idea of a separate atomic particle cannot be maintained, the observer and observed merge. Both theories agree that the world is whole, as we have found, but according to Bohm, both theories retain elements that contradict their wholistic premise. For relativity theory, fragments are retained through its emphasis on continuous orders. Also, the role of "the signal" does not fit and should be dropped for it implies some separate "thing." Einstein's "field" concept which is his basic starting point for his "unified field theory," "still retains the essential features of a mechanistic order, for the fundamental entities, the fields, are conceived as existing outside of each other, at separate points of space and time, and are assumed to be connected with each other only through external relationships" (Bohm, 1980, p. 174). For quantum mechanics, an example of its fragmentation is "the wave function, [which] is still generally taken to be a description of overall *statistical potentialities* that are regarded as existing separately and autonomously" (Bohm, 1980, p. 137). This approach and description implies "something that has a separate and autonomous kind of existence" (Bohm, 1980, p. 137). Bohm recommends dropping the basic role of the signal, and fields, and of the quantum state as old, fragmentary notions tied to the Cartesian-Newtonian system.

Bohm (1980) offers three analogies or models to help us understand his theory of wholeness, which unites relativity theory and quantum theory. His theory of wholeness and the implicate order replaces the idea of "random" order with the idea of a hierarchy of order. Bohm suggests we all know order implicitly. Order means *"to give attention to similar differences and different similarities"* (Bohm, 1980, pp. 115–116, emphasis in original). Bohm suggests we no longer use the term 'disorder,' having no order whatsoever, but instead we distinguish between different degrees of order. One scientific image he proposes to convey a wholistic view of nature is the hologram, an instrument that writes the whole ('holo' means 'whole' and 'gram' means 'to write'). A hologram is a kind of photograph. The entire scene is recorded on a holographic plate, so that each and every "part" of the plate reflects the whole and undivided order of the universe. An infinite holographic universe is one where each region is a distinct perspective, yet each contains all. This image is meant to show how the whole is reflected in the parts. It serves for Bohm in a similar way as Indra's net serves for Buddhism (see Chapter 7) to help us understand an important principle of a wholistic universe: *"Everything mirrors everything else; the universe is a looking-glass"* (Briggs and Peat, 1984, p. 112, emphasis in original).

The second analogy Bohm (1980) uses to describe his wholeness theory is a drop of dye. This analogy is used to explain his second principle of a wholistic universe: *"Wholeness is flowing movement"* (Briggs and Peat, 1984, p. 112, emphasis in original). Imagine a drop of dye is dropped in a viscous liquid like glycerine, which is encased between two glass cylinders. The outside cylinder is turned slowly, and the dye dissipates in the liquid. If we rotate the cylinder backwards the same number of turns, the drop would reconstitute itself. We will end up with the drop of dye we started with! This surprising result shows that there is a hidden implicit order. There is an order to the dye being dropped in the liquid and how it is distributed, but this order is enfolded or implicated in the 'grey mass' that we see. The parts remain in one-to-one correspondence. Bohm calls this hidden order which is spread throughout the whole *the implicate order* (from 'implicit' meaning 'to fold inward'). When it evolves into a form that can be seen it is then 'explicate' (meaning 'to unfold'), like the drop of dye. Explicit and implicit orders turn out to be two sides of the same coin, complementary notions. The explicate is what Dewey (1960) calls foreground experience and the implicate is what Dewey calls background experience.

For Bohm (1980), beneath the events described by quantum theory and relativity, are deeper movements and orders which must be described by deeper laws—laws of implicate order. Our earliest experience is of movement of an enfolded-unfolding continuous "present" (James's pure experience, Buddhism's No Mind or Big Mind). As we learn, we apply maps to this "present" (language is a highly explicate map), we become higher and higher in our degrees of explication. Beneath each explicate order lie implicate orders, as the threads of the dye drop lie beneath the dye drop itself. We can now study the relationship between explicate "relatively autonomous subtotalities" and the implicate ensembles which give rise to them (Briggs and Peat, 1984, p. 120). Bohm's implicate theory solves these paradoxes: particle vs wave (depends on how the observer looks at it), continuity vs discontinuity (unfolding is continuous and discontinuous at the same time), causality vs noncausality (everything causes everything else), locality vs nonlocality (local-explicate, has its roots in the implicate holomovement), order vs disorder or determinate vs indeterminate (both and), known vs unknown (same movement). "In Bohm's implicate universe *both the observing apparatus and the observer himself are also unfolding ensembles*" (Briggs and Peat, 1984, p. 122, emphasis in original).

The third analogy Bohm (1980) uses is of a fish tank with one fish in it and two camera views on it, a side view and a head-on view. When we look at the different camera views it appears that there are two different fish in the tank, when it is really one fish we are seeing from different angles. The images on the screens are two dimensional projections of a three dimensional reality. Similarly, 'particles' are projections of a 'higher dimensional' reality rather than separate particles existing in a three dimensional space. This analogy demonstrates his third principle: "*It is a universe of countless dimensions which embody its wholeness*" (Briggs and Peat, 1984, p. 123, emphasis in original). "For Bohm, the multidimensional reality is one unbroken whole extending through the universe and including all of what scientists call particles and fields" (Briggs and Peat, 1984, p. 125). This description of a wholistic universe is one Bohm shares in common with Buddhism's dharma of dependent co-origination, or co-arising.

We have found in my comparisons of Bohm's ideas to Dewey's, James's, Berger's and Luckmann's, and Buddhist ideas, that Bohm's implicate-order theory extends beyond the traditional domain of physics into philosophy. By its very nature, it must do so. Other scientists criticize Bohm by saying what he offers is a metaphysical theory, not a physical theory, but of course Bohm must respond by pointing out that the distinction between physics and philosophy is an artificial one that is useful in some contexts but ultimately inaccurate. Bohm cautions us not to mistake our descriptions of the universe for the universe itself, and therefore reify our theories. He believes that the distinctions between life/nonlife, animate/inanimate are only abstractions, which, again, are useful in some contexts but ultimately just reflect the mapmaking process. We are trained to screen out the implicate and focus on the explicate, the process of abstraction, the mapmaking. By focusing on the explicate we can do great things, like go to the moon, but we also learn to ignore the transitory, subtle features of existence, the nuances and differences (Briggs and Peat, 1984, pp. 129–130). "For Bohm, our universe is filled with nothing or no-things—it is a vast fluid no-thingness in which everything is" (pp. 144–145). This concept of no-thingness is one he shares with the Buddhist dharma of emptiness (śūnyata).

Bohm (1980) also shares with Buddhism the concept of egolessness of self (anatman), for he realizes that the self is an example of an explicate order adopted by consciousness. Individual consciousness is an abstraction. The implicate order applies to both matter and consciousness. All the matter in our bodies enfolds the universe in some way. "(E)ach moment of consciousness has a certain *explicit* content, which is a foreground, and an *implicit* content, which is a corresponding background" (p. 204). Bohm's science is a science of becoming, being *is* becoming. Whereas Einstein introduced us to "the space-time continuum, seeing them as one inextricably linked process, Bohm brings us the matter-mind continuum, seeing consciousness and matter as inextricably linked" (Briggs and Peat, 1984, p. 127). For Bohm, "Mind is a subtle form of matter, matter is a grosser form of mind" (p. 128).

It is time for me to leave the field of physics behind, which at this point, can no longer be distinguished from philosophy. I will turn now to chemistry, but we will find I have not really left physics (or philosophy) far behind. In particular, I want to explore J. E. Lovelock's contributions to the paradigm shift in science I am describing in this chapter, as well as contributions by Lynn Margulis, a biologist. Lovelock's Gaia theory serves as an example of general systems theories. "Systems theory" is an idea originated by Ludwig von Bertalanffy (1968), who explored how biological forms organize to sustain themselves in their environment. Thus, we will find that as we move into examples of general systems theory, physics and chemistry overlap and "leak" into the scientific field of biology as well.

General Systems Theory

James Lovelock's Gaia theory is an example of a wholistic systems theory that relies of a relational scientific paradigm. Lovelock is a British chemist (with a scientific background in biology and medicine) who works as a free-lance atmospheric scientist. He pays for his researches and exhibitions to discover Gaia, the Earth as the largest living organism, from his income for inventing and developing scientific instruments. For example, he is the inventor of the electron-capture device, which is very sensitive in detecting the traces of certain chemical substances.[3] Lovelock worked for NASA (the National Aeronautics and Space Administration of the USA) in the 1960's, helping them solve the problem of how to determine ways and means of detecting life on Mars and other planets. He turned to the atmosphere as a possible way to detect life on other planets. He discovered that Mars and Venus both have atmospheres that represent steady states of equilibrium, whereas Earth's atmosphere is in a persistent state of disequilibrium, which he argues is a clear proof of life's activity. Lovelock describes the atmosphere as "a dynamic extension of the biosphere itself," a view which was in sharp contrast to conventional geochemical views of the mid-1960's. The conventional view held that the atmosphere is "an end-product of planetary outgassing and held that subsequent reactions by abiological processes had determined its present state" (1979/1987, p. 7).

Lovelock worked for Shell Research Limited during the same time frame as his work for NASA (mid-1960's) "to consider the possible global consequences of air pollution from such causes as the ever-increasing rate of combustion of fossil fuels" (Lovelock, 1979/1987, p. 8). Again, this work was linked to his idea that the atmosphere might be an extension of the biosphere. What Lovelock's idea developed into is the hypothesis that the Earth's atmosphere is actively maintained and regulated by life on the surface, by the biosphere. By the biosphere, Lovelock means the atmosphere, oceans, and soil; "the totality constituting a feedback or cybernetic system which seeks an optimal physical and chemical environment for life on this planet" (Lovelock, 1979/1987, p. 11). A cybernetic system is one that is able to be self-regulating through the use of positive and negative feedback. If something is capable of harvesting information and of storing experience and knowledge, then it is adaptive, and can be called a cybernetic system. The term used to describe the maintenance of relatively constant conditions by active control is *homoeostasis*. Lovelock's ideas concerning planet atmospheres have developed into the Gaia hypothesis, also known as geophysiology, "the study of the planetary surface as an organismlike body in which geology and biology are ... intimately linked" (Margulis, 1998, p. 118). Lovelock named his theory 'Gaia' in recognition of the fact that his hypothesis represents a renaissance of an ancient myth about the Greek Goddess of the Earth, Gaia. Lovelock (1979/1987) argues that Gaia (the Earth) has a tendency to keep constant conditions for all terrestrial life (homoeostatis) and that she is a cybernetic system capable of adaption (p. 127). Gaia is evolving and changing.

My sources for Lovelock's theory come from his own writings, *Gaia* (1979/1987) and *The Ages of Gaia* (1988), both of which were written so that they are accessible to nonscientists such as myself. He has been strongly criticized by his colleagues in science for presenting his work this way, for they argue that Gaia has not been stated properly as a scientific hypothesis. Lovelock found that his theory was at first ignored by his colleagues. If discussed, his theory was treated with derision and condemned as teleological, suggesting that the Gaia theory of Earth's adaption required foresight and planning by the biota, thus denying the objectivity of Nature. Scientists ask, how can mere biota (the sum of all the living organisms: flora, fauna, and microbiota) possibly regulate the planet Earth? Relying on a mechanistic view of the universe, Lovelock's critics say his Gaia theory lacks a tangible mechanism of control, such as sound, light, or chemical signals interacting with carbon-containing matter. For example, Doolittle and Dawkins, two biologists, argue that "there is no way for natural selection to lead to altruism global in scale" (Lovelock, 1979/1987, p. ix). The climatologist Schneider and the geochemist Holland question Lovelock's suggestion that homeostasis is the only means of climate regulation. They suggest "that biological regulation is only partial, and that the real world is a 'coevolution' of life and the inorganic" (Lovelock, 1988, p. 34). Lovelock (1988) responded to these criticisms with his second book, *The Ages of Gaia*, which offers a model of a planet with a simple ecosystem, Daisyworld, that requires no foresight or planning, just the growth and competition of the black and white daisies on Daisyworld in order to regulate the temperature on the planet. Daisyworld is Lovelock's answer to the criticism that his theory is teleological. He shows this is a false criticism, for Daisyworld regulates itself without a mechanism for regulation. The geophysiological view of the history of the Earth is a new theory of evolution Lovelock offers as an answer to the criticism concerning current views of evolution and of theoretical ecology. Let's explore Lovelock's Gaia theory more closely.

In *Gaia*, Lovelock (1979/1987) begins his presentation of the Gaia hypothesis by considering what the Earth was like in its beginning. In *The Ages of Gaia*, Lovelock (1988) offers a more detailed description of his theory of the history of the Earth during the Archean, Proterozoic, and Phanerozoic times (from the beginnings of life through to the time when oxygen first dominated the chemistry of the atmosphere). What we know comes from the records the rocks have kept for the past three-and-a-half aeons (3,500 million years; the estimated age of the Earth is 4,500 million years, four-and-a-half aeons, and the estimated beginning of life is more than three aeons ago). Lovelock's (1979/1987) method for showing the existence of Gaia, the Earth as a single living system, comes from thermodynamics and Boltzman's redefinition of entropy as "a measure of the probability of a molecular distribution" (p. 34). In *Gaia*, he uses the example of a sand castle on a beach, to help us understand the four states: the inert state of complete equilibrium (featureless neutrality, which cannot exist on Earth as long as there is a sun that shines and gives energy to the air and sea, setting them in motion), the structured non-living 'steady state' (a beach of rippled sand), a beach exhibiting a product of life (the sand castle) is the third state, and the final state is where life is present itself (the builder of the sand castle). Lovelock's NASA problem involved the question of how do we identify something as being a product of life versus just a random structure of nature?

Lovelock (1979/1987) suggests that he found his solution to this problem through thermodynamics. In thermodynamics, Boltzman showed that 'entropy' "implies that wherever we find a highly improbable molecular assembly [like finding a sand castle on the beach] it is probably life or one of its products" (p. 34). Lovelock suggests that if we can find something that is an example of a highly improbable molecular assembly at a global level, then we are seeing life in the form of Gaia. He finds several examples of distributions of molecules so unusual as to be different and distinguishable beyond a reasonable doubt from the equilibrium state or the steady state. One example is the regulation of the Earth's temperature. Other examples are the regulation of oxygen in our atmosphere, and of salt in our oceans.

Lovelock (1979/1987) tells us, "The history of the Earth's climate is one of the more compelling arguments in favour of Gaia's existence" (p. 19). We know our climate has never been wholly unfavorable for life, and that the oceans have never frozen or boiled, for the records of life are unbroken. During this time our sun has increased its output of energy by at least 30%, following a standard evolutionary pattern of a star, yet our atmosphere has continued to maintain a steady range of temperature. Lovelock argues that "(i)f the Earth were simply a solid inanimate object, its surface temperature would follow the variations in solar output" (p. 20). This is not what has happened. Our temperature has remained constant and favorable for life, even though climates are inherently unstable and a mere 2% decrease in heat is enough to send us into an Ice Age (Lovelock, 1979/1987, p. 23). How has this maintenance of our temperature occurred so that we did not become a frozen planet or one with temperatures over 100° C? Lovelock tells us that where scientists used to think that maybe the presence of gases such as ammonia helped to conserve what heat the Earth received, it is now considered more likely that carbon dioxide served as the gas that helped us stay warm. Some scientists suggest that the Earth was darker in color earlier on and that this helped the Earth absorb and maintain heat as well. Others hypothesize that ocean plankton operates like a thermostat to keep the earth's temperature within a certain range. Lovelock's (1979/1987) point in this discussion is, no matter what the methods of control are, the fact that the Earth developed a means to actively regulate its temperature is an indication "that Gaia had emerged from the complex of parts" (p. 24).

Lovelock suggests that our atmosphere is such a curious and incompatible mixture, it couldn't have possibly happened by chance. In his 1960's NASA study of Mars, Lovelock realized that we have an unusual composition of gases on our planet. While the Earth has an atmosphere dominated by nitrogen and oxygen, Mars and Venus both have atmospheres dominated by carbon dioxide, with only small proportions of oxygen and nitrogen (Lovelock, 1988, p. 28). Mars and Venus have atmospheres close to the chemical equilibrium state whereas Earth's atmosphere violates the rules of equilibrium chemistry. "(Y)et amidst apparent disorder relatively constant and favourable conditions for life were somehow maintained"

(Lovelock, 1979/1987, p. 67–69). The oxygen we have in our air, which from a chemical point of view is our dominant gas, is especially hazardous. Oxygen makes it possible for fires to be lit almost anywhere on Earth and for birds to fly, and yet, if we only had 4% more oxygen in our air we would be in danger of burning up. For even a 1% increase of oxygen to occur in our atmosphere, our risks of fires due to lightning increases by 70%. How is our oxygen level controlled? Lovelock presents several different explanations for how this occurs, including methane gas acting as a two-way regulator of oxygen, with nitrous oxide maybe also being a counterbalance for methane, as well as nitrogen acting as a dilutant for oxygen in the air. Again, the point is not so much what are the methods of control as it is the fact that control is taking place. "The constancy of oxygen concentration suggests the presence of an active control system" (Lovelock, 1979/1987, p. 74). Lovelock's Gaia theory suggests that "the biosphere actively maintains and controls the composition of the air around us, so as to provide an optimum environment for terrestrial life" (p. 69).

A third powerful example Lovelock (1979/1987) offers is his discussion of the Earth's oceans, which cover nearly three-quarters of the Earth's surface. Over the past three-and-a-half aeons the evidence says that the total volume of water on Earth has remained unchanged, despite changes in ice caps, etc. How? Not only has the volume of water not changed, but the salt content in the ocean, which today is around 3.4%, has remained at this basic level "for hundreds of millions, if not thousands of millions of years" (Lovelock, 1979/1987, p. 92). Yet millions of tons of salt are washed into the Earth's oceans every year. Why isn't the sea more salty? This is another balance that is precariously maintained, for if there is above a 6% salt level, living cells will literally fall apart (p. 90). Lovelock argues that since the beginning of life the volume of water and the salinity of the oceans have been under biological control. Again, he offers several explanations for how these balances are maintained, but the ultimate point is the fact that the biosphere actively maintains and controls the level of water on Earth as well as the level of salt in the ocean water. The successful ability to control the levels of water and salt serves as proof that the Earth is a living organism. Lovelock concludes that innumerable biological mechanisms are responsible for the steady state of the planet, the homeostatis.

Not only is Gaia capable of self-maintenance, but she is also capable of self-transformation. Remember, she is a cybernetic system capable of adaption. Gaia is evolving and changing. The most vivid example of the Earth's ability to adapt is with the emergence of free oxygen into the air two aeons ago. Our Earth has not always had oxygen in the atmosphere, and oxygen was a poison to the life that had evolved for more than an aeon after Earth's initial formation. When oxygen began to be released into the atmosphere, life had to go underground. Archean biota has not ended; these bacteria still live all over Earth in muds, sediments, and in our intestines. Lovelock (1988) tells us that Margulis has shown that the cells themselves "are communities of microorganisms that once lived free. The energy-transforming entities of animal cells (the mitochondria) and of plants (the mitochondria and the chloroplasts) both were once bacteria living independently" (p. 18). Lovelock suggests there is reason to think Gaia is continuing to evolve and adapt to the changes humans are making to the Earth's environment.

Many of the current fears of pollution Lovelock (1988) considers irrelevant, such as the fear of depletion of the ozone layer, since ozone is continually created in our atmosphere. Lovelock suggests Gaia will take care of much of industry's pollution, as it has always had to take care of pollution. He does not recommend we lose our current technology, for our very survival at this point depends on it. Yet he does recommend a need for us to be vigilant. The worse dangers to Gaia's ability to self-regulate and adapt involve the algae of the sea and the soil surface's photosynthesis. The cutting down of the tropical rain forests for farming and the farming of the continental shelf are serious matters, for these are vital to the regulation of the oxygen-carbon cycle. Lovelock suggests that Gaia's main self-regulation occurs due to the microorganisms. He warns us that if we hasten to farm algae and kelp without understanding the planetary control systems, we can harm our planet's ability to maintain planetary homoeostatis. Lovelock recommends scientists need to get out of their university labs and go out into the environment in order to gather accurate information. Lovelock's work, like Margulis's and McClintock's below, implies a cosmic state of co-evolution in nature, a seamless cycle of mutual causality.

Lynn Margulis (1997, 1998, 1999), a microbiologist at Boston University, has championed Lovelock's Gaia theory in the United States of America, writing about this theory separately as well as co-jointly with Lovelock. Margulis is interested in Gaia theory because Gaia represents our largest example of symbiosis, and symbiosis is the focus of Margulis's own work. Margulis (1998) defines symbiosis as "the living together in physical contact of organisms of different species" (p. 2). This living together of unlike organisms is without respect to outcome (Margulis and Sagan, 1997). Symbiosis researchers do not try to prove that the relationship is beneficial, rather they focus on "whether or not the partners experience prolonged, permanent, cyclical, facultative, or casual relationships" (Margulis and Sagan, 1997, p. 297).

Margulis (Sampson and Pitt, 1999) tells us that until the 19th century even scientists thought the Earth could be alive. However, the description of the Earth being alive is one that alienates scientists today. Margulis (Sampson and Pitt, 1999) does not agree with Lovelock's formulation which says Gaia is an single living organism, because he has not defined what he means by 'organism' and she does not think Gaia is a singularity, but rather an extremely complex system (p. 120). Margulis (1998) defines Gaia as "the series of interacting ecosystems that compose a single huge ecosystem at the Earth's surface. Period" (p. 120). Yet, she does not think the criticisms that have been made against Gaia theory are fair or accurate. As we found above, scientists say Lovelock's theory is teleological, yet Margulis agrees that

Lovelock's Daisyworld answers that charge, showing a model of a world that is powerfully homeostatic, with no prior planning or foresight. Scientists criticize Gaia for being a hypothesis that can not be tested, yet Margulis suggests that clearly Lovelock has shown it can be tested, and therefore it does fall within the realm of science. Lovelock correctly predicted that there is no life on Mars, based on his Gaia theory, prior to the 1976 *Viking* probe that confirmed his prediction. Margulis (Sampson and Pitt, 1999) points out that Lovelock's Gaia theory not only allows for successful predictions, but it is also stimulating scientists to ask new questions. Gaia theory enlarges theoretical ecology, and has profound significance for biology.

Margulis (Sampson and Pitt, 1999) does not think there are fundamental inconsistencies between Gaia theory and Darwin's theory of evolution. According to Margulis (Margulis and Sagan, 1997), Darwin even anticipated symbiogenesis (the appearance of new organs, new bodies, new species by establishing long-term permanent symbiosis) with his view that "each living creature must be looked at as a microcosm" (p. 305). Margulis and Lovelock (Margulis and Sagan, 1997) agree that the laws of physics and chemistry are basic to understanding the atmosphere, Lovelock's most vivid example of Gaia's existence. However, Margulis and Lovelock (1997) insist that the laws of biology must be considered, too. The Earth's atmosphere is not inert. It has remained remarkably constant in the face of enormous potential turbulence. According to Margulis and Lovelock (1997), the maintenance of the Earth's atmosphere is performed by the biosphere. The world is a living system (or organism) of which we are a part. Such a view is certainly consistent with the Buddhist, Native American, and ecofeminist views expressed in Chapter 7.

Now that we have examined an example of systems theories, with James Lovelock's Gaia theory, I would like to move on for a closer look at Margulis's and McClintock's biological work. We will find that Margulis supplies a vivid example of a connected view of the universe, one that emphasizes collaboration, and McClintock supplies a vivid example of the need to include compassion in our relational paradigm shift in science. McClintock's compassion is found in her methodology, and it represents what I have described as caring reasoning in various chapters, and, we have learned, others describe as attention or attentive love (Weil, 1977; Ruddick, 1989), or sympathetic understanding (Dewey, 1960) and as Buddha nature.

Compassionate, Connected Science

Symbiosis

Lynn Margulis has her own theory to offer, beyond the Gaia theory, as her contribution to science's paradigm shift away from a mechanistic view of the universe toward a more wholistic view. Her work cycles from the macro (Gaia) to the micro (organelles within cells) and back again. Her (1998) theory is a symbiotic theory of evolution now dubbed SET *(Serial Endosymbiosis Theory)*. Like Lovelock's Gaia theory, Margulis's SET theory was met with resistance and was initially rejected by her peers. However, now SET is taught in high school biology classes and has become mostly accepted by the majority of today's scientists. Let us see what she proposed that stimulated a very different view of evolution from the view she was taught when she was in school.

Margulis (1998) tells us her work in microbiology was always off-center. While others were studying the inside of cells, in terms of the nucleus, she studied "the genetic systems others tended to ignore, those residing in cell structures (organelles) outside the nucleus" (p. 19). She realized science's focus was too narrow and overly focused on the nucleus. This realization became her jumping-off point. Margulis learned that mitochondria contain their own genes, and chloroplasts also have their own genes. She realized how similar the cell organelles, the plastids and mitochondria, are to free-living microbes. So, she studied microbes in the symbiosis literature and became fascinated with evolution. She enrolled into graduate school at University of California, Berkeley, in 1960, hoping to study genetics and compare bacterial cells to plant and animal cells, only to find that the bacterial geneticists did not know about plant and animal cell work and vice versa. Surrounded by what she calls "academic apartheid," Margulis (1998) discovered she was out there on her own, pursuing her intellectual interests alone (p. 27).

Margulis (1998) argues in SET *(Serial Endosymbiosis Theory)*, first published in a paper in 1966, and a few years later in her book, that most evolutionary novelty arose and still arises directly from symbiosis. The central claim of her theory "is that extra genes in the cytoplasm of animal, plant, and other nucleated cells are not 'naked genes': rather they originated as bacterial genes" (p. 37). Inside each of our cells we have what used to be four entirely independent and physically separate bacteria that now live together in permanent symbiosis. These four separate bacteria that merged together still exist today as separate bacteria as well as existing inside of nucleated cells. The four bacteria merged in a specific order to become the green algae cell. The term 'serial' in serial endosymbiosis refers to the order of the merger. Margulis (1998) presents her theory in terms of four provable postulates, three of which have been proven to be right at this point in time.

The first postulate is that "a sulfur- and heat-loving kind of bacterium, called a fermenting 'archaebacterium' (or 'thermoacidophil'), merged with a swimming bacterium, [and together they] became the nucleoocytoplasm, the basic substance of the ancestors of animal, plant, and fungal cells" (Margulis, 1998, pp. 34–35). Scientists now agree that the nucleocytoplasm of cells descended from archaebacteria, in particular mainly from thermoacidophil bacterial (this is step 1). This earliest swimming protist was an anaerobe, poisoned by oxygen, and it still lives today in muds and sand, puddles and pools where oxygen is scarce. Margulis's (1998) third postulate is that an oxygen-breathing bacterium was incorporated into the merger, which made it possible to cope with accumulating levels of free oxygen in the air (p. 36). Scientists now agree that the oxygen-respiring mitochondria evolved from bacteria symbionts call "purple bacteria" or "proteobacteria" (this is step 3). The fourth postulate is that "the complex-cell-generating series, oxygen breathers engulfed, ingested, but failed to digest bright green photosynthetic bacteria" (p. 36). The undigested bacteria survived and eventually these green bacteria became chloroplasts. Scientists now agree that the chloroplasts and other plastids of algae and plants were once free-living photosynthesis cyanobacteria (this is step 4). These three steps are now undisputed for it has been proven that plastids and mitochondria have distinct DNA that is bacterial in style and organization. What is controversial still is Margulis's step 2 of SET.

Margulis (1998) suggests that the swimming appendages, the structures associated with cell movement such as the cilia, sperm tails, sensory protrusions and other cell whips (centriole-kinetosomes) come from step 2, when the swimmer was acquired at the first. The stranger that became the centriole-kinetosome still has free-living relatives today, spirochetes. Spirochetes thrive in wet, rich, dark habitats. Her theory is that as spirochetes attached to archaebacteria, where they symbiogenetically intergrated, at the point of their attachment, that became the centriole-kinetosome of today (p. 46). This step 2 has left the least visible trail of all the steps, and is the most difficult evolution to trace. However, Margulis (1998) thinks that bacteria have left us hints of their former merger. She suggests that "(t)he crucial part of the theory begins with the cilium's underlying dot" which all centriole-kinetosomes have (p. 41). This underlying dot acts as tiny seeds. All sperm tails, cilia, and other structures responsible for cell motility extend from these little tiny seeds. Margulis (1998) suggests that "the integration of the centriole-kinetosome bacterium is what made the eukaryotic cell in the first place!" (p. 42). If she is right, symbiogenesis is what distinguishes all nucleated-cell life from all bacterial life. She tells us: "My claim is that all nucleated organisms (protoctists, plants, fungi, and animals) arose by symbiogenesis when archaebacteria fused with ancestors of centriole-kinetosomes in the evolution of the ultimate protoctist ancestor: the nucleated cell" (pp. 42–43). The DNA of the centriole-kinetosome is distinguishable from the rest of the nuclear DNA in some stages of cell development, but it joins all other chromosomal DNA during mitotic cell division, therefore leaving the faintest trail of separate ancestry (p. 48). Margulis (1998) tells us she is prepared to be wrong about step 2 of SET, but she does not think she is. Even if she is wrong, her theory of symbiosis still prevails due to her correctness on steps 1, 3, and 4. Where other biologists have proposed that the parts of the cells were formed by direct filiaton, pinching off DNA from the nucleus, Margulis's SET proposes that the parts of our cells were formed by different bacteria fusing together. SET is a theory of collaborative partnerships.

Margulis (1998) found that symbiogenesis collides directly with common presumptions of science, based on the scientific taxonomy and nomenclature historically used. This collision has delayed the acceptance of SET. She has had to criticize and then revise biological classification in order to recreate a system that is consistent and more accurately reflective of evolutionary history. She proposes a new taxonomy using the metaphor of a hand to describe evolutionary history (Margulis, 1998, Figure 4, p. 53). Her system has two tiers and five kingdoms. The base of the hand, spreading out to the thumb, represents the first tier, the base of all life, bacteria (whose cells lack nuclei). Next, spreading throughout the middle section of the hand is the second tier, all the eukaryotic others which includes all organisms with nucleated cells, which all evolved by symbiogenesis. This group includes the protoctists (algae, slime molds, ciliates, and others, composed of cells with nuclei), that spread out into the little finger of the hand. Developing from the second tier into the ring finger are the fungi (yeasts, mushrooms, molds, which develop from spores), into the middle finger are the plants (which develop from both spores and sexually), and into the pointer finger are the animals (p. 52). Margulis's taxonomy has the two tiers of prokarya and eukarya, with the five kingdoms of bacteria, protoctists, fungi, plants, and animals. Her taxonomy reflects evolutionary history for bacteria underwent "at least 2000 million years of chemical and social evolution" before any plants or animals appeared on Earth, and fungi are newer too (p. 56). To understand the evolution of animal sex requires knowledge of the protoctrists, which are ignored and seldom studied.[4]

Briggs and Peat (1989) describe Margulis's symbiogenesis as a theory of evolution based on cooperation and collaboration, not mutation and competition. It is a theory of co-evolution that does not begin with an assumption of life as made up of separate parts that are competing against each other. Margulis describes a world that is connected, a wholistic universe where everything affects everything else and partnerships are necessary to evolve. Margulis's work emphasizes an alive, multidimensional view as well as a collaborative view of an evolving universe. Her symbiotic theory emphasizes how connected we all are to our world around us, that within each of our cells there are communities of microorganisms. Let's move on to explore McClintock's contributions to the scientific paradigm shift from a mechanistic, atomistic description of the universe to a relational one.

Transposition Theory

I conclude my scientific stories by exploring Barbara McClintock's contributions to the scientific paradigm shift from a mechanistic, atomistic description of the universe to a relational one. McClintock contributes significantly to scientific understanding of genetics through her work with plant genetics, in particular maize genetics. She was awarded a Nobel prize for her contributions to physiology or medicine in 1983. However, McClintock also contributes a powerful example of a dissolving of the boundary between the observer and the observed, between the knower and the known, with her compassionate approach to science, and that is an important contribution she makes to our discussion.

McClintock began her college career at Cornell in 1919 and earned her Ph.D. in biology at Cornell in 1927. Scientists at Cornell were studying genetics through the use of maize, which produced a new generation annually, while others began studying the fruit fly, which produced a new generation every 14 days. While still a graduate student at Cornell, McClintock showed how corn could be studied for chromosomes too, and helped establish the chromosome basis of genetics. When others began to study E. coli (phage and bacteria), that produced a new generation every 20 minutes, McClintock continued to study corn cytogenetics, for by then it was her passion and it became her life-long work. One crop per year gave her all the data she could carefully analyze.

McClintock's style of working is unconventional in style and focus, by Euro-western standards, but actually very similar to the meditation practice of Buddhists. It is a methodology that relies on direct perception (intuition). McClintock described to Keller (1983), her biographer, how the more she worked with the maize chromosomes, the bigger they got. She was able to attend to so much about plant genetics because when she was working with the maize chromosomes, she would lose her 'self' and she would become part of the plant's system, as an insider rather than an outsider, down there with the chromosomes. Like Buddhist monks with their practice of meditation, McClintock learned to lose her 'self' in her work. As an insider, she was then able to see what the plant revealed to her. McClintock "knew by seeing, and saw by knowing" (Keller, 1983, p. 148). She would also try to just listen to what the plants were trying to tell her. McClintock related to the corn she planted like friends she grew to love. She grew her own corn and tended it, rather than having a research assistant do that work for her. It was important to her that she was in close touch with her corn, for the close attention she gave her corn was the source of her knowing. The people McClintock worked with say she could write an autobiography of each corn plant, she knew them so well. She turned her object of study into a subject, and instead of viewing nature as an object, to control, she related to nature as a friend she was trying to understand. Her knowing is based on a shared subjectivity. Her methodology represents a scientific paradigm shift away from Newton's mechanical science toward a relational science.

In 1944 McClintock began work on the complex processes of genetic regulation and control, which lead to her discovery of transposition, which earned her the Nobel prize. McClintock was investigating "the new mutations produced by the breakage-fusion-bridge cycle," and, seeing that there were stable patterns of instability, she guessed that something was controlling the rate of mutation. One cell was gaining what another lost. What she saw was controlled breakage. What she discovered was transposition, genetics subject to adaption and change, due to environmental influences. McClintock discovered the capacity for chromosomes to change positions, which could be controlled by regulator genes. "Transposition is a two-part process, involving the release of a chromosomal element from its original position and its insertion into a new position" (Keller, 1983, p. 127). McClintock's transposition supports a co-evolutionary theory such as Lovelock's and Margulis's, asserting "that life forms are not created piece by piece in small changes: They're dissipative structures arising spontaneously and holistically out of the flux and flow of macro and micro processes" (Briggs and Peat, 1984, p. 201). Transposition theory describes a "dance of symbiotic feedback," a "seamless cycle of mutual causality" (Briggs and Peat, 1984).

McClintock's results were totally at odds with the view of genetics at the time. Like the other scientists I have discussed in this section, McClintock became a maverick and outsider to her own field of study. It was not until the mid 1970's that people finally began to turn their attention to her work. Keller (1983) tells us that today "even the skeptics must acknowledge this much: the genome is not a static entity, but a complex structure in a state of dynamic equilibrium. And transposable elements—all having the same structural organization—are a common feature of higher and lower organisms alike" (p. 193). McClintock's life and her work are a vivid example of the realization of the connectedness of things to each other, and the importance of using compassion in aiding our understanding. Because McClintock was able to be patient and open, and she was willing to take the time to get to know what she was observing at an intimate level, she was able to develop a feeling for the organism. She was able to let the maize chromosomes speak to her and to listen to them with a level of cultivated attention that allowed her to forget her 'self.' By approaching her daily work with her heart/mind and letting go of her 'self,' she was able to break down the artificial boundary between the observer and the observed, between the knower and the known. She was able to get to know the organism intimately. Her deep emotional investment provided her with the motivational force to continue her work even when others were not listening to her, and could not share her vision.

In this chapter we discovered many examples of scientists whose works contributed and continue to contribute to a paradigm shift in science, away from a reductionistic, mechanistic description of our universe toward a wholistic and dynamic description. We have learned that in the major fields of scientific study, physics, chemistry, and biology, for example, there are new and exciting theories that bring into question key assumptions which supported separate, inert descriptions of our world. Einstein's theory of relativity raises basic questions concerning the concepts of space/time, matter/energy, and gravity/acceleration. Bohr's and others' contributions to quantum theory bring into question basic concepts of matter as continuous and discontinuous (waves/particles), and of the world as destructible and indestructible.

Bohm helps us understand with his theory of the implicate order that relativity theory and quantum mechanics complement each other, rather than contradicting each other as Einstein and Bohr thought. Einstein's theory emphasizes the order of the universe and Bohr's theory emphasizes the disorder of the universe, and both of them together describe the same wholistic and dynamic universe. All three theories lead to the same conclusion, that the universe is indissolvably whole, as does Lovelock's Gaia theory, Margulis's co-evolution theory, and McClintock's transposition theory.

The scientists discussed in this chapter were educated to embrace basic assumptions about the universe that their own work began to bring into question. Their love of science helped them to take seriously the questions their work triggered, and to follow through on their doubts and concerns to try to answer their questions. Their love of science caused them to question basic scientific assumptions they took for granted and to reexamine the criteria and standards they were employing for their research. They discovered that scientific criteria are not universally neutral, and objective, as assumed, and that scientific criteria must be continually reexamined and adjusted. Their love of their subjects caused them to attend carefully to what the subject was trying to tell them, and to listen humbly and compassionately to the subject. Their love of their subjects caused them to become aware of their own influences on their observations and to critique their own projections on to the data. Their love of their subjects caused them to question basic distinctions between the observer and the observed and again to reexamine science's assumptions of universality, objectivity, and neutrality. The scientists presented in this chapter make considerable contributions to the description of the world I am developing throughout this text. It is a unified, connected world that is dynamic and alive, always changing and in flux, a world with which we enjoy a transactional relationship. It is a complementary, complex world that we can only hope to begin to understand if we approach our inquiring with compassion and humility, in cooperation with each other.

I move on to the final chapter of this text, in which I will develop implications a relational (e)pistemological theory has for practice, in particular educational practice as experienced in USA schools.

CHAPTER 9

Educational Implications

I end this book on relational (e)pistemologies by turning to the practice that is central to my work as a philosopher: education. By no means do I wish to portray to the reader the idea that education is an afterthought in this text, for education is a main focus in my daily life. I have been a teacher and a student in some form or another most of my lifetime and plan to continue such activity as long as I am able. I agree with the many philosophers and scientists who have argued that what makes human beings unique in the animal kingdom is our ability to educate our young and pass on the cultural wealth of our societies. Education is a vitally important topic. However, my goal with this text has been to describe relational ways of knowing at a more theoretical level, with the hope that by doing so we will be better able to understand the implications a connected, wholistic theory of knowing has for our daily living. My desire has been to consider how individualized, separated, transcendent Epistemological theories, and their supporting Metaphysics, have shaped our views of "reality" by offering contrasting relational theories so we can find ways to critique this shaping and change our descriptions of "reality" to reflect its transactional qualities.

I turn now to the daily living of school life to help us check our understanding, and consider the effects a relational approach to knowing can have on our actions. I say 'can' because I do not think the majority of us living in the Euro-western world are taught to see our world in an overlapping, associated manner so I must describe mainly possibilities here, and a small number of actualities. Most Euro-westerners are educated to see themselves as separate and disconnected from their world and each other, yet we can turn to others who do embrace a more wholistic view, such as Buddhists, Native Americans, ecologists, some feminists and educators, to help guide us in this projection.

If we define education as a teaching-studenting process in which there is guided, intentional learning, then we are reminded that education takes place in many settings, not just in schools. Teachers are defined as the guides who know whatever it is that students need to know and students are defined as those who are consciously intending to know whatever they feel a need to inquire about. These needs range from basic to very complex, from how to tie a shoe, to how to drive a car, from the basics of language development to the reading of classic literature, from how to write one's name to how to write a dissertation. Teachers come in many forms, as our parents and our friends, as books we read and as animals we observe around us. Our teachers do not have to be in human form. All of us learn a great deal from teachers in a variety of settings, including more formal settings like schools or work sites or churches, where there are people actually hired to teach us. We also learn a great deal in more informal educational settings such as our homes or our neighborhood playgrounds, where our teachers are not contracted to teach us skills and give us information at a set time or place, but rather they teach us as the need arises. We also are taught on a daily basis through a process of acculturation, or what Harry Broudy (1954/1964) called 'milieu education,' as we watch television and listen to the radio, and are bathed in the sounds and sights, smells, and touches that surround us. As I turn to look at the implications of a relational theory of knowing for education I feel the need to remind the reader that schooling is only one form of education: there are many other forms in our lives. However, schooling is a powerful example of education that most of us can relate to, and it certainly has major impacts on our lives, even for those who are unwilling or unable to attend, since so many people do attend schools as children.

I will follow the pattern of our previous chapters for this discussion, and begin by considering personal relations, then social relations, w/holistic relations, ecological relations, and end with scientific relations. I will explore each of these overlapping topics from within the framework of the general definition of education I sketched above, that education is a teaching-studenting process. As such, education involves a teacher and a student (these roles are fluid and flexible and often interchangeable), something that is taught (the curriculum, the content) in some kind of setting and in some manner (the form of instruction, the context). Therefore we will need to look at how the roles of teachers and students change, given a relational (e)pistemology, and we will need to consider curriculum, as well as pedagogical and environmental issues. We will find that a relational theory of knowing has tremendous implications for all areas of schooling as we know them today in much of the world. The influence of Euro-western views, based on separated, disconnected, transcendent Epistemologies, has been felt all over the world due to the colonization of much of the world by parts of the Euro-west. Colonizers from countries such as Spain, France, Germany, England, and more recently the United States, have used schools as a means to impose their cultural beliefs upon other dominated people. These colonizers often come as missionaries under particular church banners. It is only with great effort, and the assistance of geographic isolation, for example, that instances of Indigenous peoples' wholistic approaches to education remain today for us to study and learn from.

I will rely on assorted examples available: my own and others' experiences as teachers and students, the various conversations I have shared with others concerning schools, and the tools of intuition, emotions, imagination, and reason I/we have available to help me/us constructively think of some new possibilities for schools (Thayer-Bacon, 2000). I will try to remind the reader of my own limitations and fallibility throughout the discussion, as I seek to reveal my own biases and not neglect my own contextuality.[1] I do not want to try to ignore and diminish the political power that philosophers wield in their social roles as legitimators. I do not mean to suggest that the examples I offer or the suggestions I make are in any way final or complete, for I have argued in this text for the impossibility of attaining knowledge that is certain, as well as for the impossibility of attaining knowledge that is universal. As a fallible social critic, I need others to contribute to this discussion and help me in this redescribing effort. I need a clamor of diverse voices, so I encourage your contributions to help us in our efforts to recreate anew schools that take relations to be primary.

Personal Relations

In Chapter 4, on personal relations, I focused on intimate relationships we share, as infants, with our childcare providers, and as spiritual beings with our Thou. By 'intimate' I do not mean sexual, I mean relationships that are close associations, relationships that are two-fold relations between I and Thou, between one-caring and one-cared for. I emphasized in Chapter 4 that all of us begin our lives already in relation with our biological mothers, and that this very close relationship extends for us into the early years of our lives, according to object relations theory, as we continue the psychological birthing process with our adoptive mothers. It is through our personal relationships with others that we develop a voice, an "I," a sense of who we are as unique individuals in relation to Thou. I mentioned that in her book, *Caring*, Nel Noddings (1984) does not just explore the intimate relationship of a mother and child in her discussion of caring relations, but she also considers the relationship between a teacher and student as another example of a caring relationship. She (1992) further explores the personal relationship between teachers and students in her follow-up book, *The Challenge to Care in Schools*.

Noddings's (1984, 1992) description of teacher-student relationships in terms of one-caring and one-cared-for is considered controversial in the USA because of the distinction that Americans make between private, intimate, personal relations and public relations. While it is expected that parents and their children, and friends and lovers have close, personal relationships, these are all considered examples of private relationships. Teachers and students, and bosses and their employees, are expected to have a public relationship that is therefore not intimate and personal.

In America we fear that if teachers establish personal relationships with their students this means students will be vulnerable to manipulation, and indoctrination, including physical and psychological abuse. We recognize that teachers wield great power over students in their roles as dispensers of knowledge and evaluators and judges of what students have learned. Teachers assign grades to students' work and these grades help to determine whether or not students have the opportunity for the good life, in terms of employment and higher education. We also recognize teachers are responsible for the safety and well-being of their students and we realize that teachers have great influence in affecting the quality of students' daily lives as a result of teacher interactions with others. Teachers witness and monitor students' behaviors toward each other in schools, as well as how other teachers and administrators treat students.

Yet, certainly parents (childcare providers) wield even greater power over their children than school teachers. In fact, children's very survival depends on their parents, and still we acknowledge the importance of parents establishing personal relationships with their children. We even argue that if parents are unable or unwilling to establish caring relationships with their children their children could be hindered in their growth and development and will have to find ways to compensate for this lack. If caring is so important in parental relationships with their children, even though there are many risks and dangers involved—for children are very vulnerable to their parents' manipulations as well as their physical and psychological abuse— why is the establishment of caring relationships with students not important for teachers in school settings? I want to suggest that in fact it is very important for teachers to establish caring relationships with their students. And I can even point to many examples to show that we do agree that this is important, even though it seems at times that we go out of our way to make it next to impossible for teachers to be able to establish caring relationships with their students.

One of the very important implications for education of a relational theory of knowing is that those of us working in schools, as well as those of us who make decisions which affect the quality of working conditions in schools, need to focus our attention on the relationships teachers have with their students, as well as the relationships students have with each other.[2] This is because a relational (e)pistemology describes knowers as social beings-in-relation-with-others, not as isolated individuals. As social beings-in-relation-with-others, not only must we focus on relationships, but we must also worry about the quality of these relationships in order to insure that they are caring relationships rather than harmful, oppressive ones. A relational (e)pistemology recognizes and attempts to address the political powers involved in relationships, both personally and socially.

Schools in America currently focus predominantly upon the outcomes and products of schooling. Often these are entirely disconnected from the relational processes of learning. Students become objects who must produce a certain amount and quality of products in order to graduate, and teachers become the managers of this production effort whose job security and salaries depend on how productive their students are. Current emphasis on proficiency exams in the United States, to try to hold teachers accountable and make sure all students are able to produce the outcomes and products others determine students should be able to produce at various ages, just further enhances a product focus. A relational theory of knowing insists that we must focus on the process of learning and consider very deeply how we can help students, as social beings-in-relation-with-others, become knowers. While we may all be born with the possibility of becoming knowers, we can only actualize that possibility if others, such as our family members and friends and schoolteachers, encourage and support our efforts.

I am suggesting that education at its best is a personal, relational process between a student and a teacher. I want to suggest, in agreement with Noddings, that teachers need to establish caring relationships with their students, in which students are active participants able to reject their teachers' relationships if they are not perceived as caring. While there are many false forms of caring that we all have been exposed to, a genuine caring relationship is one that is good, not harmful to either the one-caring or the one-cared-for (Thayer-Bacon, 1997). We already know from our defining of caring relationships in Chapter 4 that if teachers are to establish caring relationships with their students this means that teachers need to use caring reasoning to attend to their students and get to know them. Teachers must focus their efforts on valuing and appreciating the students' needs and learning what their interests and desires are. Teachers should suspend their own views and listen attentively and generously to their students. This is the only way they can be assured they understand their students, and can therefore help to meet students' needs to know. This effort of attending to the needs of others helps assure us that the teaching-studenting relationship will be a caring one, and not one that is manipulative or harmful to the student, or vice versa. A caring relationship is based on treating the other with respect and dignity, so that a trusting relationship can develop between the two.

Of course, it is next to impossible for teachers to establish caring relationships with their students in most middle schools, high schools, and colleges in America. The larger the population in the school is and the more students each individual teacher has, the more difficult the establishing of caring teacher-student relationships becomes. It is not humanly possible to establish caring relationships with a large number of people. There is just not enough time in each day to be able to listen attentively to everyone's needs. One teacher can only be available, approachable, and attentive to so many people, and most teachers are asked to teach more students than they can possibly get to know well. Not only are teachers and students not able to establish caring relationships with each other in most schools, but students are not able to establish caring relationships with other students as well for there are too many students in each classroom and too little time to get to know each other. Older students usually move from one classroom to another during the day, thus exposing themselves to even more students than elementary students meet each day.

Even though we make it next to impossible for teachers to establish caring relationships with their students due to the working conditions we create in schools, it is easy to point to examples that show we do value caring teacher-student relationships. Schools, including colleges, will advertise that one of their advantages is their smaller number of students, and they will boast about their student-teacher ratio as a way to attract students to their school. They will point out that the smaller the student-teacher ration is the more likely the individual student will receive the attention they need from their teachers to help them learn. Schools that offer flexible, alternative forms of scheduling where students can enjoy more time with their teachers and the possibility of having their teachers as mentors throughout their schooling experience will advertise these possibilities as ways to attract students to their campus. Again, the schools will acknowledge the value of students being able to work closely and over extended periods of times with their teachers, for it helps the students learn and succeed in school. And, campuses will offer faculty smaller numbers of classes to teach and fewer students as incentives to teach there. They will point out that if the potential faculty member teaches here they will have more time to prepare for their classes as well as more time with their students. The gift of more time and fewer students will make it more likely that the potential faculty member will be able to do a good job as a teacher and enjoy the intrinsic rewards of teaching, such as getting to know their students and watching them grow as a result of working with them. In general, the more prestigious the university, college, elementary or secondary school is, the smaller the faculty-student ratio is and the lighter the faculty teaching load is.

The closest the majority of students in public schools come to being able to establish caring relationships with their teachers and their classmates are when students are in preschool, kindergarten, and lower elementary grades. Several states in the USA have established public policies limiting the number of students that can be in lower-grade levels to no more than 20 students, and often each classroom will have two teachers or a teacher and a classroom aide (non-certified teacher). Again, this policy demonstrates that we do recognize the value of teacher-student relationships. With no more than 20 students, two adults, and most of each day to be together, there is much more of a chance for students and teachers to get to know each other and establish caring relationships with each other.

Sometimes students will have the opportunity to establish caring relationships with their teachers if they are placed in special education or bi-lingual education classes, for these teachers may teach the same students for up to three years, depending on their school's resources and policies. Also, some smaller public schools only have one art, music, foreign language, or physical education teacher, and so that teacher will have the same students for extended periods of time, sometimes stretching over the entire time the student is enrolled in the school. However, many of these teachers are severely limited in terms of the amount of time they spend with students and are even more overwhelmed by the sheer number of students enrolled in a school if they are the only gym, art, or music teacher for the entire school enrollment. Even worse, they can be the "specials" teacher for two or three schools.

As a Montessori teacher, I had even more opportunity to establish caring relationships with my students than most elementary teachers.[3] Not only were my classroom sizes smaller (the largest class I had was 23 students), and I had classroom co-teachers, as well as having the students in my classroom for most of the day, I also had the students in my classroom for three years. Three years of time with a student makes a BIG difference, and that is the typical structure for all Montessori classrooms; students ages 3-6, 6-9, and 9-12 years are together in the same room for three years. As some students graduate each year and move on, and other, younger students move into the classroom each year, the child ideally stays in the same room, with the same teacher, and a core of other students around the same age, for three years. I found that as a teacher in such a setting not only was it possible for me to establish caring relationships with my students: it was necessary. Neither the students nor I could look forward to another year of being together unless we were able to relate to each other in a caring manner. And students could not function effectively with the same students in their classroom year after year unless they were able to learn how to get along. My classroom became like an extended family, which included the students' extended family members as well, many of whom I still hear from.

I am not suggesting that teachers and students need to establish caring relationships in schools because students are lacking these experiences in their home settings, as Jane Roland Martin (1992) does in her book *The Schoolhome*, though that is sadly often true. Like Noddings, I want to suggest that even for students experiencing significant caring relationships in their home settings, all students will benefit from experiencing caring relationships with their teachers. The establishment of personal, close relationships with their teachers and other students will help students become knowers able to participate in and contribute to the knowing process. It will help them develop their own voice and learn how to express it, for they can feel confident that others will listen to what they have to say generously. And they will be able to learn from the voices that other students are expressing as well. It will help them gain confidence in their own abilities for they will feel valued and affirmed by the attention they receive. Students will thrive under such conditions. Why should only a few students be allowed the opportunity to experience close, personal relationships with their teachers and other students, those who come from wealthy backgrounds, attend Montessori schools, or live in small, isolated locations, for example? There are many things we can do to help make it possible for all students and teachers to experience caring relationships.

One suggestion is to make classroom sizes smaller, following the early childhood/younger elementary policy of no more than 20 students in a classroom. Another suggestion is to assign more than one teacher to a classroom. A third suggestion is to lengthen the time students spend in one classroom with each other and their teachers, as well as increase the number of times students can have the same teacher. Some schools are trying ideas that support these suggestions, such as changing their scheduling formats to what many are calling "block scheduling," which gives students more time in a classroom each day with a teacher. Other schools are creating "schools within schools" as ways of breaking down large student populations into smaller groups, and having the same teachers work as a team with the same students, so students can become better known in a more wholistic manner by their teachers and classmates. Some schools are creating advising/mentoring programs where all teachers are assigned a small number of students to meet with regularly and consecutively throughout the student's enrollment in school. All of these suggestions—and I'm sure there are many more we can think of—will help students and teachers have more chances to develop personal relationships with each other.

Now, let's come back to the concerns people express about the studenting-teaching relationship being a personal, caring one. In no way am I suggesting that any student, or teacher for that matter, should have to experience a teaching-studenting relationship with someone who is manipulative or abusive. Students should not have to fear their teachers or protect themselves from teachers (or vice versa). There are many people teaching who do not know how to relate to other people in healthy, constructive ways and who use teaching as an opportunity to dominate and oppress others. These people should not be allowed to harm our children. And, unfortunately, today there are many students who are so troubled due to many factors in their lives, that they are a danger to other students and teachers as well. These students should not be allowed to harm each other or their teachers. But these are extreme examples that are signs of unhealthy social conditions. The extremes do not diminish the importance of establishing caring relationships with each other; they underscore how important caring relationships are. A relational (e)pistemology describes knowers as social beings-in-relation-with-others, not as isolated individuals. It therefore emphasizes that education is a relational process between beings who are in relation with each other. Wherever people are together in relation with each other there will be political factors. A relational approach to knowing does not seek the impossible task of getting rid of political factors, nor does it try to ignore them. Rather a relational focus highlights political factors and underscores them so we can address them. I can turn to addressing political factors further by turning to a discussion of social relations, and so I move on to consider social relations in terms of schooling.

Social Relations

In Chapter 4, as we explored personal relations, we were regularly being reminded that individuals and their significant others do not exist in a vacuum. Each of us experiences personal relations with our childcare providers within a larger social context which surrounds our childcare providers and therefore us as well. Chapter 5 considers the social dimensions of our lives and their influences on us as individuals. I address Mead's (1934) efforts to avoid solipsism as well as others' fears that Mead's theory leads us away from solipsism into the hands of social determinism. We found the fear of social determinism in our previous discussion of teachers and students establishing caring relationships with each other, for a suggestion of teachers relating to students in a personal way causes us to fear teachers' influences on students. Yet, we also pointed to the dangers and harm that can occur for children if they do not experience caring relationships, especially with their main childcare providers. If children are not able to establish a relationship with an other it can affect their ability to create what Flax (1990) calls "a core identity" for themselves. This is because, as Mead argued, we gain a sense of self by having our self reflected back to us by others. Others, as strangers to us, offer us ways to gain an outsider perspective on ourselves, for we become objects to ourselves when we are able to see ourselves as others see us.

A relational (e)pistemology argues that the relationships we experience with others are both personal and social: they are what Dewey called transactional relationships. We are first of all social beings who are greatly affected by others, but we also greatly affect others with our individual influence, right from the start. We are social beings who exist in relation to others at an intimate level as well as at a generalized level. We are selves-in-relation-with-others. There is a direct transactional relation between our individual subjectivity and our general sociality. The implications of a transactional view of selves-in-relation-to-others are many. For one, we cannot focus just on the individual student, or even the student-teacher relationship, at a personal level alone, for we must take into consideration the larger social context in which both student and teacher are embedded. All of us are historical, locally situated beings. As soon as we widen our lens to take into consideration the larger social context placed within a historical timeframe, all sorts of exciting possibilities become available to us. With a larger social and historical context, we now have a variety of perspectives from which to choose. We now can have a greater understanding of our own situatedness for we can compare ourselves to others. Others draw attention to themselves and us, through their differences, for while they may have much in common with us, they also are irreducibly distinct and different from us. They offer us contrasting images, they cause ruptures in our understanding, and they cause discontinuities. These contrasts others offer allow us the chance to become more conscious of who we are and more self-reflective. These contrasts also expose us to other possibilities and differences and help to stimulate our ideas of what is possible. Then we can even change something about ourselves that we do not like. We can grow and develop further; we can enlarge our thinking, as Benhabib (1992) says.

Paradoxically, at the same time that a relational approach to knowing implies that schools need to offer students and teachers ways to develop caring relationships by lowering the student-teacher ratio and increasing the time students and teachers have with each other, it also implies that students need to be exposed to diversity. A relational (e)pistemology argues that we learn more about our own situatedness by having ourselves reflected back to us by others not like us. The more variety and differences in the others we are exposed to, the more perspective we will be able to gain on ourselves. Since we begin our lives as immature individuals who have not developed a sense of self yet, we are exposed to our culture before we are able to critique the culture we are exposed to. As Jim Garrison (1996) says, culture has us before we have it. We become acculturated by the others who care for us. That acculturation process happens unconsciously, automatically, so that we are not even aware that it is taking place. Thus, when we begin to interact with others not like us, we begin with an assumption that others are like us, not even realizing the concept of difference. We become aware of our differences through our interactions with others, through our efforts to establish common meanings so that we can communicate and relate to each other, and all the mishaps and miscommunications we experience along the way. It is others not like us who help us become more conscious and aware of our own contextuality. They wake us up and make us notice what before we had taken for granted.[4]

Therefore, while I just recommended that students need to experience small classroom sizes in the previous section, I also want to say that students need to experience diverse perspectives. What does it mean "to experience diverse perspectives?" There are many levels and degrees to diversity. Placing any two students together will create diversity for there will be differences between the two, even if they come from the same family, as any siblings and even twins can attest to. Two students from two different families already walk into a classroom with a great deal of diversity, as well as commonality, between them. Add in differences in ages or make the classroom co-educational and we now have even more differences that will be represented in the classroom. If the students come from different social economic backgrounds then even more differences will be represented, and that's without even introducing differences due to religious and ethnic backgrounds. Because the United States is a very pluralistic country with people who have immigrated here from all over the world, it is not so difficult to find classrooms with even a small number of students in them (20) that will still represent a lot of diversity. Even in more isolated parts of the country, or for other countries that are more homogenous, it is still the case that there will be differences represented which can teach us a lot.

Yet, it is possible to import even more differences into a small classroom community by assuring that diversity is represented in the curriculum. Maybe recommending small classroom sizes that are diverse is not quite so difficult after all. It requires the embracing of a multicultural curriculum.

Sonia Nieto's (1992) *Affirming Diversity* is an excellent source for considering the concept of multicultural education, and her book is used in many college classrooms across the United States that focus on helping future teachers understand what a multicultural curriculum should entail. While I have disagreements with some of Nieto's theory, in particular her Marxist critical theory, which always risks sliding into a God's-eye view of how the world should be transformed, I do think her definition of multicultural education represents a fine example of what a relational (e)pistemology implies. Nieto does not recommend that students should enroll in a class on various cultures during the time they are matriculated in schools. She does not recommend we only study various cultures, for example, during Black History month, or Latino, Native American, or Women's History month. Nieto defines a multicultural curriculum as one that is basic and pervasive and for all students, in that culture becomes a significant way for framing all subject areas taught each day. Students should not just learn about other cultures in their foreign language classes, but in their English, science, history, math, and geography classes as well on a daily basis. In all subject areas culture should not be just a "tag on," that we add at the end of each chapter, as a supplemental text, but culture should be used to frame the way we learn about the subject areas. Following her advice, students will not just learn about the American Revolutionary War, but they will learn various perspectives of the USA Revolutionary War: the perspective of the British, the Founding Fathers, the Indigenous tribes that lived in the area, the Black slaves of the Founding Fathers, and the Founding Fathers' wives, as well as the non-property owners working in America at the time. The more perspectives are introduced into a subject area, the more students will be able to be conscious that there are differences in opinions and a variety of experiences. Teaching subject areas through cultural perspectives allows students to gain a greater awareness of their own perspectives, as well as greater understanding of others. Importantly, a multicultural curriculum offers students ways to learn how to critique the various viewpoints represented, including the majority view that is easily taken for granted and allowed to remain invisible as the established norm against which other worldviews are measured.

Nieto (1992) defines a multicultural education as one that teaches students to be critical thinkers able to critique the very curriculum they are taught. By teaching students subject areas through a cultural framing, students become aware of the situatedness of the various subject areas themselves. They learn not only about science, but that the science is influenced by different schools of thought, and that there is more than one way to view science. They learn that scientific theories have changed and developed over time as scientists have gone through paradigm shifts, thus helping them not only critique past scientific theories but also making them aware that the current theories of science they are learning will change over time as well. Students learn not only the situatedness of the various subject areas they study, but they also learn of the limitations of their various sources of knowledge, their teachers, including their school teachers and their texts. Clearly, teaching students through a multicultural curriculum encourages and supports the qualified relativism I argued for in Chapter 2. A multicultural curriculum teaches students about situated truths that are qualified by as much evidence as we can offer. A multicultural curriculum teaches students that criteria and standards for judging the evidence we offer change over time and can be corrected and improved upon. A multicultural curriculum teaches students that the world in which we live is a pluralistic world supported by a variety of truths. It does not represent our struggles to gain knowledge as leading us to one final answer upon which in the end we will all agree.

We can therefore anticipate the kinds of worry a recommendation of teaching through a multicultural curriculum might trigger. Many worries will center around fears of relativism. People worry that teaching students through a multicultural curriculum will lead students to become cynical and critical of all sources once they realize no source has the Truth and all the Answers. They worry that school teachers will lose students' respect and their authority will be undermined as teachers if students are taught their teachers cannot serve as a final source of knowledge. They also worry that whole cultures will be undermined, for students will question the very culture their teachers, including their parents, are trying to teach them. Many fear that teaching a multicultural curriculum will incite the youth to civil disobedience, and it will lead to chaos and the undermining of social foundations (as Socrates was accused of in ancient Greece).

Awareness of diversity highlights our own fallibility. It emphasizes that none of us has a God's-eye view of the world, we are all embedded and embodied within the world. None of us are authorities, including our school teachers. A relational (e)pistemology implies that we must change the way we view our teachers. They can no longer be viewed as the experts. Teachers become other inquirers, along with students. Teachers become facilitators and resources and guides, but not expert authorities. At the same time, teachers are still able to critique existing knowledge, as are the students. Teachers and students become social critics, able to deconstruct and reconstruct, and offer new theories and contribute to the construction of new knowledge with the help of others.

Others worry that in teaching students about diverse perspectives students will lack a commonality and cohesiveness that pulls them together as citizens. If we emphasize our differences and strangeness, the irreducibility of our alerity, how can we ever hope to learn how to work together with each other and establish grounds of commonality, on which communities depend? And, if we teach students diverse curriculums, how will we give them a common base of knowledge from which to be able to relate and communicate with each other? Still others worry that in teaching a multicultural curriculum, there are only going to be so many perspectives we can include, simply due to lack of time, not to mention lack of resources and knowledge. So, which ones will we include and which ones will we leave out? For every perspective we include in our curriculum, there is another one we must leave out. On what grounds will we decide? For decide we must.

A relational (e)pistemology, with its emphasis on social relations, highlights our similarities with others as well as our differences. It highlights how each of us is uniquely affected by our cultural surroundings, while at the same time emphasizing that all of us share that commonality of cultural influences. A relational (e)pistemology underscores our limitations and contextuality, while at the same time pointing out that all of us are limited, contextual beings, thus showing how much we also share in common. A relational (e)pistemology is a humbling approach to knowing that insists we must always reconsider the criteria we use to make curriculum decisions about what to include and what to leave out. We must always remind our students and ourselves that we are not able to be all-inclusive, and that there are many perspectives worthy of our consideration which are beyond our reach. And yet, at the same time we must help our students learn how to critique various perspectives, once they have attempted to generously understand them, for some ideas are worth rejecting. Our theories of knowledge are qualified by as much evidence as we can socially muster so that it is not the case that we must accept anything as good, and yet at the same time we cannot accept anything as certain, fixed, and final. A relational (e)pistemology helps us critique cultural influences and avoid social determinism while at the same time our transactional relationships with others reminds us that we are not alone, we are social-beings-in-relation-with-others, thus avoiding solipsism as well.

I would like to continue discussion of curriculum issues, and bring in more instructional implications, by moving on at this point to consider w/holistic relations.

W/holistic Relations

I discussed spiritual issues in Chapter 4's consideration of personal relations, with Martin Buber's I-Thou relations, and Simone Weil's description of an anonymous relationship with God. And, in Chapter 6, when I turned to Buddhism and Native American philosophy for examples of wholistic relations, we found that these examples are spiritual examples as well. They are holistic as well as wholistic, which is why I describe their views in terms of w/holism, to emphasize that they are both. One cannot separate spirituality out of a discussion of Buddhism or Native American philosophy without being vulnerable to accusations of misrepresentation. Spirituality clearly forms the ontological categories that help to shape and give meaning to the central concepts of their philosophies, such as the concepts of big Mind and Holy Wind. For Buddhists and Native Americans, their spirituality and their philosophy are one and the same. While it is easier to see that spirituality is central to Buddhist and Native American philosophy, I want to suggest that for all of us our spiritual beliefs represent our ontological categories and our ontological categories directly affect our (e)pistemology. Americans typically equate spirituality with particular religious affiliations such as Judaism or Christianity, instead of noting that 'religion' is a concept that usually stands for organized, institutionalized forms of spirituality that involve membership and participation in the dogmas of some particular church, whereas spirituality describes one's metaphysical approach to life. What I want to explore in this section are spiritual beliefs, not any one particular church affiliation.

It is a brave person, indeed, who takes up spiritual beliefs in a discussion of schooling in American society. Ironically, though the United States was formed to help protect citizens' right to religious freedom, teachers today in America must be very cautious in discussing any kind of spiritual issues in their classrooms. In America, we have tried to separate church from state and we have told teachers they cannot teach a particular religion in our public government funded schools. However, we have never achieved this goal of separating church and state. Teachers in American public schools have historically taught a Christian curriculum, however subtly, in particular a Protestant Christian curriculum. The number of Catholic schools and Jewish schools in the USA, formed to offer an alternative to the teachings of Protestant Christian beliefs in the public schools, attest to this fact. American public schools are contradictory places where we teach religious beliefs without admitting we do so. We can find Christmas trees in American schools all over the country in December, as students and teachers prepare for their Winter Break, which just so happens to coincide with the Christian Christmas holiday. At the same time, teachers cannot openly discuss religious beliefs, without fear of being accused of violating our constitutional rights to separation of church and state. Thus, Protestant Christian beliefs continue to shape the curriculum of American schools at an unconscious and foundational level without being contested, for they are not allowed to be brought to our attentions and critiqued.

The belief that religious beliefs can be separated from the learning that takes place in schools is based on a philosophy that attempts to separate ontology from epistemology. A relational (e)pistemology argues that ontology and epistemology cannot be separated; they are connected and support each other. They are the warp and woof that form the netting we use to catch up our experiences and describe them and give them meaning. Our religious beliefs represent our spiritual views, which influence the essential categories that we use to make sense of our experiences. America has never been successful at separating church and state in our schools because it is impossible to do so. Teachers cannot leave their religious beliefs at the doorstep when they walk through their classroom doors. Teachers can try to mask their particular church affiliation, but the spiritual beliefs they embrace, which their church represents, cannot be discarded like an article of clothing they can take off and on. A relational (e)pistemology insists that teachers' spiritual beliefs as well as others' spiritual beliefs need to be made an explicit part of the curriculum, rather than be allowed to remain a hidden, implicit part of the curriculum. By making teachers', students', and others' spiritual beliefs a conscious part of the school curriculum, those spiritual beliefs can then be examined carefully, compared and contrasted, and consciously embraced or rejected. Ironically, America made the rule of separating church and state in public schools in order to try to protect people's religious freedoms, and prevent indoctrination of any one particular religion on vulnerable students. Yet, the fact that we do not allow religious beliefs to be an explicit part of the curriculum insures that religious beliefs are implicitly taught to students without submission to critique.

We can see the impossibility of separating our spiritual beliefs from our knowing and the implicit effects said beliefs have on pedagogy by pointing to many examples of practices in American public schools that represent Protestant Christian beliefs which are foundational to American public school experiences. There are many Christian practices that are subtler than Christmas trees and holiday celebrations. For example, Christians believe in the concept of original sin, that we are born sinners and have to work hard to become good. This spiritual belief in original sin is an ontological category that gives much meaning to Christians' daily practice. Protestant Christians in particular believe that we are each responsible for our daily actions and that it is through hard work on Earth in this lifetime that we will earn a place in Heaven. Over time the belief in original sin has translated into making sure children are kept busy and working hard, for idleness is "the devil's workshop." Therefore, in American public schools, which are shaped by Protestant spiritual beliefs, it is not a surprise that we find school days structured with tight schedules, with the students given very little time to pass between classes, or to socialize during lunch. We fear that if students have too much time that is "free time" they will waste that time and get into trouble. We want our students in their classrooms working hard, and we want teachers who are able to contain and control their students' behavior, and keep them working "on task." Researchers have even given a name to student behavior that involves doing things like getting a drink of water, sharpening one's pencil, chatting with one's neighbor, or just daydreaming. Such behavior is called "off-task" behavior, and it is recommended good teachers minimize off-task behavior as much as possible. Students who do not work hard all day at school are labeled lazy, unmotivated, and underachievers. They are viewed as potential discipline problems.

My Montessori classroom would make the researchers with this spiritual belief in original sin shake their heads in dismay, for my students were free to move around their room and consequently engage in plenty of "off-task" behavior, as long as they did not disturb other students' work. Many people who first observe a Montessori classroom respond to it by saying, "This feels like chaos! How is any learning taking place here?" Again, this is because most people attended schools where their behavior in the building was strictly monitored and managed and in Montessori classrooms the children learn to monitor and manage their own behavior. Maria Montessori was a very spiritual woman, who believed in the goodness of all children, not that they begin their lives as sinners. Similar to Rousseau, she had tremendous faith in children's natural instincts. She trusted children's desire to learn and saw the teacher's job as one of encouraging that desire and supporting it, rather than stopping it or trying to contain or control it. Her spiritual beliefs are reflected in the pedagogical style of teaching she developed and taught to others, once she became famous for her results. Children thrived in her schools.

In a Montessori classroom children work at their own pace, and they may choose to work with someone else or by theirselves. The children are free to move around their classroom and they may choose to work at a table or desk, or on a rug on the floor. Montessori teachers do not have a desk in the front of the room so they can monitor all students' behaviors. Most Montessori teachers do not have a desk at all. They likely carry around a clipboard where they can write down observation notes on the students, and what work they choose to do. I had a corner of our counter area as my space to keep my notes. Montessori students do not have grades either. There is no failing in a Montessori classroom. Children just work on their lessons until they have mastered them, and then they move on. The curriculum is individualized and taught in sequential stages. Concepts are taught mainly through concrete materials, at least originally, until the students are able to move on to a more abstract level of understanding. The curriculum and pedagogical style of teaching that can be observed in a Montessori classroom reflect the spiritual beliefs of Maria Montessori: children can be trusted to want to learn and that if we allow them to choose their own work and set their own pace for working, they will choose wisely and will learn a great deal. She did not believe children needed fear tactics such as threats of failing, beatings, or suspensions to motivate them to learn. Nor did she believe that children needed competition and awards to motivate them to learn. The joy of learning is its own reward. Montessori stands as a vivid example of how one's spiritual beliefs shape one's educational philosophy, and one's daily practice as a teacher working with students. She also serves as an excellent example of a teacher who made her spiritual beliefs a conscious part of the curriculum and therefore opened these beliefs up to the possibility of critique. Montessori wrote and spoke about her spiritual beliefs and how they shaped her pedagogy. She actively encouraged parents to become educated in her views and determine if they agreed with them or not. She did not allow her spiritual beliefs to remain a hidden part of the school curriculum.

Instead she articulated her spiritual beliefs, which shaped her pedagogy, so that they could be discussed openly and agreed upon, or not.

A relational (e)pistemology is supported by a relational ontology, the unifying spiritual belief that we are one with the universe. I am suggesting that the relational ontology that supports a relational (e)pistemology needs to be foregrounded as a conscious part of the curriculum, so its influence can be carefully considered and critiqued. How do we teach students that all things are interconnected and interdependent and to see themselves as jewels reflected in Indra's net? How do we help students learn to recognize appearances that we take to be existent, separate, and permanent for what they are, delusions that cause us great suffering? There are many ways to teach a w/holistic curriculum: I do not think there is any one right way. I am certainly not trying to recommend the Montessori method as the way all children should be taught. Buddhists may turn to meditation and yoga, and the studying of Buddha's teachings as ways to rid themselves of delusions. Native Americans may turn to music and dance, and storytelling, as ways to help them tune into their primal experiences of the world as one. Let me share an example from a Native American teacher, to help us see how Native American spiritual beliefs, which reflect a relational ontology and (e)pistemology, are translated into the daily practice of a school classroom and how their spiritual beliefs become an explicit part of the curriculum.

In *Look to the Mountain*, Gregory Cajete (1994) offers us spiritual insights into Native American education. Cajete is of Santa Clara Pueblo heritage, and at the time of his writing he had been an Indian educator for more than 20 years.[5] His book was the first major work by an American Indian on Indian education. Cajete tells us he wrote his book as an open letter to Indian educators. Cajete describes Indian focus in education as a relational orientation. Indian education brings out affective, subjective, communal relations, artistic and mythical dimensions, ritual and ceremony, and sacred ecology. "Education is an art of process, participation, and making connection. Learning is a growth and life process; and Life and Nature are always relationships in process!" (p. 24). Native Americans teach their children that they have mutual, reciprocal relationships between their social group and the natural world. They teach their children that relationship in community includes people, plants, animals, the whole of Nature. Cajete recommends a w/holistic approach to knowing that is process focused, and appreciative of spirituality. It is an education that shows respect for individual, cultural, and biological diversity, and seeks to establish a reflective dialogue. Cajete does not hide Native American spiritual beliefs in his discussion of Native American education; rather these spiritual beliefs are foregrounded by him so that their guiding influence can be easily seen and they can be carefully considered.

For Native Americans, according to Cajete (1994), the spiritual ecology of Indigenous education is taught through breath, language, song, prayer, and thought.

Much of this education is informal education, taught through experiences, storytelling, ritual/ceremony, dreaming, tutoring, as well as through artistic expression. Spirituality is not a religion for Native Americans, in the sense of a particular religious doctrine, but rather it is a way of life. The tools used for teaching and learning include the cultivation of senses, and the ability to use language. Cajete presents many Native American stories within his text, including the Navajo story of Holy Wind I shared in Chapter 6, and each story is presented with the deepest respect. The stories are told to illustrate Native American spiritual beliefs, and their educational implications. We have already learned in Chapter 6 that the Mountain and Wind are spiritual symbols for Native Americans. These spiritual symbols are used to orient them, and they are viewed as a source of knowledge and guidance, as well as a source of life and creation. The Holy Wind is the Navajos source of life, spiritual light, thought and wisdom, language, way of knowing, guidance, and creation.

Another spiritual belief Cajete (1994) shares with his readers is the Hunter of Good Heart. "The hunter hunts to perpetuate the life of family, clan, and community. The hunter represents the community to the world of animals and spirits; therefore, the community as well as the hunter is judged through his behavior" (p. 59). The hunter participates in the "great dance of life." Cajete shows how the Navajo deer hunting story and the Blackfoot legend of Scar Face serve to teach the lessons of how to be a hunter with a good heart. Such a hunter must learn how to prayerfully ask that a life be taken to sustain others, with the promise that those others' bodies will eventually be given back to sustain the hunted. The hunter must use intense concentration and application of skill in hunting, and the hunter must treat the prey with respect. After the prey is killed, the hunter with a good heart must celebrate and give thanks for the food received.

The orienting foundations of what Cajete (1994) calls "spiritual ecology" include: the Mythic (the tribe's language and culture), the Artistic/Visionary (winter element-deeply inward), the Environmental (connects a tribe to their place), and the Affective/Communal (summer element-outward, highly interactive, external dimension). Cajete sums up his description of Indian education as being about a journey "to find our face (to understand and appreciate our true character), to find our heart (to understand and appreciate the passions that move and energize our life), to find a foundation (work that allows us to fully [reach] our potential and our greatest fulfillment), and to become a complete man or woman (to find our Life and appreciate the spirit that moves us)" (p. 68).

With these few examples in mind, we can envision all sorts of possibilities in terms of how to teach students to view their world in a wholistic and holistic manner. Teachers teach spirituality by the way they talk to their students and treat them, by the way they move through the classroom environment and how they care for it, by the way they treat the studying of other cultures and various subject areas, by the way they model for students how to live one's life as someone who is connected and related to others including their natural world. It is impossible to separate spirituality from education, for our spiritual beliefs serve as our compasses, guiding us in the choices we make and the meaning we give to our experiences. Given the impossibility of separating (e)pistemology from ontology, we can understand the importance of making teachers, and students, spiritual beliefs, and others in comparison, a conscious part of the curriculum. Making spirituality an explicit part of the curriculum, rather than implicit, makes these various spiritual beliefs available for public scrutiny. It protects students from the indoctrination of hidden spiritual beliefs rather than making them more vulnerable to teachers' influences.

Included in a relational ontology and (e)pistemology is the concept of ecological relations, as illustrated through the description of Native American education. At this time I would like to move on to consider educational implications for schools in regards to our relationship with Nature.

Ecological Relations

A relational (e)pistemology does not separate human beings from Nature anymore than it separates sprituality from materiality. Already in my discussion of educational implications Nature has been part of the discussion, as when I pointed to Cajete's (1994) examples of the Holy Wind and the Hunter with a Good Heart. I capitalize Nature in my discussions to emphasize when the concept represents sacred spirituality, and I use 'nature' without capitals to note the times when the concept is used as it has developed historically in Euro-western science, as an object devoid of spirituality. The nature of modern Euro-western science is a nature that must be contained, controlled, and mastered. It is a nature that must be forced to reveal its secrets and be made to serve humankind. It is a nature that can be studied in textbooks, observed under a microscope, dissected and stained and experimented with. The Nature of a relational (e)pistemology is the same Nature of Buddhism, deep ecology, eco-feminism, and Native American philosophy. It is a Nature that we are connected to and associated with, that we overlap with and integrate with, that we relate to. Even describing our relation with Nature in a relational manner tends to suggest some kind of separation between human beings and Nature and I do not want to suggest any separation. We are one with Nature; we are Nature.

The Nature of a relational approach to knowing is all around us, inside and outside of us. It is our source of life, as well as our kin and our teacher. As our teacher, Nature is a tremendous source of knowledge for us. A relational (e)pistemology implies an ecological educational focus for students where the walls of the classroom and school building must be broken down so that there are no outside/inside boundaries separating us from Nature. There is no ontological split between humans and Nature in a relational (e)pistemology, and thus no potential for us to create a hierarchy as well, with Nature in a subordinate role. An ecological education teaches us to treat Nature with reverence and respect, as we treat ourselves, for we are mutually dependent, we are interrelated. To oppose Nature is to oppose ourselves.

Let me further define an ecological education by returning to Cajete's (1994) advice for Indian educators. We learned in Chapter 7 that Native Americans do not separate spirituality from Nature. For Native Americans, in particular, Nature is sacred, the true ground of spiritual reality. In *Look to the Mountain*, Cajete (1994) devotes a chapter to the topic of "Environmental Education," as he explains to us how the environment, connecting a tribe to their place, serves as one of the orienting foundations of Indian education. Environmental understanding is directly tied to the cosmologies of Tribal life. Nature's cycles of life, death, struggle, and survival represent Tribal metaphysics. How Indians answer the questions of survival and sustainability reflects their understanding of Nature.

From Chapter 7, we know that Indigenous people possess a tremendous wealth of environmental wisdom that they have preserved and passed down to their children. Their knowledge is gained from Nature, received directly from animals, plants, and other living and non-living entities. One implication of environmental education is that it must involve daily contact with animals, plants, and the land. Cajete (1994) laments that Native Americans no longer spend their lives in daily contact with animals, plants, and the land, and this loss of daily contact affects them in many ways. They become ignorant, for they lose touch with their sources of knowledge. They become ill, due to a loss of dynamic balance. They experience disharmony, disrespect, dishonor, disturbance, and misuse or misconduct.

Native American environmental education involves teaching students how to maintain a harmonious relationship with their land. Living in a harmonious and sustainable relationship with the land is considered a sacred responsibility. Students are taught that they have a responsibility to respect and preserve the web of life. They need to learn that their relationship with Nature is one of mutual reciprocity. Nature, as kin, establishes the context, the set of relations that connect everything in their lives. If they lose their contact with Nature, as many Native Americans have, they lose what gives their lives meaning, what connects them and relates them to everything else in their lives. Students are taught:

> Nature is sacred, humans share the breath of life with other living things, we exist within and are affected by the mutually reciprocal web of interrelationships in a natural community. Plants, animals, and other natural phenomena and entities are imbued with power; the natural world creates through the interplay of opposite yet complementary primal energies, and there exists a guiding creative force in Nature that affects everything. (Cajete, 1994, p. 91)

This thought is symbolized by such metaphors as "look to the mountain," the title of Cajete's book, for the mountains are sacred places of vision and orientation.

Teachers can help to encourage a sense of wonder and affinity for the living world, and they can nourish that affinity. Teachers can teach students to be fond of the outdoors, to aesthetically appreciate Nature, and to see things in their wholeness. How can teachers accomplish all of this? It is very important for students to experience the natural world at an early age with the help of teachers who can serve as role models for loving Nature. We have to experience the natural world in order to understand it. Teachers can teach students that life is sacred, and they can teach students an attitude of care for Nature. Cajete reminds us that students need to develop a sense of place, which requires direct contact with the natural aspects of a place (soil, wildlife, landscapes), so that students can learn how to live well in a place. We need intimate knowledge of our landscape. We need to study the natural history of our location at a micro level. We need to establish a dialogue with a place, as Thoreau did with Walden, in order to develop a sense of rootedness, responsibility, and belonging. Some may worry, isn't this studying of a particular place inherently parochial and narrowing—but this need not be a concern, for the study of a particular place should be only part of a larger curriculum which includes the study of the relationship between places. The study of place at a micro *and* macro level can promote diversity of thought and a wider understanding of interrelatedness. It can lengthen our perceptions of time and help to keep us together as communities.

Ecological theorists teach us that students need to realize they are part of Nature. Through direct experiences, participation, and open dialogue with Nature, students can learn to understand and comprehend the world of Nature. The Native American example I offer in this section stresses the importance of teaching students that life is sacred, and that we need to learn to live simply and with care. We must learn to live in harmony with Nature, understanding our relationship with Nature as one of mutual reciprocity rather than seeking to dominate nature. We must learn that we have a responsibility to respect and preserve Nature. These are spiritual lessons that teach us how directly connected we are to the natural world, that we are part of the natural world, that we are one with Nature. An ecological curriculum must be interwoven throughout the entire curriculum and throughout all the operations of the school, not taught in just a few scattered courses. A relational (e)pistemology and ontology implies that our curriculum and pedagogy must be shaped by a focus on ecological relations.

We have learned in this section that an ecological curriculum will help us teach students the discipline areas with an integrated and connected emphasis, connecting the mind, hand, and heart. The final section on scientific relations will serve to help develop further the relational (e)pistemological implication that teachers need to teach an integrated, multidisciplinary curriculum that connects the mind, hand, and heart.

Scientific Relations

In Chapter 8 I offered a description of the universe as dynamic, transactional, and whole with the help of several famous scientists who have contributed significantly to the dismantling of the reductionistic, mechanistic description of the universe they inherited from Newton and others. We learned from these scientists that the universe is a complicated, complementary web of relations that must be understood as an undivided whole, rather than analyzed into parts. Einstein's relativity theory dissolves the boundary between space and time, as well as the boundary between matter and energy. The quantum mechanic physicists realized that light and electrons are both particles and waves, for atoms are not solid, nor are electrons. They prove Newton's concept of separate, independent objects is wrong, as well as the idea of subject/object distinction. Bohm links mind and matter as a continuum with his theory of wholeness and the implicate order, helping us understand how consciousness and matter are inextricably linked. Lovelock demonstrates that our Earth, Gaia, is an example of an open system not in a state of equilibrium that is able to maintain order amidst apparent disorder by functioning as a cybernetic system continually adjusting to feedback it receives from the air, water, land, and other life forms. Margulis shows us that our very cells within our bodies are communities of microorganisms that contain several separate bacteria that use to live independently, thus breaking down the boundaries between animal and plant life as we learn that we have co-evolved in a complementary fashion together. And, McClintock's transposition theory teaches us that even the genes within our cells are not static entities, but rather another example of a dissipative system that is able to maintain a state of dynamic equilibrium and bring order to the chaos of changing forces which cause genetic mutations. McClintock learned about genetic mutation and regulatory genes by using a scientific methodology that broke down the boundaries between herself and her objects of study, thus modeling for us a way to inquire and research this alive, dynamic, multidimensional universe with her compassionate approach to science.

The scientists discussed in Chapter 8 all share in common the quality of having their work cross discipline boundaries, causing them to be labeled as mavericks within their own disciplines. Bohm helps us understand that relativity theory and quantum theory have brought back together two disciplines that were separated—science and philosophy. Lovelock's Gaia theory brings together the separated scientific fields of chemistry, geology, and biology, in what he calls 'geophysiology.' Margulis's symbiosis theory brings together evolutionary theory and microbiology, and within microbiology, her work connects bacterial genetics to plant and animal cell studies. Lastly, McClintock's transposition theory is based on a life-time of singular work in maize cytogenetics but her approach to science is one that breaks down the boundaries between science and spirituality, or what some refer to as mysticism, as she relies on her exceedingly strong feeling for the oneness of things to guide her work.

A relational (e)pistemology, with its emphasis on connection, overlap, association, integration, comparison, and reference, implies that schools need to have curriculums that are multidisciplinary. The scientists considered in Chapter 8 serve as examples to reinforce this implication, for in order to solve the problems that interested them, they had to consider solutions that were "outside" of their specific discipline areas. However, I also want to suggest that a relational (e)pistemology implies that schools need to have curriculums that are focused, so they can teach students how to immerse themselves in a problem, and address it with compassion, rather than try to solve a great many problems at a superficial, surface level. The scientists discussed in Chapter 8 also serve as examples of people who learned to address their problems in focused, deeply compassionate ways. At first glance these two recommendations may seem to be in tension with each other. Doesn't a multidisciplinary curriculum suggest a curriculum with a wide variety of subject areas? And, doesn't a focused curriculum suggest a curriculum that is narrowed down and limited in its considerations? Let me expand on these recommendations by addressing them first one at a time and then together in order to show how they can function in schools and not be in tension with each other. In discussing both of these final implications for schools, we will find that all the qualities that help to define education, the teacher, student, curriculum (content), and methods of instructing (context), will come together in this final section.

As public schools exist today in the USA, no matter at what age level, we find school curriculum programs designed in a conveyor belt fashion, or another metaphor often used is that schools are like shopping malls. Students go from class to class picking up separate bits of information from each class. At the elementary level students spend most of their day in one classroom, but the curriculum within that classroom changes for them in slots of 30–60 minutes. Elementary students have the separate subjects of math, history, science, reading, writing, spelling, handwriting, etc. They also have the "specials" of art, music, gym, and maybe foreign language. In junior high/middle school and high school, students move from classroom to classroom and their classes last around 45–60 minutes. Students sign up for classes and are assigned random time slots that fit into a master schedule. It is up to chance or convenience when in the day students are assigned their classes, or in what order. In this shopping mall format each student is taught the curriculum as a group of separate discipline areas. Rarely are the subject areas integrated together. Students are generally left to their own devices to figure out how these various subject areas relate to each other. Rarely do students have more than one course with the same teacher, or have teams of teachers that work together trying to integrate their subject areas. Rarely do teachers show students how problems cross disciplinary lines, and consider connections.

In general, our public schools are not designed to support a multidisciplinary approach. Students generally receive a narrow, discipline-defined, segmented education. If they are able to pull their knowledge together into some kind of cohesive whole, it is not because the schools help them do so, but because they are able to do so on their own. Yet, a multidisciplinary approach to education is exactly what a relational (e)pistemology implies. When knowing is described as a process of associating and relating, and the universe is described in a wholistic manner, then the emphasis in school curriculums must be placed on how various subject areas connect to each other. Sharp boundaries between disciplines must be softened, and the porous nature of these boundaries must be demonstrated. Students need to learn that discipline boundaries are socially constructed categories that people have developed over time to help them sort their booming, buzzing, confusing experiences into manageable, understandable chunks. These boundaries do not really exist. While they help us try to contain and control our experiences, the boundaries also hinder us, for they artificially narrow our understanding of our experiences. Discipline boundary lines serve as ontological categories helping us catch up our experiences in certain ways and not others. They help us define our experiences but they also artificially limit the range of our definitions for they limit the range of our thinking. They help us find ways to focus on parts, but cause us to lose sight of the whole.

There have been efforts to teach classes in ways that cross discipline lines and encourage more of a multidisciplinary approach in schools. I am certainly not the first to point out a need for a multidisciplinary approach to education. Some schools have tried teaching more than one subject area together in a scheduled block of time with a team of teachers working together. In the USA it is not unusual to find 11th grade English and History classes that are taught in a block with the English class focusing on American Literature while the History class focuses on American history. Unfortunately, the only cross-over many of these classes experience is with a final paper assignment that is graded by both the history and English teachers. At the elementary level it is not unusual to find classrooms that have learning centers strategically placed around the room that may include assignments that cross disciplinary boundaries. However, it is often the case that students are only allowed to work in the learning centers after they have completed their discipline-based assignments. The learning centers serve as an "extra" tagged on to the students' regular assignments, rather than being allowed to shape the curriculum as multidisciplinary.

I have observed schools, especially elementary and middle schools, that choose a theme, and in all their subject areas they try to address this theme throughout the school year. For example, the theme might be water, or the seasons, or holidays around the world, or a particular author. I have also seen schools that choose a particular project or social problem to work on all year in all their subject areas. This project may be adopting a sister city in Russia to work with, or choosing the problem of racism to attempt to address. I have also witnessed schools that teach all their curriculum through multidisciplinary learning centers, even to the point of creating a central multi-purpose room that all students have access to, and where they meet regularly to share what they are learning across the various discipline boundaries. These are important examples of how to teach students in multidisciplinary ways. We can point to many examples that have been successful at achieving multidisciplinary approaches, and can even document the exciting creative results of having students work in these ways. But, all too often the examples become exceptions that are added on top of discipline-based requirements, and they lose their base of support as confidence in them becomes eroded by evaluative systems that demand discipline-based results.

It is not too difficult to find factors that help to erode multidisciplinary approaches to education. One only needs to look as far as our reward and gate-keeping systems. In the USA we are currently greatly enamored with proficiency exams, which were designed to help make sure that students graduate with the skills and knowledge they are supposed to acquire in schools, and that teachers are held accountable for teaching students the skills and knowledge they are expected to learn. These tests are designed as discipline-specific tests. As long as we rely on discipline-specific tests to determine if students graduate and teachers keep their jobs, then teachers will be doing a disservice to their students, as well as themselves, if they do not teach from a discipline-based approach.

If we want to encourage multidisciplinary approaches to education, we need to make sure we consider how we assess students and teachers and reward them, so that a multidisciplinary approach is encouraged rather than undermined. We need to not only teach students in ways that emphasize how subjects relate to each other, but also ask students to demonstrate their understanding of the various subjects they have studied in multidisciplinary ways. If we grade students on their abilities to exhibit their understandings across disciplinary lines, as Ted Sizer's (1992) "exhibitions" idea suggests in *Horace's School*, then students will be encouraged to view inquiry topics through a variety of disciplines, rather than through just a singular discipline focus. Like Sizer, I am suggesting a complete revamping of the way teachers teach subjects and require students to demonstrate what they have learned. I am suggesting a complete rethinking of how we reward students and teachers for their work with each other. In order to encourage a multidisciplinary approach to education, we need to consider ways we can open up time for people to be able to work together and explore various connections between different fields of study. We need to allow students time to follow a theme or problem in all the various directions it might lead them, so they can begin to discover connections and associations and overlaps between discipline areas.

What we begin to realize is that a multidisciplinary approach to education does not necessarily mean piling on more subjects for students to study. In fact, increasing students' subject exposure will likely result in giving students more and more to learn about various disciplines and less time to really understand any discipline in depth, let alone help them make connections between disciplines. Instead, a multidisciplinary approach to education suggests that there is a need to open up more time for students to explore a variety of ways to solve problems. Rather than teaching students more subjects so they can begin to discover connections between subjects, the solution is to teach subjects through particular themes and problems, and allow students the time to explore those few themes and problems in depth and breadth. I am reminded of Sir Alfred North Whitehead's advice, which was an inspiration for Sizer's (1984, 1992) school restructuring suggestions, that students need to learn a few things well instead of trying to do all things and doing them poorly. This is where the second implication for education comes into our discussion, for besides recommending a multidisciplinary curriculum, a relational (e)pistemology also implies that students need the chance to learn how to focus their attentions on their studies and gain a depth of understanding they might otherwise not achieve.

We learned from Evelyn Fox Keller (1983) that Barbara McClintock has an unusually strong ability to focus her energy on a problem and concentrate. She can tune in to her subject matter at a very deep level and lose herself in her studies. She becomes one with her subject, and establishes a compassionate relationship with the object of her interest. She listens attentively to what her subject tries to tell her, and lets it tell her its secrets. Her methodology for research is not one of imposition, but rather one of respectful receptivity and absorption. McClintock models for us the value of teaching students how to focus deeply on problems and help them learn how to concentrate and follow their inquiry through to conclusion. She also models for us the importance of not approaching problems with preconceived answers, or we will miss what the objects of our inquiry are trying to tell us. The other scientists we explored in Chapter 8 also found that they could not solve their problems of inquiry by imposing their assumptions on to their objects of inquiry. They could not force their subjects to fit into the molds they had already constructed; they had to stop trying to shape their subjects and let their subjects be their guides. They had to let go, and lose their preconceptions, so they could understand things in new ways. How can we help students learn how to focus their interests intently on a subject, lose themselves in their efforts to attend to the subject, and learn how to compassionately listen and attend to their subjects? How can we help our students learn how to let go of their preconceptions and allow themselves to be surprised by a new perspective?

Again, I turn to Montessori schools as the best example I know of to help us imagine how schools can be restructured so that they support students' efforts to focus and concentrate on their problems attentively and deeply, allowing students enough time to follow their interests through to completion. Maria Montessori helped to solve the problems of time I point to in profound ways, by encouraging her teachers to think of their curriculums in terms of sensitive periods of time, as well as in terms of returning spirals. Montessori was trained as a scientist, not an educator, and so she approached her studies of students as a scientist and formed her conclusions about students by first observing them. She noticed times when students were more interested in certain subjects and could easily learn particular skills, such as learning how to read, and other times when they were less interested and the learning was more difficult. She called these times of heightened interest 'sensitive periods.' During a sensitive period, when a child is interested and ready to learn, she will learn easily and well. During that sensitive period the child will become deeply absorbed in her learning process, if allowed to do so. When deeply absorbed in the learning process, usually through some activity the child is doing, it is not easy to break the child's concentration, and in fact it is painful to the child to have her concentration broken. If the teacher allows the child to follow her interest to completion, the child will come to an end in her learning on her own, as if coming out of a dream, with a deep sense of satisfaction and fulfillment, and a deeper level of understanding. Montessori noticed that adults are continually interrupting children when children are concentrating on a task. Adults frame what the child does as "play" and therefore not important, and therefore justify that it is okay to interrupt the child. Montessori reframed what the child was doing as "work" and made it a rule with her teachers that they should avoid interrupting a child's concentration if at all possible and respect the child's need to complete their task to their satisfaction. Montessori students are often complimented for their strong abilities to concentrate and focus on their work. However, it took someone who could see what children do as important work worthy of respect and attention, to create a school structure where children have as much uninterrupted time as possible to work at their own pace and choose their own work. One of the most important rules in a Montessori school is not to interrupt a child's work cycle. Each child learns to respect others' needs to concentrate and be left alone.

At the same time that Montessori observed children have sensitive periods for learning, and that they have strong abilities to concentrate, she also observed that students will come back to previous lessons again and again, if allowed to. By structuring her classrooms as multiage classrooms with three ages together in one room, she encouraged her teachers to think of their curriculum in terms of three-year cycles, and to spend each year doing a few subjects in as much depth as the childrens' interests allowed. The teachers no longer had to feel like they had only one year to teach the students all they could. They knew they had three years, and that in the course of those three years they could come back to various subject areas many times. The teachers also learned that they did not need to teach the children all they could; they needed to teach them how to be good inquirers and researchers. Once the children learn how to be good researchers, they can continue to follow their own interests way beyond the Montessori classroom. The curriculum in a Montessori classroom is described as a spiral, and subject areas are taught again each year with different focuses. Maybe in science this year the focus will be on the human body and on plants and animals, maybe next year the focus will be on weather and the seasons, etc. Over the course of the three-year cycle the children have the opportunity to be exposed in a multidisciplinary way to a variety of different subject areas, to varying levels and degrees, depending on the children's interests, abilities, and needs.

As adults, most of us can relate easily to these insights. We know the joy of uninterrupted time to focus on a task and see it through to completion, and we know the frustration of trying to concentrate and finding ourselves continually interrupted. We also know that when we are deeply interested in a topic we can concentrate on it to the point that we can actually tune out a certain level of distraction, and that when we are not very interested in a topic we can easily be distracted by the slightest movement or noise. Yet in our schools, we give students little time to learn and in general we do not hesitate to interrupt their learning for such things as announcements from the office. We teach them that learning comes in half-hour segments, believing that younger kids have short attention spans, and in 45–60 minute segments when they are older, still believing students cannot concentrate for long. We dispense knowledge in fast, efficient, disjointed ways, using what Paulo Freire (1970) called "the banking method." We teach students that we have the right to interrupt their concentration whenever we see fit, and that we, as teachers, get to choose the topics for study, not them. We stop students from following their interests, not allowing them to explore and inquire further, because it is time to move on to the next subject. And then we wonder why students refuse to engage in the inquiry process, and they resist our efforts to teach them. We wonder why they will stall and chat with each other rather than get to work. Students can tell time. They know the bell is going to ring in five minutes.

Students need time to immerse themselves in the inquiry process, and lose themselves in their efforts to concentrate on their questions, so that they have the chance to listen and be receptive to what their subject is trying to tell them. Students need time to follow ideas through to completion and not be continually interrupted in their efforts. If we, as teachers, stop trying to teach them so much, and instead try to teach them a few things well, I think we will be pleasantly surprised at the depth and breadth of students' understanding, at their abilities to make connections across various disciplines, and the incredibly creative, new ways they will help us understand this dynamic, multidimensional universe. The recommendation of teaching a multidisciplinary curriculum through the study of themes and real problems so as to integrate subject areas together does not have to conflict with the recommendation that we open up students' time so they can follow their work through to completion. We can meet both recommendations by doing a few things well. We can teach students how to inquire, and do research, through some specific examples to which they can devote their time. Then we must trust that students will be able to use those same research skills with other questions they will pursue on their own. We can allow students to choose topics of interest to them and show students how to approach those topics in a variety of ways, thus encouraging them to make connections and associations between subject areas. Then we must assess students on how they are able to demonstrate their multidisciplinary understanding in a variety of integrative ways. Teaching students subject areas through a focused, multidisciplinary content and context will enhance their subject-specific knowledge as well as their multidisciplinary understanding of this living, breathing world in which they reside.

Conclusion

There is much more that can be said. But, it is time for me to stop talking and let others join in the conversation. I have focused this final chapter on some specific recommendations for schools that a relational (e)pistemology implies. If this discussion has helped to connect theory with practice, enhance the reader's understanding of the relational theories presented in previous chapters, and demonstrate the kinds of impact a relational (e)pistemology can have for our daily living, then I have achieved my goals. I chose education as my focus, in particular schools, because education is so central to the continuance of any society and education is the central focus of my own philosophical work. How we teach our children has such a profound effect on how they will relate to the world as adults.

The specific recommendations I made in this chapter include:

- teachers need to establish caring relationships with their students
- all students need to be exposed to diversity through a multicultural curriculum
- spiritual beliefs need to be made an explicit part of the curriculum
- all students need the chance to develop their relationships with this organic universe through an ecological curriculum
- schools need a curriculum that is multidisciplinary, reflective of this connected and transactionally related universe
- schools need a focused curriculum that teaches students how to be compassionate inquirers

I end this book by returning to the beginning. I remind the reader that I did not offer a traditional Epistemological theory in this text, for it was never my goal to do so. Traditional Epistemological theories strive to establish the criteria and standards necessary to prove the validity of truth claims, and they mean Truth in the absolute sense of warranted assertions that are justified as necessarily so. I question that it is possible to accomplish what traditional Epistemologists claim to be able to do. I suggest, in agreement with many others, that none of us can know what is True or Real in a universal sense. I also did not offer an extensive argument for the demise of traditional Epistemology here, preferring to refer the reader to others such as Dewey (1938) and Rorty (1979) who have already done that work for us. I am very grateful for the careful and extensive arguments they have already successfully made.

At the same time that I have agreed with pragmatists, feminists, and postmodernists that we can never find absolute Truth, I have also argued that we cannot divorce ourselves from epistemological and ontological questions, for they form the net that we use to catch up our experiences and give them meaning. Our epistemology and ontology will affect what we decide to inquire about, and how we inquire, and therefore what our results will be. So, while I have not offered a traditional Epistemological theory here, I have not let go of traditional Epistemological concerns of standards and criteria for warranting arguments and determining truths from falsities. Instead, I have reclaimed these concerns in order to make them visible and hold them accountable for the power they assume. I have argued for standards and criteria that are pragmatically useful on socially constructed grounds, not on transcendental grounds.

According to Berger and Luckmann (1966), my role as a philosopher is one of social legitimation and universe-maintenance. I understand my role as one of cultural critic. I use the study and analysis of other cultures to help me question and critique conformities that have become so habituated that they are taken to be Reality or Truth. I want to help develop ideas to deal with the actual crises of our lives. I join the efforts of many other feminists and postmodernists in seeking to uncover the philosopher's assumption of power. My task here was to contribute to efforts to redefine *epistemology* in a manner that does not assume absolutism, as (e)pistemology, and that is where I directed my energy. I attempted to describe my own feminist (e)pistemological theory, a relational way of knowing, as well as other relational (e)pistemologies such as those of Buddhists and Native Americans. I offer these descriptions in contrast to traditional Epistemological theories, to help us in our efforts to critique major contributors to the crises with which we currently live.

I have offered a feminist (e)pistemological theory that insists that knowers/subjects are fallible, that our criteria are corrigible, and that our standards are socially constructed, and thus continually in need of critique and reconstruction. I have argued that an (e)pistemology that rests on an assumption of fallibility entails pluralism, both in terms of there being no one final Answer at the end of inquirying, and also in terms of the need to be open and inclusive of others, in order to help us compensate for our own limitations. I have worked to help us understand caring's connection to (e)pistemology, with caring reasoning, which I have compared to similar ideas such as Dewey's 'sympathetic understanding,' and Benhabib's 'enlarged thinking.' I have also tried to further develop Dewey's idea of transactional relationships, and compare transactional relations to concepts such as 'mutual causality.'

I hope the comparisons I have made to not only philosophical theories, but also psychological and sociological theories, Buddhist and Native American philosophies, deep ecological, eco-feminist, as well as scientific theories help the reader make connections and associations beyond the ones I have presented here. I look forward to continuing this conversation with others. I am excited about the many more sources others will suggest of which I am unaware. I began this project with only a vague sense of how some of the theories presented here are related. I have learned so much as I have read and discovered more and more of the work that is already in print. It is clear to me, and I hope it is clear to the reader too, that there is a wealth of scholarship that already exists which relies on relational approaches to knowing. I could spend a great many more years just reading what has already been written in support of a relational, wholistic description of this flowing universe. And think of what exciting possibilities are still out there waiting to be created and constructed and shared with others!

Notes

Introduction

1. The following description is an altered version of what was first published as: Thayer-Bacon, B. (1997, Spring). The nurturing of a relational epistemology, *Educational Theory*, 47(2), 239-260.

Chapter 1

1. Historically, logical reasoning has been equated with critical thinking, which is associated with the mind, as opposed to emotions, which are associated with the heart, and intuition, which is associated with the Mind's eye, and imagination, which is associated with the spirit. I discuss logical reasoning in great detail in (2000) *Transforming Critical Thinking*.
2. I use the term "Euro-western" to specify what has been traditionally referred to as Western thought. This is a political decision, due to the fact that without naming Western thought as European-based thought, other peoples' cultures are invisibily included in that category. Africa, and North, Central, and South America are continents in the Western hemisphere of our world, and yet they have their own cultures and traditions which predate European influence. All of the Western hemisphere has come under European influence, due to the colonization of the Western hemishpere by European countries such as Spain, France, and England. However, there remains significant differences among cultures in the Western hemisphere, and not all of these cultures are European-based today.
3. I first wrote about the Burbules/Siegel debate in "Navigating Epistemological Territories," presented at the 1995 Philosophy of Education Society conference and published in: (1996). Navigating epistemological territories, *The Philosophy of Education Society Annual Proceedings 1995*, 460-468.
4. I would like to acknowledge many helpful discussions with Jim Garrison concerning Siegel's Epistemological theory.
5. I follow Belenky et al.'s lead, from *Womens Ways of Knowing* (1986), in using the term *voice* to describe a person's worldview. 'Voice' is meant to include all that contextually makes up who we are, so it is more than one's spirit, or mind, or soul, it is the bodymind as one, within the context of our own unique experiences. I agree with Belenky et al. that 'voice' helps shift us away from ocular images, is more direct and overtly physical, and is more supportive of a social (e)pistemological theory which seeks to emphasize the importance of community and conversation. I will use *voice* throughout the text.

6. I refer the reader to Simone de Beauvoir's *The Second Sex*, as well as more recent work contributing to the analysis of the androcentric voice (the 1960's): Betty Friedan's *The Feminine Mystique*; (the 1970's): Nancy Chodorow's *The Reproduction of Mothering*; (the 1980's): Belenky et al.'s *Women's Ways of Knowing*, Susan Bordo's *Flight to Objectivity*, Carol Gilligan's *In a Different Voice*, Jean Grimshaw's *Philosophy and Feminist Thinking*, Sandra Harding's *The Science Question*, Evelyn Fox Keller's *Reflections on Gender and Science*, and Sarah Ruddick's *Maternal Thinking*. There are even more contributions in this decade, for this work continues to the present.
7. Feminists coined the phrase "view from nowhere/view from everywhere" to represent the absolutism/relativism debate. Code credits Haraway with this phrasing ("Situated Knowledges," Fall 1988), others credit Bordo, but the terminology can be traced back to the title of Thomas Nagel's book *A View From Nowhere*, 1986.
8. More recently Code has described her epistemological view as an ecological one in a paper she gave at the International Association of Women Philosophers in Boston, MA, August, 1998, titled "Ecological Thinking, Responsible Knowing."
9. All of these authors have essays in Alcoff and Potter's (1993). *Feminist Epistemologies*.
10. Other standpoint theorists include: Nancy Hartsock, Patricia Hill Collins, and Dorothy E. Smith. A more recent discussion of feminist standpoint theory was published in the Winter 1997 edition of *Signs*. Hartsock, Collins, Smith, and Harding all respond to an essay by Susan Hekman. My discussion of Harding's work stems from Chapter 5 of *Transforming Critical Thinking*.
11. This phrase is originally Audre Lorde's, from a speech she gave titled "The Master's Tools Will Never Dismantle the Master's House" which can be found published in (1981, 1983) *This Bridge Called My Back* (pp. 98-101).
12. Seigfried embraces James' definition of truth as 'satisfactory resolution,' and I am in agreement with her, but the mistaken fears this wording triggers for professional philosophers who equate 'satisfaction' with personal feelings and neglect temporal considerations is worthy of a longer, separate discussion. See Chapter 2.

Chapter 2

1. My discussion of Peirce, James, and Dewey is derived from a paper I wrote for the Ohio Valley Philosophy of Education Society, "Pragmatism as Qualified Relativism," which I further developed into a book chapter: "A Feminist Re/examination of William James as a Qualified Relativist," (2002). *William James and Education*, J. Garrison, E. Bredo, and R. Podeschi (Eds.) pp. 97-114. NY: Teachers College Press. Some of the roots of this discussion can be traced back to Chapter 2 of *Transforming Critical Thinking* (2000).
2. Siegel references Susan Haack (1993, pp. 203-205) for this distinction between conduct and products of inquiry.
3. I use here Siegel's shortened wording from his outline used during his presentation and distributed to the attending audience.

Chapter 3

1. Dewey (1938/1965) describes his transactional theory as the "principle of interaction" in *Experience and Education*. Interaction "assigns equal rights to both factors in experience—objective and internal conditions. Any normal experience is an interplay of these two sets

of conditions. Taken together, or in their interaction, they form what we call a *situation*" (pp. 38–39, emphasis in original). Later in the same chapter, Dewey goes on to say: "The conceptions of *situation* and of *interaction* are inseparable from each other. An experience is always what it is because of a transaction taking place between an individual and what, at the time, constitutes his environment . . ." (p. 4, emphasis in original). He later in his career recommended the use of the term "transaction" in *Knowing and the Known* (1949/1960), with Arthur Bentley.
2. Some will argue that child-rearing practices are changing dramatically and mother-child relationships are not so predominant today, but there is a great deal of evidence supporting patriarchal child-rearing patterns even today. For many families where mothers have joined the ranks of the working, few men have gone home to take care of their children for extended periods of time. Instead, children are being raised by nannies and in childcare facilities where women are predominantly employed. Jane Roland Martin discusses the issue of changing families at length in *The Schoolhome* (1992).
3. Plato and Aristotle both wrote about intimate, personal relationships between teachers and students. See, for example: Plato's *Symposium* and *Phaedrus*, and Books 8 and 9 of Aristotle's *Nichomachean Ethics*.
4. I use italics for *I, Thou, I-Thou,* and *I-It* within my description of Buber's theory because that is what he does in his text. When I move away from the text to my own discussion of it, I will capitalize the words without italicizing them, for ease of reading.
5. Buddhist and Native American beliefs represent religious views in the sense that they concern themselves with spiritual life as well as material life. However, it is potentially misguiding to describe their spiritual emphasis as a religion, for religions suggest particular dogmas and Buddhism and Native American spirituality are not saturated with dogma as Judaic, Christian, and Islam religions are. 'Spiritual' is a better term to use to describe them than religious.

Chapter 4

1. This discussion on caring's role in (e)pistemology is derived from my "Caring Reasoning."
2. Again, I use italics for *I, Thou, I-Thou,* and *I-It* within my description of Buber's theory because that is what he does in his text. When I move away from the text to my own discussion of it, I will capitalize the words without italicizing them, for ease of reading.
3. Emmanual Levinas (1986, 1994) embraces Buber's (1958) distinction between I-Thou relations and I-It relations, and he reaffirms the primacy of interpersonal relations. He agrees that the self cannot survive alone or find meaning within its own being-in-the-world. However, Levinas disagrees with Buber that relationality is reciprocal and mutual, that it is a symmetrical copresence. He emphasizes the asymmetry of relations by introducing a third person to consider in relations, the other. The other is our neighbor with whom we come face-to-face. The other is always a stranger to us, is always exterior to us, and is phenomenologically irreducible. Levinas argues that our ethical relation to the other is prior to our ontological relation to ourselves and the world around us. The other's existence has priority over ours. He does not mean this "ethic of heteronomy" to place us in a servitude relation with others, but to insure that we include others in our ethics by beginning with our responsibility to others. However, his description of relations as asymmetrical risks placing the self in either a subjugated role to the one-cared-for, or in an arrogant role of protector of the other. I insist, in agreement with both Noddings and Buber, on the mutuality of relations, the transactional nature of relations that are reciprocal. This mutuality

preserves the two-foldness of relations. It insures the alerity of the other as well as prevents the I from being reduced or subsumed by the other (or Thou).

Chapter 5

1. Jane Roland Martin uses this concept in her discussions of the role of women in philosophy. See, in particular, her *Reclaiming a Conversation* (1985), and *Changing the Educational Landscape* (1994). She credits Lorraine Clark with first introducing her to this phrase. See Clark, L. (1976).
2. I do not offer an indepth discussion of each of these philosophers' dismissal of women and children. Flax (1983) offers a detailed discussion in "Political philosophy and the patriarchal unconscious," which I pointed to in Chapter 4. Another excellent source, besides Jane Martin, for more on this issue is Susan Okin's *Women in Western Political Thought* (1979). Many feminists have contributed to the exposure of Euro-western's androcentric biases, and their work is referenced throughout this text.
3. Seyla Benhabib (1992) contributes further to an understanding of the tension between the generalized other and the self. She rightly criticizes Mead for reducing the otherness of the other (their alterity), with his concept of 'the generalized other.' Benhabib highlights the irreducible distinctness and difference of the other, whereas Mead underscores the commonality of the generalized other. She introduces the concept of "the concrete other" in order to point to how each of us are unique individuals and to argue that we cannot assume to know the concrete other from our own perspective; we must listen to the other's self-definition. The other is a stranger to us and listening to the other's unique voice will help to enlarge our thinking. We cannot assume that our vocal gestures solicit a symmetrical response and are symmetrically reflective, as Mead assumes. To do so denies what is unique and different about each one of us. While Mead emphasizes that we gain a sense of a unified self from the generalized other, Benhabib turns his concept upside-down by arguing that the standpoint of the generalized other is abstracted from the individuality and concrete identity of the other. Mead's approach is meant to avoid the problem of solipsism. If we argue that individuals are antecedent to the social process then how do individuals ever learn how to communicate with each other through a public language? Benhabib's approach is meant to avoid the problem of social determinism.
4. Karen Hanson (1986) thinks Mead has done a good job of describing the philosophical problem of socialization, speech, and self, but she disagrees with his solution in terms of vocal gestures. She proposes that the reflexivity needed in order to develop a self is achieved through an act of imagination. Thus, we find that she agrees with Mead that the self is essentially reflective: we gain a sense of self by being able to take on the attitude of the other, and become an object to ourselves. Their differences lie in Mead's efforts to maintain a behavioristic framework for his theory, studying the individual from the point of view of his conduct as it is observable by others, while Hanson does not hold such a commitment. Unfortunately, Hanson errs in the same way as Mead, whom she criticizes so effectively, for she relies solely on the imagination to explain the development of the self, instead of recognizing that we rely on many tools to help us develop a sense of self, including the imagination, but also our emotions, intuition, and reasoning, as well. Hanson discards Mead's generalized other as being oppressive and overbearing and instead she presents a description of the self that grants the complexity of persons and acknowledges the difficulty and instability of individual and community alignment. Her description of a mosaic self is a significant contribution to the discussion.

5. I have changed Mead's and Dewey's language to reflect gender neutrality in much of their discussion in the previous section, even though both of them use the term 'man' to signify 'human beings,' as was the custom at the time of their writing. However, given that this section will be questioning the androcentrism of sociological theory, it is important that I let that androcentrism be more visible by *not* changing the language Berger and Luckmann use in their description.
6. Seigfried's definition of pragmatism is taken from her contribution to Audi, R. (Ed.). *The Cambridge Dictionary of Philosophy*. She uses specifics from John J. Stuhr's *Classical American Philosophy* definition of pragmatism to help shape this definition, pp. 4-11.
7. Susan Bordo (1987, 1989, 1990) uses Foucault's analysis of power to show how the discipline and normalization of the female body is a strategy of social control. She restores a focus on female daily practice in order to help us resist gender domination.

Chapter 6

1. I use the term 'Native American,' a White man's term, as my generic term even though natives have informed me that they prefer to use the term 'Indigenous people.' I do so because there are indigenous people on every inhabited continent and I want to specifically address indigenous people of North America. I will use particular tribal names when I am talking more specifically, but it is important to note here that those tribal names are also White man's language, not the name originally used by the specific indigenous tribe or nation. For example, Navajos call themselves "Dineh," meaning "the people."
2. Trungpa's lectures on the topic of egolessness in *Glimpses of Abhidharma* (1978) can help the interested reader further understand the Buddhist understanding of ego. The Buddhist *abhidharma* explains the psychological pattern of ego; it presents a survey of the psychology of the human mind. The *abhidharma* is part of the basic philosophy of Buddhism, common to all schools. It is part of "the three baskets," the three bodies of teaching that constitute the Buddhist scriptures. The first basket is the *vinaya* (*vinayapitaka*) which is concerned with the discipline, the practicalities of how to live one's life. The second basket is the *sutra* (*sutrapitaka*) which deals with meditative practices. The third basket is the *abhidharma* (*abhidharmapitaka*) which works on the background philosophy and tells us how to communicate with others. The *abhidharma* (which means "pattern of dharma") is a very precise way of looking at individual mind, not Big Mind, in terms of the five *skandhas*. It is based on the point of view of egolessness, the absence of ego and the absence of the projections of ego. Egolessness is a by-product of seeing the transitory and transparent nature of the world outside (which are projections of the ego). The ego manages to maintain its identity by means of its projections (Trungpa, 1978, pp. 7-8). Without the projections of the ego, the ego has no reference point.
3. I use 'literature' here in the traditional sense of "written work." Paula Gunn Allen (1986), as a foremost Native American literary critic, redefines 'literature' to include oral traditions such as songs, dances, and stories. With this redefinition, Natives have a longer history of literature then Buddhists.
4. I will come back to the Navajo creation story with my presentation of Farella's work. Farella adds much more texture to the story, but I do not want his details to shape McNeley's presentation of the Holy Wind.
5. Changing Woman is sometimes described by the Navajo as being the daughter of First Man and First Woman, and sometimes she is described as the granddaughter, with Sky and Earth as her parents. In the stories about her leaving to live with the Sun in the west, she

is placed in the daughter role, and Sun is the son-in-law. Farella (1984) tells us that the Navajos are a society that emphasizes matrilocal residence, and Changing Woman's leaving to live with Sun represents one pattern for marriage and a cause for strife, a child's debt to her parents that cannot be paid, ensuing guilt, and anger and sadness on the parents' side (p. 61).

Chapter 7

1. Arne Naess's (1989) *Ecology, Community and Lifestyle*, is translated and edited by his student, David Rothenberg. Rothenberg tells us in his preface that many sections of the English version were revised and rewritten by Naess and himself in an attempt to clarify the original text, so the English text is not a literal translation of the original Norwegian text.
2. The term *ecofeminisme* was coined by Françoise d'Eaubonne in 1974 "to bring attention to women's potential for bringing about an ecological revolution" (Warren, 1990, pp. 125-126). For an example of d'Eaubonne's work, see d'Eaubonne, 1980.
3. See Chapter 4 for an indepth discussion of Martin Buber's (1923/1937/1958) description of an I/Thou relationship.
4. As I write this text, Mary Daly is in the news for refusing to teach male students in her Boston University classes. She is willing to teach males on an individual, independent basis, but finds their presence too disruptive to the classroom culture and curriculum she wants to address. From her perspective, she is trying to teach a class for battered women, and does not want the batterers in her class at the same time. She is accused of reverse sexism and is being forced to retire, although she is fighting Boston University's decision. For Daly, this is a battle for academic freedom and an attack on radical feminism. This is not the first battle she has fought concerning academic freedom for her controversial radical feminist views. The year she wrote *Gyn/Ecology*, 1975, she was denied promotion to full professor because her work was judged to not be scholarly enough, or making a significant contribution to her field. There were great protests and demonstrations over this decision, and Daly took an unpaid leave of absence from Boston University, and wrote *Gyn/Ecology* (1978/1990), while things simmered down again. She shares the context of her writing of *Gyn/Ecology* in detail in the introduction which is added to the 1990 edition of the book. Ironically, since her work was already being judged by the academy to be unscholarly, the result was a creative surge of freedom on Daly's part. *Gyn/Ecology* is not written as a more traditional piece of scholarship, it is as poetic as it is theoretical, crossing many genres to create its own. It brings together and demonstrates the interconnectedness of these various fields of study: theology, mythology, philosophy, history, and medicine.

Chapter 8

1. I will use the term 'science' throughout my discussion in this chapter, but I think it is important to note at the beginning that what I am discussing is Euro-western science. Science does not distinguish itself this way, but instead reports to make empirical claims that apply across cultures, etc. However, given the important differences between the descriptions of the universe offered by 'scientists' and the descriptions of the universe offered by Buddhists or Native Americans, for example, I want to note that when I am discussing 'science' I am discussing science as it has developed out of the Euro-western tradition.
2. While Descartes and Newton can be fairly credited with helping to inspire a mechanistic

paradigm shift, certainly the seeds of this view can be traced back to Plato's and Aristotle's ancient Greece, as Merchant (1980) and others (Thayer-Bacon, 2000) have demonstrated.
3. Rachel Carson (1962) used Lovelock's electron-capture devise to collect her data for *Silent Spring*, her very moving description of how chemicals such as DDT are harming our environment which was very influential in stimulating today's deep ecological movement as well as the ecofeminism movement (see Chapter 7).
4. Margulis (1998) does not include viruses in any of the five kingdoms because they are not alive, since they are not able to generate their own metabolism but must depend on living cells to metabolize for them (p. 63).
5. For example, in *Women's Ways of Knowing,* Belenky et. al. (1986) discuss McClintock as a vivid example of a constructive knower.

Chapter 9

1. Please see my biographical statement to find out more about my background. I do not try to hide who I am from my readers in my writing, and often I share personal stories as a way of contextualizing myself. I am a United States of America citizen and will be speaking from that perspective. I am also a White, middle class, near-sighted, middle-aged, heterosexual, woman, twice married, mother of four children, Unitarian Universalist, middle child, military brat, Sagittarius, born the year of the snake in the Chinese calendar, and the list goes on.
2. Due to space limitations, and for ease of discussion here, I will limit myself mainly to teacher-student and student-student relationships. But this relational approach to schooling includes the relationships teachers have with each other, administrators have with teachers, students, and parents, and parents have with students, teachers and administrators, etc.
3. I am an American Montessori Society (AMS) certified elementary Montessori teacher, and I taught in Montessori schools from 1981–1987. My own children all attended Montessori schools from around the age of three for as long as they were able to attend, depending on where we lived at the time. Sources for information on the Montessori method of instruction include Montessori (1972, 1977) and your nearest Montessori teacher training program. Listings of teacher training programs can be found by contacting the American Montessori Society (AMS) and the International Association of Montessori Societies (IAMS).
4. See Maxine Greene's work for wonderful discussions on the idea of helping students become awake and aware, especially her *Teacher as Stranger,* 1973, and *Releasing the Imagination,* 1995.
5. I use the term 'Indian' here because that is the term Cajete uses.
6. David Orr (1992) offers another perspective on environmental education which focuses on the concept of 'ecological literacy' (also the title of his book). While I do not completely agree with Orr's approach to ecological education, I am troubled by his universalizing philosophical style and his anthropocentric approach to "solving" our ecological problems, I do think he offers another interesting example for how to approach environmental education.

Bibliography

Alcoff, L. and Potter, E. (1993). *Feminist epistemologies*. NY and London: Routledge.
Allen, P. (1986). *The Sacred Hoop: Recovering the Feminine in American Indian Traditions*. Boston: Beacon Press.
———. (1990). The woman I love is a planet; The planet I love is a tree. In I. Diamond, and G. Orenstein (Eds.). *Reweaving the world: The emergence of ecofeminism* (pp. 52–57). San Francisco: Sierra Club Books.
Arendt, H. (1958). *The human condition*. Chicago: University of Chicago Press.
———. (1977, 1978). *Thinking* Vol. 1 of *The life of the mind*. New York: Harcourt Brace Jovanovich.
Bar On, B-A. (1993). Marginality and epistemic privilege. In L. Alcoff and E. Potter (Eds.). *Feminist Epistemologies* (pp. 83–100). NY and London: Routledge.
Belenky, M., Clinchy, B., Goldberger, N., & Tarule, J. (1986). *Women's ways of knowing*. New York: Basic Books.
Benhabib, S. (1992). *Situating the self: Gender, community and postmodernism*. New York: Routledge.
Berger, P. L. & Luckmann, T. (1966). *The social construction of reality: A treatise in the sociology of knowledge*. Garden City, NY: Anchor Books, Doubleday & Company, Inc.
Berry, W. (1981). *Recollected Essays, 1965–1980*. San Francisco: North Point.
Bertalanffy, L. von. (1968). *General systems theory*. New York: Braziller.
Bettoni, E. (1961). *Duns Scotus: The basic principles of his philosophy*. Bernardine Bonansea (Trans. and Ed.). Washington, DC: Catholic University of America Press.
Bredin, R. (1999). Learning to weave and to dream—Native American educational practices. In C. Titone and K. Maloney (Eds.). *Women's philosophies of education: Thinking through our mothers* (pp. 131–147). Upper Saddle River, NJ: Prentice-Hall, Inc.
Broudy, H. (1954, 1961, 1964). Definition of education and philosophy of education. In *Building a philosophy of education*. Englewood Cliffs, NJ: Prentice Hall.
Bohm, D. (1951). *Quantum theory*. New York: Prentice-Hall.
———. (1957). *Causality and chance in modern physics*. London: Routledge & Kegan Paul.
———. (1965). *The special theory of relativity*. New York: W. A. Benjamin.
———. (1980, 1995). *Wholeness and the implicate order*. London and New York: Routledge.

Boler, M. (1997, Spring). Disciplined emotions: Philosophies of educated feelings, *Educational Theory*, 47(2), 203-227.

———. (1998). Taming the labile other: Disciplined emotions in popular and academic discourse. In S. Laird (Ed.). *Philosophy of Education 1997* (pp. 416-425). Urbana, IL: Philosophy of Education Society.

———. (1999). *Feeling power: Emotions and education*. New York: Routledge.

Bookchin, M. (1982). *The ecology of freedom: The emergence and dissolution of hierarchy*. Palo Alto, CA: Cheshire Books.

———. (1984). Toward a philosophy of nature—The bases for an ecological ethics. In M. Tobias (Ed.). *Deep ecology* (pp. 213-239). San Diego, CA: Avant Books.

———. (1988). Social ecology versus deep ecology. *Socialist Review (3)*, 9-29.

Borden-King, L. (1989). Peirce's philosophy in relation to the idea of change. Unpublished paper given at fall colloquium, Indiana University, Bloomington, IN.

Bordo, S. (1987). *The flight to objectivity: Essays on Cartesianism and culture*. Albany, NY: State University of New York Press.

———. (1989). The body and the reproduction of femininity: A feminist appropriation of Foucault. In A. M. Jaggar and S. R. Bordo (Eds.). *Gender/Body/Knowledge: Feminist reconstructions of being and knowing* (pp. 13-33). New Brunswick and London: Rutgers University Press.

———. (1990). Feminism, postmodernism, and gender-skepticism. In L. Nicholson (Ed.). *Feminism/Postmodernism* (pp. 133-156). New York and London: Routledge.

Briggs, J. and Peats, F. (1984). *Looking glass universe: The emerging science of wholeness*. C. Tavernise (Ills.). New York: Simon & Schuster, Inc.

———. (1989). *Turbulent mirror: An illustrated guide to chaos theory and the science of wholeness*. Tavernise (Ills.). New York: Harper and Row, Pub.

Buber, M. (1923, 1937, 1958). *I and Thou*, 2nd edition. Ronald G. Smith (Trans.). New York: Charles Scribner's Sons.

Burbules, N. C. (Spring, 1991). Rationality and Reasonableness: A Discussion of Harvey Siegel's Relativism Refuted and Educating Reason, *Educational Theory*, 41(2): 235-252.

———. (1992). Two perspectives on reason as an educational aim: The virtues of reasonableness. In M. Buchmann & R. E. Floden (Eds.). *Philosophy of Education 1991* (pp. 215-224). Norman, IL: Philosophy of Education Society.

Butler, J. (1990a). Gender trouble, feminist theory, and psychoanalytic discourse. In L. Nicholson (Ed.). *Feminism/postmodernism* (pp. 324-340). New York and London: Routledge.

———. (1990b). *Gender trouble: Feminism and the subversion of identity*. New York: Routledge.

Cahn, S., Ed. (1977). *New studies in the philosophy of John Dewey*. Hanover, New Hampshire: University Press of New England, for the University of Vermont.

Cajete, G. (1994). *Look to the Mountain: An ecology of indigenous education*. Durango, CO: Kivakí Press.

Callicott, J. & Ames, R. (Eds.). (1989). *Nature in Asian traditions and thoughts: Essays in environmental philosophy*. Albany, NY: State University of New York Press.

Capra, F. (1975). *The Tao of physics: An exploration of the parallels between modern physics and Eastern mysticism.* Boulder, CO: Shambhala Publ, Inc.

———. (1992). *The turning point: Science, society, and the rising culture.* New York: Simon and Schuster.

Card, C. (Spring 1990). Caring and evil. Review Symposium of Caring, *Hypatia,* 5(1): 101–108.

Carson, R. (1962). *Silent spring.* Boston, MA: Houghton Mifflin Co.

Cheney, J. (1987). Eco-feminism and deep ecology. *Environmental Ethics,* 9, 115–145.

Chodorow, N. (1976). *The Reproduction of Mothering.* Berkeley, CA: University of California Press.

Clark, L. (1976). The rights of women: Theory and practice of the ideology of male supremacy. In W. Shea and J. King-Farlow (Eds.). *Contemporary issues in political philosophy* (pp. 49–65). New York: Science History Publications.

Code, L. (1987). *Epistemic responsibility.* Hanover and London: University Press of New England, for Brown University Press.

———. (1991). *What can she know? Feminist theory and the construction of knowledge.* Ithaca and London: Cornell University Press.

———. (1993). Taking subjectivity into account. In L. Alcoff and E. Potter (Eds.). *Feminist Epistemologies* (pp. 15–48). New York and London: Routledge.

———. (1998, August). Ecological thinking, responsible knowing. Paper delivered at International Association of Women Philosophers, Boston, MA.

Cohen, R. (Ed.). (1986). *Face to face with Levinas.* Albany, NY: State University of New York Press.

Collins, P. (1990). *Black feminist thought.* Boston: Unwin Hyman.

Cook, F. (1989). The jewel net of Indra. In J. Callicott, and R. Ames (Eds.). *Nature in Asian traditions and thought: Essays in environmental philosophy* (pp. 213–229). Albany, NY: State University of New York Press.

Daly, M. (1978, 1990). *Gyn/ecology: The metaethics of radical feminism.* Boston: Beacon Press.

de Beauvoir, S. (1952, 1980, 1989). *The second sex.* H. M. Parshley,(Trans and Ed.). New York: Vantage Books, Random House, Inc.

de Lauretis, T. (1986). Feminist studies/critical studies: Issues, terms, and context. In T. de Lauretis (Ed.). *Feminist studies/critical studies* (pp. 1–19). Bloomington: Indiana University Press.

d'Eaubonne, F. (1980). Feminism or death, in E. Marks and I. de Courtivron (Eds.). *New French feminisms: An anthology,* Amherst: University of Massachusetts Press.

Deleuze, G. (1986, 1988). *Foucault.* S. Hand (Trans.). Minneapolis, MN: University of Minnesota Press.

Deloria, Jr., V. (1995). *Red earth, white lies: Native Americans and the myth of scientific fact.* New York: Scribner's Sons.

Derrida, J. (1973). *Speech and phenomena.* D. B. Allison (Trans.). Evanston, Ill. Northwestern University Press.

———. (1976). *Of grammatology.* G. C. Spivak (Trans.). Baltimore: John Hopkins Press.

———. (1978). *Writing and difference*. A. Bass (Trans.). Chicago: University of Chicago Press.

———. (1981). *Positions*. A. Bass (Trans.). Chicago: University of Chicago Press.

———. (1982). *Margins of philosophy*. A. Bass (Trans.). Chicago: University of Chicago Press.

Dewey, J. (1916, 1944, 1966). *Democracy and education*. New York: The Free Press, Macmillan.

———. (1922). *Human nature and conduct*. New York: Henry Holt and Company, Inc.

———. (1925, 1981a). Experience and nature. In J. Boydston (Ed.). *John Dewey: The later works, 1925–1953*, Vol. 1 (pp. 1–326). Carbondale, IL: Southern Illinois University Press, symbolized in the text as LW.

———. (1925, 1981b) Experience and philosophical method. In J. Boydston (Ed.). *John Dewey: The later works, 1925–1953*, Vol. 1 (pp. 10–41). Carbondale, IL: Southern Illinois University Press.

———. (1927, 1954). *The public and its problems*. Athens, OH: Swallow Press.

———. (c 1934, 1958). *Art as experience*. New York: Capricorn Books.

———. (1938, 1955). *Logic: The theory of inquiry*. New York: Henry Holt and Company, Inc.

———. (1938, 1965). *Experience and education*. New York: The Macmillan Co.

———. (1960). *On experience, nature, and freedom*. Indianapolis, IN: Bobbs-Merrill Co., Inc.

Dewey, J. and Bentley, A. F. (1949, 1960), *Knowing and the known*. Boston, MA: Beacon Press.

Diamond, I. and Orenstein, G. F. (Eds. and contributing authors). (1990). *Reweaving the world: The emergence of ecofeminism*. San Francisco: Sierra Book Club.

Duran, J. (1991). *Toward a feminist epistemology*. Savage, MD: Rowman & Littlefield Publishers, Inc.

Farella, J. R. (1984). *The main stalk: A synthesis of Navajo philosophy*. Tucson, AR: The University of Arizona Press.

Flax, J. (1983). Political philosophy and the patriarchal unconscious: A psychoanalytic perspective on epistemology and metaphysics. In S. Harding & M. B. Hintikka (Eds.). *Discovering reality* (pp. 245–281). Dordrecht, Boston, London: D. Reidel Publishing Company.

———. (1990). *Thinking fragments: Psychoanalysis, feminism, and postmodernism in contemporary West*. Berkeley, LA, Oxford: University of California Press.

Foucault, M. (1972). *The archaeology of knowledge and the discourse of language*. A. M. Sheridan Smith (Trans.). New York: Pantheon Books.

———. (1973). *The birth of the clinic*. A. M. Sheridan Smith (Trans.) London: Tavistock and New York: Pantheon.

———. (1979). *Discipline and punishment: Birth of the prison*. A. M. Sheridan Smith (Trans.). London: Allen Lane and New York: Vintage.

———. (1978, 1984). *The history of sexuality*, Vol. I. R. Hurley (Trans.). New York: Pantheon and Harmondsworth: Penguin.

———. (1965, 1967). *Madness and civilization*, Vol. I. R. Hurley (Trans.). New York: Random House and London: Tavistock.

———. (1980). *Power/Knowledge*. New York: Pantheon.
———. (1985, 1986). *The use of pleasure*. R. Hurley (Trans.). New York: Random House and Harmondsworth: Viking.
Freire, P. (1970). *Pedagogy of the oppressed*. R. Howard (Trans.). New York: Herder and Herder.
Friedan, B. (1963, 1974). *The feminine mystique*. New York: Dell Publishing Co.
Galtung, J. and Ikeda, D. (1995). *Choose peace: a dialogue between John Galtung and Daidaku Ikeda*. R. L. Gage (Trans. and Ed.). London, East Haven, CT: Pluto Press.
Garrison, J. (1994, Jan-Feb). Realism, Deweyan pragmatism, and educational research. *Educational Researcher*, 23(1), 5–14.
———. Ed. (1995). *New scholarship on Dewey*. Dordrecht, Boston, London: Kluwer Academic Publishers.
———. (Winter 1995). Deweyan pragmatism and the epistemology of contemporary social constructivism. *American Educational Research Journal*, 32(4), 716–740.
———. (1996). A Deweyan theory of democratic listening, *Educational Theory* 46(4) 429–451.
———. (1999a). Dangerous dualisms in Siegel's theory of critical thinking: A Deweyan pragmatist responds, *Journal of Philosophy of Education*, 33(2), 213–232.
———. (1999b). Reclaiming the Lógos, considering the consequences, and restoring co-text, *Educational Theory*, 49(3), 317–337.
Gilligan, C. (1982). *In a different voice: Psychological theory and women's development*. Cambridge: Harvard University Press.
Goldberger, N., Tarule, J., Clinchy, B., and Belenky, M. (Eds.). (1996). *Knowledge, difference, and power: Essays inspired by Women's Ways of Knowing*. New York: Basic Books, HarperCollins Publishers, Inc.
Greene, M. (1973). *Teacher as stranger: Educational philosophy for the modern age*. Belmont, CA: Wadsworth Publishing Co.
———. (1988). *The dialectic of freedom*. New York: Teachers College Press.
———. (1995). *Releasing the imagination: Essays on education, the arts, and social change*. San Francisco: Jossey-Bass Publishers.
Griffin, S. (1978). *Woman and nature*. New York: Harper & Row.
Grimshaw, J. (1986). *Philosophy and feminist thinking*. Minneapolis, MN: University of Minnesota Press.
Haack, S. (1993). *Evidence and inquiry: Towards reconstruction in epistemology*. Oxford: Blackwell Publishers.
Hanson, K. (1986). *The self imagined*. New York and London: Routledge & Kegan Paul.
Haraway, D. (Fall 1988). Situated knowledges: The science question in feminism and the privilege of partial perspective, *Feminist Studies* 14(3): 575–599.
Harding, S. (1986). *The science question in feminism*. Ithaca and London: Cornell University Press.
———. (1991). *Whose science? Whose knowledge? Thinking from women's lives*. Ithaca, NY: Cornell University Press.
———. (1992). What is feminist theory? In H. Crowley and S. Himmelweit (Eds.). *Knowing women: Feminism and knowledge* (pp. 338–355). Cambridge and Oxford: Polity Press, The Open University.

———. (1993). Rethinking standpoint epistemology: What is "strong objectivity"? In L. Alcoff & E. Potter (Eds.). *Feminist epistemologies* (pp. 49-82). New York and London: Routledge.

Harstock, N. (1983). The feminist standpoint: Developing the grounds for a specifically feminist historical materialism. In S. Harding and M. B. Hintikka (Eds.). *Discovering Reality* (pp. 283-310). Dordrecht, Holland, Boston and London: D. Reidel Publishing Co.

Hoagland, S. (Spring 1990). Some concerns about Nel Noddings' Caring. Review Symposium of Caring, *Hypatia*, 5(1), 109-114.

Hobbes, T. (1968). *Leviathan*, C. B. Macpherson (Ed.). Baltimore: Penguin.

hooks, b. (1984). *Feminist theory: From the margin to the center*. Boston: South End Press.

Hookway, C. (1997). Logical principles and philosophical attitudes: Peirce's response to James's pragmatism. In R. A. Putnam (Ed.). *The Cambridge companion to William James* (pp. 145-165). Cambridge, UK: Cambridge University Press.

Houston, B. (Spring 1990). Caring and exploitation. Review Symposium of Caring, *Hypatia*, 5(1), 115-119.

Hungry Wolf, B. (1980). *The ways of my grandmothers*. New York: Quill.

Hytten, K. (1999). Using whiteness studies in the knowledge debate: An exploration of epistemological racism, *Philosophical Studies in Education*.

Illich, I. (1973). *Deschooling society*. New York: Harper & Row.

Irigaray, L. (1974, 1985). *Speculum of the other woman*. G. Gill (Trans.). Ithaca, NY: Cornell Press.

———. (1985). *This sex which is not one*. G. Gill (Trans.). Ithaca, NY: Cornell Press.

Jaggar, A. (1989, 1992). Love and knowledge: Emotion in feminist epistemology. In A. Garry & M. Pearsall (Eds.). *Women, knowledge, and reality: Explorations in feminist philosophy* (pp. 145-171). New York, London: Routledge.

———. (1995). Caring as a feminist practice of moral reason. In *Justice and care: Essential readings in feminist ethics*, V. Held (Ed.). (pp. 179-202). Boulder, CO: WestviewPress, HarperCollins Publishers.

James, W. (1890,1950). *The principles on psychology* (Vol. 1). New York: Dover.

———. (1909, 1975a). *The meaning of truth*. Cambridge, MA: Harvard University Press.

———. (1907, 1975b). *Pragmatism*. Cambridge, MA: Harvard University Press.

———. (1912, 1976). *Essays in radical empiricism*. Cambridge, MA: Harvard University Press.

———. (1909, 1977). *A pluralistic universe*. Cambridge, MA: Harvard University Press.

Kaufman-Osborn, T. V. (1993, Spring). Teasing feminist sense from experience. *Hypatia*, 8(2), 124-144.

Keller, E. (1983). *A feeling for the organism: The life and work of Barbara McClintock*. New York: W. H. Freeman and Company.

———.(1985). *Reflections on gender and science*. New Haven: Yale University Press.

———. (1992). *Secrets of life, secrets of death*. New York and London: Routledge.

Kheel, M. (1990). Ecofeminism and deep ecology: Reflections on identity and difference. In I. Diamond and G. Orenstein (Eds.). *Reweaving the world: The emergence of ecofeminism* (pp. 138-154). San Francisco, CA: Sierra Club Books.

Khema, A. (1999). *Be an island: The Buddhist practice of inner peace*. Boston: Wisdom Publications.

King, R. (1991). Caring about nature: Feminist ethics and the environment. *Hypatia*, 6(1), 75–89.

King, Y. (1981). Feminism and the revolt, *Heresies*, 12–16.

———. (1987). What is ecofeminism? *The Nation*, 245(20), 702, 730–732.

———. (1989). The ecology of feminism and the feminism of ecology. In J. Plant (Ed.). *Healing the wounds: The promise of ecofeminism* (pp. 18–28). Santa Cruz, CA: New Society Publishers.

———. (1990). Healing the wounds: Feminism, ecology, and the nature/culture dualism. In I. Diamond and G. Orenstein (Eds.). *Reweaving the world: The emergence of ecofeminism* (pp. 106–121). San Francisco: Sierra Club Books. Also published in A. Jaggar and S. Bordo (Eds.). (1990). *Gender/body/knowledge* (pp. 115–141). Rutgers University Press.

Kongtrül, J. (1992). *Cloudless sky: The Mahamudra path of the Tibetan Kagyü Buddhist School*, R. Gravel (Trans.). Boston and London: Shambhala.

Kuhn, T. (1962, 1970). *The structure of scientific revolutions*. Second edition. Chicago: University of Chicago Press.

Leonard, A. (1949). *A sand county almanac*. New York: Oxford University Press.

Levinas, E. (1987, 1993, 1994). *Outside the subject*. Michale B. Smith (Trans.). Stanford, CA: Stanford University Press.

Longino, H. (1990). *Science as social knowledge: Values and objectivity in scientific inquiry*. Princeton: Princeton University Press.

———. (1993). Subjects, power and knowledge: Description and prescription in feminist philosophies of science. In L. Alcoff and E. Potter (Eds.). *Feminist epistemologies* (pp. 101–120). New York, NY: Routledge, Chapman and Hall, Inc.

Lorde, A. (1984). The master's tools will never dismantle the master's house. In *Sister outsider*. Freedom, CA: Crossing. Reprinted in C. Moraga, and G. Anzaldúa (Eds.). (1981, 1983). *This bridge called my back* (pp. 98–101). New York: Kitchen Table: Women of Color Press.

Lovelock, J. E. (1979, 1987). *Gaia: A new look at life on Earth*. Oxford, New York: Oxford University Press.

———. (1988). *The ages of Gaia: A biography of our living earth*. New York, London: W. W. Norton and Co.

———. (1999). Gaia as seen through the atmosphere; The Earth as a living organism. In P. R. Samson and D. Pitt (Eds.). *The biosphere and noosphere reader* (pp. 115–120). London and New York: Routledge.

Loy, D. (1988). *Nonduality: A study in comparative philosophy*. New Haven and London: Yale University Press.

Lugones, M. (Summer 1987). Playfulness, 'world' traveling, and loving perception. *Hypatia* 2, 3–19.

Lyotard, J. (1984). *The postmodern condition: A report on knowledge*. Minneapolis: University of Minnesota Press.

Macy, J. (1991). *Mutual Causality in Buddhism and General Systems Theory: The dharma of natural systems*. Albany, NY: State University of New York Press.

Margulis, L. (1982). *Early life*. Boston, MA: Science Books International, Inc.
——. (1998). *Symbiotic planet: A new look at evolution*. Amherst, MA: Sciencewriters, Basic Books.
——. (1999). Jim Lovelock's Gaia. In P. R. Samson and D. Pitt (Eds.). *The biosphere and noosphere reader* (pp. 120–122). London and New York: Routledge.
Margulis, L. and Sagan, D. (1986). *Microcosmos: 4 billion years of evolution from our microbial ancestors*. New York: Simon & Schuster.
——. (1997). *Slanted truths: Essays on Gaia, symbiosis, and evolution*. New York: Copernicus, Springer-Berlag New York, Inc.
Martin, J. R. (1985). *Reclaiming the conversation: The ideal of the educated woman*. New Haven, CT: Yale University Press.
——. (1992). *The schoolhome: Rethinking schools for changing families*. Cambridge, MA: Harvard University Press.
——. (1994). *Changing the educational landscape: Philosophy, women, and curriculum*. New York and London: Routledge.
Marx, K. and Engels, F. (1848, 1964). *Communist manifesto*. New York: Pocket Books.
——. (1848, 1970). *The German ideology*. New York: International Publishers.
McCarthy, C. (1997). When you know it, and I know it, what is it we know? Pragmatic realism and the epistemological absolute. In Frank Margonis (Ed.). *Philosophy of Education 1996* (pp. 21–29). Urbana, IL: Philosophy of Education Society.
McNeley, J. K. (1973). The Navajo 'wind' theory of life and behavior. Ph.D. dissertation, University of Hawaii, Honolulu, HI.
——. (1981,1997). *Holy wind in Navajo philosophy*. Tucson, AR: The University of Arizona Press, 5th printing.
Mead, G. H. (1934). *Mind, self, and society: From the standpoint of a social behaviorist*, C. W. Morris (Ed.). Chicago: University of Chicago Press.
Merchant, C. (1980). *The death of nature: Women, ecology, and the scientific revolution*.
——. (1989). *Ecological revolutions: Nature, gender, and science in New England*. Chapel Hill, NC: The University of North Carolina Press.
——. (1990). Ecofeminism and Feminist Theory. In I. Diamond, and G. F. Orenstein (Eds.). *Reweaving the world: The emergence of ecofeminism* (pp. 100–105). San Francisco: Sierra Club Books.
——. (1992). *Radical ecology: The search for a livable world*. New York: Routledge.
Montessori, M. (1972) *The discovery of the child* (2nd ed., M. Josephy Costelloe, Trans.). New York, Ballantine.
——. (1977). *The secret of childhood* (2nd ed., M. Josephy Costelloe, Trans.). New York, Ballantine.
Morgan, K. P. (1996). We've come to see the wizard! Revelations of the enlightenment epistemology. In Alven Neiman (Ed.). *Philosophy of Education 1995* (pp. 27–35). Urbana, IL: Philosophy of Education Society.
Naess, A. (1973). The shallow and the deep, long-range ecology movements. *Inquiry, 16*, 95–100.
——. (Fall 1984). A defense of the deep ecology movement. *Environmental Ethics, 6*(3), 265–270.

———. (1985). Identification as a source of deep ecological attitudes. In M. Tobias (Ed.). *Deep Ecology* (pp. 256–270). San Diego: Avant Books.

———. (1986). The deep ecological movement: Some philosophical aspects. *Philosophical Inquiry*, 8(1–2), 10–29.

———. (1989). *Ecology, community and lifestyle*. David Rothenberg (Trans. and Ed). Cambridge: Cambridge University Press.

Nagel, T. (1986). *A view from nowhere*. Oxford: Oxford University Press.

Narayan, U. (1989). The project of feminist epistemology: Perspectives from a nonwestern feminist. In Alison Jaggar and Susan Bordo (Eds.). *Gender/Body/Knowledge* (pp. 256–269). NJ: Rutgers University Press.

Nelson, L. (1990). *Who knows?* Philadelphia: Temple University Press.

———. (1993). Epistemological communities. In L. Alcoff and E. Potter (Eds.). *Feminist epistemologies* (pp. 121–159). New York, NY: Routledge, Chapman and Hall, Inc.

Noddings, N. (1984). *Caring: A feminine approach to ethics and moral education*. Berkeley, CA: University of California Press.

———. (Spring 1990). Review symposium: A response. *Hypatia*, 5(1), 120–126.

———. (1992). *The challenge to care in schools: An alternative approach to education*. New York: Teachers College Press.

Okin, S. (1979). *Women in Western political thought*. Princeton, NJ: Princeton University Press.

Orr, D. (1992). *Ecological liiteracy: Education and the transition to a postmodern world*. Albany, NY: State University of New York, SUNY Press.

Pagano, J. (Fall/Winter 1999). Taking our places, *Educational Studies*, 30(3/4), 251–261.

Peirce, C. (1933–58). *Collected papers of Charles Sanders Peirce*, Charles Hartshone, and Paul Weiss (Eds.). Cambridge, MA: Harvard University Press, 5, 6. Symbolized in the text as *CP*.

———. (1958). *Values in an universe of chance: Selected writings of Charles Sanders Peirce (1839–1914)*, P. P. Wiener (Ed.). Garden City, NJ: Doubleday & Co, Inc.

Plato. (1970). Meno. In S. Cahn (Ed.). *The Philosophical Foundations of Education* (pp. 7–35). New York: Harper & Row, Publishers.

———. (1979). *Republic*, Raymond Larson (Trans. and Ed.). Arlington Heights, IL: Harlan Davidson Inc.

Plumwood, V. (1991). Nature, self, and gender: Feminism, environmental philosophy, and the critique of rationalism. In *Hypatia*, 6(1), 3–27.

Potter, E. (1993). Gender and epistemic negotiation. In L. Alcoff and E. Potter (Eds.). *Feminist epistemologies* (pp. 161–186). New York, NY: Routledge, Chapman and Hall, Inc.

Prakash, M. (Spring 1994). What are people for? Wendell Barry on education, ecology, and culture. *Educational Theory*, 44(2), 135–157.

Quine, W. . (1960). *Word and object*. Cambridge, MA: M.I.T. Press.

———. (1981). *Theories and things*. Cambridge, MA: Harvard University Press.

Rorty, R. (1977). Dewey's metaphysics. In S. Cahn (Ed.). *New studies in the philosophy of John Dewey* (pp. 45–74). Hanover, NH: University Press of New England, for University of Vermont.

———. (1979). *Philosophy and the mirror of nature*. Princeton, NJ: Princeton University Press.

———. (1982). *Consequences of pragmatism.* Minneapolis, MN: University of Minnesota Press.
———. (1985). Habermas and Lyotard on postmodernity, in *Habermas and modernity.* R. Bernstein (Ed.). Cambridge, MA: M.I.T. Press.
———. (1989). *Contingency, irony, and solidarity.* Cambridge: Cambridge University Press.
———. (1991). Feminism and pragmatism, *Michigan Quarterly Review,* 30(2), 231–258.
Rorty, R., Critchley, S., Derrida, J., and Laclau, E. (1996). *Deconstruction and pragmatism,* Chantal Mouffe (Ed.). London and New York: Routledge.
Rosenberg, J. (1993). Raiders of the lost distinction: Richard Rorty and the search for the last dichotomy, *Philosophy and Phenomenological Research,* 53(1), 195–214.
Ruddick, S. (1989). *Maternal thinking: Toward a politics of peace.* Boston: Beacon Press.
———. (1996). Reason's "femininity": A case for connected knowing. In Goldberger, N., Tarule, J., Clinchy, B., and Belenky, M. (Eds.). *Knowledge, difference, and power: Essays inspired by Women's Ways of Knowing* (pp. 248–273). New York: Basic Books, Harper-Collins Publishers, Inc.
Sarris, G. (1989). *The last woman from Cache Creek: Conversations with Mabel McKay.* Dissertation at Stanford University, Palo Alto, CA.
———. (1993). *Keeping slug woman alive: A holistic approach to American Indian texts.* Berkeley: University of California Press.
———. (1994). *Mabel McKay: Weaving the dream.* Berkeley: University of California Press.
Seigfried, C. (1978). *Chaos and context: A study in William James.* Athens, OH: Ohio University Press.
———. (1990). *William James's radical reconstruction of philosophy.* Albany, NY: State University of New York Press.
———. (1996). *Pragmatism and feminism: Reweaving the social fabric.* Chicago: University of Chicago Press.
———. (1997, April). Beyond epistemology: A pragmatist feminist inquiry, paper presented to EnGendering Rationalities Conference, University of Oregon, Eugene, OR.
Sessions, R. (1991). Deep ecology versus ecofeminism: Healthy differences or imcompatible philosophies? *Hypatia,* 6(1), 90–107.
Shaner, D. (1989). The Japanese experience of nature. In J. Callicott, and R. Ames (Eds.). *Nature in Asian traditions and thoughts: Essays in environmental philosophy* (pp. 163–182). Albany, NY: State University of New York Press.
Siegel, H. (1987). *Relativism Refuted: A Critique of Contemporary Epistemological Relativism.* Dordrecht & Boston: D. Reidel Publishing Co.
———. (1988). *Educating Reason.* New York: Routledge.
———. (1992). Two perspectives on reason as an educational aim: The rationality of reasonableness. In M. Buchmann & R. E. Floden (Eds.). *Philosophy of education 1991* (pp. 225–233). Norman, IL: Philosophy of Education Society.
———. (1997). *Rationality Redeemed?* New York: Routledge.
———. (Winter 2000). Afterwords, *Educational Theory,* 50(1), 129–131.
Sizer, T. (1984). *Horace's compromise: The dilemma of the American high school.* Boston: Houghton Mifflin.

———. (1992). *Horace's school: Redesigning the American high school.* Boston: Houghton Mifflin.

Sleeper, R. W. (1986). *The necessity of pragmatism: John Dewey's conception of philosophy.* New Haven and London: Yale University Press.

Smith, D. (1987). *The everyday world as problematic: A feminist sociology.* Boston: Northeastern University.

———. (1990). *The conceptual practices of power: A feminist sociology of knowledge.* Boston: Northeastern University.

———. (Winter 1997). Comments on Hekman's "Truth and method: Feminist standpoint theory revisited," *Signs,* 22(2), 392–398.

Stuhr, J. J. (Ed.). (1987). *Classical American Philosophy.* New York: Oxford University Press.

Suzuki, S. (1970). *Zen mind, beginner's mind.* Trudy Dixon (Ed.). NY and Tokyo: Weatherhill.

Thayer-Bacon, B. (Summer 1993). Caring and its relationship to critical thinking, *Educational Theory* 43(3), 323–340.

———.(Spring 1997). The nurturing of a relational epistemology, *Educational Theory,* 47(2), 239–260.

———. (1997). The power of caring, *Philosophical Studies in Education,* Ohio Valley Philosophy of Education Society, 1–32.

———. (2000). *Transforming critical thinking: Thinking constructively.* New York: Teachers College Press.

———. (2002). A feminist re/examination of William James as a qualified relativist. In Bredo, E., Garrison, J., and Podeschi, R. (Eds.), *William James and education,* pp. 97–114. New York: Teachers College Press.

———. (2002). Using the 'R' word again: Pragmatism as qualified relativism. *Philosophical Studies in Education,* 33, 93–103.

———. (Summer 2000). Caring reasoning. *Inquiry: Critical Thinking Across the Curriculum,* 19(4), 22–34.

Toynbee, A. and Ikeda, D. (1989). *Choose life: a dialogue between Arnold Toynbee and Daisaku Ikeda.* R. L. Gage (Ed.). Oxford: Oxford University Press.

Trungpa, C. (1978). *Glimpses of Abhidharma.* Boulder, CO: Prajñā Press.

———. (1988). *The myth of freedom, and the way of meditation.* John Baker and Marvin Casper (Eds.). Boston and London: Shambhala.

Warren, K. J. (1987). Feminism and ecology: Making connections, *Environmental Ethics,* 9, 3–21.

———. (1988). Toward an ecofeminist ethic, *Studies in the Humanities,* 15, 140–156.

———. (Spring 1990). The power and the promise of ecological feminism, Environmental Ethics, 12(1), 125–146.

Warren, K. and Cheney, J. (Spring, 1991). Ecological feminism and ecosystem ecology. *Hypatia,* 6(1), 179–197.

Watson, R. A. (Fall 1983). A critique of anti-anthropocentric biocentrism, *Environmental Ethics,* 5(3), 245–256.

Weinstein, M. (1992) Reason and refutation: A review of two recent books by Harvey Siegel, *Studies in Philosophy and Education,* 11(3), 231–263.

Weil, S. (1977). *The Simone Weil Reader*, George A. Panichas (Ed.). New York: David McKay Co., Inc.

West, C. (1989). *The American evasion of philosophy: A genealogy of pragmatism*. Madison, WI: The University of Wisconsin Press.

Williams, P. (1989). *Mahāyāna Buddism: the doctrinal foundations*. London and NY: Routledge.

Index

absolutism
   absolutism/relativism dichotomy, 49, 56, 58, 63
   vulgar vs. non-vulgar, 19–20, 21, 23
Alcoff, Linda, 15–16
Allen, Paula Gunn, 195, 197–198, 205, 207
androcentrism, 27, 29
Aristotle, 17–18, 60, 157

beliefs (philosophical concept), 17, 51, 62, 63, 66
Berger, Peter L., 1–2, 11, 83, 140–142
Bergson, Henri, 59–60
biology (science of), 98–99, 236
   See also Margulis, Lynn; McClintock, Barbara
Bohm, David
   criticisms of, 229–230
   and knowing, 226–227
   and matter, 225–226
   and quantum theory, 97, 214, 220
   and wholeness theory, 228–229
   and the w/holistic universe, 220, 227
Bohr, Neils
   and matter, 223
   and quantum theory, 96, 216, 217, 220–221
   and theory of complementarity, 224
   and the w/holistic universe, 218
Buber, Martin
   I-It relations, 123–124
   I-Thou relations, 122, 123–124, 192
   Noddings, Nel; compared to, 125
   relationality, 76
   and religious belief, 81
   scholarly background, 122–123
   Spiritual Beings, 85
   Weil, Simone; compared to, 124–125
Buddhism
   beliefs of, compared to Navajos, 181
   "big Mind" and compassion, 164–165
   dependent co-origination, doctrine of, 159, 166, 187–188
   and duality, 86
   and education, 259
   and gender bias, 154
   human/nature inseparability, 90–91
   Mahäyäna Buddhism, 157–158, 164, 165
   and meditation, 155, 156
   and the mind, 86, 160–161
   and nature, 183–184
   Noble Truths, 160
   and non-violence, 189
   and physics, 216, 220, 230
   and the self, 92, 162–163, 192
   storytelling practices, 155
   types of, compared, 87
   Zen Buddhism, 163, 164
   See also w/holistic relations
Burbules, Nicholas, 21–22

Cajete, Gregory, 259–260, 262–263
Capra, Fritjof, 215, 216, 220, 224
caring reasoning
   Buddhist "compassion," compared to, 165

contextual perspective, as a means to, 120–121
definition of, 120, 122
and ecological relations, 211
examples of, 121–122
and Native American beliefs, 173
chemistry (science of). *See* Gaia theory; Lovelock, James
childrens' games and development of the self, 132–133
Christianity, 207, 208, 256
Code, Lorraine, 5, 28–29, 30
"concepts" in definitions of reality, 59–60, 61, 85, 155–156
"context" defined by Dewey, John, 36, 37

Daly, Mary, 201, 202, 205–210
de Beauvoir, Simone, 26–27, 199, 201, 204
de Broglie, Louis, 216, 217, 222
deconstructionists, 41
deep ecology
   criticisms of, 194
   definition and tenets of, 190–191
   and nature/human split, 193
   origin of the term, 189
   and the self, 192
   and women and girls, 198
Deloria, Vine, Jr., 186, 196–197
Descartes, Rene, 18, 26, 49, 112, 144
Dewey, John
   art as a model for inquiry, 70
   and community of inquirers, 36
   and context, philosophy's neglect of, 2, 14, 37, 40
   criticisms of, 64
   democratic communities, 64–65
   epistemology, rejection of, 3, 38
   and experience, 47, 62
   and feminists, 34, 64
   habits, views on, 135–136
   immaturity, definition of, 137
   and inquiry, 4, 6, 39–40, 120
   and interdependent relationships, 83
   and logic, 38–39
   Mead, George Herbert; friendship with, 135
   and pragmatism, 45, 48

and relationality, 76
Rorty, Richard; criticisms of, 47
sympathetic understanding, 120
transactional relations, 136, 138–139, 251, 273
and truth, 9
See also experience (philosophical concept)
Dirac, Paul, 217
domination, logic of, 200, 206, 210

ecofeminism
   and deep ecology, 194
   and natural determinism, 210
   and nature/human split, 184
   and ontological/epistemological reorientation, 94
   and power relations, 198, 205
   and radical cultural feminism, 204–205
   women and nature, 197–202, 204, 205
ecological relations, generally, 89–94
   See also Buddhism; Native Americans; nature
ecological theories, 185
Ecosophy T, 190, 191, 192, 193
   See also Naess, Arne
education (practice and theory)
   and caring reasoning, 247
   church and state separation, 256–257
   curriculum issues, 255, 265–267, 270
   definition of, 243
   and diversity, 252–253, 254–255
   ecological education, 261–263
   I-Thou relations, 245
   multicultural education, 253–254
   proficiency exams, 247, 267
   and Protestant faiths, 257
   reforms, 250
   relational learning, 246–247
   and social renewal, 136–137, 138
   and spirituality, 255–261
   student-teacher ratios, 247–249, 252
   teacher-student relationships, 244, 245–246, 250
   See also Montessori schools; teachers
Einstein, Albert
   and de Broglie, Louis, 222

"field" concept, 228
  relativity theory, 95–96, 216
  space-time continuum, 218
  and the w/holistic universe, 217–218, 219–220
environmental philosophy
  and Buddhism, 187, 188
  exclusion of Asian philosophies, 186–187
  nature/human split, 192–193, 194
  origins of, 186
  and socialism, 203–204
  See also deep ecology; ecological relations, generally
epistemological fallibilism, 32, 49, 54
epistemological pluralism and pragmatists, 54
epistemology/Epistemology
  caring concepts, importance of, 119
  definitions of, 17
  distinguished from sociology of knowledge, 2–3
  dualisms in, 7, 35, 48
  "Epistemology" and "(e)pistemology" distinguished, 3–4
  and gender issues, 34
  and morality, 28
  naturalistic epistemology, 40
  and nature, 11
  and philosophy, 14
  and postmodernists, 42
  socially constructed standards, 6
  subjects, importance of, 28
  and truth, 17, 18
  See also relational epistemology
ethic of care, 108–109
ethics, value of in hierarchy of philosophy, 15
experience (philosophical concept)
  and Buddhism, 87, 155
  Dewey, John; views of, 38, 63
  foreground vs. background, 207–208
  James, William; views of, 57–58
  and knowing, 58
  and Native American beliefs, 155
  and nonduality, 157
  and spirituality, 85–86
  and theory/practice dualism, 35, 37

fallibilism
  Dewey, John; views of, 62
  differing views of pragmatists, 49, 51
  and inclusionary discourses, 70
  key concepts, 35
  Siegel, Harvey; views of, 20–21, 22, 23
  See also epistemological fallibilism
Farella, John, 88–89, 174, 175, 177
feminist epistemologies
  androcentrism, in response to, 26
  "caring" and women, 119
  and collapse of absolutist epistemology, 32
  and context, 41
  criticisms of, 16
  and epistemology, need to redefine, 34
  gynocentric epistemology, 33
  James, William; influence of, 71
  and Marxism, 30–31
  and pluralism, 8
  proponents of, 5
  "S knows that p" statements, 28–29
feminists
  empiricist feminists, 29–30
  and experience, 46–47
  and private vs. public realms, 128
  and psychoanalytic theory, 110–111
  and race, 206
  and radical pluralism, 70
  and research methods, 69
  and scientific/scholastic community, 66
  social feminists, 202–204
  standpoint feminists, 5, 30, 31, 32
  See also Allen, Paula Gunn; Code, Lorraine; Daly, Mary; de Beauvoir, Simone; ecofeminism; Flax, Jane; Gilligan, Carol; Harding, Sandra; King, Ynestra; Margulis, Lynn; McClintock, Barbara; Merchant, Carol; Noddings, Nel; Ruddick, Sara; Seigfried, Charlene Haddock; Smith, Dorothy; Warren, Karen; Weil, Simone
Firstness, 55
Flax, Jane
  on child care, 100
  core identity, 251
  infants, 101
  mother-child relation, 79

Flax, Jane *(continued)*
  object relations theory, 111
  patriarchy and knowledge, 112–114
  theoretical bases, 110
Foucault, Michel, 1, 41–42, 84, 149–151

Gaia theory, 97–98, 230–236
Garrison, Jim, 24, 25, 38, 252
gestures, 82, 130–132
Gilligan, Carol, 106–107, 122
goddesses, 207, 208–209
God's-eye view
  and deconstructionists, 41
  and Dewey, John, 70
  and feminist standpoint epistemology, 5, 31
  and multicultural curricula, 254
  and Siegel, Harvey, 20
gravity and physics, 219
Griffin, Susan, 205
Grimshaw, Jean, 104–105

Harding, Sandra, 29–30, 31–32
Heisenberg, Werner, 96, 217, 221, 222–223
Houston, Barbara, 120–121

inclusionary discourse, 66–71
indigenous people, definition of, 196
infant and child care
  caregivers, definitions of, 101–104
  and relationality, 77–79, 82, 107–108
  treatment of in philosophy, 100
intellectualism, vicious, 59
I-Thou relationships, 81, 123–124, 192, 245
  See also Buber, Martin

James, William
  absolute chance, 52
  criticisms of, 53, 64
  feminists, influence on, 71
  Peirce, Charles S.; contrasted with, 49, 60, 61
  and pluralism, 60, 61
  radical empiricist ontology, 56–57, 58
  radical pluralism, 58–59, 70
  relation of beliefs to truth, 52–53

  and the subject, 36
  and truth, 9
Judeo-Christian ontology, 183

Kaufman-Osborn, T.V., 46
Keller, Evelyn Fox, 98–99
Khema, Ayya, 165, 167
King, Ynestra, 194, 199–200, 204–205, 210–211
knowledge (philosophical concept)
  and communities, 64
  Dewey, John; views of, 62–63, 76
  and oppression, 93
  and patriarchy, 112–113
  and power (Navajo gods), 178
  and relationality, 73
  and scientific facts, 226–227
  scientific knowledge defined, 94–95
  social contexts of knowing, 7–8
  types of, 60
  warranted assertability, 63

language
  as cultural matrix of inquiry, 65, 70
  and experience, 46
  and fragmentation of thought (in science), 227
  and mistranslation, 182
  and self-consciousness, 82, 132
legitimators, 1, 142
logic, 38–39, 62
Lovelock, James, 97–98, 215, 230–236
Luckmann, Thomas, 1–2, 11, 83, 140–142

McClintock, Barbara, 98–99, 215, 239–240, 241, 268
McKay, Mabel, 87–88, 170–174, 195
McNeley, James, 88–89, 174
Margulis, Lynn, 98, 215, 235–236, 237, 239
maternal thinking, 78, 102
  See also Ruddick, Sara
Mead, George Herbert
  "co-operative activity," 131
  criticisms of, 135
  and development of the self, 82–83, 129–131, 132–134, 251
  scholarly background, 129

social behaviorism, 129-130, 134
meditation, 161, 167
Merchant, Carol, 201, 202-205, 206
metaphysics
    and abstraction, 15
    and the assumption of absolutism, 18
    breakdown of, 42
    Dewey, John; views of, 47
    and experience, 63
    Mead, George Herbert; views of, 135
Montessori schools, 249, 257-258, 268-270
Morgan, Kathryn, 69

Naess, Arne, 91-92, 189-193, 193-194
NASA (National Aeronautics and Space Administration, 230-231
Native Americans
    and animals, 186, 196, 260
    and Christianity, 208
    creation myth stories, 208
    and education, 259-260
    and gender issues, 154-155
    and gynocentrism, 197-198
    and nature, 183-184, 194-196, 262-263
    nature/human split, 198
    oral tradition, 87, 168, 196-197
    plants, use of, 196
    stories, importance of, 155, 169
    women and nature, 205
    See also McKay, Mabel; Navajos; Pomo Indians
nature (natural world)
    and anthropocentrism, 194
    in Asian art, 188
    and classification, 200-201
    and diversity, 192-193
    and education, 261
    and Euro-western philosophy, 183, 184
    mechanistic view of, 203, 212-213
    nature/human split, 184
    and social feminism, 204
    and women, 199, 200-203, 205, 207
Navajos
    alkéé naá aashii concept, 89, 180-181
    beliefs of, compared to Buddhists, 181
    Changing Woman, 179
    First Man and First Woman, 155, 176, 178, 179-180
    gender in beliefs, 178
    gods of (Holy People), 177-179
    Holy Wind concept, 89, 175-177, 195, 260
    and nature, 195
    population, 89, 174
Newton, Sir Isaac, 218, 224
Nieto, Sonia, 253-254
Noble Truths (of Buddhism), 160
Noddings, Nel
    and the caring attitude, 108-109
    Gilligan, Carol; compared with, 106-107
    relational ontology, 79-80, 81
    Ruddick, Sara; compared with, 109
    scholarly background, 106
    teacher-student relationships, 245
nonduality, 156-157, 161, 181, 182

object relations theory, 111, 113, 114

Pauli, Wolfgang, 217, 221
Peirce, Charles S.
    absolute truth, 52
    fallibilism, 20, 51
    on ideas and experience, 37-38
    James, William; contrasted with, 60, 61
    Pragmatic Maxim, 49, 143
    relation of beliefs to truth, 51
    and Scotistic realism, 54-56, 61
    and synechism, 60-61
    and triadic ontology, 55
    and truth, 18
    truth as determined by a community of scholars, 65-66
personal relations, generally, 77-80
philosophers
    as cultural critics, 2, 41, 272
    feminists, 15
    roles of, 5, 17, 43, 45
    See also individual philosophers
philosophy (academic discipline)
    change agents within the field, 84
    definitions of, 14-15, 14-15, 36
    fallacies in, 37
    and females, marginalization of, 26, 31, 42, 67-68, 69

philosophy *(continued)*
  and feminists, 15
  as the foundational discipline, 17
  and infancy, neglect of, 100
  and Native Americans, marginalization of, 197
  and transformative theories, 84
  value of abstraction, 15
  See also environmental philosophy
physics
  and causality, 226
  and light, 221, 222
  and perception, 226
  quantum mechanics, 221–222
  and relationality, 95–98
  relativity theory, 216–217, 218, 219, 227
  transcendence of a mechanistic view of the universe, 214
  and the w/holistic universe, 223, 225
  See also Bohm, David; Bohr, Neils; Einstein, Albert; quantum theory
Plato
  and duality, 157
  Forms, 183
  and intellectualism, 59
  and knowledge, 17
  mind/body split, 15, 26
  value of abstraction, 112
  and women and girls, 127
Pomo Indians, 89, 169–170, 171–172
Potter, Elizabeth, 15–16
pragmatism
  definitions of, 51, 143
  Dewey, John; contributions of, 64
  and feminists, 45, 46
  origins of, 49, 70
  and relativism, 54
  transforming effect on philosophy, 144
  See also James, William; Peirce, Charles S.
pragmatists, 35, 41, 42, 71–72

qualified relativism, 53, 54, 61
quantum theory
  and complementarity, 224
  Einstein's criticisms of, 217
  formulation of, 95–97, 220–221
  and probability, 223
  relation to relativity theory, 218
  and the w/holistic universe, 227

radical empiricism, 56–57, 58–59, 63
radical pluralism, 58, 70
rationalism, distinguished from empiricism, 57
rationality (philosophical concept)
  contrasted with maternal thinking, 102, 105
  four dimensions of, 33
  and James, William, 59
  and Siegel, Harvey, 24
  substantive conception of, 21, 22
reality (philosophical concept)
  and embeddedness, 10
  as a social construct, 9, 140–142, 150, 207–208
  as a social construct (in science), 216, 224
relational epistemology/(e)pistemology
  definition of, 9–10
  educational recommendations, 271
  and mysticism, 77
  role of subjects to objects of knowing, 12
  and teachers, 254
  transactional nature of knowing, 76
relationality and power, 150
relations, generally, 73–76
  See also education
relations of ruling, 146–147
relativism, criticisms of, 19
Rorty, Richard
  advice to feminists, 41, 46
  as change agent, 84
  and demise of epistemology, 3
  and demise of philosophy, 4
  Dewey, John; criticisms of, 47
  and history of epistemology, 42
  "ironists" vs. "liberalists," 128
  and knowing, 42–43
  and ontology, 48
  particular/universal distinction, 44
  postmodernist positions, 43
  and pragmatism, 45
  private vs. public realms, 127–128
  on the role of philosophers, 4–5
Ruddick, Sara

attentive love, 117–118
and caregivers, 101
and connected knowing, 106
on maternal thinking, 78, 102, 104, 105
Noddings, Nel; compared to, 109
See also infant and child care

Sarris, Greg, 88, 170–171, 174
schools, role of, 137
See also education
Schrödinger, Erwin, 216–217, 222
science
cross-discipline milestones, 264–265
detrimental effects of, 214
dualisms in, 213
in history, general characteristics, 212
and knowledge, 226
and marginalization of females, 213
scientific knowledge defined, 94–95
w/holistic view of universe, 241–242
See also biology (science of); Gaia theory; Lovelock, James; physics
Scotus, Duns, 55, 56
Secondness, 55
Seigfried, Charlene Haddock, 5, 33–34, 53, 143
the self
"borderline syndrome," 110
and Buddhism, 86, 87, 92, 166, 188
and communities, 64–65, 82, 83, 133–134
and deep ecology, 191–192
and early childhood development, 79, 114
and identification with nature, 193
I-Thou relations, 123–124
and knowing, 7
and language development, 82
and physics, 230
postmodernist definition, 43
and reified roles, 141
and relationality, 114, 192
and the scientific method, 51
and scientific research methods, 240
self-consciousness defined, 132
self-realization, 91–92
and social embeddedness, 8, 11, 32, 251
transactional nature of, 122
See also Mead, George Herbert

Sessions, Robert, 194
SET theory (serial endosymbiosis theory), 236–239
See also Margulis, Lynn
Siegel, Harvey, 67
Burbules, Nicholas; debate with, 21–22
conduct/product distinction, 68, 69
and dualism, 24
epistemological theory, 16, 18–21, 22
and fallibilism, 20, 22
feminist allies, 29
Garrison, Jim; debate with, 24
and inclusionary discourses, 66, 67, 69
and performative contradiction, 25–26
on postmodernist positions, 43
Rorty, Richard; criticisms of, 44, 144
and truth, 25
Weinstein, Mark; debate with, 23–24, 33
"S knows that p" statements, 17, 27, 28–29, 100
Smith, Dorothy, 84, 145–149
social behaviorism. *See* Mead, George Herbert
social contexts of knowing, 8
social determinism, 139
sociology, 1, 145–148
See also Foucault, Michel; Smith, Dorothy
synechism, 60–61, 62, 65, 66
Systems theory, 230

teachers
in Buddhism, role of, 167
caring relationships, 80, 246, 247–250
definition of, 243–244
duties of, 246
new roles, 254
student assessment, 267
See also education
"Theories R Us," 69
Thirdness, 55
transactional relations. *See* Dewey, John
transcendental philosophy, 3, 5–6
transposition theory (biology), 240–241
truth (philosophical concept)
absolute/relative dualism, 53
and Buddhism, 159

Truth (*continued*)
   and epistemology, 272
   James, William; as defined by, 52–53
   and knowledge, 9
   and the personality, 117, 118
   and science, 213
   Siegel's "non-epistemic conception" of, 25
   subjective/objective dualism, 53
   and warranted assertions, 63
   See also Peirce, Charles S.
tychism, 61

von Bertalanffy, Ludwig, 230

warranted assertability, 63
Warren, Karen, 199, 200–202, 205
Weil, Simone, 80–81, 115, 116, 117–118, 119
Weinstein, Mark, 23–24, 33
Whitehead, Sir Alfred North, 268
w/holistic relations, generally, 85–89
   See also Buddhism; Native Americans
Williams, Paul, 157–158

About the Author

Barbara J. Thayer-Bacon is currently a professor of philosophy of education on the faculty of the University of Tennessee in Knoxville. She was a faculty member at Bowling Green State University from 1991 to 2000. She teaches courses on philosophy and history of education, social philosophy and cultural diversity, feminist epistemology and critical/constructive thinking. She received her Ph.D. in education from Indiana University in 1991. Prior to that she was an elementary Montessori teacher for seven years, as well as a public school teacher one year, and she still serves as a consultant for local schools, visiting them regularly. She is an active member in numerous professional organizations, such as American Educational Research Association, American Educational Studies Association, and Philosophy of Education Society, and presents papers regularly at their annual conferences. She is past president for the Ohio Valley Philosophy of Education Society and president-elect for the Research on Women and Education and Philosophical Studies Special Interest Groups of AERA. She is the author of several chapters in essay collections and over fifty journal articles published in professional journals such as *The Journal of Thought, Educational Theory, Studies in Philosophy and Education, Inquiry, Educational Foundations,* and *Educational Studies.* She has written two previous books, *Philosophy Applied to Education: Nurturing a Democratic Community in the Classroom,* with Dr. Charles S. Bacon as contributing author (Upper Saddle River, NJ and Columbus, OH: Merrill Publishing, Prentice-Hall, Inc., 1998), and *Transforming Critical Thinking: Constructive Thinking* (New York, NY: Teachers College Press, 2000).

Studies in Criticality

General Editor
Shirley R. Steinberg

Counterpoints publishes the most compelling and imaginative books being written in education today. Grounded on the theoretical advances in criticalism, feminism, and postmodernism in the last two decades of the twentieth century, Counterpoints engages the meaning of these innovations in various forms of educational expression. Committed to the proposition that theoretical literature should be accessible to a variety of audiences, the series insists that its authors avoid esoteric and jargonistic languages that transform educational scholarship into an elite discourse for the initiated. Scholarly work matters only to the degree it affects consciousness and practice at multiple sites. Counterpoints' editorial policy is based on these principles and the ability of scholars to break new ground, to open new conversations, to go where educators have never gone before.

For additional information about this series or for the submission of manuscripts, please contact:

> Shirley R. Steinberg
> c/o Peter Lang Publishing, Inc.
> 29 Broadway, 18th floor
> New York, New York 10006

To order other books in this series, please contact our Customer Service Department:

> (800) 770-LANG (within the U.S.)
> (212) 647-7706 (outside the U.S.)
> (212) 647-7707 FAX

Or browse online by series:
> www.peterlang.com

www.ingramcontent.com/pod-product-compliance
Lightning Source LLC
Chambersburg PA
CBHW050621300426
44112CB00012B/1606